The Practical Guid… …ng Human Resources in Hospitality, Hotels and Events

Taking a practical approach, this insightful book provides key guidance and insights from HR professionals working in hospitality, hotels, and events, showing how aspects of HR are facilitated in the working world, using case studies and practical examples to elucidate theory. With contributions from a range of industry HR professionals, this volume aims to enhance the comprehension of a range of practical HR-related issues facing the hospitality, hotels, and events industries. This includes guidance on the recruitment process, fair recruitment practices, contract types, onboarding, training, appraisals, reward and performance management, amongst many other topics. This book will contain real-life experiences, complementing the ideal process that HR follows when recruiting, onboarding, training, monitoring performance, and when rewarding staff. The book also considers legal issues faced by an industry which continues to handle staffing challenges, alongside post-Brexit and Covid pandemic shortages. International in scope, this volume is a pivotal resource for college and university-level students studying hospitality, hotel, or events management subjects, as well as those with a general interest or career in HR or management, such as those with an involvement in planning hospitality staffing, or individuals responsible for planning corporate, charitable, or private events.

Jennifer Kaye has over 30 years' industry experience in restaurants, hotels, bars, and events. Jennifer has worked for recognised hospitality brands including Whitbread, Hilton, and Crowne Plaza, Centreplate, Sodexo, and a leading corporate travel agency, as well as working across various independent brands in the UK and overseas, including Australia and the US. Jennifer manages weddings and private events in her spare time, as well as volunteering at sporting events to ensure her teaching content is current.

Jennifer is currently lecturer at the Edge Hotel School, University of Essex, UK; the first hotel school in the UK. Jennifer's passion in academia is for human resources and leadership, having launched modules in these subject areas. As module leader for Human Resource Management on both undergraduate and postgraduate programmes, alongside her ongoing casual work in the events industry, Jennifer's experience enables the delivery of industry-informed pedagogy.

Jennifer's MBA focused on Zero-Hour Contracts and staff motivation and her PhD research is in perimenopause and menopause and impacts on the workforce.

Jennifer has contributed book chapters, 'Management of Catering Outlets', in *The Practical Guide to Managing Event Venues* (Berners, 2019, pp. 77–87), and 'Revenue Management in Licensed Retail', in *The Practical Guide to Understanding and Raising Hotel Profitability* (Martin, 2020).

The Practical Guide to Events and Hotel Management Series

Series Editor: **Philip Berners,** *Edge Hotel School, University of Essex, UK*

The Practical Guide to Organising Events
Philip Berners

The Practical Guide to Managing Event Venues
Philip Berners

The Practical Guide to Understanding and Raising Hotel Profitability
Adrian Martin

The Practical Guide to Achieving Customer Satisfaction in Events and Hotels
Philip Berners and Adrian Martin

The Practical Guide to Managing Human Resources in Hospitality, Hotels and Events
Jennifer Kaye

For more information about this series, please visit: https://www.routledge.com/tourism/series/PGE

The Practical Guide to Managing Human Resources in Hospitality, Hotels and Events

Jennifer Kaye

Routledge
Taylor & Francis Group
LONDON AND NEW YORK

Designed cover image: Getty Images

First published 2026
by Routledge
4 Park Square, Milton Park, Abingdon, Oxon OX14 4RN

and by Routledge
605 Third Avenue, New York, NY 10158

Routledge is an imprint of the Taylor & Francis Group, an informa business

British Library Cataloguing-in-Publication Data
A catalogue record for this book is available from the British Library

Library of Congress Cataloging-in-Publication Data
Names: Kaye, Jennifer, (Academic lecturer) author
Title: The practical guide to managing human resources in hospitality, hotels and events / Jennifer Kaye.
Description: Abingdon, Oxon; New York, NY : Routledge, 2026. |
Series: The practical guide to events and hotel management |
Includes bibliographical references and index.
Identifiers: LCCN 2025023392 (print) | LCCN 2025023393 (ebook) |
ISBN 9781032745527 hardback | ISBN 9781003469803 ebook
Subjects: LCSH: Hospitality industry—Personnel management | Hotel management |
Special events—Personnel management
Classification: LCC TX911.3.P4 K39 2026 (print) | LCC TX911.3.P4 (ebook)
LC record available at https://lccn.loc.gov/2025023392
LC ebook record available at https://lccn.loc.gov/2025023393

ISBN: 978-1-032-74552-7 (hbk)
ISBN: 978-1-032-74551-0 (pbk)
ISBN: 978-1-003-46980-3 (ebk)

DOI: 10.4324/9781003469803

Typeset in Iowan Old Style
by codeMantra

Access the Support Material: www.routledge.com/9781032745510

I dedicate this book

To my brother, Andy Rayner 1979–2024, who will be forever 44.

To my dad, Graham Rayner 1950–2010, who ignited my passion for travel and the hospitality industry.

To my grandparents, whose warmth and kindness inspired me to work in the service industry, so I could look after people.

Contents

Figures

Tables

Contributors

Adrian Martin, Deputy Head of School, Edge Hotel School, University of Essex.

Alexandros Paraskevas, PhD, Professor in Strategic Risk Management, University of West London.

Edward Gallier, Head of Learning & Development, Leonardo Hotels (UK and Ireland).

Emily Timbrell, Head of Learning and Culture, Nobu Hotel, London, Portman Square.

Frazer Gander, Assistant Head of People & Culture, De Vere.

Gorm Larsen, Tourism and Sales professional.

Holly Lockyear, People and Culture Executive, The Royal Air Force Club.

Holly Marston, Learning & Development Manager, Leonardo Hotels.

Julia Greenwood, Policy and Engagement Lead.

Julie Norris, Cluster HR Manager, Leonardo Hotels.

Katie Owlett, Head of Talent Acquisition, De Vere.

Loredana Burdulea, Cluster HR Manager, Leonardo Hotels.

Lucy Potts, Hotel Manager, Leonardo Hotels.

Megan-Ellis Smith, Hotel Management graduate, Edge Hotel School, University of Essex.

Mike Dalley, Assistant Director of Talent & Culture, The Chancery Rosewood Hotel (contribution from HRaddict).

Dr Mostafa Marghany, Lecturer, Edge Hotel School, University of Essex.

Nirmeen Elmohandes, PhD Researcher, University of Debrecen and Canterbury Christ Church University.

Paula Musson, Assistant Group HR Manager, Leonardo Hotels.

Penelope Lynn Ananiadis-McAravey, Beyond HR Consulting & Xsellerate (contribution from HRaddict).

Dr Philip Berners, Associate Professor in Events Management, Edge Hotel School, University of Essex.

Philip Wicebloom, Event Manager, 5-star hotel, London.

Rachel Matthews, Director of People and Culture, The Royal Air Force Club.

Sarah Powell, Human Resources Director, Le Manoir aux Quat'Saisons.

Sophie Linin, Deputy Head of Events, Royal Museums Greenwich.

Tamsin Parker, Events Management graduate, Edge Hotel School, University of Essex.

The team and contributors at HRaddict.com

Tim Claydon, Events Manager, sports venues.

Zed Karoui, Doctoral Researcher and Lecturer in Hospitality Management, University of West London.

Series Editor Introduction

This book is the fifth title in the Routledge series, *The Practical Guide to Events and Hotel Management*.

Each book in the series is written in a logical format and contains practical tips drawn from real-life industry examples, case studies, industry leaders, and the author's extensive background working in events and hotels.

The Practical Guide to Managing Human Resources in Hospitality, Hotels and Events is ideal for students of the management of events, hotels, hospitality, or tourism, to be used as a practical resource alongside existing theoretical textbooks. It is also an essential tool for anybody working in the customer-facing industries.

Philip Berners
Series Editor

Acknowledgements

I wish to thank my mum and papa, and my support network for helping push me forward. Philip Berners for guidance and enabling this project to become reality. The incredible industry professionals, colleagues, and friends who kindly contributed their expertise for this book, and to the hundreds of inspirational students I've taught over the years and our future industry leaders.

Thank you,
Jenny Kaye

Introduction

The hospitality industry is one of the fastest growing industries globally, incorporating hotels and other lodgings, restaurants, cafés, pubs/bars, and nightclubs. Hospitality is interrelated with events and travel industries, with food and drink offerings, transport, and accommodation often needed, alongside events.

Hospitality, hotels, and events are part of everyday life. Whether we visit a café, attend a concert, visit a bar or restaurant, or stay in a hotel, each of these businesses, employ others to support daily operations.

Employees, or staff, are central to business success in hospitality, hotels, and events. Many of these staff are employed in customer-facing roles, responsible for decision-making, customer service delivery, and operations across our industries, and are therefore the 'face' of an organisation.

Staff are relied upon for organisational success, and it is essential to employ talented individuals who are motivated to make informed decisions, provide excellent customer service, and upsell to maximise profit.

The workforce supports organisational success and competitive advantage, and therefore needs to be carefully deployed and managed. Given ongoing challenges across industry in terms of staff retention, economic crises, and political uncertainty,

DOI: 10.4324/9781003469803-1

managing employees is challenging. The Human Resources department, or in smaller firms, the manager/director, has overall responsibility for employees.

Human Resources (HR) is unique in hospitality, hotels, and events, due to being part of the service industry, operating unsociable hours, irregular shift patterns, use of precarious contracts, and use of volunteers and agency staff. In addition, expectations of staff, brand standards, and operations across cultures and countries vary, alongside legislative requirements. The hospitality industry also faces unprecedented staffing issues with skills shortages, a transient workforce, and pressure applied by post-pandemic migration of staff away from industry. Every event, client, geographical location, and venue is unique, and no two days are the same in hospitality, hotels, and events.

Human Resources is a fundamental aspect of any business, and part of our daily working lives as Human Resources practitioners, managers, employees, and students. *The Practical Guide to Managing Human Resources in Hospitality, Hotels and Events* provides practical application to the hospitality, hotels, and events industries to support knowledge and understanding, develop career readiness, and identify best practice in industry in terms of Human Resources. This book provides a practical perspective of Human Resources to raise the knowledge and skill set of aspiring undergraduates and postgraduate students, early career hospitality managers, and Human Resource practitioners. It can be difficult to obtain work experience in Human Resources, therefore college and university-level students pursuing hospitality, hotel or events management subjects, and those with a general interest or career in Human Resources or people management, can use this book as a resource for guidance and insights into industry practices whilst raising the profile of careers within Human Resources. This book is for anybody with an involvement in planning hospitality staffing, or individuals responsible for planning corporate, charitable, or private events.

This book provides key insights and case studies from industry professionals working in hospitality, hotels, and events. Contributions are also drawn from doctoral academic staff in the research team at the Edge Hotel School, who have vast industry experience. Collectively, this will enhance the comprehension of a range of practical Human Resource related issues facing the event and hotel industries.

The Practical Guide to Managing Human Resources in Hospitality, Hotels and Events makes Human Resources easy to understand and to put into practice.

As this book is perspective based, it is not a basis for legal guidance, but rather a guide on best practice and experiences of industry and academic professionals. As culture, best practice, policy, and law varies from country to country, please check with your employer/managers or seek legal advice where necessary before implementing any guidance or templates within your workplace. For legal guidance for students, please research employment law in your region which you may find on government websites.

Chapter 1

The Role of Human Resources

1.0 Introduction

This first chapter outlines the roles and responsibilities of Human Resources within hospitality, hotels, and events. Chapter 1 will outline the different roles and tasks that Human Resources are responsible for. It will also analyse the role of the manager in small organisations in managing Human Resources and the role agencies play in supporting the Human Resources' function. Recruitment agencies are discussed alongside staffing agencies to ensure staffing levels are maintained. Strategic Human Resources Management is discussed which aligns Human Resources with the strategic needs of the organisation. The historical shift from welfare and personnel to Human Resources and now People and Culture is outlined – pertaining to a more people-focussed culture in modern organisations.

Human Resources (HR) are a core functional department within hospitality, hotel, and event businesses that help manage an organisation's core asset – its people.

Human Resources are primarily involved in attracting and retaining talent, and staff deployment, effectively utilising the skills and experience of the workforce to enhance productivity and achieve business success.

DOI: 10.4324/9781003469803-2

The primary focus of Human Resources is therefore effective utilisation, development, and management of human capital to achieve strategic organisational goals.

Today, and considering the rapidity of globalisation, Human Resources are influenced by external factors that impact daily operations and competition, including industry-wide recruitment challenges, international trade and labour agreements, differing labour laws, changing minimum legal pay and wage costs, increased levels of post-pandemic remote and hybrid working (working from home, or WFH), and changes in technology.

1.1 Analysis of the Different Job Roles and Responsibilities of Human Resources

Some people might assume the main job role of Human Resources is recruitment, but the role is much more varied, and the role undertaken by the Human Resource department might be tasked across multiple departments such as Payroll or Training and Development, or by individuals such as a single manager or business owner, or even outsourced to an agency.

Human Resources are responsible for a variety of activities including, but not limited to, employee relations, employee welfare, recruitment, and selection (which involves aspects such as hiring, deploying, and managing employees), onboarding, training and development, performance management, succession management, promotions, internal recruitment, pay, rewards, and benefits. Human Resources are also involved with policy-writing, performance investigations, grievances, disciplinaries, bullying, harassment or victimisation investigations, termination of employment, health and safety, diversity and inclusion, record keeping, and legal compliance. Consulting a relevant employment law specialist will be essential (when employing others) to ensure legal due diligence for tasks such as contract-writing or employee dismissal. Legal firms will provide guidance and support to ensure adherence to relevant laws.

The Human Resources manager or team will work with departmental managers in many aspects, such as the recruitment and selection process, to ensure consistency, fairness, and compliance. The role of Human Resources might also be carried out by an individual manager or business owner, especially in smaller firms. The manager will identify staffing needs and, together with Human Resources, will write job descriptions which outline the key aspects of the role, and person specifications to profile the ideal candidate. The main criteria from the job description and the person specification will then be added to a job advertisement for the vacant role. Once applications are received, applicants will be shortlisted against the key criteria and invited to interview.

INDUSTRY VOICE

Dr Philip Berners, Associate Professor in Events Management

An advertised job role needs to attract only the most suitable candidates to apply. This means that the person specification needs to show the essential and desirable criteria.

A candidate's CV informs the recruiter that this person meets or exceeds the criteria.

Thereafter, the interview allows the recruiter to judge the candidate's personality and whether they would fit with the culture of the existing team. This is why personality is important and a candidate needs to show their personality at the interview. Even if their personality doesn't fit, it is better to identify this at interview stage rather than find out later.

Once an employee is appointed, Human Resources will create onboarding (induction and training) programmes, policies, and procedures enabling managers to implement standard procedures and help settle the candidate into their new role. Human Resources will also set performance management expectations, ensuring consistency in evaluations, and managers will facilitate appraisals based on these criteria, reviewing employee performance using a standard format. Whilst managers should identify where employees have learning or development needs, Human Resources will design and implement training. If performance issues are identified by managers, Human Resources will provide guidance on training needs, any probationary periods in place, and any further support needed.

Human Resource personnel should also provide guidance to managers on conflict management and difficult conversations and will help conduct investigations and implement policies such as disciplinary procedures. Where staff are recognised for hard work by managers, Human Resources will identify suitable benefits and reward packages.

It can already be seen, therefore, that the role of Human Resources is diverse and relies on good communication between managers and Human Resources to ensure successful management of the workforce.

1.2 The Role of the Manager and Human Resources in Small Businesses

In smaller organisations, Human Resources may be the responsibility of the company owner/s, the manager or other senior personnel. Considering many hospitality, event, and accommodation providers operate as micro or small businesses, staffing numbers may be limited, therefore removing the need for a Human Resources department. Instead, the owner or appointed manager will adopt associated responsibilities, such as recruitment, policy writing, onboarding, training, and other employee issues. They will play a crucial role in fostering positive employee relations, helping to resolve any conflict, supporting employee well-being, team cohesion, and performance monitoring. This will help ensure smooth functioning of the business through a productive workforce and maintain a positive workplace culture.

Managers will need to have sound understanding of relevant employment laws to ensure compliance in terms of hiring practices, pay and benefits, and employee rights as examples. As with all organisations, employment law specialists will need to be consulted to ensure due diligence and legal compliance in matters such as fair recruitment practices, health and safety requirements, termination of employment, and fair wages.

Managing the workforce, once recruited, requires a variety of leadership skills, including adopting a flexible approach to leadership and changing the leadership style depending on who is being managed and the situation. Leadership is therefore situational and whilst some staff are more skilled and experienced and able to work independently with little instruction or guidance, others will need close supervision or additional training.

Sometimes, difficult decisions will need to be made for the greater good of the organisation, such as performance management and termination of employment. The manager will also have to facilitate this role.

Therefore, the role of the manager in smaller organisations varies. Not only will they potentially act as Human Resources, they could line-manage individuals as well.

This requires a variety of leadership and management skills including emotional intelligence, communication, people skills, and resilience, whilst keeping the bottom line and strategic intentions in mind.

INDUSTRY VOICE

Dr Philip Berners, Associate Professor in Event Management

I view the termination of an employee as a failure of management.

Termination must be the last resort if all else fails. But, before reaching the decision to terminate a member of the team, I will ask questions of the employee to identify how I can help them perform better. It might be something outside the workplace which is affecting their job such as caring for a relative or even having to arrive late due to the availability of public transport. I will always try to accommodate a person's needs.

I will provide training, coaching, mentorship… whatever it takes to improve performance before having to terminate. After all, this person was recruited into the organisation in the first place, so if nothing else works, it is still a failure of management: in the recruitment process.

If I do terminate a member of my team, I will reflect on why it didn't work out. What can I improve? How can I adjust my recruitment process so that I don't recruit a candidate who might not work out?

1.2.1 People Management in Small Businesses

Contribution from Philip Wicebloom, Event Manager in a London 5-star hotel

Ask any person, 'What is the most important element in hospitality?', invariably, the answer is 'service'. It isn't! Like all businesses, the single most important element is money. Without it, there is no business.

The second most important element is communication. Without clear, efficient dialogue between all stakeholders, nothing gets done. The best five-star hotel, or from the poshest restaurant to a local café, all rely on communication to run efficiently, provide good service, and in turn make money. It is a constantly turning circle and an engine that never stops running.

Whatever the establishment, it needs staff/team members/colleagues. The collective noun may differ, but the purpose does not. Staff are there to carry out their duties according to role and job description, in return for pay. At base level, the equation is simple: staff give their time in exchange for money. In the events industry, event volunteers may not be financially rewarded, and therefore management of these individuals and motivating them becomes more difficult.

Managers must consider myriad factors relevant to the organisation, for example motivation, ongoing training, and promotion potential.

In smaller establishments, having a team that works well together as an efficient unit, communicates effectively with each other, and creates a harmonious working environment is vital to the success of the business. This applies to whether the organisation is operating a one-day event, a temporary pop-up restaurant or bar, or a permanent hospitality event, or hotel venue.

The Hospitality/Hotel/Event Manager in a smaller business may deal with many of the Human Resource tasks that a dedicated Human Resources department would undertake in a larger organisation.

Smaller establishments can represent lines of management responsibility that are blurred, with wider duties undertaken, and decisions can often be made quickly and less formally than in larger organisations. Staff will also be able to share concerns or participate in decision-making more easily due to the smaller hierarchy and have more access to managers than in a large organisation. This helps staff to feel heard and valued. However, the opposite could also be true where relations between staff members and a manager are strained, and they do not have another manager or Human Resources department they can share concerns with to resolve conflict or issues.

Managers must also act in a manner that presents the establishment in the best possible light. Treating staff poorly would undoubtably result in a poor local reflection and reputation. Retaining staff and recruiting within the local community would then become very difficult.

There is no magic formula, but happy and motivated staff are excellent ambassadors for any organisation. As staff are often deployed in customer-facing roles, in a smaller business service expectations will increase, so being a positive ambassador for the brand is imperative. A guest staying at a hotel with 20 bedrooms would have expectations to be recognised by name and be remembered throughout their stay. Maybe this is not such an expectation in a 400-bedroom hotel.

In a small business, each member of staff is key, and the impact of an absent employee is magnified. If an employee is off work due to sickness, or is on annual leave for example, this can impact operations in the following ways:

> There will be less opportunity for other colleagues to 'cover' for a missing role due to limited staffing numbers, and existing staff might need to work longer hours to cover shifts. Working longer hours results in overtime payments (or additional wage costs for hourly paid staff or when agencies need to be used). So potentially, there is no cost saving compared to saving the absent employee's wages.
>
> If no overtime payments are granted, then resentment will quickly follow from the team. Working longer hours creates fatigue amongst existing staff.

This is not only a tiredness factor but also causes resentment at spending less time with families, or less time for recreation and outside interests. In turn, this leads to lack of motivation, poor performance, and a decline in standards. If it is an ongoing issue, present staff could decide enough is enough and leave.

INDUSTRY VOICE

Philip Wicebloom, Event Manager, 5-star London hotel

Recruitment is essential to business success. In my career, I have predominantly managed the recruitment of head waiters and event managers. Senior managers have at times suggested leaving a role open for a couple of months to 'see how you go' and save the wage, rather than covering with overtime or recruiting for a vacant role. I have steadfastly pushed back against this type of penny pinching, as it is self-defeating for the reasons just given.

After the 9/11 terrorist attack in 2001, the impact on hospitality, hotel, and event businesses was devastating. At that time, I was working in a central London hotel and our event revenue dropped dramatically. Redundancies followed, and the event management team dropped from three to two: me as Head of Department and one Event Manager. After three months in the doldrums, business levels resumed and rapidly rose to normal levels. The two of us were struggling to cope but my authority to recruit for another Event Manager was refused. So, two were doing the job of three, working 80-hour weeks, with no overtime compensation and both of us were fed up and our motivation was dwindling. Only an impassioned appeal to the group's Managing Director resulted in an admission that the situation could not reasonably continue, and I was permitted to recruit the all-important third position. I did that with some haste.

The role of a hotel manager or event manager in a small hospitality venue may involve them in Human ResourcesCase studies related tasks. In doing so, they must be versed in current and relevant Human Resources legislation. They must also act in a manner that presents the establishment in the best possible light.

There is no magic formula, but happy and motivated staff are excellent ambassadors for any organisation. This is magnified in smaller businesses.

Smaller hospitality establishments can benefit from social media exposure. This can be in the form of:

- Management posts on social media platforms, promoting the establishment for its product, or telling the story of a special event they have hosted
- Posting job vacancies
- Guests posting on their own social media accounts of their experience
- Staff posting on their own social media accounts

The latter can be an asset and beneficial if positive, appropriate, and in line with the inherent values. However, posts cannot infringe on guest identity or privacy, be abusive, or reflect a negative impression.

Larger establishments have clear policies when it comes to a colleague's online presence, often needing a signature when joining. Smaller businesses, though, may have a less formal approach, but some direction should be given as to expectations of an online profile when it comes to place of work.

There are myriad circumstances where managers are potentially led into Human Resources territory. Each incident needs to be treated according to its context and merits. However, there are always two sides to a story. To offer a fair reflection of any given situation, the facts are key. Each person involved needs to have the opportunity to put their perspective forward. Only after each side has delivered their version of events, can an accurate analysis of the facts be achieved. Depending on the situation, the investigation process can be time consuming and require some degree of patience. However, it is important that both parties feel they have been given a fair hearing.

Management is never finite. There is always more to experience and learn.

1.3 The Role of Agencies for Human Resources Support

In some firms, an external contractor might be appointed to provide Human Resources support and legal guidance. This is known as an agency or contractor. An agency can provide a range of services depending on business needs. Different agencies will provide different specialist services. Using an agency is beneficial where specialist skills are lacking or if cost savings can be made compared to employing permanent Human Resources staff to fulfil the role.

An agency that specialises in Human Resources provides a range of services, including recruitment and selection, which involves advertising job vacancies, shortlisting, screening candidates, and facilitating interviews. The agency would assist with contract or policy writing, support with legal matters and employee relations such as conflict resolution, which includes performance issues and disciplinaries, bullying and harassment investigations, and employer/employee conflict or termination of employment.

A recruitment agency, job agency, or staffing agency is another service that can be used, especially where there are skills shortages or job vacancies. There are differences between a recruitment agency and a staffing agency:

1.3.1 Staffing Agency

A staffing agency provides agency staff for ad hoc shifts, or on a regular basis in exchange for a fee, but legally employs the staff themselves. Use of a staffing agency tends to be more expensive than employing your own staff due to agency fees alongside paying wages for hours worked. There will be wider considerations here such as ensuring the appointed agency is paying fair and legal wages, and rights to work checks are being completed to ensure the individual is legally allowed to be employed given their age or resident status. It is imperative an employer is aware of the reputation and legal compliance of suppliers within the supply chain – which includes use of staffing agencies.

1.3.2 Recruitment or Job Agency

A recruitment or job agency is one which is used as a platform for employers to broaden the reach of a job advert to a wider pool of potential candidates. Some agencies have physical offices and others are online platforms only. An agency can filter applications prior to sending them to the hospitality or events business, whether for a full-time role, for hourly paid staff, or for temporary roles. Recruitment or job agencies typically charge a percentage of the salary or a set fee in exchange for their services.

Recruitment agencies can also assist with headhunting and profiling ideal candidates for any job openings (also known as an executive search). This helps with appointing candidates into senior roles such as executives, directors, and managers, but also for operational roles where needed. This may be a specialist headhunting agency or a general recruitment firm.

Other agencies provide consultancy services to help improve policies, procedures, or compliance, or to support strategic changes in staffing.

Outsourcing Human Resources to an agency, consultant, or contractor, can save an event, hotel, or hospitality manager's time, can save costs, and ultimately provides specialist services and support needed that are outside the company's expertise or skill set.

1.4 Strategic Human Resources Management (competitive advantage, strategy, and culture)

Human Resource Management (HRM) and Strategic Human Resource Management (SHRM) are related concepts, slightly differing in terms of scope and focus. Whereas HRM is people focused, SHRM aligns Human Resource practices and policies with overall organisational strategic goals, with the intention of supporting attainment of a company's vision and aspirations.

Strategic goals are pertinent to Human Resource Management, which is a strategic approach to Human Resources, with the intention of maximising productivity in line with organisational strategy, whilst being concerned with maintaining employee motivation and well-being. These goals in hospitality, events, or hotels enhance competitive positioning and will therefore include goals such as exceptional customer service, sustainability, profit growth, product or service quality, community engagement such as fundraising, or employee satisfaction. Employee satisfaction should help ensure organisations retain talented staff, which in turn reduces recruitment costs and maintains desired levels of customer service. Therefore, Human Resource Management seeks to achieve organisational needs whilst enhancing staff morale to help achieve strategic goals.

When utilised effectively, and when in alignment with business strategy, the Human Resources department, alongside policies, targets, training, and brand standards, helps guide employee behaviour, utilise skills, and maintain employee motivation, helping to achieve strategic goals. For example, during the annual appraisal process, targets will be set for individuals and teams to achieve, to meet company expectations. Targets relate to customer service or profit, for example, and each employee can receive set targets such as upselling to improve both the customer experience and sales.

Overall, the role of Human Resources is to maximise the performance of the organisation through effective utilisation of its employees. Human Resources incorporates effective utilisation of an organisation's human assets – its employees – whilst fostering a positive working environment which helps maximise productivity, overall company strategic intent, and achievement of company goals.

1.5 The Historical Shift from Industrial Welfare and Personnel

In the eighteenth and nineteenth centuries, change in technological, economic, and social developments occurred during the Industrial Revolution, which saw the rise of manufacturing lines and mass production. Prior to this, many firms were family owned, homebased businesses, or small businesses with few employees and the employer–employee relationship more personalised but labour intensive.

With advancements in machines and the growth of factories, employment of a larger number of people became necessary. Amidst concerns for safety, worker welfare became more important, driven by humanitarian, religious, philanthropic, and social movements, alongside business needs. Due to social disconnection between employers and employees, there was very little regard to employee well-being, safety, or concerns.

This led to the Progressive movement in the United States because of pressure from these groups alongside employee uprising due to poor labour policies and safety concerns during this time. The same concerns were being raised in the United Kingdom regarding dangerous and challenging working conditions in factories and coal mines. Furthermore, rapid industrialisation led to labour exploitation and increased poverty as productivity and financial concerns were prioritised instead.

During these periods, more stringent workplace safety regulations and social well-being motives were implemented to protect workers, resulting in the emergence of 'Industrial Welfare'. People wanted fairer wages, fairer taxes, better housing, and education.

During this time, Industrial Welfare focused on the employer–employee relationship and involved trade-union negotiations, which helped negotiate employee rights, working conditions, and fair pay.

Developments continued during both world wars in the early twentieth century given the rise in women workers.

Alongside Industrial Welfare, individuals were employed to manage 'employee relations', also known as 'industrial relations'. Employee relations helped analyse the job roles and work of the individual, and employment offices were set up to help with hiring staff, payroll, and record-keeping.

In the late 1900s the terms 'Personnel', or 'Personnel Department', and 'Personnel Management' became the new name for employee relations as the job role expanded.

'Personnel' were responsible for a variety of tasks including recruitment and selection, training and development, and performance management. Performance management involves monitoring of staff performance, identifying strengths and areas for development, and opportunities for progression.

This review of performance, or performance review is now what we refer to as the 'appraisal process' or 'appraisal'. Appraisals include setting standards of work, often involving targets which align with strategic goals. During this process, achievements of employees will also have been recognised. The role of Personnel, therefore, also included benefits or rewards management, in recognition of work inputs.

Employee relations and dealing with conflicts and disputes were also pivotal to the Personnel role, considering peer relations and employer–employee relations and other employment issues such as pay or working conditions. This involved compliance with labour laws and health and safety compliance, including the creation of health and safety policies and equal opportunities within the workplace.

Keeping confidential records of employee details, employment history, and performance records was also necessary as part of the Personnel role.

Finally, workforce planning, which involves recruitment of the right number of employees with the right skills at the right time was a necessity of the Personnel role (further discussed in Chapter Two).

The term 'Human Resources' replaced what was formally known as 'Industrial Welfare', then 'Personnel', names which continuously adapt as society progresses and is now being referred to as 'People and Culture', as outlined in Figure 1.1.

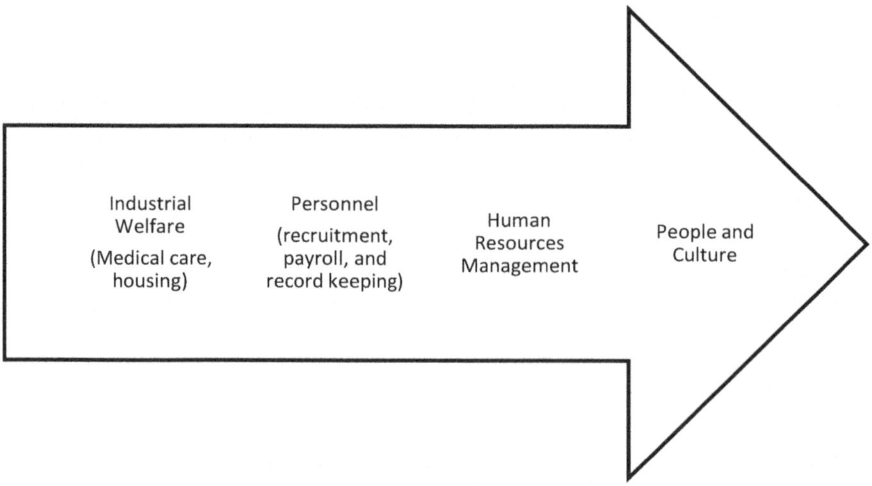

Figure 1.1 The Emergence of Human Resources

1.6 People and Culture – the Modern Human Resources Department

Today's Human Resources department is commonly known as People and Culture, as the focus shifts from being organisation-oriented to people-orientated, and managers increasingly recognise the value of people in achieving strategic goals. The way in which hospitality, event, and hotel organisations manage employees, influences employee behaviours and organisational performance. People and Culture therefore highlights the importance of employees within an organisation in achieving organisational success. Staff can also be referred to as 'human assets' or 'human resources', and are considered as important as financial capital, facilities, equipment and goods, or services offered.

Whilst it is recognised that different terms have been used to describe what we commonly refer to as Human Resources, and a shift to People and Culture, People and Services, or People Operations, the general shift is towards recognition of the contributions individuals make to a company.

In service industries, hospitality, event, and hotel staff are frontline staff and can be seen as the face of the company, normally engaged in customer-facing roles. As such, staff have influence over guest interactions, service standards, and customer satisfaction, and it is important to consider staff as an asset and recognise and value their contributions to guiding positive organisational behaviour. Their decisions, behaviours, and actions can impact customer satisfaction, and therefore business reputation, sales, and success. Putting staff at the centre of the organisation, alongside customers, will result in increased staff motivation, enhance the psychological contract with the employer, and stimulate productivity and loyalty. A committed employee who feels valued will reduce staff turnover and absenteeism. Alongside investments in training, this will result in fewer mistakes, higher productivity, better sales skills and customer service skills, customer loyalty, and a more reputable organisation, thus contributing to business success.

People and Culture recognises the value of staff, and seeks to drive staff satisfaction, retention, well-being, motivation, and productivity, whilst recognising how this influences overall culture, whether a company chooses to value people (staff, customers, or wider society), profit, quality, business growth, or even sustainability. If employees feel valued, they are more likely to embrace company goals, and be accepting of change, and will strive to provide excellent customer service and excel in their job role, contributing to organisational success.

Chapter 2

Recruitment and Selection

DOI: 10.4324/9781003469803-3

Part 1: Workforce Planning, Key Recruitment Documents, and Shortlisting

2.0 Introduction

This chapter provides insight into workforce planning and techniques used to determine staffing levels. The recruitment process is also outlined, with a guide as to how to ensure a fair recruitment process and the role of key recruitment documents such as the person specification, job description and interview analysis forms, and interviews. The chapter will also cover shortlisting and screening of candidates, employment checks, and recruitment of volunteers.

Recruitment and Selection are core functions of Human Resources and typically what people think of first when considering what the HR department does within a business.

Whilst the scope of Human Resources is much broader than recruitment and selection alone, ultimately an organisation needs employees and therefore recruitment is fundamental, whether for an independent small business requiring few staff, or a large international chain requiring many staff.

Recruitment refers to the process of finding and encouraging applicants to apply for a given job vacancy.

Selection involves identifying the most suitable candidate to fulfil the vacant role.

Before the recruitment and selection process can commence, workforce planning and forecasting is used to determine how many employees are needed at any given time and what skills are required to fulfil the tasks of the vacant role.

2.1 Workforce Planning and Forecasting

Workforce planning is the process of determining current and future staffing needs within an organisation. This entails finding the right number of staff, with the right skills, in the right place, at the right time.

Workforce planning is necessary to ensure business needs are met in accordance with operational requirements and in terms of demand for services. Consideration will also need to be given to 'gaps' in staffing needs, such as covering staff days off, annual leave requirements, staff turnover, sickness and absenteeism, and other factors such as retirement, and death in service.

Forecasting, therefore, is the process of determining how many staff are needed at any given time and will be strongly influenced by demands of the business.

Workforce planning and forecasting is more complex for the hospitality, event, and hotel industries, which fluctuate in terms of demand and are seasonal, and more staff are needed at certain periods of time before demand again reduces.

Events, especially, are seen as 'pulsating' organisations which recruit staff for an event (swell) and release them after the event has happened (reduce) and is why the events industry is largely made up of freelance professionals.

The summer season sees a notable increase in music festivals, food and drink festivals, weddings, and other outdoor events, with warm weather leading to an increase in demand for beer gardens/outdoor venues and increased attendance at outdoor events. Events such as international sporting competitions also influence the demand for venues such as bars and pubs screening sports. Staffing needs pulsate with fluctuations in demand.

Demand for resort hotels will increase in school holidays, and entire holiday resorts will close during the winter 'off' season, for example in locations such as Greek islands where workers move back to the mainland when the summer season is finished. Many of these workers do not receive any income for the winter season or move to other locations to earn money.

INDUSTRY VOICE

Gorm Larsen, Tourism and Sales Professional

Working in Rhodes within the tourism industry is so rewarding, and I love meeting so many different people from around the world. The tourist season typically lasts from April until October, so employment is limited to these months.

Being from Denmark I am free to travel and work around Europe so have worked in a few countries seeking roles in hotels, restaurants, and time-share resorts.

I'm fortunate, as during the peak tourist season, working in sales, I earn commission, which is not your typical role in hospitality and tourism. When tourist numbers drop towards the end of the season, my wages will suffer and financially things can become difficult. I therefore have secondary employment in customer services to maintain my income and sometimes move to a winter sun location to continue earning.

Other hotels experience demand from different types of guests during different days, such as business guests on weekdays and leisure guests at weekends. Hotels, for example, in the financial district of a city will be busy during weekdays business travel, but quiet at weekends, and coastal towns busy at weekends for leisure travel but quiet during the week. Some locations will benefit from both business and leisure guests, and in other situations business clientele will extend their stay or visit attractions in the area. Hotels will need to adjust staffing depending on demand.

Travel that combines work and leisure is what is now referred to as 'Bleisure' or blended travel, where leisure activities, extended stays beyond work, or friends and family accompanying the individual are possible. Therefore, typical tourist areas such as areas of cultural significance or cities will benefit from *bleisure* travel in terms of hotels and extended stays, tourist attractions, restaurants, and shopping areas. Hotels, restaurants, cafes, tourist attractions, and licensed venues need to maintain consistent levels of staffing in tourist hotspots.

In all instances, despite what type of business or geographical location it operates within, staffing will need to be flexible to meet operational needs. Every hotel, event venue, bar, restaurant, or travel company will be busy at different times and will need to fluctuate staffing according to business demands. This is known as 'numerical flexibility' where staffing numbers can be increased or decreased according to business needs, such as reducing staff numbers during quieter periods, and increasing them during busier periods or where there is a sudden increase in demand. Having numerical flexibility will help save labour costs, which is one of the biggest expenses for hospitality and events organisations.

Many hotels, bars, and restaurants will utilise a variety of employment contracts to achieve numerical flexibility in terms of staffing numbers. These include full-time permanent contracts and part-time contracts, where staff are employed on a permanent basis but work fewer hours.

Casual labour is also used: casual workers tend to be employed on Zero-Hour Contracts, commonly used in some parts of Europe such as the UK. Zero-Hour Contracts are where staff are paid an hourly rate, and only paid for hours worked – which enables firms to quickly increase staff numbers when needed, whilst providing cost savings for this reason.

Some organisations also use agency staff to increase the number of workers, for example for a large-scale event in a hotel or for catering outlets in sports stadia. In other instances, volunteers will be used to increase staffing, for example for major events such as the London Marathon where hundreds of marshals are distributed throughout the course.

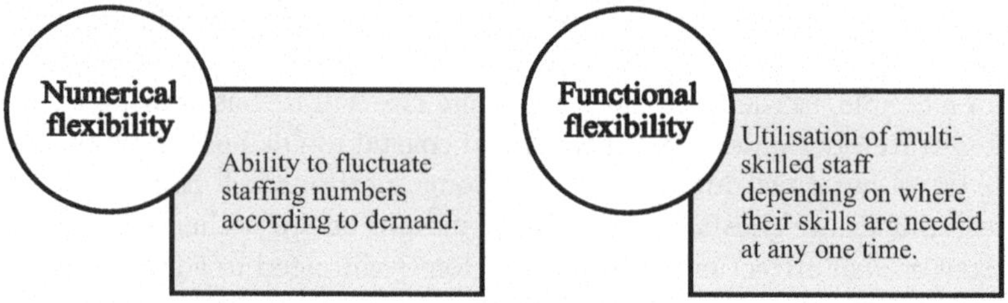

Figure 2.1 Numerical and Functional Staffing

Functional flexibility is beneficial where staff are trained across multiple areas or departments within the business. Multi-skilled and cross-trained staff enable managers to move staff to areas within the organisation that are busy, such as reception staff also being trained in restaurant or bar, so they can flexibly do both jobs as and when required within a hotel; or airline crew being able to board passengers and operate food service; or kitchen porters being able to support with food preparation (see Figure 2.1):

2.1.1 Approaches to Workforce Planning and Forecasting

Workforce planning requires an audit of the current workforce and an analysis of the future workforce in terms of the number of workers available in the workforce and in accordance with demand. Any gaps in the labour pool will need to be filled in each department or area of the business, regarding the duties they carry out, and their skills. This can be done through multi-skilling of staff, recruitment of new employees, or with transfers from other sites as examples.

There are several ways to determine required staffing levels, including managerial judgement, trend analysis, ratio analysis, budgets, computerised forecasts, and efficiencies.

Managerial judgement is where a manager uses their experience and knowledge of business volumes and historical demand to predict how many staff are needed at any given time. Consideration will be given to general staffing needs and other busier periods such as events, seasonality, staffing costs, and skills.

Trend analysis involves looking at past data and demand, looking at historical staffing numbers and productivity. It involves looking at customer numbers, sales data, queues, complaints, and stock levels as examples. This will determine whether staffing should be increased, decreased, or remain the same for the future.

INDUSTRY VOICE

Tim Claydon, Catering Manager, Sports Stadia

As Catering Manager, I had the responsibility for determining staffing levels and used trend analysis method to determine staffing numbers, as well as budget. I based this on my experience and knowledge of previous match days.

Two weeks before the match, I would look at match day ticket sales to determine how busy the bars, food kiosks, and hospitality areas would be. I would also look at previous attendance, sales, staffing numbers, and service times and complaints for when the rivals previously played.

In sports stadia in the UK, we can only serve alcohol pre-match and at halftime which only leaves limited-service times. If service was quick enough, given time constraints, and tickets sales are similar, I have a base to start with in terms of staffing numbers – if there were complaints and delays, I knew more staff would be needed next time.

I would always aim to set staffing numbers three matches at a time (normally 2–3 matches a month) and send reminders to staff by email a week before the game. Sometimes, there are two matches in a week, so I would need to be more organised at those times.

Some events and other hospitality venues may use apps for their staffing, where shifts are uploaded and staff can claim or drop these, and this will automatically send shift reminders.

Ratio analysis can be used whereby staffing numbers are determined by service quality. A fine dining restaurant or VIP event will require higher staffing levels to ensure higher standards of service and attentive staff. A chain of family restaurants and fast-food restaurants can adopt lower staffing numbers and have a lower ratio of staff to customers, to save costs as well as matching staffing numbers to the service styles and operational demands. For example, a restaurant that operates a buffet will be self-service or partial self-service, and only require staff for drinks service, replenishing buffets, and clearing tables as examples rather than fully attentive table service. Fast-food chains are similar, and customers now order via touchscreen, or an app and food is collected from a counter.

AUTHOR'S VOICE

When working as an intern in a resort hotel in Missouri, USA, I was on rotation in the Banqueting department. Ratio analysis was used for staffing depending on clientele budget and service requirements.

I was a server for a corporate function requiring a sit-down meal, attended by a few hundred guests. I was allocated 60 guests across six tables to serve for a more relaxed, casual service. So, a low ratio of staff to guests.

On other shifts, I had one or two tables for more exclusive high-end events.

One day, the hotel had high-profile guests from a well-known beer brand who wanted private dining on the roof terrace of the hotel. Three staff were allocated for less than four guests to maintain an attentive and high-quality service, resulting in a higher ratio of staff to guests.

In this situation, staff to guest ratios varied depending on service standards, event purpose, client budget, and style of service required.

Budgets are another factor to determine staffing levels, as monitored by Human Resources or managers/owners. If sales are high during the previous week, this will increase the weekly budget for the next week's staffing. Likewise, finances determine affordability of staff and therefore budgets will dictate staffing levels depending on affordability and profit targets.

Computerised systems can be used to predict future demand and to forecast sales, predict how much of a service or product is needed, and suitable numbers of staff to achieve this. The computerised system considers historical data, such as demand, sales, budgets, and forecasts for a given typical period to identify how many staff are needed.

Efficiencies. Staffing needs may also be amended according to observed efficiencies and capability of the current workforce. If staff are productive, it might be necessary to maintain or reduce staffing numbers. If there is a notable increase in mistakes, wastage, delays in service, or customer complaints, it would indicate further staff numbers (or training) is needed to improve the effectiveness of the workforce. This will improve skill set, ensure time efficiencies, or reduce mistakes.

2.2 Recruitment Process

Once staffing numbers and vacancies are identified, Human Resources (or the manager/owner) will need to apply the recruitment process. Recruitment and selection of talented staff require several steps to be taken, utilising key recruitment documents that follow fair recruitment processes, and a consistent and efficient recruitment process.

Organisations can recruit internally and externally where feasible:

Internal recruitment is when an organisation recruits from their own pool of staff. This helps employees progress within the organisation, which can enhance motivation and commitment. The employee is familiar with the company, so the onboarding process becomes easier, and leads to less risk and disruption as the employee (and their skill set) is known to the company. Progression can be into a more senior role, different role, or new location. Within international hospitality, hotel, and event brands this would enable an employee to transfer to another location and act as an incentive whereby they can travel and work.

There are disadvantages to recruiting internally, such as the original role needing to be filled, so there is still an additional need to recruit. Also, the promoted employee might lack additional ideas on how to lead the company to success and will continue to work how they always have, not knowing potential alternative ways of more efficient working, or lacking creative or strategic ideas. Furthermore, internal recruitment can cause conflict or demotivation issues for those who were not successful or not able to apply for the higher role. This will impact on teams or manager/employee relationships.

External recruitment may be preferable as external candidates bring new and innovative ideas to enhance the organisation and its operations. It means a wider pool of talent can be shortlisted and considered for the role.

This is time consuming and costly, however, requiring formal adverts to be published, which may take a few days to authorise or up to a few weeks in larger organisations. Also, if a successful candidate is not found, the vacancy will have to go out again, further delaying the appointment. Then, interviews need to take place utilising a manager's time and expense, and notice periods before the new employee can arrive, which further delays start dates. This will leave potential skills shortages and put pressure on remaining team members.

2.2.1 Fair Recruitment Practices

Fair recruitment practices ensure that the recruitment process is free from discrimination and bias. Different legislation will apply country to country, but in general refers to principles of equality, and a recruitment process that does not discriminate on the grounds of protected characteristics such as gender, race, religion, disability, age, marital status, pregnancy, or maternity, gender reassignment, or sexual orientation: under British law for example the Equality Act would apply.

Fair recruitment will maintain and protect the rights of current employees in accordance with employment legislation. This includes, but is not limited to, employment terms and conditions, redundancy rights, fair pay, progression, dismissal, training, holiday entitlement, and safe working conditions.

However, indirect discrimination or direct discrimination could occur during the recruitment process, whether intentional or not. This usually relates to a protected characteristic and can also occur due to work practices, systems, or procedures.

Indirect discrimination is usually unintentional. Where working practices and policies are the same for everyone, to ensure fairness and equality, treating people as the same can create a disadvantage for someone. An example of indirect discrimination is by stating a minimum number of years' experience required in a job advert, which would exclude young people from applying for the role. Other examples include fewer opportunities for training, progression, less favourable working conditions, or less earnings' potential and benefits. Perhaps, for instance, training is offered in a restaurant at 3 p.m., and for a working parent or caregiver, often females, this might be at a time where they collect their child from school. This creates a disadvantage to the worker in terms of sex discrimination, whose working hours fit around the school day.

Direct discrimination is when someone is disadvantaged or experiences unfair treatment because of a protected characteristic. Direct discrimination occurs when a protected characteristic, perceived protected characteristic, or association with someone with a protected characteristic is discriminated against. An example of this would be advertising that a man is needed to work in a bar due to heavy lifting of beer barrels, assuming females are not strong or able to carry a heavy load. This is sex discrimination.

Perhaps a person in a wheelchair is rejected from a job because of access issues, despite being the most suitably qualified and experienced person for the role. In this case reasonable adjustments should be made, such as adapting the reception desk so that it is lower, installing a ramp for access, adding an elevator, and providing accessible toilets. If they are refused the job due to their disability, this is disability discrimination.

Another example is to advertise a job stating the applicant must be from a specific country: 'French worker required', which discriminates on the grounds of race. The language skills are the requirement rather than the country they were born, and the job advertisement should instead state 'must be able to speak fluent French'. Therefore, anyone with French language skills may apply.

When creating the required recruitment documents to advertise, and shortlist against, the entire recruitment process must be free of discrimination and unfair practices, and careful consideration given to wording, employment law, and fair recruitment practices.

2.3 Job Analysis

The first step of the recruitment process is to create a job analysis, from which the job description, person specification, and subsequent job advertisement are created.

The purpose of a job analysis is to gather information about a specific job and can be used to help redesign a job role to enable efficiencies, be used within the recruitment process, and help determine training requirements, performance standards, and renumeration package.

A job analysis involves identifying the tasks and responsibilities, reporting lines, skills, qualifications, and order of work required to fulfil any job roles. The analysis is a document detailing the job, the purpose of the job, the tasks that need to be completed within a given job role, and how the job role fits into the organisational structure. It will also include what skills and aptitudes, qualifications, experience, or personality may be needed to carry out the work. The job analysis should also include any physical or mental requirements of the job, indicating any hazards, such as noise, where applicable.

A job analysis not only identifies the responsibilities and tasks of the job role but considers how each job fits into the overall organisation, in terms of purpose.

A job analysis can be conducted by observing an employee complete their day-to-day tasks, asking them to complete a work diary or journal, by talking to managers, by interviewing the employee, or from conducting a staff survey. Whilst it may be difficult to complete a comprehensive guide on every responsibility or task involved in any job, the idea instead is to gather information that can be used when determining pay and benefits, hours of work, and general tasks and skills needed.

It is important to capture how to carry out the work, processes followed (flow of work), lines of authority (reporting lines within the staffing structure or hierarchy), and working conditions such as long hours, shift patterns such as split shifts, evenings, or weekend work, hot or cold temperatures, noise, repetitive work, and other physical attributes such as carrying and lifting or standing for long periods. It is also important to capture what skills, knowledge, or experience is required to carry out the role, including qualifications or professional certifications.

A job analysis is then used when creating the **job description**, detailing general work demands and skills required to be able to fulfil the role. And the **person specification**, a profile of the ideal candidate which captures their skills, qualifications, experience, and aptitudes required within the role.

Overall, the job analysis helps a hospitality, hotel, or events organisation effectively utilise staff through effective job design, matching candidates to suitable roles, performance monitoring, and aligning job roles to corporate goals to help achieve strategic intent.

Table 2.1 contains an example of a job analysis template that can be used by organisations to conduct a job analysis.

Table 2.1 Example Job Analysis Template

Job Analysis Form	
Job title	
Job purpose (overall contribution/gist of the role)	
Level of responsibility – where the post fits into the structure of the organisation (reporting lines)	
Location	
Salary	
Hours of working (also outline if unsociable/variable hours/eve/weekends etc)	
Duties/tasks	
Skills & competencies	
Training/qualifications	
Knowledge and understanding (systems/processes etc)	
Personal attributes (personality traits)	
Any physical attributes of job (long hours/standing/temperate/repetitive work, etc.)	

2.4 Job Description

The job description (JD) stems from the job analysis (if one is conducted) and is the second stage of the recruitment process in terms of documentation, after the job analysis.

The aim of the JD is to provide an outline of a specific job role. The JD provides an overview of the job role including the job title, department, location of work, overall job purpose, and how the role fits into the organisation, and duties and responsibilities including the main duties and tasks. Some companies will specify the importance or priority of each task.

A JD also shows reporting lines. Reporting lines will include who the candidate will report to in terms of managers or supervisors, and who they are responsible for if supervising or managing other staff.

The company hierarchy or levels of responsibility provide an overview of where the employee fits into the organisation structure, alongside the significance of the role within the company. This also establishes if opportunities exist for progression within the hierarchy and will help motivate employees if they can see clear routes of progression.

The JD also outlines the annual salary or hourly rate of pay, and any pay scales where applicable. Not all organisations will state salary but simply state 'competitive salary' which might be in line with competitors but could waste the time of applicants where this does not meet their expectations once disclosed during the interview process. Remember, the purpose of recruitment is to identify and select the right applicants, so if the salary is not mentioned, it might not attract that candidate. If a candidate is interviewed on the basis of 'competitive salary' and later finds that the salary offered does not meet their expectations, this is wasteful to both the candidate and the recruiter.

Benefits should be identified within the JD to motivate candidates as this indicates opportunities for increasing earning potential and helps candidates to determine the financial feasibility of the role.

It may be necessary to also state conditions of work such as long hours, shift patterns, or other climatic or physical factors so that a prospective candidate can determine if they can manage within their abilities. For example, if the role involves heavy lifting or standing for long periods, the candidate may decide they are unable to meet these criteria. However reasonable adjustments might be needed to maintain an accessible workplace, for example providing a chair where feasible, wheelchair access, or accessible toilets.

The job description is necessary for applicants when deciding whether to apply for a vacancy, helping an individual to determine their suitability for the role, and therefore helps to filter unsuitable candidates at an early stage. It is helpful if the applicant can make these determinations before they decide to apply, so it is a 'self-filtering' process. This lessens the need for the recruiter to make these determinations during the interview process.

The purpose of the JD is to match candidates to specific job roles where vacancies exist. Potential applicants who feel they can fulfil the duties are more likely to apply, increasing the likelihood of talented prospects applying for the role.

When applications are received, shortlisting will consider whether the candidate is competent, experienced, or has potential to fulfil the required tasks and responsibilities associated with the role considering key criteria outlined within the application when compared to the JD.

The job description is also used when creating job advertisements, with the key information being added to the advert to attract applications alongside key skills or qualifications required for the role as outlined within the person specification. The overall purpose of the job and key tasks associated with the role will be outlined in the advert such as *'providing exceptional customer service and food and beverage service to clients'*. Some candidates will naturally feel more confident carrying out some tasks than others and this will determine if they apply in some instances.

The job description is used to clarify expectations of employers and managers, providing key criteria in which to measure employee performance. If certain tasks are not completed to standard, or the candidate lacks experience, training can be offered to enhance competency. The JD can therefore act as a useful tool when there is a dispute, such as a disciplinary or grievance, as both parties can refer to the job description when determining whether obligations have been met and duties performed as required.

Through the provision of a clear job description, the document highlights key skills, knowledge, and duties associated with the role, which is useful for determining training requirements or opportunities to help upskill staff. Training, if delivered effectively, shows the organisation's commitment to developing individuals, who will in turn feel valued and more committed to the organisation, and boost their confidence and morale, thus enhancing job satisfaction and commitment to the company. This also reduces staff turnover, reduces mistakes, leads to increased sales, ensures higher guest service, and ultimately creates competitive advantage.

The job description determines pay based on the documented key responsibilities and duties of the role, ability to make decisions, consideration as to whether the employee has responsibility for others and therefore their financial worth in line with affordability and market rates, and legal minimum wage. In short, the more responsibility and involvement in key strategic decisions, the more risk, and the higher the pay grade in general.

A job description therefore enables an organisation to structure and manage roles in a standardised way, increasing efficiency and effectiveness of recruitment, training and development, organisational structure, workflow and activities, and customer service in hospitality, hotels, and events.

A job description which contains a list of benefits attracts a higher number of skilled applicants, and where this is traditionally listed near the bottom, can now feature nearer the top of the document. Listing benefits demonstrates wider compensation for work efforts and will demonstrate company culture towards valuing employees.

Over time, the job role can change so it is important to keep the job description up to date, and whilst it cannot list every task or responsibility, an additional caveat can be added to include any other reasonable duties. A file reference can also be added to the bottom of the document to show when it was last updated and identify how current the latest version is.

Table 2.2 shows an example of a job description template that can be used by organisations to create a job description.

Table 2.2 Example Job Description Template

Job Title or strapline Job Description	
Job title:	Insert job title.
Location of work:	State location or if multiple sites or if any travel.
Department:	Department name such as Food and Beverage, Banqueting, Housekeeping, Marketing.
Hours of work:	Full-time/part-time/zero-hours? These may not always be included as these may vary, and may be in a separate contract of employment.

(*Continued*)

Table 2.2 (Continued)

Job Title or strapline Job Description	
Job title:	Insert job title.
Salary and/or Pay Grade/ Band:	Best to state actual hourly rate or salary or salary range to attract high-quality candidates and a higher number of applications to prevent wasted time if salary does not meet needs. For organisations with pay scales best to note which pay band or scale the job fits into.
Benefits:	List benefits and other compensation available.
Responsible to:	Reporting lines: what supervisors/managers they will report to (job title).
Responsible for:	Reporting lines: what job roles they will supervise/manage (job titles).
Job purpose:	Overall contribution of the role to the organisation. This may include key responsibilities and what makes the job role impactful within the organisation.
Main duties and responsibilities:	List of main responsibilities and duties. Each duty or task starts with a verb.
Other duties / tasks:	Add a caveat/clause as to other reasonable duties that may be expected should other duties arise.
Special requirements:	Include special requirements such as standing for long periods or if hours include evenings or weekends/unsociable hours/shift patterns.
Title or reference to show if up-to-date version of document:	JD/Receptionist/September2025.

2.5 Person Specification

A person specification (or personnel specification) (PS) is a document that outlines the profile of the ideal candidate for the role, including level of education, qualifications, experience, knowledge, and competencies required for the job role.

As a standardised document, the PS reduces bias and discrimination as the person specification provides recruiters with a tool to systematically consider candidates against the same set criteria when shortlisting candidates for interview.

The PS also helps prospective candidates to determine their suitability before deciding to apply, much like the job description. It is therefore a further tool to filter who applies for the role before the recruiter is required to do so.

The following criteria will often be shown in the person specification:

Qualifications

Can typically be gained with education, or through professional training and experience. Qualifications include high-school qualifications / certificates such as numeracy and literacy, college education (further education, or FE), or university degrees (higher education, or HE). Qualifications also include work-based professional qualifications such as health and safety or food hygiene, licences such as alcohol licences, or other professional certifications awarded by accredited bodies. The PS must be specific about level of qualifications or grades where necessary.

Personal Attributes

These relate to attitudes and personal characteristics. In hospitality, hotels, and events this would typically include traits such as attention to detail, customer oriented, personable, adaptability, emotional intelligence, communication, and charisma.

Experience and Knowledge

This relates to the level of experience or knowledge an applicant should have to be able to carry out the role. This includes experience in a specific industry, job role, specific tasks, or type of venue, or a certain level or number of years of experience, especially for management roles or specific tasks.

In terms of number of years' experience, this should be carefully considered, if necessary, as it could constitute age discrimination for younger applicants who will not have as much experience as older applicants. Instead, they could be asked to demonstrate experience or competency.

Knowledge includes the knowledge or experience of using specific IT systems such as electronic point of sale (EPoS/PoS) systems such as *Oracle, Fidelio, Squirrel,* or Microsoft Office software including Word, Excel, and Outlook.

Competencies

This may be an additional heading or be placed within other criteria such as 'skills'. Competencies tend to be more detailed than skills and involve the behaviours and knowledge that enable individuals to be successful in the role. Competencies include language skills, budgeting, demonstrating an ability to communicate, honesty, dependability, problem-solving, teamwork, leadership, and relationship building.

Other or Physical Attributes or Requirements

This may state specifics such as standing for long periods, repetitive work, hot or cold working conditions, or manual handling as examples, which enable the applicant to determine if they are able to fulfil these criteria.

This may also outline shift patterns, or unsocial hours such as working evenings or weekends, or flexibility around working patterns.

A person specification typically lists criteria in two separate columns: **'Essential'** and **'Desirable'**.

Essential demonstrates to prospective applicants what is necessary for the role.

For example, for qualifications and education there is often a minimum educational level required and will be listed under the 'essential' column, and these criteria must ideally be met to be shortlisted for interview.

Desirable (sometimes listed as 'preferred') refers to attributes that would be useful for the job.

Desirable criteria are qualifications, skills, or experience that would supplement an application and make it stronger but are not essential. Desirable criteria enhance a candidate's application if met but are maybe not 'essential' as they can often be gained in-post once recruited.

Marginal applications that meet some, but not all, of the essential criteria may still be considered for interview, as applicants could have potential, and other skills can be gained in post, whilst training can also be given. A marginal applicant might be interviewed if stronger candidates decline interviews or withdraw from the application process (which is common in competitive environments where they have since accepted a different job or have been enticed to remain in their current employment).

Shortlisting applications against the person specification ensures fair and consistent hiring practices.

The PS is therefore pivotal in demonstrating fair recruitment practices when considering fair employment law and prevention of bias or discrimination as candidates are systematically judged against essential and desirable like-for-like criteria such as skills, qualifications, and experience relevant to the specific needs of the role. This prevents the risk of bias and discrimination against protected characteristics of the Equality Act such as age; race including colour, nationality, ethnic or national origin; gender or gender reassignment; religion or belief; pregnancy; disability; sexual orientation; and marital status.

See person specification in Table 2.3 and Table 2.4 for example templates. Criteria is placed under headings or uses ticks for essential and desirable and criteria as listed under the essential/desirable columns.

Each organisation will format their job description and person specification differently. Leonardo Hotels, for example, do not list criteria under essential or desirable, and the two documents are combined in one as seen in Table 2.5.

Table 2.3 Example Person Specification Template

Meetings and Events Operations Supervisor Person Specification		
	Essential	Desirable
Qualifications/ training	List educational requirements such as minimum qualifications and grades required. GCSE Maths and English grades A-C grades 4–9 or equivalent. Relevant hospitality degree or college-level qualification.	Supplementary qualifications or training. First Aid certificate. Food Hygiene.
Knowledge/ experience	Relevant work background such as experience of customer service or use of Microsoft packages. Supervisory experience or a strong conference and events team member looking for additional responsibility.	Experience or knowledge of specific practices or systems such as specific Point of Sales systems (POS). Knowledge of revenue management and reservations systems.
Skills	List technical skills such as proficiency in client databases, or social media tools. Excellent communication skills. Good people and interpersonal skills. Excellent customer service skills.	List supplementary skills such as proficiency in client databases, or social media tools. Sales skills.
Personal attributes	Other key competencies such as adaptable to change, working under pressure, attention to detail. Customer service oriented. Strong ability to work independently.	List other supplementary key competencies. Results driven.
Special requirements	Shifts patterns/ physical or other demands. Ability to work flexible shift patterns including evenings and weekends. Standing for long periods. Manual handling.	

Table 2.4 Adaptation of Industry Person Specification Template courtesy of Wivenhoe House Hotel, Colchester, UK

General Manager Person Specification		
Qualifications/training	Essential	Desirable
• A hospitality or related qualification.		X
• English and maths school-level certificates or equivalent.	X	
Knowledge/experience		
• Proven track record of budgeting and achieving performance targets.	X	
• Visionary in leading the brand to success and implementing positive change to improve operations and service.	X	
• Experience of mentoring and coaching team members.	X	
• Experience in a similar role across hospitality or events operations.	X	
Skills		
• Team working and ability to lead a team.	X	
• Self-motivated and can-do attitude.	X	
• Excellent management and leadership skills.	X	
• Problem-solving skills with an ability to manage issues with a flexible approach.	X	
• Well-developed communication skills and interpersonal skills.	X	
Personal attributes		
• Excellent work ethic and results driven.	X	
• Able to respond to guests and staff in positive manner.	X	
• Service oriented.	X	
Special requirements		
• Ability to work flexible shift patterns including evenings and weekends.	X	
• Ability to stand for long periods.	X	

Table 2.5 Industry Example of a Job Description courtesy of Edward Gallier, Leonardo Hotels

Cluster Human Resources Manager Job Description	
Job Title	Cluster Human Resources Manager
Grade or Pay	Competitive salary
Reports to	Assistant Group Human Resources Manager/ Group Human Resources Manager
Company Vision	To be the first choice for everyone who values genuine hospitality
Company Values	Consistent, Friendly, Genuine, Positive and Willing
Summary of Role	
The Cluster Human Resources Manager will direct the HR strategy within the cluster, as well as managing day-to-day HR operations. As part of your clusters senior management team you will develop and maintain close working relationships with the full management team within your cluster to ensure quality HR support is provided and aligned with business needs. You will focus on ensuring that a consistent employee journey is provided with a view to retain and develop our team. You will act as an ambassador for the Leonardo Hotels brand, reflecting the company vision, mission and values at all times. You will lead your cluster on compliance with employment law, benefits and payroll regulations.	
Main Tasks	
– Develop, train, coach and support managers within all areas of people management to ensure a good understanding and a consistent approach in line with company policies, procedures, best practice and legislation. – Lead, train and coach the local HR team to ensure a good understanding of their role and a consistent approach in line with company policies, procedures, best practice and legislation. – Drive the company strategies and business objectives within the cluster including HR, ESG, DEI, Wellbeing, recruitment, engagement and reward & recognition strategy and employer branding, utilising companywide systems and initiatives alongside local activity, feedback and celebrations. – Lead on local HR strategy appropriate for each hotel or function within your cluster, identifying key challenges and trends and implementing appropriate actions both proactively and reactively. – Host regular people strategy meetings with the General Manager/Hotel Manager/Head of Function to review key people metrics and issues, and agree future activity.	

(Continued)

Table 2.5 (Continued)

– Lead on local recruitment strategy to ensure that each hotel/function is resourced appropriately and recruitment is prioritised and managed in a timely manner by directing internal resources and working with third party organisations as appropriate. – Ensure compliance with all HR policies, procedures, best practice and legislation across the cluster, in particular employment law, benefits and payroll regulations, including Right to Work and National Minimum Wage regulations. – Ensure that a quality induction is delivered to all new starters through line managers, team coach and the face to face HR induction, ensuring all new starters receive the face to face induction within their first 6 weeks of employment – Promote development opportunities for all employees and ensure succession planning is in place throughout the cluster. – Drive continuous professional development and progression for yourself and the cluster HR team, with regular feedback, recognition and succession planning for your team. – Take overall responsibility for payroll being processed accurately and in line with the deadlines each month. Ensure that all relevant managers and the HR team are trained on the payroll systems and processes. – Provide leadership, guidance, coaching and advice in all aspects of employee relations. Work closely with Group HR and the ER Panel on complex or high-risk cases as appropriate. – Promote an open door policy, sign posting employees to relevant support and ensuring awareness of how to contact HR as required. – Managing the cluster HR team to ensure consistent and sufficient coverage of all hotels and functions within the cluster including during periods of leave and turnover within the HR team. – Lead on maintenance of HR and people systems, ensuring accurate and up to date at all times. – Ensuring self and cluster HR team identify and direct queries through the correct channels, including directing employees to their line managers where appropriate, taking action as required for example recommunicating correct channels – Travel to each hotel within the cluster regularly and as required, ensuring maximum visibility and on-site support from self and cluster team. – Travel across the estate for meetings and training as required. – Any other reasonable task.
Person Specification
– Comfortable working within brand guidelines to deliver results – Ability to handle multiple challenging priorities and deadlines – Focus on nurturing and developing individuals – Experience in a similar role – Excellent communication, inter-personal and influencing skills

(Continued)

Table 2.5 (Continued)

– Experience in managing and resolving ER issues – Excellent computer skills, previous use of HR systems is an advantage – Ability to manage and coach team members and managers – Ability to analyse situations, make independent judgements and use own initiative – Excellent presentation skills – Ability to work as part of the senior management team, have presence, generate credibility and build effective working relationships – Ability to travel to property locations in your cluster and other locations as required – Previous experience in hospitality is advantageous – Previous experience in a managerial level role – Up to date knowledge of relevant employment legislation – Is discreet and understands the importance of confidentiality in HR – CIPD qualified or working towards this is desirable
Measurable Performance Indicators
– Meeting agreed KPIs – Regular review meetings with line manager – Compliance with legislation including Right to Work and National Minimum Wage – Retention and turnover statistics – Employee absence statistics – HR Inductions held regularly – Engagement Survey scores and feedback – Activity to promote the employer brand – Mandatory and People Programme training completion – Accuracy of HR Data and systems
Ongoing Learning
– Online BELONG induction and development courses – Management induction – The People Programme – Passion 4 People programme – External training to keep updated with current legislation – HR Qualifications – Job Skills Checklist – HR induction – Buddying from another Cluster HR Manager – Coaching and guidance from line manager and Group HR – External courses, training and webinars – Self-learning and continuous professional development (CPD)

2.6 The Job Advertisement

Using the key information from both the person specification and job description, a job advertisement (advert) is then created.

The job advert highlights the key tasks/responsibilities for the role as taken from the job description, alongside key criteria from the person specification such as education and qualifications, skills, and aptitudes required for a role. The advert will often detail the location of work and pay and benefits to attract high-quality candidates to apply. Details of how to apply need to be included with application deadlines noted.

Hospitality, hotels, and events organisations may supply just an advert, or provide a job description and the person specification to potential applicants. These can be grouped within a 'job pack' or 'application pack' for candidates to review. Generally, the more information advertised to prospective candidates, the more refined will be the applications received.

Using information from the job advert, the job description, and person specification if provided, these documents help candidates determine their suitability for the role, helping to filter unsuitable candidates at an early stage which saves time, cost, and disappointment for both the candidate and the recruiter.

When pay and benefits are disclosed within the job advert, it attracts high-quality candidates. However, failure to specify pay can deter applications due to vague information. When 'competitive salary' is stated, this could waste the applicant's and recruiter's time, when it does not meet a candidate's expectations. The pay might be lower than their current wages, or not cover necessary costs such as travel, if commuting for example, or where the job is based in a city where living costs may be higher. But even a lower salary should be disclosed for applicants to make that decision. If it is revealed later in the process, it will demotivate the candidate and waste time and productivity of the recruiter(s).

A job advert must be free of discriminatory language, such as specifying gender – for example 'waitress' (waiting staff can be any gender), or 'must be English' as opposed to 'must be able to speak fluent English' which can apply to anyone who can speak English as opposed to discrimination based on ethnicity. This complies with equal opportunities employment law which requires related job-based competencies, skills, qualifications, and experience to protect characteristics such as age, gender and gender reassignment, ethnicity, disability, sexual orientation, marital status, pregnancy, and religion.

The job advert should clearly outline the job title, company branding and values, what the role involves, any skills, qualifications, experience or other personal aptitudes that are relevant, where the job is based, how to apply, an application deadline, and pay and benefits.

The job advert should follow the A.I.D.A principles: Attention, Interest, Desire, and Action. The advert should be visually stimulating to capture Attention; be easy to read and capture the Interest of high-quality applicants. The inclusion of the job title, benefits, tasks, and personal attributes required, should provide applicants with the Desire to apply. And details of how to apply and by when should be provided for the candidate to Action their application.

Traditionally, job adverts were placed in newspapers, trade publications, job centres, recruitment agencies, on radio, or television. These traditional methods of advertising tend to be expensive. With the rise of the internet, tablets, computers, and mobile devices, platforms to promote job vacancies have evolved. The most common platforms today include company websites, agencies, professional networking sites such as LinkedIn, and social media platforms such as Facebook, Instagram, WeChat, and TikTok. Word of mouth, however, is a common way of securing employment through professional and personal networks.

INDUSTRY VOICE

Dr Philip Berners, Associate Professor in Events Management

I have only ever secured jobs for events through my professional networks. This is why I advise people to find jobs through their networks – and if they don't have a network such as LinkedIn, then I urge them to begin building one!

There is an art to building your professional network. Link with people in your industry or who have the same professional interests as yourself. This way, you will network with people in their network which is how it grows.

And you will begin to recognise who is who in the industry – not only people, but names of organisations and things like job titles. You will be up to date with industry news – including job vacancies.

I feel that in today's society, 'cold' applications are dying out. We don't apply without knowing someone in the organisation, or being referred by someone else, or by knowing someone who happens to have a job opening. I call it 'warm' job searching.

Figure 2.2 provides an example of a job advert and Figure 2.3 an online job agency advert example.

Bartender

add logo

Salary: £27k a year

Location: London

Job type: Full-time contract

Apply Online!

About us:

At XYZ brand, we pride ourselves on creating warm, welcoming restaurant and bar providing exceptional service to our guests. We are a family restaurant situated in central London providing a relaxed environment to eat or drink and we are looking to expand our team. We are seeking a friendly, professional and charismatic Bartender to join our front of house team to provide memorable experiences for our guests.

As a Bartender you will be responsible for creating and serving drinks to our guests at the bar and restaurant. You will be responsible for guest interactions, drink recommendations, drinks preparation and sales for effective bar operations.

Key responsibilities:

- Greet and serving guests with a friendly demeanour
- Prepare and serve a range of beverages
- Maintain an organised, clean and hygienic bar area
- Take customer orders, offering recommendations, and high quality standard of drinks
- Prepare a range of garnishes for drinks and cocktails
- Maintain stock levels in bar fridges, the cellar and stock room using old stock first
- Work with the bar team and front of house team to establish a strong team and communications
- Check deliveries and create orders from suppliers
- Reporting inventory needs, shortages, or discrepancies to the Bar Manager
- Process payments through the till system
- Adhere to licensing requirements, health and safety regulations and other relevant legislation such as Weights and Measures and hygiene and age verification requirements
- Ensure all bar tools and glassware are cleaned and glasses replenished throughout your shift
- Assist with bar opening and closure procedures

Requirements:

- Previous bartending experience preferred but not essential
- Good understanding of a variety of soft drinks and alcoholic beverages and mixers
- Excellent communication skills
- Exceptional customer service skills
- Good organisation skills and able to multitask
- Able to work flexible shift patterns including evenings and weekends

Benefits:

- Competitive salary plus gratuities
- Free meals on shift on shift and staff discounts
- Full bar training and cocktail making masterclasses.
- Team social events
- Long service awards
- Additional paid day off on your birthday

To apply for this role as Bartender, please click apply online and upload an updated copy of your CV with cover letter or email your application to email@XYZCompany.com by 12 August.

Figure 2.2 Example Job Advertisement Template

Meeting & Events Operations Supervisor

add logo

City of London

£ **Competitive salary + gratuities**

Apply

At Leonardo Hotels, we are recruiting for a Supervisor role to join our great team in the Meeting & Events Operations areas. We are looking for an enthusiastic, genuine, and friendly person who really enjoys working in hotels and wants to provide great hospitality to our guests, contributing to them having a memorable stay with us.

As Meeting & Events Operations Supervisor

We want you to be part of a great and diverse team working together to provide great hospitality and products to our guests in the restaurant, bar or conference departments. We set high standards for ourselves so that we can surprise and delight our customers and deliver a great experience.

What we want you to have-
• Supervisory experience or be a strong Meeting & Events team member looking to take on additional responsibility
• Great communication skills so you can chat to our guests and of course the team
• Flexibility – to enjoy working different shift patterns and seeing the operation on different days of the week including the weekends as well as mornings, or evenings (no split-shifts here)
• The ability to recognise what our customers want and need and be able to provide it
• Good people skills – to work well in a team - we want work to be fun for all of our employees
• Have a genuine interest in providing hospitality to our customers
• Confidence with systems and taking payments
• To be able to work well under pressure at times and multi task in a fast paced environment
• Ensure prompt resolution of customer complaints

The job -
• To supervise the activities of the Meeting & Events Operations Crew, ensuring they are aware of their responsibilities and performing duties to a high standard
• To be familiar with the days business, restaurant, and conference bookings so that you can prepare the team, the department and be ready for action
• To serve food and drinks and give excellent customer service, being a role model to the team demonstrating great hospitality
• To have a visible presence within the hotel to ensure that all customer requests and queries are responded to promptly and effectively and to keep all areas clean and tidy at all times
• To deal with guest complaints in a friendly and efficient manner, ensuring guest satisfaction at all times
• Training and motivating team members
• Ensuring all cash, charge, float, and till procedures are carried out correctly.

Why come and work for us – to receive practical training, development, and progression within a dynamic and rapidly expanding company. If you want a career in Hospitality then look no further, we have great programs to support your development towards a long and successful career.

Some of the great benefits of working for us include:

• Varied and interesting work- no day is the same at Leonardo Hotels
• Flexible working hours- shift working is what we do but not split shifts – we want you to have a work-life balance too
• Having the chance to work with and around friendly people
• Birthday cards every year- we celebrate everything
• The opportunity to work for a well-respected brand where people development is at the heart of our culture
• Lots of locations in the UK and Ireland which mean that if you want to develop or just fancy a change of scene, we can help you to move and provide relocation support
• A smart Uniform
• Meals on duty
• Monthly engagement activities- we like to have fun while working hard
• Annual Charity Event Day- we help and support our communities
• So many training courses that your brain may not be able to squeeze them all in
• Employee of the month earning you a little bonus and fame for the month.
• Leo Points – earn points and claim them back on gifts that you want
• Stay at one of our hotels for a hugely discounted rate and get a reduced rate for friends and family if they want to stay too
• 28 days holiday entitlement including bank holidays, increasing with service to a maximum of 33 days
• Sensible benefits that could save you money - Pension Scheme, Life assurance, wellbeing support, wedding leave.

Figure 2.3 Industry Example of an Online Job Advertisement via an Agency

2.6.1 *Talent Acquisition and Job Advertisements*

Contribution from Katie Owlett, Head of Talent Acquisition, De Vere Hotels

Most companies' Human Resources teams now include dedicated Talent Acquisition (TA) teams who lead all recruitment activities, from job advertising, interview design and delivery, to training and employer branding. Employers' websites normally include a careers page where you can find out more about available careers and the benefits on offer; these tend to be owned and managed by the TA team.

While the TA team is linked with the Human Resources team with its key focus on people and culture-related activities, the roles involve many marketing-related tasks to positively promote the brand as an employer of choice.

Job advertising is another aspect of marketing, and it is worth noting that good recruiters may not necessarily have good creative-writing skills. Talent Acquisition teams might therefore attend some form of job advert copywriting course or work closely with their company's marketing team to ensure their adverts are correctly worded to resonate with candidates and provide insight into the company and its culture. The artificial intelligence (AI) writing programmes, such as *ChatGPT*, have proved a useful tool for many job adverts, but it is best used to only provide inspiration or suggestions if you want the company's tone to be authentic.

First and foremost, the headline or job title of the advert is crucial. If this is not right, then your advert might not even get read. Talent Acquisition teams spend time researching the most searched job titles in their industries to ensure candidates see their companies' job roles and that their adverts feature in jobsite keyword searches. Once you've got the right job title, your job advert needs to be well thought out.

Job adverts need to be brief and to the point because research suggests you have only about eight seconds of someone's attention before they decide whether it's for them, and that the optimum number of words for a job advert is between 150 and 300. Deciding what to include and in what order is therefore very important and will vary depending on your target market and for generational recruitment must be very well thought out.

Currently, if you are looking to appeal to Gen Z candidates (born between 1997 and 2012), you need to be clear within the first scroll about what the job will offer them. Companies have in recent months moved the 'benefits' from the bottom of their job adverts to much nearer the top. It is important to highlight the benefits being offered and other information relating to work–life balance, hybrid working options, and flexibility, as these are increasingly important to candidates.

Believe it or not, an ongoing hot topic is whether to advertise the rate of pay or salary or leave showing this as competitive. However, whilst many employers still choose to hide this information, a *talent.com* survey showed that 98 per cent of 2,000 people they surveyed said they would not apply for a job if they did not know the salary – would you?

The outline of the role should be brief and interesting – not a copy and paste of the job description. A couple of sentences about what the job involves should be all you need, followed by up to five bullet points about any related skills or experience required. Remember, the focus of the advert is to generate applications, but you also want them to be suitable applicants, so make sure you include important details like the working hours, days, and location.

Diversity and inclusion are another very important area for consideration with regard to job adverts, and TA teams often use language-checking tools before publishing content to ensure it appeals broadly, with many jobsites offering free tools. Many employers now include statements in their job adverts noting they are equal opportunities employers and that all applications are welcomed. However, good employers will go one step further, outlining their Diversity, Equality, and Inclusivity (DE&I) initiatives to demonstrate the positive actions they have taken.

Finally, deciding where to place your advert is also extremely important, and costs differ dramatically between online jobsites and other methods. This area should always be given due research and analysis, again taking into consideration your target market for the specific job role. You should review the sources of your existing workforce and new-hires on a regular basis, as well as the number of applications you receive from different sources and the conversion of these applications-to-hires. This information will help you decide where best to advertise your vacancy.

2.6.2 Application Methods

The job advert should state how to apply for the job vacancy.

An application form may be the preferred option or application with Curriculum Vitae (CV) also known as a Resume (or Résumé) accompanied with a cover letter. This could be a hard copy posted to the organisation, or uploaded to an online application system, whether internal or via a recruitment agency.

An application form is often chosen by organisations as it captures standard information from all candidates, making it easier to compare candidates and assess their suitability. An application form is also useful to assess neatness and intelligence (when handwritten) and provides an opportunity for candidates to express themselves and demonstrate their personality traits. Application forms establish candidate motivations, aspirations, and achievements. However, poorly designed application forms might mean there is not enough space to write answers, questions are complicated to understand and answer, and it is not clear how much information is required.

Applicants should be advised that they can ask for large-print application forms or braille or any other adaptions as required as reasonable adjustments – and demonstrates that the organisation is compliant with ED&I, and welcoming and thoughtful.

Alternatively, applicants can be asked to apply using a CV (with or without a cover letter). CVs and application forms will be filtered against set criteria based on competency to perform in the job role and potential for development. Online platforms attract large volumes of applicants, so shortlisting against set criteria helps filter applicants.

Whether online or done manually, applications received will be filtered according to criteria such as experience, qualifications, personal attributes, and skills – to avoid bias. Not all applications received by agencies or online agencies will be forwarded to the recruiting firm to ensure only the most suitable candidates are shortlisted.

Recruitment agencies are often used alongside the company website to attract high-quality and higher volumes of candidates. A recruitment agency may be an online platform or physical recruitment office, and each will charge fees such as a percentage of the job vacancy salary, or a set fee (flat fee) for their search and select recruitment services. Recruitment firms will help with recruitment documents, upload the advert to their own site, and will sort through their database to find suitable candidates and email job opportunities to potential candidates.

Recruitment agencies often require candidates to make appointments to visit physical recruitment offices and may provide work immediately or put forward applications to the recruiting hospitality organisation to consider. A recruitment agency may also interview on behalf of the employing organisation.

For specialist or more senior roles, a headhunting agency (also referred to as 'Executive Search') can be used to identify and approach candidates on behalf of the employing organisation. Head-hunters are hired to provide specialist recruitment services to source talented individuals who meet specific job requirements. This helps find passive talent who may not have been actively job hunting.

Word-of-mouth might also be used, and an employee reward scheme put in place for staff to recommend a job to their professional contacts, friends, or family members. If that individual is then employed and retained within the business for a specific period, a finder's fee will be offered. Word of mouth is now one of the most common ways of sourcing candidates, alongside company websites, social media, and online recruitment agencies. This is also known as 'referrals'.

Popular trade publications such as the *Caterer* online and other trade journals are useful for targeting individuals with an interest in hospitality, hotels, and events specifically, and an advert placed for a fee.

Professional networking platforms such as *LinkedIn* have grown in significance for recruitment. *LinkedIn* allows for peer-to-peer professional networking, private messaging, following individuals with similar careers, or Human Resources professionals and managers who advertise vacancies. *LinkedIn* has a jobs section, enables individuals to upload multiple CV's and a profile of professional skills, alongside providing recommendations for others. The platform has options to highlight that an individual is 'open to work' or is 'hiring'. *LinkedIn* has quick 'apply' options so that a CV can be uploaded, whilst other job adverts redirect to company websites or online recruitment platforms that can be auto populated with information from the CV or need to be manually typed.

Once applications are received the shortlisting process can commence.

2.7 Shortlisting and Screening (of Applications Received)

Shortlisting is the process of filtering applications to determine who to invite for interview.

Some companies use screening processes such as telephone calls or video calls to further determine suitability for the role where there are several applicants, or applicants who meet the criteria as noted in the person specification and experiences that support competency in terms of the job description (or job advert where these documents are not used).

Ideally, applicants will be shortlisted for interview using the Essential and Desirable criteria in the person specification (see Section 2.5), sorting applicants into 'suitable, 'marginal', and 'unsuitable' for interview.

Suitable candidates will have demonstrated all, or a majority, of the criteria in the Essential column such as key qualifications, skills, experience, knowledge, and aptitude. The Desirable criteria do not have to be met to be shortlisted but will enhance an application such as a hospitality or events degree, which is not necessary for employment but demonstrates wider industry knowledge and skills.

Marginal applicants will meet some of these criteria and could still be interviewed if suitable applicants withdraw from the process, or still be interviewed based on potential.

Unsuitable applicants will not meet the required criteria and will not be shortlisted for interview.

This selection process enables fair recruitment practices whereby applicants are being shortlisted against standard criteria, according to task-based criteria and the profile of the ideal candidate, as opposed to risking exposure to selecting (or rejecting) due to protected characteristics such as ethnicity, age, or gender.

Shortlisting can be done manually by the recruiting team or manager, by sifting through CVs, or reading application forms where used, comparing the applicant profiles to the pre-determined criteria outlined in the person specification (or advert if no person specification exists).

The application is usually supported with a cover letter which is a further opportunity for the candidate to highlight their suitability for the role, their motivation for applying for the role, and their desire to work for the organisation.

Cover letters are a further tool for recruiters who can ascertain individual traits of applicants by their approach to writing their cover letter.

INDUSTRY VOICE

Philip Wicebloom, Event Manager, 5-star London hotel

When recruiting new colleagues, consideration must be given to the person's education level (if relevant to the role), current skill set, prior experience, and their suitability to the role. Before meeting a candidate, their suitability really is a guess. A CV/Resume, even a well written one, can be a remarkably poor representation of a person compared to meeting them in person.

I view CVs just as a means of identifying prospective candidates, who may vaguely fit the criteria.

As Senior Events Manager of a prestigious central London hotel, with a large event business, every time we needed to recruit an Event Manager, I was faced with going through hundreds of CVs which is time-consuming. Each one was graced with 20 seconds of my attention due to the volume received.

The best gauge when selecting candidates is simply instinct. You just never really know until the interview.

On occasion, I have selected candidates on the basis of a really impressive CV. Yet on meeting them, that impression was disappointing.

INDUSTRY VOICE

Dr Philip Berners, Associate Professor in Events Management

When I was a recruiter for event venues, I was not reading CVs. I was looking for reasons to reject a CV. This was the only way to get through the sheer volume of CVs sent to me. It was selection by elimination.

Events management is about details – planning, organising, communicating, leading, executing... it's all about detail. If presented with a CV with incorrect detail, how can I give you a job managing my events?

This is why I advise people to have an excellent CV free from errors, incorrect grammar, or spelling mistakes. Because, if I received that CV with a spelling mistake, I would put it on the 'reject' pile and move on to the next CV. It may be brutal, but it is efficient.

Besides, if a CV contains any errors, it shows that the applicant has a deficiency with their eye for detail – especially when promoting themselves for a job which is when I would expect personal pride in the detail!

2.7.1 Shortlisting and Screening Applications Using Agencies and Technology

Where an agency is used, shortlisting and screening may be completed by the local or online recruitment agency, who will forward only suitable applicants to the employing organisation. This reduces time spent by the employing company when recruiting but does incur a fee.

Alternatively, shortlisting can be facilitated using artificial intelligence (AI) or computer-based systems which search for keywords within applications such as 'communication skills', 'customer service', 'people management', or job-specific terms such as bartending, events management, systems knowledge, and reservations. Computerised systems speed the shortlisting processes, but in some instances, systems may have text boxes or text inside tables which cannot be read and therefore applications will be rejected for failing to meet the required criteria. Likewise, if keywords are used for filtering, and different wording is used by an applicant, this will also not be picked up.

AI can provide Human Resources and managers with helpful tools to write recruitment documents, contracts, and policies, but as with all technology, there are risks. AI and other shortlisting systems can make mistakes, as they can only be as accurate as the information they have access to, and all documentation generated using such systems should be checked for accuracy.

AI and computerised systems may be deployed by the employing organisation or by a third party such as a jobsite, so applicants might apply via third-party agents such as *indeed.com* and *Global Hospitality*. However, when applications are made through third-party websites, some of the applications received will not be seen by the employing organisation as the third-party has shortlisted on their behalf.

INDUSTRY VOICE

Rachel Matthews, Director of People and Culture, The Royal Air Force Club

Having worked in businesses that utilise both manual and computerised methods for screening and shortlisting candidates during the recruitment process, I can attest to the effectiveness of both approaches in finding the right fit for a role.

A preference will depend on factors such as the size of the company, budgets available, volume of recruitment, and desired outcome. However, one outcome remains paramount: any method followed must ensure a process that is free of discrimination and is objective and fair.

Online screening and shortlisting methods in particular have risen in popularity due to the technology now available to serve this purpose and the timesaving element. Popular methods include Applicant Tracking Systems (ATS) or Artificial Intelligence (AI).

We must however remain vigilant to some of the pitfalls to using online methods for recruitment purposes. These can include: a lack of a 'personal touch' during the process; relying on technology working all the time; and all candidates having access to the right technology, specifically in terms of screening and shortlisting candidates.

Other pitfalls may include not setting the correct shortlisting criteria; candidates not responding accurately to set criteria; challenges with technology being able to select all the correct data; and ensuring the technology is set up to avoid bias.

Online systems can be extremely useful but should not replace the human element when selecting the right candidate for a role.

2.7.2 Other Screening Methods

Trial Shifts and Showcasing Skills

It is common practice in hospitality and events to require prospective recruits to undertake a trial shift. Trial shifts involve inviting the applicant to work a full shift, part of a shift, or to demonstrate a particular skill. This is commonplace for operational front-of-house roles.

Historically, many venues have not compensated candidates for the trial shift which has led to widespread concerns over organisations using trial shifts to potentially fill labour gaps and abuse free labour: making applicants work for free. Anyone who completes a trial shift should be fairly paid for their time.

Instead, an applicant can showcase competency and skills, such as making coffees in a café, serving food or drinks, or clearing tables in a restaurant, a short time behind the bar, serving food at a banquet, or showcasing cooking skills such as making an omelette for a catering job.

INDUSTRY VOICE

Dr Philip Berners, Associate Professor in Events Management

I have never asked a prospective employee to work a trial shift. What's the point?

Firstly, I consider myself perceptive enough to consider an applicant's CV, their history, their experience, and their qualifications. Then, at interview, I can consider their personality and 'fit' with my team. What more should I need?

On top of this, if I make them an offer of employment, I can determine very quickly whether it will work out – don't forget they are on 'trial' during their probation period, anyway.

If I have made a mistake and it isn't working out, I now have the opportunity to find solutions and offer support such as training, coaching, mentoring, or buddying with an existing employee.

Finally, nobody performs well during a trial shift. The situation for the applicant is false, frightening, and unfamiliar. They will not know where anything is or who anybody is. It's traumatic.

But, not to pay them for their trial shift? That is unforgivable. Everybody deserves something for the work they have done; the time they have given up; the contribution they have made to the profit of an organisation. Okay, their reward might be to get the job, but if they don't get the job, they should be paid double for the trial shift they have worked for you.

Assessments

Whilst interviews themselves could be classed as a form of assessment allowing for a face-to-face or online meeting between recruiter and applicant to assess personality and fit with the organisation, other assessment methods can be used such as psychometric testing, including aptitude tests and personality tests and telephone screening.

Psychometric testing involves the use of tests which can be administered and systematically scored to assess personality, aptitude, and intelligence. This can be useful in determining an individual's cognitive ability or identifying specific personality traits needed for the role. These should correlate with job performance measures such as attitude towards a customer complaint, or ability to complete administrative tasks.

There are two categories of psychometric testing, **aptitude tests** and **personality tests**.

Aptitude tests assess cognitive abilities such as problem-solving skills, numeracy, literacy, verbal reasoning, diagrammatic reasoning, and logic. This involves issuing tests such as tax calculations, profit calculations, identifying patterns, or proofreading for literacy errors in guest communications.

Personality tests assess the personality, attitude, behaviours, and motivations of applicants. These are designed to establish work-based behaviours in line with the job requirements. This helps ascertain how they would respond to situations at work such as attitude towards complaint handling, conflict or difficult conversations, and relationships with peers or managers as examples. The *Myers-Briggs Type Indicator* and emotional intelligence tests are commonly issued to candidates.

The *Myers-Briggs Type Indicator* (MBTI) identifies 16 personality types which helps identify whether an individual is introverted or extroverted as examples, which assesses how they would deal with certain scenarios or approach their work and working relationships. This will help judge an individual's personality and attitude relevant to the role to determine if they are suitable for the vacancy.

Emotional intelligence tests identify an applicant's ability to understand and manage their own emotions, and their ability to understand and empathise with the emotions of others. Self-awareness, self-regulation, and the ability to understand the emotions of others, helps enhance working relationships, necessary within the working environment of hospitality, hotels, and events, especially given the social environment of the service industry, the need for teamwork and working under pressure, and the volume of customer-facing roles.

Essentially, employers use psychometric testing to evaluate applicant skills and personality traits compared to other applicants, and interviews to objectively assess candidate suitability for the role and reduce bias.

Psychometric testing helps predict performance within the workplace, how applicants will perform in the job role, and if their values align with that of the employing organisation, and can be used to help shortlist candidates for interviews.

They are typically issued prior to interviews and will often be online. Some job roles, including graduate schemes, require applicants to complete timed assessments to determine competence in relevant language proficiency or numeracy, as examples. If the test is not completed in the required time, or minimum pass marks not met, the candidate will not be successful in the application process. This initial screening provides information on candidate skills necessary for the role, and any test that is failed identifies shortcomings in certain skills. It is advisable for applicants to practise example tests readily available online before attempting an official one, so they are better prepared for what is expected in terms of questions and timings, and to help overcome nerves.

Telephone Screening

Telephone screening is a process used by the hiring manager to determine if an applicant meets the required criteria to be shortlisted for interview. In the early stages of the interview process, the manager, Human Resources, or recruitment agency where used, will arrange a telephone call as a means of an initial screening of applicants. This is useful where there are a large number of applicants, or marginal applicants who do not meet all criteria but demonstrate potential, or as a less-formal interview to help shorten the list of candidates for interview.

Once shortlisting has been completed, a list of candidates to take forward to interview should be created, outlining their name, contact details, summary of key competencies against the set criteria determined in the person specification where needed as a candidate summary, and availability for interview. This can include a score or other information for each of the criterion such as education, experience, or key skills required for the job. An example template for shortlisting can be seen in Table 2.6.

Alternatively, a form for each candidate may be created during the initial screening process that is more specific and detailed, as per the example in Table 2.7.

Table 2.6 Example Shortlisting Template

Name of applicant	Criterion 1	Criterion 2	Criterion 3	Interview Yes / No	Comments

Table 2.7 Example Applicant Shortlisting Template

<table>
<tr><td>Applicant Shortlisting Document
Vacancy applied for: [insert job title]
Date: [insert date]

Interviewer: [insert name]</td><td colspan="2">Rating system:

1: Poor, does not meet basic requirements
2: Fair, meets some of the basic requirements
3: Good, meets most criteria, some training needed
4: Very good, meets requirements
5: Excellent, exceeds all requirements</td></tr>
<tr><td>Applicant Name</td><td>Email</td><td>Phone number</td></tr>
<tr><td>[insert name]</td><td>[insert email]</td><td>[insert phone number]</td></tr>
<tr><td colspan="3"></td></tr>
<tr><td>Criteria (copied from person specification)</td><td>Summary or tick box if criteria met</td><td>Score if relevant 1–5 (with 1 being the lowest and 5 the highest)</td></tr>
<tr><td>Qualifications/training
[List key qualifications/ training or professional memberships or qualifications such as high-school literacy/ numeracy and state-level/ grades. Relevant degrees of professional affiliations]</td><td>Summary of candidate's qualifications/training</td><td>Score 1–5 or numbered boxes to tick</td></tr>
<tr><td>Knowledge/experience
[List criteria such as knowledge of systems, profit and loss accounts, menu planning, managing teams]</td><td>Summary of candidate's relevant experience</td><td>Score 1–5 or numbered boxes to tick</td></tr>
<tr><td>Skills
[List each skill separately e.g. customer service, communication]</td><td>Does the candidate have the required skills? Yes/ no or tick box against each or summary</td><td>Score 1–5 or numbered boxes to tick</td></tr>
<tr><td></td><td></td><td>Total score=</td></tr>
<tr><td colspan="3">Recommendation: Shortlist/reject</td></tr>
<tr><td colspan="3">Comments/notes</td></tr>
</table>

2.7.3 Shortlisting at De Vere

Contribution from Katie Owlett, Head of Talent Acquisition, De Vere

During the shortlisting process, all candidates need to be benchmarked on the same criteria which should have been discussed and agreed before the job was advertised, but certainly should be before any shortlisting or screening commences.

It is important to note that the criteria will vary for each different position being advertised. For instance, the formatting and spelling of a Curriculum Vitae (CV)/Resume might be an essential element of criteria for someone applying for an administrative or sales role. As these roles involves communication with clients, attention to detail is necessary, especially for written communication. Spelling of client names, accuracy of function sheets, or when writing a response to complaints is essential to the role, so if mistakes are present in an application or CV, this demonstrates a lack of attention to detail, or a lack of motivation in their application.

Spelling and grammar may become much less important for someone applying for operational back-of house-roles such as in the kitchen or housekeeping and in that case literacy errors become less relevant.

Other areas for consideration when shortlisting might include:

- Relevant experience in industry or similar
- Qualifications / Education / Professional Memberships
- Related or Transferable skills
- Length of service in previous roles

De Vere initially screen the CV/resume applications received and shortlist candidates for a screening interview. This initial screening interview might take place by telephone or video call depending on the role.

The purpose of the screening call is to not only gauge the suitability of the candidate and whether they should be invited to a face-to-face interview, but to check that the role is right for the candidate.

If contacting someone without notice for a telephone interview, always start with introductions and the company name, explaining the purpose of the call, and how long the call will take, and ask if it's a good time for the candidate to talk. If it's not, a more suitable time to contact them can be agreed. Sometimes, applicants may have applied for more than one role in more than one organisation, so it is best to state a name and reason for calling.

Some examples of De Vere screening questions include:

1. Please could you start by telling me what interested you in the role and led you to apply.
2. Why are you looking to leave your current role?
3. What do you know about our Company?
4. Please talk me through your understanding of the job you have applied for and then I can help by filling in any gaps for you if needed… – it's important the candidate understands the role properly to ensure it's the right role for them.
5. How long would it take you to get to and from the location? How would you be commuting?
6. This role involves working xxx – are these shifts suitable for you? Are there any restrictions around the days or hours you are available for work?
7. The pay rate for this position is xxx – how does this compare with your current salary?

Throughout the call, not only listen to the answers given, but also the way the candidate communicates, the language used, and their tone of voice. A candidate who has researched the company and travel location is preferable as it demonstrates a genuine interest in working with the company. Although, in some cases an organisation may still consider someone who needs to do further research, and to ask this question again at the next stage – the in-person interview.

An example of a telephone screening form can be seen in Table 2.8.

Table 2.8 De Vere Telephone Screening Form

TELEPHONE SCREENING FORM

Candidate Name:	Position Applied for:
QUESTION	RESPONSE
Check/discuss current role on CV Why do you want to leave your current role?	
What attracted you to apply for this position?	

(Continued)

Talk me through your understanding of the role (fill in any gaps in knowledge & check still interested) and any relevant experience			
Why do you want to work for the Company/what do you know about us already?			
Are you legally entitled to work in the UK? Do you require a visa to work in the UK?			
How would you travel to and from the Hotel/Venue? Check commute time			
How does the pay/ salary on offer compare to what you have been earning?			
What is your notice period?			
If shortlisted for the next stage: When are you available to attend an interview?			
TELEPHONE INTERVIEW FEEDBACK/NOTES In addition to the above consider their telephone manner & communication style			
OUTCOME (Circle as appropriate)	PROGRESS TO ON SITE INTERVIEW	REGRET AFTER TELEPHONE INTERVIEW	APPLICATION WITHDRAWN
Screened by:	Date:		

After the screening interview, it is then determined who to invite to attend a face-to-face interview. These generally involve meeting two members of the team for team members/supervisors and up to four people for senior managerial roles. This is known as a panel interview where there are two or more interviewers.

It is recommended to take note of the reason any applications are declined (at any stage), and to keep all candidates informed of the outcome of their application. Informing candidates of their application status helps demonstrate good communication, advising if applications are still under review, or not successful, to hopefully reduce applicant frustrations and leave a positive impression of the brand.

Under the Equality Act (UK law), it is illegal for employers to discriminate at any stage of the recruitment process. There will be similar requirements globally.

At De Vere, hiring managers are required to attend a 'Talent Acquisition Masterclass' to help consistently deliver a fair recruitment process and to in turn foster a diverse and inclusive culture. During the training session, protected characteristics and discrimination are covered, alongside conscious and unconscious bias, to highlight the danger of stereotyping and preconceived notions and the risks of them overlooking talent. For example, you may assume certain behaviours are typical, such as if they are nervous or if they share similar experiences, thus causing the 'halo effect' whereby the applicant is perceived as preferable due to individual comparable lived experiences, thereby leading to bias.

Part 2: Interviews, Interview Analysis, Offers of Employment, Right to Work Checks, Contracts, and Volunteer Staff

2.8 Interviewing

Invites should be sent to applicants once shortlisted for interview, advising of date of interview, time, location, and instructions, such as car parking or other transport arrangements, waiting areas, and notifying someone upon arrival, such as reception or security.

Interviews can also take place by telephone or videocall, in which case time zones, connectivity, timings, and online links should be provided in advance of the interview.

An interview is an opportunity for the candidate to impress the employer, and applicants are their own marketing tool, promoting themselves as the most suitable candidate for the role. If a candidate does not believe in their own skill set and qualities, neither will the employer.

However, interviews are also important in terms of the impression the employer gives, and interviewers should leave a positive impression of the organisation. Interviewer(s) should also leave a good impression and maintain professionalism throughout, whilst providing information on the organisation and the role.

INDUSTRY VOICE

Dr Philip Berners, Associate Professor in Events Management

A CV should be strong and impressive to win an interview. The interview is for the candidate to now show their personality.

Although interviewers usually go through the candidate's CV at the interview, that information is already known – and is why the candidate has been invited for an interview. The purpose of the interview is for the interviewer to see the candidate's personality; their response to questions; their confidence; their professionalism; and their fit for the role and the organisation.

It is important, therefore, for the candidate to relax and allow their personality to show. And the interviewer should be mindful to allay nerves and coax the personality to shine.

If the candidate's personality isn't right, it needs to be seen to make the employment decision. After all, if the candidate doesn't fit the role or the organisation, it won't be a long and successful employment relationship and it is better for both the candidate and the interviewer to identify this at the earliest stage. That is what an interview is for.

An interview should be a two-way meeting with both the interviewer(s) and interviewee having the opportunity to ask questions and provide information. An interview only provides a snapshot of an applicant's abilities and different judgements will be made throughout the interview.

INDUSTRY VOICE

Philip Wicebloom, Event Manager, 5-star London hotel

When interviewing applicants who may come across well on their CV, the interview can then be really disappointing.

There can be several reasons. A primary one is poor preparation for the interview. For Event Manager roles, I typically ask candidates to imagine they are organising an event in The Ballroom. What does that event look like?

If the answer indicates that the candidate has no knowledge of The Ballroom and cannot formulate any basic response, then the interview does not last much longer. It is politely terminated, and I explain why and give guidance as to their future interview preparation.

Candidates must research the establishment for which they are being interviewed. They must demonstrate knowledge of the hotel, its history, values, etc., plus some departmental information. Such intelligence is easily obtained from a website.

A desire to work at a particular business is also key. Skills can be taught, attitude cannot.

INDUSTRY CASE STUDY

Philip Wicebloom, Event Manager, 5-star London hotel

Sharon is applying for a job within food and beverage at a local small hotel.

Her CV shows a diploma in beauty therapy. Following college, Sharon obtained a role in a local hair and beauty salon but recently was promoted to an informal management position, deputising when the owner is off duty or on holiday.

Sharon's covering letter states that she recently experienced fine dining and was completely overawed by the occasion. It sparked her interest in food and beverage, and she is fascinated by the hospitality industry and desires a change in career. She thought about becoming a chef but feels more comfortable front of house, as she loves talking to clients.

Worth an interview? Absolutely. Sharon is pure gold as a candidate. A negative attitude would be – no relevant experience, discard.

Positives are:

- She has communication skills, honed by talking to clients in the salon
- Shown progression in her role there, being entrusted as manager on occasion
- Is passionate about food and beverage and wants a starting role
- Will be an adaptable team member in the interest of learning all she can, as quickly as she can

Remember, skills can be taught, attitude cannot

Sharon is the sort of team member that would be ideal in a small hospitality business. She would need to be nurtured to retain her, after time. As a person motivated to progress in hospitality, she may be hard to keep. Such an ambitious colleague should be identified, encouraged, and promoted after reaching key achievements along her work pathway. That one-time Food and Beverage Assistant could turn out to be the General Manager in just a few years.

2.8.1 Interview Planning

Each candidate invited to attend an interview should be sent an interview confirmation email outlining the details of the interview, what they need to do when they arrive, and what to bring with them.

Reasonable adjustments should be noted such as needing forms in large print, braille, or if a hearing loop is required. Car parking and access requirements should be checked.

A suitable time and date should be arranged, and confirmation sent to the applicant of where to go, including notifying reception when they arrive.

The candidate will ideally be escorted to the interview room, but interviews can take place in meeting rooms, a bar area, back office, or coffee shop, depending upon how formal it is.

Remember, the interview reflects the employer as well as the candidate. This is the hospitality/event industry so make the candidate feel comfortable (do not forget you want to reveal their personality). Offer water or a hot drink. When they arrive, ask the candidate if they would like to use the bathroom – they may have travelled for some time. Ask this again when the interview is concluded – they may have a long journey home.

Interviews must be carefully planned, considering timings, availability of interviewers, their working hours, and their rest breaks. Furthermore, in our service industry, operational needs need to be considered, especially if managers are conducting interviews and may be called upon to support operations during busy periods. Interviews vary in length, but an hour is typical to allow for full discussion. Timings must consider how long it takes to collect applicants from the waiting area, delays, rest breaks, and lunch breaks.

Conducting six interviews over one day may be suitable, but due to time constraints, some organisations will conduct more, and some less. Some interviews will be conducted in one day, others across multiple days. Some recruitment processes involve multiple stages and therefore multiple days, such as group assessments, individual assessments, and individual interviews.

To ensure equality and fair treatment, applicants should be asked in advance of the interview if any reasonable adjustments need to be made such as wheelchair access, large print or braille documents, or a hearing loop.

If interviews are conducted by videocall – for example on *Teams* or *Zoom*, the online link for the meeting must be sent to the candidate.

Interviews can be confirmed with candidates by telephone, calendar invite, letter, and/or email as examples. Candidates should be asked to confirm their intent to attend.

When in-person interviews are used, the location of the interview room and seating arrangements should be considered, and the room should be quiet and free from interruptions. A desk between the applicant and interviewer creates a barrier, but formalises the interview, whilst sitting in a coffee shop will create a less formal environment if desired.

When interviewing online, for example by videocall, interviewers must consider environments that are free from noise and disruption, and consider internet stability for both the interviewers and interviewee and establish the process if connectivity is lost, or if audio or cameras do not work. Both parties should be aware of their background, and blur or consider a more professional setting where necessary.

Considering the rise in home working, some applicants or interviewers have children or pets which can cause disruption and distraction. In such situations, patience and understanding is required.

Telephone interviews can take place at a mutually convenient date and time, and background noise and locations when making the call should be carefully planned.

In all types of interviews, it is important to have a predetermined set of questions, and pen and paper or other means of writing notes available. Best practice involves using a formal interview analysis form listing key criteria to write notes against, so candidates can be fairly compared against one another using a standard set of criteria with which to capture responses of the candidates and to score candidates against.

The manner of the interview should be considered such as a 'hot seat' or 'easy' interview, with the former involving an ongoing list of questions for the candidate to answer, and the latter being less formal and relaxed. Care should be taken to avoid asking multiple questions in one, so as not to confuse or overwhelm the interviewee.

Whichever format is used, interviews should involve two-way conversation between the interviewee and interviewer(s) and opportunities should be given for the candidate to ask questions. The hiring team should be able to answer more specific details about the job role, organisation, benefits, and working conditions.

2.8.2 Types of Interviews

A job interview may be structured or unstructured.

Unstructured interviews are when the candidate talks freely, and the hiring team does not prepare questions, thus allowing for free-flowing conversation. Interviews in an unstructured format result in a less-formal discussion to get to know the applicant and for the applicant to get to know the interviewing manager or ask questions about the job role and company.

Generally, an applicant is allowed to talk freely and little interviewer preparation is required. An informal unstructured interview puts candidates at ease. Informal unstructured interviews result in the applicant being more relaxed as formalities are reduced.

However, unstructured interviews make the conversation difficult to control and may not result in capturing the right information from interviewees. If there is no structure and multiple interviews take place, it will be difficult to fairly compare one candidate to the next or remember strengths and shortcomings of each applicant.

The risk with unstructured interviews is in not being able to demonstrate fairness and non-bias if this becomes challenged. A rejected candidate could complain that the interview or indeed the hiring decision was discriminatory or unfair – especially if decisions are subjective and not comparable with other candidates.

Structured interviews are more formal and require the interviewers to prepare questions in advance. This is preferable in terms of fair recruitment practices and makes it easier to compare candidates when determining which candidate provided the strongest answers and evidence of competency to fulfil the role.

A standard set of questions are created based on key attributes and skills needed to fulfil the role as taken from the job description and person specification. Each candidate is asked the same standard set of questions. This ensures candidates are only asked questions relevant to the role and reduces the risk of bias and discrimination. This format tends to be better perceived by candidates.

Candidates will then be scored using a rating or Likert scale on an interview analysis form, as discussed in Section 2.8.5. These forms can then be referred to when comparing candidates and the person with the highest score should be the person employed. Structured interviews can result in a more effective predictor of potential performance in the workplace.

Semi-structured interviews are often used to enable the recruiter to ask similar questions candidate to candidate, but adapt questioning depending on individual responses, experiences, and the application. Some questions will be tailored to the individual being interviewed, their experiences and qualities. Further questions will result from specific responses a candidate provides, to probe more information, or to develop rapport.

Structured and semi-structured interviews may be perceived as more professional by the candidate with the recruiter showcasing professionalism, planning, and organisation skills, resulting in the candidate feeling more valued, especially when personal achievements and career history is known. This can enhance perceptions and brand reputation.

2.8.2.1 INTERVIEW BIAS

Due to structured interviews being more formal and unnatural, it is common for candidates to feel under pressure. An applicant may experience anxiety or stress and come across as nervous or unable to fully answer questions because nerves may change their outward behaviours. Consequently, the applicant might be judged due to this, and an unfair biased interview occurs.

This is referred to as **temporal extension effect** where interviewers assume a candidate's behaviour (such as nerves) during an interview is typical of their general behaviours.

The recruiter might also associate specific groups of people with specific traits or characteristics. Whilst this may be an unconscious bias – such as a name, educational background, age, or gender – it can lead to assumptions about the applicant and is known as the **stereotype effect**.

Affinity bias is where the interviewers and applicant may share a similar background, education, or career. An individual recruiter may favour a candidate if they identify with them due to similarities and may then give preference to this applicant.

The **halo effect** can lead to bias and is where a similar, more favourable, trait or positive impression overshadows the poor qualities (horns).

The **horn effect** is when bias occurs due to a single negative trait which leads to overall negative judgement of the individual.

2.8.3 Ways to Conduct Interviews

One-to-one is where the interview consists of a single interviewer and the applicant. This is useful for two-way conversation but risks bias where there is just one person to consider how suitable the applicant is for the role.

Small group interview is where two or three people interview the applicant but could also be referred to as a panel interview. This may consist of one member of Human Resources who would ask CV-based biographical questions, and departmental managers asking specific job-based competency questions. In this instance, there are multiple perspectives of each candidate reducing the risk of bias. It can also be useful for the other interviewers to write notes as another asks the questions.

Panel interviews are similar to small group interviews but usually consist of a larger number of interviewers. This is where several people interview the applicant which is usual for high-level executive roles and where numerous managers want to meet candidates. Again, a range of views are sought, reducing the risk of bias. Large panels can cause stress, however, and put applicants under pressure where they are being judged by a number of people.

Candidate group interviews are where several applicants are interviewed together – this format helps when large volumes of applications are received. This may involve all applicants answering the same questions in front of each other (but is unfair on those who answer first, as latter applicants can improve their own response or copy previous answers) or individual questions. Alternatively, it might involve a group activity such as panel discussions, or group assessment centre-based activities, assessing key competencies required for the job, such as teamwork, communication, or leadership qualities. Group assessment activities include problem-solving competences such as puzzles, working together as a team to solve a problem, a simulated roleplay, or game.

CASE STUDY: GROUP ASSESSMENT CENTRE ACTIVITY

Several applications have been received and a group assessment centre activity is being used to shortlist candidates against one another in teams. The winning team will be taken forward to the next round of interviews.

A box of *Lego* bricks is disseminated to each team. The number of bricks is the same for each team, for example 25 bricks, and each team is briefed to build the tallest tower using the least number of bricks available in the shortest time possible. The tower needs to be freestanding.

The concept is that each brick is a commodity which costs money, and the time taken to build the tower amounts to labour costs. The tower needs to be tall and freestanding to ensure product or service quality. The objective is to build a tower with the highest profit to win.

The teams start at the same time, and are covertly assessed by the hiring team on factors such as communication, leadership, problem-solving, and strategy (traits relevant to the job role).

When the first team finish, their time is recorded; then the second; third; and so on.

The hiring team will then record tower height, alongside how many bricks were used.

Materials. Each brick costs £1.00 irrespective of its size.

Labour. Calculate the time it takes to make the tower in minutes (x 10).

Height. Measure (x 2)

The winning team is calculated as per the above:

Profitability: = Height (x2) – ((labour x10) + bricks))

Team 2 wins: = £74.00 – (33.20+25) = £15.80 profit

Table 2.9 Case Study, Group Assessment Activity, Illustration of Team Results

	Team 1:	Team 2:	Team 3:
Time (labour costs)	1minute 06seconds (£10.60)	3minutes 32seconds (£33.20)	6minutes 20seconds (£62.00)
Bricks used (costs)	14 bricks (£14.00)	25 bricks (£25.00)	22 bricks (£22.00)
Height (profit)	13cm (*2 = £26.00)	37cm (*2 =£74.00)	15cm (*2 =£30.00)
Profit =	£1.40	£15.80	-£54.00

During the debrief, the hiring manager would highlight each team's strengths and weaknesses, for example:

Positive team traits: delegating tasks (brick building), discussing how to make the tower sturdy, changing the way the tower is rebuilt if it falls the first time, using fewer resources/bricks, focussing on height, brick costs, and time: stacking single bricks one on top of the other or not.

Less desirable traits: team members not contributing, building the tower repeatedly the same way with the same results (tower falling over), using too many bricks, spending too much time on the task, and poor building technique. A team which uses multiple bricks in one layer will use more bricks which costs money in terms of number of bricks used (commodity costs) and does not add height.

The most profitable team will be announced, and this is the team who go forward to the next round of interviews which may be individual interviews or an individual assessment.

Example group interview

Group interview scenario: Managing a Busy Reception

Context: You are working in a busy resort hotel and a coach with 50 guests has arrived with all guests needing to check in. There is also a wedding taking place in the hotel with guests arriving, and the lobby is busy. Guests are becoming frustrated waiting at reception to be attended to, and with only two receptionists working, tension is building. The team needs to find solutions for efficient check in for the coach party at the same time as the wedding guests, whilst ensuring everyone feels valued and is satisfied with service.

Candidate Instructions:
Work together as a group to manage the situation described. Determine how you would manage both the group of guests checking-in and the wedding guests to ensure efficient operations and guest service standards. Consider (1) the guest experience and problem-solving skills; (2) teamwork and delegation of tasks; (3) communication; (4) complaint handling; (5) time management.

De-brief or discuss the following with candidates:

- What approaches did the group use to manage the situation?
- How was guest service handled?
- How did you delegate tasks?
- How did you communicate issues and problem solve?

Candidate evaluation:

- **Customer service:** how guests were prioritised, service standards met or exceeded
- **Teamwork:** to work together, keep calm, communicate, and delegate roles
- **Problem-solving:** solutions that were used to deal with the issues; how were complaints handled?
- **Communication:** clear, polite communication with guests and team members
- **Time management:** resolving service-time issues and quick service of guests

Telephone or online interviews are mainly used as an initial screening procedure prior to formal interviews and are useful where applicants do not live locally. Telephone interviews have evolved with technology and whilst *Skype* was commonly used, this has been replaced with online videoconferencing software such as *Teams* or *Zoom*. Face-to-face interviewing using online videoconferencing software is more useful than voice calls because facial expressions and body language can be assessed and are generally more personalised with the ability to see one another.

Online waiting rooms can be utilised for applicants to be held until interviewers are ready in the main meeting room online.

Issues may include poor connection, image, voice time lag, and connection loss. Regardless of whether the interview is by phone or online software, time zones might also present issues and must be considered.

AUTHOR'S VOICE

Whilst studying my Hospitality degree I completed an internship and chose to work overseas in Missouri, US. The resort hotel employed many international students within reception, events, and restaurants so it would have been impractical to interview in person.

Human Resources called me at a pre-arranged and agreed time and interviewed me by telephone to assess my personality, skills, and to discuss which departments I would be most suitable to work within. We built a strong rapport on the phone, and I was made to feel at ease and was offered the internship within the food and beverage department rotating between Conference and Banqueting and their two restaurants.

2.8.4 Interview Questions

Interview questions will typically be created from the applicant's CV, their application form, the person specification, and the job description. This will ensure the interview questions are based on both competency and experience.

Generally, questioning will begin with Human Resources asking CV-based questions, asking about previous work experience and qualifications. Departmental managers will then ask job-specific questions to assess whether the candidate is the right fit for the organisation in accordance with the job description and person specification. Managers would assume all these roles in the absence of Human Resources.

Some interviews are informal and questions not pre-prepared. Others will be semi-formal with a set of questions being asked but will then ask secondary or alternative questions based on the candidate's answers.

Formal interviews are structured, so all candidates are asked the same set of questions to ensure candidates can be fairly compared against one another in line with fair recruitment practices.

Prior to the interview, interviewers will prepare a standard set of interview questions where a more formal interview format is being utilised. The types of questions which may be asked include **biographical, situational,** and **behavioural** questioning.

Biographical questioning involves asking the candidate to confirm previous work experience, education, and qualifications. This is normally led by the Human Resources professional but can be performed by the recruiting supervisor or manager. Such questions may be posed as: *'Tell me about yourself'*; *'Talk me through your previous job role/what did you enjoy most about working for XYZ company'*; or *'Talk me through your CV'*.

Situational questioning is where an interviewer asks the candidate to state what they would do in a certain scenario or hypothetical situation. This may involve asking questions such as *'How would you deal with.../What would you do if...'* Questions should be relevant to skills or experience required within the advertised job role, so if customer service skills were essential, this may involve asking: *'How would you deal with a customer complaint if they were unhappy with the service received?'* This establishes problem-solving skills, confidence with customer service, and when working under pressure, as well as communication which may all be skills required for working in the service industry such as in events, restaurants, or hotels.

Behavioural questioning is similar to the situational style, but the candidate is asked to give an example of their own practice/experience. This may be an important decision or reaction to a given scenario: *'Tell me about a time when you provided excellent customer service'*; or *'Explain to me how you dealt with a difficult customer or complaint'*. This assesses personality and aptitude to different work situations relevant to the role.

Interview questions can be closed or open-ended. Closed questions require a yes, no, or one-word answer. These determine specific information but lack detailed information that more open or probing questions will achieve. An example may be *'Have you ever dealt with a complaint?'* This requires a yes or no answer and lacks information as to how they dealt with the complaint which would establish their aptitude and work-based behaviours.

Therefore, open-ended probing questions are useful for capturing more information from the candidate in assessing their suitability for the role.

Open-ended questioning involves asking questions which enable the candidate to talk more freely, such as *'Talk me through your work experience'*; or *'Tell me about your role at XYZ company'*.

Probing questions are similar in nature but with the aim of obtaining further specific information about a skill or quality needed for the role. This aligns with situational and behavioural style questions to assess competency, for example *'How would you/did you deal with a complaint that you experienced within your role.'*

Here is an example list of common questions starting with biographical CV-based questions:

1. Talk me through your CV.
2. How would you describe your current level of experience in hotels/events/hospitality?
3. What did you like most about working at XYZ Company?
4. Describe a time when you have used your [skill] e.g. customer service.
5. How do you ensure a positive guest experience?
6. How do you deliver excellent customer service?
7. If a customer was dissatisfied, how would you deal with their complaint?
8. Please tell me about a time when you faced a difficult challenge from a previous job role and how you dealt with it.
9. What do you enjoy the most about working in XYZ job role?
10. How do you manage working under pressure during busy periods?
11. What difficult decisions have you had to make at work?
12. Please explain how you would deal with a deadline/unreasonable deadline.
13. Please discuss a time when you have worked effectively in a team.
14. How would you describe your relationship with co-workers/managers?
15. How would your current employers/colleagues describe you?
16. What are your strengths/weaknesses at work?

17. What is your long-term career goal?
18. How do you see yourself in 5/10 years' time in terms of career goals if we were to employ you?
19. Having recently left education, how prepared are you for the working environment? How have/are you prepared?
20. Why do you want to get into hospitality/events/hotels, this career path?
21. Why do you want to work for us?
22. What do you know about our company?
23. Are you willing to travel?
24. Are you able to work flexible hours/shifts/overtime?
25. What are your hobbies/pastimes/interests/passions?
26. Name a time when you have been criticised, describe how you felt and what you did/would do in future.
27. How do you feel this interview went for you?

2.8.4.1 BEST INTERVIEW QUESTIONS TO ENSURE A COMPREHENSIVE INTERVIEW

Contribution from Mike Dalley, HR, Learning and Development Expert, HRAddict.com

Job interviews are heavily reliant on asking the right questions. Doing so, uncovers valuable information about candidates' skills, experience, and what they can add to the organisation's culture. The best interviews contain a mix of questions designed to gauge experience through examples, hypothetical scenarios, aspirations, and motivations.

HRAddict propose 20 of the best interview questions to ask a candidate to ensure a balanced and comprehensive recruitment process. We will cover why these questions are an important part of an effective interviewing technique and what you as a hiring manager can learn from the way applicants answer them.

1. 'What attracted you to this organisation?'

   This question is a good way to open an interview, as it gauges candidates' attitudes towards the organisation and allows you to see how they align with your core values and purpose. The question will also allow you to understand how prepared the candidate is, as well as what research they have done about the organisation and the role.

   If a candidate answers this question by demonstrating organisational knowledge and alignment with your purpose and shows plenty of research, this will affirm to you that they are very interested in the role — and for the right reasons.

2. 'Tell me about yourself.'

   This question is useful to understand the candidate's work biography and give them the chance to bring their résumé to life and allows you to ask questions to follow up and deep dive into aspects that are aligned with the job.

   This question tells you a lot about candidates but is especially useful to see how they can add context to their work history and narrate their biography in a way that demonstrates to you they understand the job description and what you as an interviewer need to hear.

3. 'What motivates you?'

   Gauging what motivates a job candidate is vital, as it allows you to see if they find motivation in your organisational culture, in terms of how it rewards and recognises employees. You can also use this question to see if the candidate will be a good fit with their manager and how they like to manage people.

   Look out for candidates who explain how they approach self-motivation and how they expect to be motivated by their manager and see if this is a good fit for how your business operates.

4. 'How do you evaluate success?'

   This question can give you insights into how candidates approach goal-setting, motivate themselves, and lead people or respond to leadership. You can also assess their approach to problem-solving, commitment, and work ethic. When candidates answer this question, you will be able to pick up insights into how they handle tasks, approach continuing professional development, and their attitude to work–life balance.

5. 'How do you handle stress?"

   This question aims to assess a candidate's ability to cope with pressure and demands at work; because of this, it is a great question to ask if the role is especially stressful or intense. The question can also help you gauge a candidate's attitude to time-management and resilience.

   Their answer to this question will give you information about a candidate's stress management techniques, their attitudes to work–life balance, how they might work on their own or in a team, and their fit for the culture in your organisation.

6. 'How would your boss describe you?'

   This question assesses a candidate's interpersonal skills, their self-awareness of strengths and development areas, their cultural fit to the organisation, and their general professional approach in the workplace. It is a useful question, as it is a good all-rounder to ask and allows candidates to be a little reflective in their answer.

When candidates answer this question, look for examples or achievements of anything they have raised, and try to glean an understanding of balanced feedback (e.g. if they offer a combination of positive and negative traits).

7. 'What are your hobbies and interests?'

   This question might not seem very work-related but in fact it can tell you a lot about candidates. Their answer will help you understand more about the candidate's personality and cultural fit, as well as their preference for work–life balance and how well-rounded they are as a person.

   The question is also useful, as the candidate's preference for hobbies and interests will reveal information about what transferable skills they have. Finally, the question can often relax candidates and make a personal connection – vital to the flow of an interview.

8. 'How do you handle negative feedback?'

   This question can help interviewers assess candidates' receptiveness to feedback, their attitude to change management, and the level of their emotional intelligence. It can also be used to understand their approach to problem-solving.

   In the candidate's answer, look for signs regarding how they process feedback, especially through understanding, acknowledging, and acting on it. You will be able to glean their approach to reflecting on challenges and how they learn from tricky situations.

9. 'Why should we hire you?'

   This question is a very useful one to ask, as it covers quite a few areas of competency at once. These areas include cultural fit, skills, experiences, and motivations.

   When the candidate answers this question, you will be able to discern information regarding their fit to organisational values, the level of their self-awareness and confidence, motivations, and general enthusiasm about the role.

   You should probe for specific achievements and assess how the candidate's answer aligns with other information about their competencies that you have taken from the interview so far.

10. 'What are your greatest strengths?'

    This question gives candidates a chance to candidly boast in the interview! It is useful because it will give you an opportunity to clearly understand the candidate's strongest areas or key qualities, and how they align with the role they are interviewing for.

When assessing the candidate's answer, take time to seek contrary evidence (i.e. have they spoken about anything in the interview that contradicts these strengths?). Assess their level of confidence, and how self-aware they are of their competencies. Finally, seek clarification from the candidate on any strengths that you are not sure would be in alignment with the job description.

11. 'How do you manage deadline pressure?'

    Another especially useful question for high-pressure environments, this question assesses a candidate's time-management skills, their resilience, ability to work to multiple deadlines or under pressure, and organisational ability.

    When they answer this question, you will be able to assess how candidates respond to stress and what coping mechanisms they use, how they manage their work, how they solve problems, and determine their work ethics and reliability. Ensure candidates give examples of these areas when they answer the question.

12. 'What are some of your short-term goals?'

    This question is a good one to ask, as it gives insight into a candidate's strategic planning abilities. Candidates can share both their personal and professional objectives, and this gives insight into how they organise themselves, what they prioritise, and how their approach to planning might align with the role and organisation.

    When they answer this question, you will be able to assess a candidate's approach to motivation, and how (and where) they take initiative. You will also be able to assess how they set goals, which will give insight into their planning ability and organisational skills.

13. 'What do you know about our company?'

    This question is a great one to ask, as it gives candidates a chance to demonstrate what research they have done about your organisation and, based on this, why they feel they might be a good fit for the company and the role.

    When they answer this question, you will be able to gauge their level of preparedness for the interview, and whether they can use the information they discovered to demonstrate that they fit – and want to fit – into the organisational culture and its purpose. You can also use their answer to assess if the candidate is aware of the organisational changes that might impact the role.

14. 'What are your salary expectations?'

    This is one of the most important questions to ask in the interview, as it will ensure the candidate and yourself share the same expectations when it comes to money and they have not been invited to the interview in vain. Asking this question can mean that both parties do not waste their time on a process if the salary cannot be agreed upon.

When asking this question, employers can use the exchange to understand how gaps in salary versus expectation can be bridged, such as seeing if other benefits like healthcare or bonuses can be used to make the role more attractive to the desired candidate.

15. 'How do you learn new skills?'

    This question gives insight into how candidates approach continuing professional development. It is useful because it will help you understand the candidate's attitude to skill gaps and their awareness of areas they need to develop.

    When assessing a candidate's answer to this question, consider their learning style and how this aligns with the learning culture of the organisation. Consider their attitude to learning (i.e. is it reflective or proactive?) and assess their skill gaps and general level of enthusiasm about doing more than is required.

16. 'How would your co-workers describe you?'

    This question gives valuable insight into how candidates work with others. It can demonstrate the levels of a candidate's teamwork skills, and provides an opportunity for the candidate to assess their competencies from the opinions of others. Therefore, it is a powerfully reflective question to really get candidates thinking.

    There is a lot to discern from how candidates answer this question. You will be able to see if they would be a good cultural fit for the organisation and its people, and how they might get along with their stakeholders. You will also get an insight into their competencies, and how these align with the job description.

17. 'Describe your ideal work environment.'

    This question is crucial to understand how candidates like to work. It will get them to share insights about how they like to work, their perfect organisational culture, how they like to be managed, and what motivates them.

    In their answer, you will be able to consider whether your organisation is the right choice for candidates, based on their response. You can strike up a discussion during this question, informing them about the culture and working environment, and whether this aligns with what they are seeking. This allows the candidate to decide whether they proceed with the application or self-select out of the process.

18. 'Why do you want this job?'

    This question assesses a candidate's motivations for the role, and why they have chosen to apply in the first place. It also encourages the candidate to share what they know about the organisation and the role, encouraging them to be honest and sincere.

    When you ask this question, ascertain the candidate's reasons for applying for this job. If they give detailed reasoning, assess its alignment with your organisational values. If they talk a lot about your culture and cite this as a reason for applying, this is also a good sign. Probe into answers that are vague or seem too generic.

19. 'How do you define effective teamwork?'

    With teamwork being so critical to many roles, this question aims to allow candidates to explain how they like to work in a team, their interpersonal skills, and what their expectations are regarding collaborating with others.

    The candidate's answer to this question will enable you to understand how they approach teamwork and if this aligns with your organisational culture. You will also get an idea of their conflict-management skills, and how they might approach leading teams if this is part of the job description.

20. 'Have I answered all your questions?'

    This question is used at the end of the interview. It is typically asked to understand if the candidate has any concerns that have not been addressed, and to gauge the candidate's interest in the role. It is an important question, as it clears the air and closes the interview naturally.

    Use the candidate's response to clarify any concerns they have and prevent any misunderstandings. You can also assess their engagement in the interview so far and get a feel for their enthusiasm for the role.

    Using these top interview questions will ensure that you create a balanced and detailed interview experience that will get the best out of every candidate. Remember to probe into candidates' answers and use your interviewing skills to extract the best answers from candidates who might be nervous or unsure of the best way to answer questions.

    Using a mix of questions like the ones I have provided will ensure that you discover every dimension of the candidate, helping you make a balanced and fair assessment that will ultimately result in making great hiring decisions.

Contribution from Katie Owlett, De Vere

De Vere Hotels provide their managers and Human Resources with role-specific questions for interviews alongside questions that link to their key values as an organisation. These questions can be found over the next few pages.

Interview questions guide

If someone has already conducted a screening interview, try not to duplicate the same questions.

General opener questions

- Tell me a bit about yourself.
- What interests you most in this position?
- What have you enjoyed most in your current position?
- What has been your best job to date and why?
- Why are you looking to leave your current role?
- What have been the biggest challenges you have faced in your current role? How did you overcome these challenges?
- This role involves working [explain required shifts and days] – are there any restrictions around the days or hours that you are available to work?
- What shifts have you been used to working previously? How did you find those shifts?
- What are three most important things to you from your next role?
- Tell me about what you know of the brand/this property, and why do you aspire to work for us?

Technical / role specific questions

This is your opportunity to ask role-specific questions relating to probe a candidate's skills and experience.

If someone has no prior work experience, you can use the following questions:

- Talk me through your understanding of the role and what it involves.
- What do you understand might be the challenges you might face within this role?
- What skills or experience do you have that would be relevant for this position?
- In what areas do you think you would need the most support or training?

Your technical/role-specific questions include systems/IT skills but are also useful to draw out experience in other areas such as:

Health & **Safety:**

- Talk me through your health and safety responsibilities in your last role.
- Tell me about some important health and safety training you have received / attended in the past – what did you learn from this?
- What steps do you take to ensure the safety and security of guests while they are on your property or under your care?
- Describe a time when you had to accommodate a guest with a specific dietary requirement or allergy. How did you ensure their experience was safe and enjoyable?
- What was your role in maintaining a clean and welcoming environment? How did this contribute to the overall guest experience?
- Describe a time when you had to handle an unexpected crisis or emergency, such as a power outage, evacuation, or accident in the workplace.

Product Knowledge:

- How do you stay informed about local attractions, events, and dining options to assist guests in making the most of their visit? Can you give me an example of when your local knowledge enhanced a guest's stay?
- How do you keep informed on industry trends and best practices?
- What is a current trend you are aware of?

Sales/Upselling:

- Please describe a time when you had to upsell or promote additional services/products to guests/customers?
- How did you approach the upsell and what techniques did you use to convince the guest?

Rota Scheduling, Questions for Management Roles:

- Can you describe your experience with creating work schedules or rotas for a team?
- How did you ensure the rotas were fair and balanced whilst meeting business needs?
- Tell me about a time when you had to adjust a work schedule or rota at short notice due to unexpected circumstances. How did you communicate the changes to your team? How did it impact the team's productivity and morale?

- Describe a situation where you had to balance labour costs with staffing needs when creating a work schedule/rota.

Training / Inducting Team Members, Questions for Management Roles

- Can you describe your role in overseeing and co-ordinating the induction process for new employees in your previous role?
- Give me an example of a successful departmental team training session you have facilitated. How did you engage participants and ensure the training had a positive impact on their performance?

Targets Financials / Budgets, Questions for Managers

- What targets have you had to work to previously?
- Tell me about a time that targets proved challenging and actions you took/implemented to turn this around.
- Talk me through your previous budgeting responsibilities.
- Discuss your approach to setting and achieving performance targets and KPIs. How do you ensure that the team are focused on meeting these goals?
- Describe a challenging financial situation or budgetary decision that you had to navigate and what you did.

Hotel Management (or Event/Other Hospitality Role)

- Have you completed Hotel / Events / Restaurant / Bar Duty Management shifts? If so, what did this involve?
- Tell me about the most challenging Duty Management shift you have experienced and what happened.
- Can you describe your role and responsibilities as a member of the management team?
- Discuss your approach to communication and information sharing within the management team.
- Give me an example of a successful project or initiative where you played a significant role within the management team.

De Vere Values Questions

You should choose between two and no more than five questions for each Value the organisation has for use during the interview. The below is related to De Vere so should be adapted for the employing organisation.

HEART & SOUL

Craft Level

- Can you share an example of a time when you went above and beyond to ensure a positive experience for a guest or customer and received some good feedback?
- Have you gone above and beyond for a guest/customer? What was the situation and what did you do?
- Tell me about a time you went out of your way to help a colleague – what did you do?
- Talk me through how you make guests/customers feel welcome and comfortable – what specifically do you do?
- What do you think sets you apart from other candidates in terms of your natural hospitality skills and your ability to create memorable guest experiences?
- In your opinion, what are the most important qualities for someone in a hospitality role to possess? Why do you think these qualities are crucial?
- How do you stay motivated and maintain a positive attitude during long shifts or busy periods in the hospitality industry?

Supervisory / Management

- How do you create a sense of belonging and make people feel welcome in your team?
- How do you ensure guest satisfaction is a top priority for all team members?
- What do you personally do as a Supervisor/Manager to help inspire your team to put their heart and soul into their work?
- Tell me about a time you had to speak to a member of your team about their performance as you did not feel they were putting in their greatest effort.
- What do you look for when recruiting team members? What interview questions do you like to ask to gauge someone's suitability?

INTUITIVE APPROACH

Craft Level

- Can you provide an example of a time when your proactive approach enhanced a guest's experience?

- Tell me about a time when you proactively identified a potential issue or opportunity and acted before it became a problem or before it was requested of you.
- How do you normally respond if you do not know the answer to a customer's question? Can you give me a specific example?
- How do you prioritise tasks and manage your time effectively when dealing with a busy workday in a hospitality role?
- How do you handle time-sensitive and high-pressure situations, such as multiple requests? Can you provide an example of when you successfully managed such a situation?
- How do you adapt your communication style when interacting with different types of guests or customers? Can you give me an example of a time when you had to modify your approach to meet someone's needs?

Supervisory / Management

- Can you describe a situation where you had to make a quick decision without all the necessary information? What was the outcome?
- In your previous role, can you provide an example of a time when you relied on your instincts to resolve a team issue or make a significant business decision? What was the result?
- Can you tell me about a time you had to deal with a difficult guest or team member and how you balanced your intuitive judgement with company policies/procedures?
- Describe a scenario where you had to trust your intuition when hiring or promoting someone. How did your intuition influence the decision-making process and what were the results?

VALUED RELATIONSHIPS

Craft Level

- Tell me about a time you have worked as part of a team. What role did you play?
- Describe a time when you built a genuine and lasting relationship with a colleague, guest, or supplier. What steps did you take to nurture that relationship?
- How do you help to make new colleagues feel welcome and part of the team?

- Can you share an example of a time when you had to work with a challenging or demanding colleague or team member? How did you collaborate effectively?
- Give an example of a time when you built a strong rapport with a difficult colleague or customer. How did you approach the situation and foster a positive relationship?
- Share an example of when you collaborated with team members from diverse backgrounds or with different skillsets.

Supervisory/Management

- Tell me about a time when you had to take on a supervisor/leadership role within a team.
- Share an experience when you had to delegate tasks or responsibilities within a team. How did you ensure that tasks were allocated effectively and fairly?
- Discuss your approach to effective communication within a team.
- How did you communicate with your team to ensure everyone had a clear understanding of their roles and responsibilities?
- Tell me about a time when you had to provide constructive feedback to a team member. How did you approach the conversation, and what was the impact on their performance?
- How do you ensure that all team members have the opportunity to contribute their ideas and perspectives during team meetings?
- Give me some specific examples of things you have done in the past to motivate your team.
- Share your experience with celebrating team successes and achievements. How did you acknowledge and reward the efforts of your team members?
- Tell me about a time you have had to manage and resolve conflict within a team?

EVERY DETAIL CONSIDERED

Craft Level

- How do you demonstrate attention to detail in your work?
- Can you provide an example of when your attention to detail made a significant difference to a guest's or customer's experience?
- Tell me about some specific brand/service standards you have had to adhere to in the past.

- Describe a situation where you had to adapt or evolve your approach based on feedback or changing circumstances to improve the guest experience.
- Tell me about a time you were faced with a difficult customer issue. How did you resolve the situation?
- What strategies do you employ to maintain a positive attitude and remain patient, even when faced with challenging or demanding guests?
- Share an instance when you received feedback that required a change in your work habits or behaviour. What steps did you take to implement those changes?

Supervisory/Management

- Tell me about a time you had to respond to a written complaint and the process you followed.
- How do you gather guest feedback and use it to continuously improve and evolve your approach?
- Can you provide an instance where you successfully implemented a process or system to streamline operations and improve overall efficiency without compromising the guest experience?
- Tell me about a time you have had to speak with a member of your team about the accuracy of their work? How did you review their progress after the conversation?
- When delivering feedback, how do you ensure you fully understand the other person's perspective?

2.8.5 Interview Analysis

As previously outlined, when considering best practice, the person specification, alongside the job description and resumé/curriculum vitae (CV) is used to determine interview questions. In the instance of a structured, or semi-structured job interview, each candidate is asked the same set of questions.

The answers from candidates can then be compared consistently and fairly to determine the strongest applicant. The responses to interview questions can be captured within the interview analysis form (see Tables 2.10 and 2.11) and a scoring system used to identify the strength of answers given.

The responses provided by candidates help demonstrate job-based competencies in terms of experience and attitude towards work, whilst affirming qualifications and other skills and experience. The scores can then be compared against one another and the applicant(s) with the highest score taken forward to the next round of interviews or be hired.

This ensures fair recruitment practices are used as candidates are judged only on key competencies and skills required for the job, as opposed to personal traits such as protected characteristics which include gender, age, religion, or sexual orientation.

The interview analysis form can be used to evidence due diligence and legal compliance with the Equality Act concerning protected characteristics, whereby the firm has done everything as reasonably practicable to prevent bias or discrimination during the recruitment process. The interviewee with the highest score is the candidate offered the role demonstrating competence across all key criteria identified in the job description and person specification, the ideal traits and experiences required to be successful in the job role. An example interview analysis form can be seen in Table 2.10 and an industry example from Leonardo Hotels in Table 2.11.

Table 2.10 Example Interview Analysis Form

Interview Analysis form Vacancy applied for: [insert job title] Candidate Name: Date: [insert date] Interviewer: [insert name]		Rating system: 1: Poor 2: Fair 3: Good 4: Very good 5: Excellent
	Total score =	
Criteria (copied from person specification)	Comments	Interview Score
Qualifications/training [List key qualifications/ training or professional memberships or qualifications such as high school literacy/ numeracy and state-level/ grades. Relevant degrees of professional affiliations]		Score 1–5 or numbered boxes to tick. 1 2 3 4 5 ☐ ☐ ☐ ☐ ☐
Knowledge/experience [List criteria such as knowledge of systems, profit and loss accounts, menu planning, managing teams]		Score 1–5 or numbered boxes to tick. 1 2 3 4 5 ☐ ☐ ☐ ☐ ☐

Skills (Skill 1) [List each skill separately e.g. customer service/ communication/ multitasking] e.g: Communication Skills How well does the candidate communicate verbally? Is the candidate articulate and clear in their responses? Does the candidate actively listen and respond thoughtfully?		Score 1–5 or numbered boxes to tick. 1 2 3 4 5 ☐ ☐ ☐ ☐ ☐
Skills (Skill 2)	Summary of response	Score 1–5 or numbered boxes to tick. 1 2 3 4 5 ☐ ☐ ☐ ☐ ☐
Skills (Skill 3)	Summary of response	Score 1–5 or numbered boxes to tick. 1 2 3 4 5 ☐ ☐ ☐ ☐ ☐
Special requirements		
Outcome	Employ ☐ Reject ☐	
Comments/notes (or strengths and areas for improvement)		

Table 2.11 Industry Example, Interview Analysis Form (adapted), provided by Edward Gallier, Leonardo Hotels

Interview Summary Page	
Candidate name	
Interviewer's Name	
Role Applied for	
Note-taker Name	
Date	
Career	**Score (total 3 points)**
Experience	
Competency Questions	**Score (total 18 points)**
Initial Questions	
Previous Experience	
Teamwork	

(Continued)

Pace & Positivity		
Customer Service		
Role-specific questions		
Red **11 points or below**	**Amber** **12–16 points**	**Green** **Above 17–21points**
Benefits	**Concern**	
Overall summary		
Outcome of interview – Offer Regret Hold Work Trial (Please circle)		

Overall Rating			
0	1	2	3
No evidence provided	Gave some evidence, needed prompting. Little evidence	Strong evidence, little prompting, linked to our behaviours	Excellent evidence, no prompting
Welcome and introductory questions			
Introduce yourself to the candidate. Describe the structure of the interview: • Starting the interview • Career/college discussion • Scenario questions • Additional questions • Ending the interview Ask the candidate if they have any initial questions about the structure of the interview.			
Initial questions			
1. How did you hear about the position? 2. What made you apply when you saw the role? 3. What is your perception of the role you have applied for? (If no knowledge, explain role) 4. What do you know about our brand? (if no knowledge, discuss brand) Notes:			

(Continued)

Overall Rating			
0	1	2	3
No evidence provided	Gave some evidence, needed prompting. Little evidence	Strong evidence, little prompting, linked to our behaviours	Excellent evidence, no prompting

Previous experience
1. Tell me about your previous experience and roles a. Listen for transferrable skills. 2. What part of your current/previous role did you enjoy the most? 3. Why are you looking for a new role? Why did you leave your last position? 4. What has been your biggest achievement or what are you most proud of? Notes:

Overall Rating			
0	1	2	3
No evidence provided	Gave some evidence, needed prompting. Little evidence	Strong evidence, little prompting, linked to our behaviours	Excellent evidence, no prompting

Scenario questions
Tell the candidate that you now have several scenario- based questions to ask them. Explain that these questions are based on some of the competencies that are important for this role. We are looking for examples either in the workplace or outside where you may have experienced or been in these situations. Try to think of real-life examples of what you did rather than what you would do.

Team work
1. Tell me about a time you worked as part of a team, what was your role in that team? Was it successful? 2. How do you think you would add value to this team? Notes:

Overall Rating			
0	1	2	3
No evidence provided	Gave some evidence, needed prompting. Little evidence	Strong evidence, little prompting, linked to our behaviours	Excellent evidence, no prompting

(Continued)

<table>
<tr><th colspan="4">Pace and positivity</th></tr>
<tr><td colspan="4">1. Describe a busy day, how do you organise your day to complete all your tasks?
2. Give me an example of a complaint that you have dealt with. Or a complaint you made. What did they do well in this situation?

Notes:</td></tr>
<tr><td colspan="4">Overall Rating</td></tr>
<tr><td>0</td><td>1</td><td>2</td><td>3</td></tr>
<tr><td>No evidence provided</td><td>Gave some evidence, needed prompting. Little evidence</td><td>Strong evidence, little prompting, linked to our behaviours</td><td>Excellent evidence, no prompting</td></tr>
<tr><th colspan="4">Customer service</th></tr>
<tr><td colspan="4">1. Describe what have you done to ensure the highest standards are delivered in your roles.

Notes:</td></tr>
<tr><td colspan="4">Overall Rating</td></tr>
<tr><td>0</td><td>1</td><td>2</td><td>3</td></tr>
<tr><td>No evidence provided</td><td>Gave some evidence, needed prompting. Little evidence</td><td>Strong evidence, little prompting, linked to our behaviours</td><td>Excellent evidence, no prompting</td></tr>
<tr><th colspan="4">Role-specific questions based on role profile</th></tr>
<tr><td colspan="4">Q1.
Q2.
Q3.

Notes:</td></tr>
<tr><td colspan="4">Overall Rating</td></tr>
<tr><td>0</td><td>1</td><td>2</td><td>3</td></tr>
<tr><td>No evidence provided</td><td>Gave some evidence, needed prompting. Little evidence</td><td>Strong evidence, little prompting, linked to our behaviours</td><td>Excellent evidence, no prompting</td></tr>
<tr><th colspan="4">Closing questions</th></tr>
<tr><td colspan="4">1.Confirm shift patterns, hours of work, and salary expectations.
2. If successful, when could you start?
3. Do you have any pre-booked holidays?</td></tr>
</table>

(*Continued*)

Information to supply at this point:

- About the company and our brand
- Departments
- The Role & Benefits – Staff rates/ rewards / social events & meals on duty
- Learning & Development opportunities / career opportunities
- Uniform / travel / parking (where applicable)
- Holidays XX days including bank holidays (based on working full time)
- The next step of the process; give a timescale of when you will get back to them

Ask the candidate if they have any questions and answer appropriately.
Thank the applicant for their time and inform them that we will be in contact with the outcome (within 5 days).

An interview rubric (scoresheet) may also be used. A rubric is a tool used to add objectivity to the interview process to effectively evaluate the key job competencies outlined within the job description and person specification.

A rubric provides a structured approach to interview analysis matching the key criteria to candidate responses during interviews, similar to the interview analysis form.

As per a standard interview analysis form, the rubric requires a standard set of questions to be asked of all candidates to ensure fairness in the recruitment process. It also requires a list of key competencies such as qualifications and skills, a Likert scale to determine competence against these criteria (such as, 5 = excellent and 1 = poor). Examples can be noted on the rubric for interviewers to determine competency levels.

The rubric can be for an individual applicant or for scores to be identified for comparison across all candidates. The criteria would be adapted for each job role and tailored to the needs of the organisation and role.

See Table 2.12 for an example rubric with example typical skills required within hospitality. This can include other key criteria such as qualifications, education, aptitude, and experience.

The rubric can also be used to compare candidates against one another by providing an overview of overall scores for each area and can be used to assist decision-making on which candidates to hire. During interviews, it can be difficult to remember each candidate and their answers, so the interview analysis form and rubric captures this information.

Table 2.12 Interview Rubric

Competency	Poor 1	Fair 2	Good 3	Very good 4	Excellent 5
Communication	Little eye contact made, unclear or restricted answers given.	Some attempt at communication but with some restrictions or issues.	Communicative and clear, good eye contact.	Very good, strong answers and strong communication skills. Lots of eye contact and able to lead some discussions and ask questions.	Excellent, confident, and clear communication with comprehensive answers. Maintained eye contact and able to lead discussions and ask questions.
Customer Service	Lacks knowledge or understanding of complaint handling or how to enhance the guest experience.	Some ability to be able to deal with customer complaints and able to give limited examples of good guest experience.	Confident in handling guest complaints and how to enhance guest experience with some examples given and justification.	Strong understanding of personal role in handling guest complaints and guest service with examples. Demonstrates awareness of procedures and standards with justified answers.	Exemplary understanding of guest complaints and service delivery with examples, and awareness of procedures and standards and personal impact.
Problem-Solving	Unable to give examples or answers unclear or restricted.	Can somewhat deal with fast-paced environment with some demonstration of problem-solving skills.	Demonstrates a good ability to deal with a fast-paced environment and problem-solving of some common problems.	Demonstrates very good ability to deal with a fast-paced environment and gives examples of problem-solving a variety of problems.	Demonstrates a strong competence in dealing with a fast-paced environment, gives examples of resolving complex problems and ability to multitask.
Teamwork	Does not like to work within teams or answers unclear or restricted.	Has some experience or knowledge of the importance of teamwcrk.	Good understanding of the importance of teamwork with some examples of impact.	Good level of teamwork skills demonstrated whilst recognising the value of teams and impact.	Demonstrates strong competence in working with or leading teams, recognising the value of teams and impact giving examples.

The rubric displays scores for each candidate on one form, providing a quantitative overview of interview performance on which to make hiring decisions. During an interview, due to the halo effect (see Section 2.8.2) or other types of bias, it can be difficult to capture an objective view of each candidate. The interview analysis form and rubric overcome this problem, helping to ensure a fairer recruitment process free from the risk of bias and discrimination.

If recruitment decisions are questioned or challenged at a later stage, such forms and processes demonstrate hiring decisions are free from bias. These documents could be used in a court to demonstrate how fair processes have been followed to ensure fair and transparent recruitment practices. Incorporating key criteria from the job description and person specification relevant to the job role during these processes, and when applied to shortlisting, interview questions, and interview analysis, provides evidence of due diligence and legal compliance during the recruitment process. This helps prevent libels against the hospitality, hotel, or events organisation.

When a rubric or other scoring system is used such as the one in Table 2.13, the scores for each candidate can be summarised in a secondary document, summarising candidate scores in a simple clear table for comparative purposes to assist in recruitment decisions. This form can be amended to include the questions asked and/or criteria being assessed such as communication and customer service skills.

The candidate with the highest score is taken forward to the next stage of the recruitment/interview process, or to determine who to appoint into the vacant role. This form can also be shown in a court to demonstrate recruitment practices are free from bias and discrimination, should a case be raised against the firm for unfair or discriminatory recruitment practices.

Table 2.13 Example Candidate Interview Comparison

Competency	Sue	Ahmed	Andreas	Kristi	Tristian
Communication	3	5	5	4	2
Customer Service	4	3	4	4	2
Problem Solving	4	3	4	5	4
Teamwork	3	4	5	3	5
Total	14	15	18	16	13

Different organisations will use different processes, with some being more formal and others being less so. This will inevitably vary country to country also, with different laws and processes being applicable.

De Vere is a British collection of hotels and events estates and the process for recruitment is outlined below:

2.9 Interviews at De Vere

Contribution from Katie Owlett, De Vere

The candidate should be given an outline of how long the interview will last (approximately) and what it will involve. This includes a mixture of competency and behavioural questions, but for our Graduate Management Programme it also involves a group exercise and written task.

We always ask candidates to bring proof of their right to work in the UK to their interview, so that we can check and verify this prior to any offer of employment being made.

Our interview invitations also include a note for the candidate to contact us in advance of the interview if they have any queries or special requirements. This ensure all candidates have the opportunity to make us aware of any reasonable adjustments that may be required from a disability perspective. A recent example of this was a Graduate Management Programme candidate who requested the use of a computer when completing a written task on the assessment day due to severe dyslexia.

The format of the onsite interview follows the popular W.A.S.P model of interviews which is used to teach interviewers how to facilitate an interview, and acts as a checklist for interview facilitation. The process of the W.A.S.P. model is Welcome, Ask, Supply, and Part and is used as follows:

Welcome: welcome the candidate and help them to feel comfortable. Personality is important to us and so it is important we help people relax so that they do not feel nervous and can be themselves.

Acquire (or Ask): ask the pre-planned questions along with some follow-up probing questions to gain evidence of the candidate's previous experience and behaviours.

Supply: towards the end of the interview, we encourage our hiring managers to answer any questions the candidate may have and to share important information about the role and working with De Vere. Ask the candidate if they have any questions or require any further information. Be prepared to answer these questions as an interviewer.

Part: as the interview finishes, it is important to let the candidate know what the next steps are, when they can expect to hear from us, and to thank them for their time and interest in working with our company.

After the interview, our hiring managers are encouraged to score the candidate. Our questions relate to company values and a score of 1–4 is given in relation to each of our four values, as well as on any relevant technical job skills (with 1 being the lowest and 4 being the highest score). The form acts as an interview analysis form to compare candidates against one another.

All interview notes should be retained in line with the data retention policy. At De Vere, candidate data is retained for 12 months, unless the candidates request otherwise, in line with policy which is outlined on the De Vere careers website and application acknowledgement email. It is worth noting that job applicants have 12 months should they wish to make a discrimination claim, so it is worthwhile retaining relevant supporting information for this duration (such as the interview analysis forms).

2.9.1 The Candidate Experience

Candidate experience underpins the recruitment process. A candidate's application experience reflects on the employer brand and will likely influence their opinion of the company. This not only affects whether an applicant wants to work for the brand, but also the message they portray to other people and even whether they would spend money with our company in the future.

A candidate's journey might start from visiting a careers website or seeing a job advert through to the outcome of their application – whether they go on to join the company or their application is unsuccessful.

Every aspect of an applicant's journey needs to be considered, from the ease of the use of the website and application process to communication, and how they are made to feel throughout the recruitment process, regardless of the outcome.

Lengthy application forms or processes should be avoided, and websites should be mobile-friendly and ideally offer one-click apply functionality, so as not to deter people from applying.

It is also important to communicate with candidates in a timely manner, and as a recruiter in a competitive market, it is recommended to contact candidates within 48 hours of their application. To ensure a positive candidate experience, a brand should also ensure that all applicants receive a response to their application, even if not shortlisted for interview.

2.10 Offering Employment and Conducting Reference Checks

Once the decision is made as to which candidate to hire, an offer of employment should be made by telephone, email, or letter. This is usually subject to obtaining satisfactory references from a previous employer or educational establishment. It is common practice to seek two references, normally from the most recent employers, or one from recent employment and one from the academic institution.

If the employee has been in employment for a long period, or out of education for a long period, it may be that one reference can be provided, normally from an employer (or volunteer organisation where applicable). Likewise, a recent graduate would likely be able to only provide an academic reference.

It is advisable to have another applicant to consider as a contingency, in case a job offer is turned down by the first successful candidate. A candidate may withdraw from the recruitment process even at this stage and be offered more favourable terms with their current employer or offered a vacancy with a competitor.

A candidate with a job offer might negotiate with their current employment for better terms when the current employer is made aware of the employee's intention to leave. Negotiations such as increased pay or benefits may be counteroffered, and therefore the applicant chooses to stay with their current employer.

References confirm factual and accurate information about the candidate. The job role and nature of the job that was undertaken can be confirmed, such as relevant duties, period of employment, reasons for leaving where applicable, pay, reliability, and attendance (or absences).

The reference can be obtained by sending referees an electronic questionnaire or form attached to an email, for the referee to complete. Some firms request a reference with or without guidance notes and questions about what they are seeking. It is advisable to request standard information as outlined previously.

References can also be obtained by telephone. The conversation should then be kept on record using notes of the telephone call within the employee file or recruitment record.

Whilst some applicants worry what an employer may say, it is advisable for the candidate to ask permission prior to naming referees within their application.

INDUSTRY VOICE

Dr Philip Berners, Associate Professor in Events Management

I advise applicants not to show the name and address of referees in their CV. This is because it is discourteous to the referee if they receive a request which they were not expecting or prepared for. Therefore, if the applicant wants to demonstrate to the prospective employer their thoughtfulness, they will not provide that information.

The CV should simply state, 'Excellent references available upon request.'

Of course, if a job offer is made, the applicant will contact their referees to inform them of a request from 'x' company.

However, there are exceptions. Perhaps the applicant wants to show who the referee is on their CV because the prospective employer might know that person or be impressed that the applicant is using that person as a referee – especially if it is someone well known in the industry. In which case, the referee should be informed that they might receive a reference request from 'x' company.

Subjective views of performance are not always accurate, and not all referees are able to provide an accurate overview of a successful applicant, especially where they did not work closely with one another, or in larger organisations or educational establishments. Or in the case of being close personal friends, biased subjective views may be given.

It should be noted, therefore, that a reference is an additional tool to confirm information or highlight any potential issues or inaccuracies. There are other tools that determine the 'fit' of a new employee such as the probationary period, so it is not all reliant on the reference.

It is not advisable for a referee to provide a poor reference due to legal implications and potential accusations of defamation of character. Instead of a poor reference, then, an employer might refuse to provide a reference which, essentially, does the job of providing a poor reference.

Despite how large the hospitality, hotel, and events industries are, they can appear small due to the number of personal and professional connections across organisations: people get to know each other within the socio-professional construct of an industry. In this instance, there is nothing to prevent an informal conversation between two managers at different hotels who are professional friends, for example, unofficially discussing an applicant. However, this could cause bias towards the applicant whether this causes a positive or a detrimental influence.

In the situation of a candidate asking a friend or family member to pose as an employer, if discovered, this would be considered as fraudulent and could result in withdrawal of the offer of employment or termination of a contract. This is considered as a false reference.

References obtain information as to employment history, qualifications, experience, and the candidate's suitability for the role. The recruiting team may seek further information on length of employment, job title, and responsibilities, competence, performance, punctuality and time management, and reason for leaving. An example reference request form is seen in Table 2.14.

Table 2.14 Example Reference Request Form

REFERENCE REQUEST PRIVATE AND CONFIDENTIAL	
Candidate name:	Vacancy applied for:
Referee name:	Referee job title:
Referee relationship to candidate:	Referee company name:
Telephone number:	Email address:
What was the applicant's job title?	
Employment from:	Last date of employment:
What was the applicant's reason for leaving?	
If given the opportunity, would you rehire the candidate again? Yes/No (please delete)	

How would you rate the Applicant with regards to:

	Excellent	Good	Average	Poor
Professionalism	☐	☐	☐	☐
Punctuality and attendance	☐	☐	☐	☐
Interpersonal skills	☐	☐	☐	☐
Teamwork	☐	☐	☐	☐
Customer service	☐	☐	☐	☐

Would you re-employ? Yes/No (please delete)	If not, why?
Any additional comments:	

Signed:	Date:

As well as taking up references, employers may need to carry out other pre-employment checks such as relevant convictions and whether time has been spent in prison, or other criminal record checks to determine suitability for the role when working in specific roles, for example that involve working with children or vulnerable adults. This ensures safer recruitment decisions. It is illegal to refuse to employ an individual who has a spent conviction.

2.10.1 Right to Work Checks

Once references have been obtained and the formal offer of employment has been issued, the Right to Work checks can be carried out to determine legal right to work and will prevent liability if an individual is employed who is not permitted to work, which is usually due to immigration status.

The Right to Work checks vary country to country, depending on local laws. In countries with regulated employment practices such as in the United Kingdom, United States, and European countries such as France, specific documents are needed to demonstrate an individual is legally allowed to work.

In cases where workers do not have necessary permissions, workers may be subjected to exploitation, modern slavery, and wage exploitation as examples. Human trafficking can also occur. The hospitality, hotel, and event industries are vulnerable to such exploitations due to the number of international workers, language barriers, and use of contractors.

As an example, if a cleaning contractor firm is used to clean a hotel, the hotelier may want to consider checking company reputation and credentials – as the supplier may be in breach of employment law. It could be that passports are withheld from the workers to stop them leaving the country, wages withheld, cramped or poor living conditions provided, or other modern slavery and exploitation practices in place.

To complete the necessary Right to Work checks, original documents such as a passport or working visa need to be shown and checks made to ensure photograph identification matches the individual, and that the birth date and appearance are consistent with evidence within these documents.

Documents that may be used (also vary country to country) include:

- A passport demonstrating citizenship of the home country
- An immigration status document indicating the person is allowed to stay indefinitely / has residency in the country
- A birth certificate or adoption certificate and government-issued documents proving the right to work

- Working visas or work and travel visa
- Sponsor documentation

Other documents may be needed such as National Insurance (UK) / Social Security (US), proof of settled status (European Economic Area (EEA)), or similar schemes, depending on which country applies, birth certificates, military identification, and a driving licence as examples.

It is necessary to take photocopies of original documents for company records, in accordance with relevant data protection and employment laws.

2.10.2 European Workers and the Impact of Brexit on UK Employers

The European Union (EU) is a group of 27 countries affiliated for political and economic alignment, making it easier to work, travel, and trade across the European bloc, with most member states adopting one common currency, the Euro, for ease of trade. The United Kingdom joined the European Union in 1973.

The 27 countries joined as a single market bloc, comparable to a supermarket where a range of goods can be purchased from a variety of suppliers in one store, or an online marketplace such as *Amazon*, where consumers buy goods from a range of suppliers online.

The single market within the EU was established to reduce barriers in terms of trade, money, and movement of people across member countries. This meant free movement of people, goods, services, and capital. Therefore, employing workers from all over Europe became easier due to the free movement of people.

The Schengen Agreement enables free movement in terms of travel, living, and working within the EU to 450 million EU citizens, and non-EU nationals living in or visiting the EU for tourism, study, or work. The Agreement means guaranteed travel without being subject to border checks (European Commission, 2025).

Britian voted to leave the EU on 23 June 2016 following concerns by British citizens and political parties for a range of reasons including economic conditions and other factors such as rising immigration in the United Kingdom (UK). There was also a financial impact of being a member state which required the country to contribute significant funds as one of the conditions of being a member state.

Soon after the vote to leave the EU, coined Britian's Exit or 'Brexit', the British currency fell sharply against the US Dollar, making it more expensive to import goods to the UK. For the hospitality, hotel, and events industries, this led to a considerable rise in the cost of commodities, impacting profit margins with around 25 per cent of all food consumed in the UK being imported.

For tourists, however, the UK became cheaper to visit, helping achieve record visitor numbers to the UK in 2019 before the COVID-19 pandemic struck (however, numbers have since risen). This resulted in an increased number of tourists booking flights, hotels, events, eating out, and visiting tourist attractions, contributing positively to the economy.

For Human Resources and recruiting managers, legal challenges surrounding Brexit were presented in relation to the rights of EU workers who were no longer able to remain in the UK unless they were entitled to settled status, were sponsored to stay, or were granted working visas. EU citizens with five years of UK residence by the point the country was due to leave (1 January 2021) or who entered the country before this time, were eligible for settled status. EU citizens were required to register for settlement by 30 June 2021. This would mean a visa was not required for EU workers and their family to live and work in the UK and employers did not need a licence to employ those with settled status. Other EU citizens would be able to stay until the five-year threshold was met.

Given staffing shortages are one of the significant challenges the industry faces, Brexit led to further skills shortages, with hospitality particularly affected with around 15 per cent of the workforce comprising workers from the EU. Hospitality businesses in London, including restaurants and hotels, relied on migrant workers who made up around 35–40 per cent of the workforce. In some businesses this statistic would have been considerably higher.

As an industry with a historical reputation for paying low wages, alongside unsociable working hours including evenings and weekends, and variable shift patterns, Brexit presented further significant challenges for employers.

As an industry which has a high reliance on a transient workforce (students, young people, and migrant workers), this inevitably resulted in further pressures whereby the transient workforce is temporary in nature. Students and young people gravitate to employment in hospitality whilst studying or training for another industry and therefore employment is short lived. Migrant workers, however, tend to stay for longer periods, as per work visa conditions and are more motivated due to leaving their home country, and potentially supporting others at home financially due to better pay and working conditions in some cases than in their home country.

The focus on staffing therefore became a two-fold problem. The first was to determine how to retain British workers in industry; and the second, how to overcome new legal and financial challenges to employ EU workers (alongside other international workers).

The first can be tackled by visiting schools, colleges, careers fairs, offering apprenticeships, work experience, or internships to promote careers in hospitality. Young people often confuse hospitality with hospitals and are largely unaware of career options, so once informed this may influence future applications to work in the hospitality, hotel, and events sectors.

Paying above the minimum legal wage and offering better work–life balance compared to traditional shiftwork or long hours, and training or progression, help attract and retain employees.

Training and development programmes, benefit packages, and other perks help to retain staff, alongside opportunities for progression and becoming more people orientated.

Recruitment is evolving to become applicant-led, with younger generations stipulating employment conditions which employers are becoming more adaptive towards.

The second challenge, to continue to employ migrant workers, required organisations to adapt further to new government requirements. Recruiting skilled workers from the EU would become more difficult and work permits meant recruitment of this demographic became costly and time consuming.

To employ EU and other international workers, British companies must obtain a sponsorship licence from the UK Home Office. This will be a Skilled Worker licence or temporary licence if the contract is short term.

There are certain criteria businesses need to meet to be eligible to obtain their licence. Criteria include being a legitimate and legally compliant business operation that does not pose a threat to immigration control, has not had a sponsor licence revoked, and has an organised recruitment team which complies with sponsorship requirements. There is an Immigration Skills Charge applicable.

The employing organisation such as the hotel, restaurant, or events venue must issue a Certificate of Sponsorship to the prospective employee.

The employee will use this Certificate to apply for a Skilled Worker visa to work in the UK, and roles must meet certain skills levels (such as college-level qualifications), and salary levels determined by the Home Office or average industry pay (whichever is highest). The hospitality industry has some exceptions such as certain chef roles whereby visas can be granted, but lower-skilled hospitality roles neither meet the minimum skills level nor salary threshold.

When applying for a visa, the employee must be proficient in the English language, whether from education or by taking an English language test. This will need to be evidenced on application and a fee paid when applying for a Skilled Workers Visa. This must be done within three months of being issued with their Certificate of Sponsorship using the reference number cited on the certificate.

Employees on inter-company transfers within multinational firms have requirements under the Intra-Company Transfer route. This tends to apply to those who are on graduate programmes or for senior positions. The individual applying to work in the UK as intra-company transfer will need to be sponsored as such and would still be subject to the salary threshold and skills requirements. The applicant would need twelve months' experience working for a multinational firm which operates overseas and in the UK in terms of ownership, and fulfil the requirement of being an undergraduate (level 6). This application is temporary, and the employee cannot stay in the UK for more than five years in any six-year period.

Intra-company transfers employed on graduate training programmes can apply for the Graduate Trainee route with some exceptions as to experience and salary.

The Right to Work checks will still be carried out for all EU and international workers.

2.10.3 Students Studying in the UK

Students on student graduate visas, having graduated within the UK, can work in the UK for up to two years (three years for PhD students). Thereafter, they can be sponsored by their employer for a further three years.

2.10.4 Youth Mobility Scheme

Particularly useful for the hospitality, hotel, and events industry is the Youth Mobility Scheme which allows young people aged 18–30 from the EU to work in the UK for up to two years.

2.10.5 Medical Questionnaire

An applicant will normally complete a medical questionnaire to ensure they are fit to work. Medical examinations may be required for some roles in other industries but are generally not required in the hospitality, event, or hotel sectors.

There are 22 countries whereby medical tests are mandatory, however. Medical assessments identify whether the employee can fulfil the requirements of the job and work safely. For example, medications may make it dangerous to work with certain equipment, or a back injury would be difficult in a role that requires manual lifting.

In most circumstances, certain reasonable adjustments should be made to make it both safe and easier to fulfil the job role. In a kitchen, for example, it might not be safe for someone with mobility issues to be employed within this area. However, they could be employed within reception or guest services. Likewise, in the instance of a wheelchair user, it would be a reasonable adjustment, and sometimes a legal requirement, to provide ramp access, an elevator or ramp, accessible toilets, and a lower section of the reception desk to accommodate the wheelchair and for ease of dealing with guest enquiries.

An employer is not permitted to discriminate on disability grounds but does have a legal responsibility to ensure the health, safety, and well-being of all employees.

2.10.6 Criminal Record Checks

An employer may be required to complete criminal record checks especially when work involves health care or social work, working with children, or working with vulnerable adults as examples. This will check for convictions spent or unspent, or an enhanced check to determine convictions relevant to the role (such as fraud for when an employee will be dealing with money). In some circumstances, an applicant can be denied employment in some roles such as those previously mentioned.

Criminal record checks assist managers to make more informed hiring decisions to determine suitability for the role alongside ensuring safety and security, for example if the applicant is a sexual offender.

In the case of a multinational industry with individuals working overseas, different processes need to be followed, and an agency might be used to access records such as law enforcement agencies, courts, and other public records or intelligence databases.

A hiring manager should consider conducting checks as this reduces the risk of hiring someone who may, for example, steal from the organisation or take part in other criminal activity which would create liability risks for a firm. It enables a company to prevent, where feasible, harm to company reputation where negative publicity occurs when a crime is committed and helps prevent legal action.

2.10.7 Equal Opportunities Monitoring

Applicants may also be asked to complete an equal opportunity monitoring form.

Whilst not necessarily a requirement to monitor equal opportunities, if personal data is collected this must be used in line with data protection laws.

Equal opportunity monitoring enables an organisation to monitor applications from different groups of people, including their protected characteristics. The data can be analysed to determine differences between groups based on protected characteristics such as race, gender, or sexuality, and be used in investigations where necessary.

An equal opportunity monitoring form will identify inequalities within the workforce, help identify discrimination, whether intentional or not, and enable review policy and procedures for new hires to provide opportunities for all within the workplace.

It also helps to comply with fair employment legislation and ensure the organisation and managers adopt a company culture of diversity and inclusion. Data can also be used to determine if individuals are being fairly progressed within the organisation.

The data would need to be protected and confidentiality maintained, in compliance with relevant data protection legislation.

Employing individuals from a diverse range of backgrounds across a range of protected characteristics demonstrates fair employment practices in terms of equality and can lead to recognition and awards for being an equal opportunities employer. This may further attract talented recruits and help with employee retention whilst boosting company reputation, not forgetting there are benefits from a diverse workforce, such as social acceptances and experience from other cultures.

As outlined within equality law, it is illegal in most parts of the world, with some exemptions, to treat someone less favourably due to protected characteristics such as gender, age, marital status, sexual orientation, or religion. This is classed as discrimination, and discriminatory practices include not hiring someone, or paying unfair wages due to a protected characteristic, or bias towards redundancy of an individual during economic downtown due to a personal characteristic such as those mentioned.

2.10.8 Contract of Employment

When the candidate accepts the offer of employment it is usual to issue a contract of employment.

A contract of employment is a legal agreement between the employer and employee which stipulates terms and conditions of employment.

A contract will typically contain the job title and description of the job role, specifying duties and responsibilities. A start date will be noted, and an end date if it is a fixed-term contract but not a permanent position. Work hours, location of work, and any probationary periods will also be stated.

The amount of salary (or pay), payment methods, and payment frequency should be given alongside summary of benefits, holiday pay, and other entitlements, such as sick pay, redundancy, paternity/maternity leave, and notice period.

Disciplinary procedures and grievance procedures will be outlined or provided within separate policies with any references to relevant legislation such as health and safety.

The contract should be signed and dated. However, even if not signed, turning up to work on the first day, demonstrates agreement with contractual obligations and a contract does not need to be signed to be legally binding.

The contract may not be a legal requirement but it is best practice to have a written contract in place so rights are made clear to both parties and can be used to refer to, should a dispute arise.

When changes of employment are necessary, notice of changes to the contract should be given in writing. This may include change in pay, the job role, or working hours. In the United Kingdom this notice period is one month.

A contract is typically signed before the first day of employment, and whilst laws do not exist in all countries that govern this (such as in the US, Canada, Australia, and India), an employee can request a contract and best practice is to issue the contract prior to the employee starting their job, or on their first day of work.

A summary of these laws has been provided in Chapter 11, 'Employment Law'.

2.10.9 The Difference Between an Employee and a Worker

Hospitality, hotels, and events sometimes differentiate between a worker and an employee. Whilst this book uses both terms interchangeably, legally they can be considered as different from each other.

Employment status can be as either an employee or a worker (but someone can also be self-employed). An employee and a worker will be subject to different employment rights in some countries and will have different responsibilities imposed upon them.

An **employee** has more rights than workers or self-employed people and more obligations towards their employer. An employee is required to work unless on leave and should expect regular work and is not allowed to turn work down. They will receive holiday/vacation pay, be subject to disciplinary and grievance procedures, and the employer is responsible for how the work is carried out and providing resources to do the job. The employee must give notice when leaving employment or going on a period of extended leave such as maternity leave.

A **worker** is someone who carries out work on a casual basis and may not have work made regularly available. There is no strict obligation to accept work in these instances, but once work has been agreed this should be carried out. A contract should still be issued, and they are entitled to legal minimum wages, and paid holiday/vacation entitlement, but they may not have a notice period, or be entitled to claim sick pay, maternity pay, or redundancy rights in some instances. Agency workers would be considered under this type of arrangement, sometimes Zero-Hours contracted staff (but can also be considered as an employee), or someone who takes up less regular work with less commitment than someone under a Zero-Hours Contract.

2.10.10 Volunteer Staff

Staffing in the events industry can be different from hotels, restaurants, coffee shops, and airlines, for example, due to the temporary nature of many events. Events require different planning in terms of staffing, which varies according to the size and scope of each event, the venue where the event takes place, and attendee numbers. This is why the events industry is considered as a 'pulsating' workforce which expands whilst the event is happening, and contracts after the event has happened.

Events such as a festival or organised marathon often require a temporary increase in staffing numbers. In these instances, whilst a core team may be employed to plan the event, on the event day itself, the event organisers will likely have high numbers of staff to fulfil a variety of roles.

Such roles may be fulfilled by employing workers through several means including full-time permanent staff, temporary or fixed-term contracts, Zero-Hour Contracts, through an agency, contractor, or volunteers. These contracts are explored further in Chapter 4.

Many events rely on volunteers to fulfil large-volume roles such as marshals at music festivals and sporting events such as Parkrun, a weekly timed 5 km run happening throughout the world on Saturday mornings. Such events typically promote opportunities for volunteering via their website and a social media campaign.

INDUSTRY VOICE

Dr Philip Berners, Associate Professor in Events Management

The charity event sector relies on volunteers because of free labour helping reduce staffing costs that would otherwise impact the fundraising efforts of a charity. Anything which can offset costs is a benefit to a charity such as sponsorship, donations, donated prizes, and of course volunteer unpaid labour.

Many people volunteer for altruistic reasons. Usually, they want to devote time to a charity which has touched them or helped them in some way – to 'give something back' as it were.

There are benefits for volunteers to work other than receiving payment. It might be that they get good work experience (such as an internship) which they can then place on their CV to enhance their employability. Or it could be the opportunity to attend an event by volunteering to work there – festivals such as Glastonbury offer volunteering, so they get free labour in exchange for the opportunity to watch the bands and live acts.

Typically, a formal recruitment process will not be followed here, and instead roles will be allocated at random on the day of the event, or according to the skills and experience of those volunteering. Therefore, the person specification, contracts, and pay become irrelevant.

However, as events requiring volunteers are temporary in nature, in most instances training might not be given, and therefore basic training may be needed on the event day, which can cause time pressures and stress if training during the event itself.

INDUSTRY VOICE

Dr Philip Berners, Associate Professor in Events Management

It can be problematic to train or brief staff on an event day – particularly if it is a very early start time or there are very many staff.

Where there is a need for many staff, it is usually in situations of marshals on routes such as sports events, marathons, and other challenge events. In such cases, volunteers are used because such large numbers of paid staff would be too costly making the event prohibitive or unfeasible.

It is therefore better to brief the volunteers pre-event which would either be the day before the event takes place or even the week before. It makes sense logistically of course and can be done at ease without the pressures of the event day itself. It allows for planning the briefing or training and can be done over a longer period.

Remember, volunteers are unpaid so there are no costs incurred with bringing them in a day or a week early for the briefing or training, whereas, requesting paid staff to attend a pre-event briefing or training session activities will incur costs. This is why, mostly, staff briefings are conducted on the day of an event where possible (the difference between pre-event briefing and onsite briefing).

Volunteers usually demonstrate loyalty to an event or charity which is helpful because retaining event volunteers and recruiting loyal repeat volunteers is key to event success. Where volunteers have worked previously, they will be familiar with processes and will not need retraining (unless refresher training or updates are required). Also, returning volunteers can train or mentor new volunteers.

Volunteer attrition is when volunteers do not turn up on event day. Around 25 per cent of volunteers can often not turn up on an event day. This is a problem where volunteers are unpaid so might change their mind or have chosen to do something else. It is the lack of reward or incentive which is the issue. Even if it happens to be raining on the event day, volunteer staff might not turn up. It is therefore important to add value to volunteers to counteract their lack of pay or reward, such as offering free merchandise, uniform, food and drink, discounts, free passes or tickets for future events, or time-off during the event to enjoy the event – for example a couple of hours to watch a music festival.

AUTHOR'S VOICE

Being a regular volunteer at events, my role and compensation has varied.

Parkrun: I have volunteered for several years as a core team member of a parkrun in the UK. My role involves recruiting around 15 volunteers by putting a post on social media and an email appeal via the database of previous runners and volunteers. I complete a basic online rota for roles such as course marshals, timekeepers to time the events, someone to issue finish tokens, people to scan tokens, and a team to set up the course prior to the run. I then deliver basic training on the day as to how to use the parkrun volunteer app, and I help close the event at the end. There is no compensation for this role, but I benefit through social interaction within the community and participating in regular exercise to support my physical and mental health.

Local half-marathon: having been on the committee for a couple of years, my role has been to help source 200 volunteers and to manage volunteers at the finish line. A social media campaign helps source volunteers from the local fitness community, and managing the finish area includes setting up a post-event water station, snack stations, and awarding medals. Motivation and reward come from the event atmosphere, the social element, and receiving leftover race t-shirts and snacks!

Local obstacle and mud race: my role was allocated on the day, and I was asked to be on baggage drop to help race participants drop off their bags before the race started. I was also rotated to medals at the finish line and removing the chip timers from participants' shoes at the end. I was given a free lunch bag and soft drink, free pizza, and a choice of a voucher for merchandise, free race entry for another race, or a branded outdoor jacket. The choice of compensation for this event results in a waiting list of people keen to volunteer on event days. I was sent online videos to watch prior to the event day as basic training and to maintain my interest as a volunteer, and an onsite briefing on the event day to help me settle into my roles.

Bibliography

European Commission (2025). *Schengen*. Available from: https://home-affairs.ec.europa.eu/policies/schengen/schengen-area_en/

Chapter 3

Payroll

Adrian Martin

3.0 Introduction

Hospitality, hotels, and events businesses are very labour intensive, and wages tend to be the most significant cost on a profit and loss (P&L) statement.

Payroll costs are a constant challenge for business owners/managers as they vary as a total depending on business volumes, sickness levels, and staff turnover, as well as government policies, such as legal minimum wage, pension contribution, national insurance contribution, and other oncosts which include holiday pay.

Payroll may be administered by a specific department such as Human Resources, Payroll, Accounts, or it might be managed by an accountant, managers, or owners.

Most hotels, as an example, work to a payroll cost of between 30 and 35 per cent of revenue depending on the style of the hotel (budget/mid-scale/luxury), yet this figure may rise due to pension policies, minimum wage legislation, and casual workers' holiday entitlements. Not surprisingly, General Managers are very conscious of this cost measure which has been challenging to control as it has risen much faster than inflation (the average rise of prices of all goods in a country). Consequently, many hotels have not been able to pass this rise on to the customer. Hotels will need adequate staff to ensure customer service levels are maintained whilst balancing room occupation and seasonal demand.

DOI: 10.4324/9781003469803-4

A restaurant may have slightly lower staffing costs depending on service style: a fast-food restaurant will employ fewer staff than a full-service fine-dining restaurant, for example.

Events could balance staffing costs with volunteers who do not require payment. However, events often require large volumes of paid staff such as management, support staff, operational staff, casual staff, technical crew, professional staff, and security teams, who will all be on the payroll.

This chapter outlines how hotels control and reduce payroll costs and provides some commonly used techniques to save money whilst maintaining and sometimes improving quality. The chapter identifies how to calculate payroll percentage, payroll, staff turnover, and staffing levels, what to pay, training costs, and employee motivation.

3.1 Calculating the Payroll Cost Percentage

Each time a wage bill is paid, either through a fixed salary or from casual labour, the bookkeeper (or whoever manages payroll) will allocate it to the payroll section of the venue's costs.

However, these are not the only costs, as pensions, employer contributions (such as National Insurance in the UK), as well as benefits (such as health care insurance), redundancy settlements, training, uniform, holiday pay accrued, and bonuses, will all add to the cost of employment. These are known as 'on-costs'.

The total of direct and on-costs becomes the figure in the payroll line of the profit and loss statement, but the Key Performance Indicator (KPI) (a KPI is a measurable indicator of performance such as a financial target to achieve, or a cost limit to adhere to) calculation as a percentage is quite simple:

Payroll Cost %

Total Payroll Costs ÷ Total Revenue x 100 = Wage Cost %

Once this figure has been calculated it needs to be tracked monthly to identify and investigate peaks and troughs and avoid the result being a shock at the end of the financial year.

It is useful to be aware whether the payroll cost percentage is above or below industry averages. There is a range of data available on the average wage costs of an industry (generally between 30 and 35 per cent) but they tend not to be separated into sectors (e.g. for hotels: luxury, budget, hotel chain, versus independent hotels) so it uses the data as a guide rather than the rule.

3.2 Reducing Payroll Costs from the Turnover of Staff

Every time a member of staff leaves an organisation there will be costs and these will be incorporated into the payroll figure.

Recruiting and advertising for a replacement member of staff has a cost, as will training a new employee, and moving through the initial 'new staff' period where they are less productive – not forgetting the impact on service during the lag time between someone leaving and the replacement starting.

There may also be uniform costs, the impact on fellow employees taking time to mentor, train, and support new staff, and any errors made by the new staff member during their first few months in the job.

There have been several studies on this issue, quoting average recruitment and onboarding costs as high as six to nine months of the employee's annual salary each time a staff member leaves.

With staff turnover in hospitality varying between 30 per cent and 70 per cent, and higher in some venues, according to contrasting statistics being reported online, turnover is significantly higher in hospitality, hotels, and events compared to other industries, with staff turnover rates of around 15 per cent comparable to hospitality (70% retention in hospitality compared to 85% retention in other sectors). This means that 30 per cent (or more) of all staff will leave each year as a guideline, mainly due to unsocial hours, low pay, and lack of career progression.

To reduce these costs there are several strategies to prevent employees reaching that tipping-point of leaving the organisation. It may seem that an employee leaves because of one issue, but usually it is a slow build-up of multiple factors:

Job specifications: being clear, transparent, and honest at the outset about what the job entails (particularly if it involves unusual or late hours) is a useful way of attracting candidates who are clear about the role and genuinely interested in it. Raising false expectations may increase the number of applications but will mean employees feel disappointed and will not remain.

Career development: ensuring employees know that their current role will develop them with training and a wide range of experiences, and that they will receive the opportunity for advancement within the company will help employees consider the role as a longer-term prospect. Having a career progression or succession plan shows an employee the potential for career advancement, and in many cases acts as motivation for good performance to achieve those goals.

Consultation: keeping channels of communication open, either through staff meetings, employee satisfaction surveys, or using employee representatives is a good way to ensure there is nothing niggling at staff either collectively or individually. Part of this process is the exit interview to capture the reasons why a member of staff has chosen to leave the organisation.

Flexibility: within reason, adjusting and accommodating special requests from staff demonstrates an understanding employer and creates a two-way relationship at times when additional help or flexibility might be required of employees.

Well-being: maintaining a sense of work–life balance. Some employees need to be told to go home sometimes, no doubt while protesting they still have so much to do, but it can be unhealthy to their well-being (burnout) and they will appreciate the gesture. Others may need support at critical times in their life, and an employer needs to be aware and empathetic of this.

Fairness: always a critical point as the feeling of unfairness within the workplace will grate with staff and some will leave because of it. Clear and transparent policies are essential to prevent this from becoming an issue. Consistency is important and treating all staff in a consistent way will prevent feelings and accusations of bias, unfair treatment, or discrimination.

Protect the firm: pay well, reward with benefits, have team socials, organise staff festive celebrations, and encourage an atmosphere of belonging to part of a team – all these contribute to making it a more difficult decision for a team member to consider leaving. Such activities add value to a job so that the staff feel that if they leave, they will lose much more than their pay: they will lose the social interaction and 'family' feel of the job.

3.3 Calculating Levels of Staff

Workforce planning is an important part of reducing payroll costs as having too many staff on a shift is never a good thing because it is an unnecessary drain on profits. Yet, neither is too few staff as it can reduce the overall quality and service and cause complaints which is detrimental to the business – especially when profit is compromised because complaints cause refunds, plus the loss of business due to negative word-of-mouth and harm to reputation.

The process of deciding how many staff are required can vary according to department, different events, and restaurant bookings for example, and often varies week-to-week. For this reason, many bars, cafes, hotels, restaurants, clubs, events, and leisure attractions employ casual staff (such as Zero-Hour Contracts) who can be called to work on a flexible basis during busy periods.

Managers should be aware that it is rare for a head of department to admit they are overstaffed, yet individuals are very quick to complain when short-staffed.

It is comfortable to have a few spare hands around and less stressful when there are sudden let-downs such as no-shows, bouts of sickness, holidays to cover, or turnover of staff, which is why a head of department wants to be overstaffed. As a manager, however, allowing this to occur directly raises wage cost percentage, impacting overall bottom-line net profit.

Workforce planning can be straightforward: look at what the business needs, look at the current workforce, and determine if there is a gap or a surplus. However, the needs of the business can be difficult to determine, hard to predict, and volatile week-to-week – and staff will have differing levels of effectiveness, reliability, and motivation.

Yet most departments can calculate the minimum level of labour required and then use a flexible workforce to cope with peaks and troughs in demand:

Example Workforce Planning Calculation for Housekeeping

Key Information

Number of rooms	100
Average occupancy	80%
No. of rooms cleaned per person, per hour	2
Holiday entitlement	30 days including public holidays.
Average sickness levels	5%

Business need hours = 100 rooms x 80% x 365 days = 29,200 rooms to clean x 0.5hr = 14,600
= Public areas 5 hrs per day x 365 = 1825
= Laundry / Administration 2 hrs per day x 365 = 730
= **17,155 hours p.a. (per annum)**

Workforce = 12.5 FTEs (Full Time Equivalent staff)
= 5 days per week x 7.5hrs a day x 46 weeks a year (6 weeks holiday) = 1725 x <please move>12.5
= 1725 – sickness levels = (1725 – 5%) = 1638.75 x 12.5
= **20,484.38 hours p.a.**

Surplus = Workforce 20,484.38 hrs - Need 17,155hrs = 3,329.38 Surplus
= 3,329.38 ÷ FTE hrs 1638.75
= **2 FTE staff too many**

Other departments such as kitchen and reception may work on a time-basis work need, that is it does not matter how busy the venue is, there needs to be always one receptionist, or two chefs required for food service whether there are 10 or 100 guests in events, a restaurant, or hotel. In this case, the calculation is slightly different:

Example Workforce Planning Calculation for Reception

Key Information

Number of shifts to cover rooms	2 (early/late shifts each day)
Holiday entitlement	30 days including public holidays
Average sickness levels	5%

Business need	= 2 x 365 days = 730 shifts p.a. = Admin / Ledger activities = 1 shift per week = 52 shifts p.a. = **782 shifts p.a.**
Workforce	= 4 FTEs = 5 shifts x 46 weeks a year (6 weeks holiday) = 230 x 4 FTEs = 230 – sickness levels = (230 – 5%) = 218.50 x 4 FTEs = **874 shifts p.a.**
Surplus	= Workforce 874 shifts – Need 782 shifts = 92 shifts = Surplus 92 shifts ÷ FTE hrs 218.50 = **0.4 FTE staff too many**

There may be valid reasons for the surplus in staff: perhaps, it is difficult to recruit in high-season periods and it is better to be overstaffed at times rather than trying to recruit when competitors are also recruiting; sometimes, staff are involved in other departments or roles at quiet times; or it is not uncommon for staff to be involved in refurbishment off-season. Nonetheless, the exercise can uncover overstaffing in areas which, when identified and corrected, either through natural loss of staff (retirement, or leaving for other opportunities), or redundancy, can reduce the wage cost percentage.

AUTHOR'S VOICE

My advice is to talk to friendly competitors in other venues about how many rooms their housekeepers clean and how many tables their waiting staff serve as examples.

When a manager is adamant that they are short-staffed, it can be very convincing, even when you know from your own work history that it is unlikely.

The thing to remember is that having a stable team that consistently delivers, has value and may be worth more than a slightly reduced wage bill. Yet, often managers are far too cautious and it is a tough conversation, but will make a significant difference to your bottom-line net profit.

3.4 Calculating What to Pay

Every business would like to pay the best rates and attract the best staff. Pay forms part of the total rewards package, as discussed in Chapter 7.

Most venues need to calculate a fair salary which attracts the right candidates but keeps within wage cost limits, and this may be a financial challenge.

The rate of pay will need to be equal to, or greater than, the current minimum wage level per hour where this exists (and will vary country to country).

After completing the exercise described here, the business will know how many staff are needed. Multiplying every position by its pay scale will then give the gross wage bill.

However, there are other costs (on-costs) that come with employing someone, and these need to be accounted for:

Calculating the cost of an employee (UK example – amend rates for other countries)

Salary	£15,000 p.a. (per annum)
Holiday entitlement cover	30 days including public holidays = 11.5%
Average sickness levels cover	5%

Income tax (National Insurance in the UK)	13.8% (for earnings above £9,100)
Pension contribution (minimum)	3%
Training costs (typical)	5%
Uniform / equipment costs (typical)	5%
Estimated total typical on-costs	50%

Calculating this figure exactly does not really have great value as many of these costs will be estimated, but it is clear to see why many businesses add 50 per cent additional costs to payroll for the on-costs. This means that a member of staff with a salary of £15,000 should be accounted for at £22,500 for budgeting purposes.

If a department's projected income is £500,000 then it is simple to calculate the desired pay scales that could be paid to achieve the wage percentage target:

Calculating How Much Employees Could be Paid

Projected restaurant revenue	£500,000	
Wage % KPI	30%	
Total wage budget	£150,000	
Staffing required		
Restaurant Manager salary	£30,000 p.a.	
Deputy Manager salary	£25,000 p.a.	
Waiting staff x 3		£15,000 p.a. = £45,000 p.a.
Total		**£100,000 p.a.**
On-costs 50%		£50,000
Actual total		**£150,000**

These figures can now be adjusted depending on levels of business in-year or as an overall strategy. For instance, if the restaurant were over-achieving on revenue it may get to the stage where it employs another staff member, or it could offer incentives to get more out of its current staff or invest in labour-saving devices. By contrast, an under-achieving restaurant will need to make a staff cut to meet its payroll target.

AUTHOR'S VOICE

It can be difficult for some managers to grasp that the best way to increase staffing levels is to bring in more revenue. Upselling in a restaurant or upselling events tickets to packages, selling bedrooms, or increasing sales in a bar, adds revenue which increases the wage budget.

If staff fully appreciate this, it leads to incremental sales and in turn the business will always be fully staffed and will help them to drive sales.

3.5 Training Costs

Some businesses separate training as another line on their profit and loss account; others include it as one overall figure within payroll costs. Nevertheless, training staff is another area of the profit and loss that is vulnerable to being cut as it is difficult to immediately quantify the benefit and can mean losing staff from their duties during periods of training. Training also forms part of an employee's overall benefits package (intrinsic reward helping enhance employee skills set, productivity, and employability). Just like marketing, there is an argument for renaming this as an investment as the benefits are significant but often long term:

- Job satisfaction – doing a job well and efficiently reduces stress and gives employees a sense of pride that can be infectious.
- Quality standards – well-trained staff will improve the overall service quality and impact the levels of returning customers and recommendations.
- Motivation – training is an investment in an employee and will often be returned with higher levels of loyalty and effort.
- Efficiency – a well-trained member of staff might be able to do the work of more than a typical employee and either relieve short-staffed departments or justify a cut.
- Technology – new equipment and processes will be implemented and taken advantage of far more when staff are fully trained.
- Staff turnover – staff are more inclined to be loyal to a firm that invests in them.
- Brand image – higher quality increases the overall brand image supporting competitive positioning and the value of the brand which has a monetary value.

- Risk management – training reduces risks by adherence to legislative requirements as well as possible litigation from sexual harassment, diversity issues, and wrongful dismissal to name a few.

Just like any other investment, there is a return on investment (ROI) to be calculated before deciding how much to spend on this area. This is not straightforward with training, however, as the benefits we have mentioned are difficult (arguably impossible) to quantify return on investment, and the impact of one session may differ from another, and from one employee to another.

Many hospitality, hotel, and event providers have found ways to invest in training whilst saving money though employing apprentices (who take a day a week away from work to attend tuition but are paid less in return) and using online courses that can be completed in induction, for instance, which saves costs.

INDUSTRY VOICE

Edward Gallier Head of Learning & Development, Leonardo Hotels (UK & Ireland)

Training expenditure needs to be controlled like any other cost, and yes, some types of training are far more effective than others and this needs to be monitored closely.

Yet, employees who are trained feel valued, empowered, and motivated and become more efficient and loyal, and have higher standards.

Successful hotels that are serious about high standards and looking after their employees, always put a higher priority on allocating a training budget and resources, in my experience.

3.6 Motivating Employees

Historically, businesses adopted the viewpoint that pay motivates employees and the employer has effectively done their job by transferring funds each month with a payslip. Modern businesses, however, take a more holistic approach and find additional ways to get the best from their employees:

1. Communication – receiving feedback and ideas from staff through regular meetings, newsletters, and transparent communication processes to help staff feel valued and part of the business.

2. Feedback – whether this is constructive criticism or praise, feedback ensures employees know where they need to improve and that their efforts are being noticed and appreciated.
3. Recognition – 'Employee of the Month', teambuilding trips for hitting targets, all embed the feeling that the organisation appreciates employees who go above and beyond.
4. Empowerment – trusting employees to make decisions and react in the moment (particularly when dealing with customer complaints, for instance) improves business performance, as well as staff motivation. If limits of empowerment are set – such as they can discount up to 5 per cent – there is no risk to the business from staff empowered to take such decisions.
5. Following policy and procedures – a feeling of unfairness demotivates and causes conflict, so it is important to have, publish, and follow company policies.
6. Training and developing – staff who feel invested in and have aspirations that are being met long-term will be more motivated and stay longer.
7. Vision and mission – be transparent about how the company is doing, where it wants to be in the future, and how it will get there. Communicate the vision, goals, and objectives – and publish them – they are not secrets!

There is further discussion of Rewards in Chapter 7.

Chapter 4

Types of Employment Contract

4.0 Introduction

This chapter outlines different types of employment contracts, such as permanent contracts and Zero-Hour Contracts, contractual and legal rights under different contract types, the use of agency workers, flexible work, and freelancers and contractors, and provides a summary table of contracts at the end.

When a contract of employment is issued, new recruits can be employed under a variety of contractual agreements which stipulate hours of work they have been employed to fulfil, alongside legal rights and wider rights and obligations which may be stated in the contract or a separate document containing wider terms.

The type of contract issued will depend on the needs of the business, role requirements, the time frame over which the employee is needed, and financial constraints. There are many types of employment contracts including full-time, fixed-term, and Zero-Hour Contracts. Each contract will meet different operational needs and is dependent on factors such as budget, specialist skills or facilities, service requirements, and client needs.

4.1 Permanent Contract

The most typical contract an employee will be given is an indefinite or permanent contract, which has no end date, and will expire when an employer or employee

DOI: 10.4324/9781003469803-5

ends the contract (for example, the employee exits the business). Typical rights under this type of contract include entitlement to be paid the minimum legal wage, paid annual leave, sickness pay, paternity or maternity pay, and redundancy pay. These will vary country to country.

4.1.1 Working Hours

A permanent contract of employment may be considered a full-time contract, and the employee will work, for example, 40 hours per week, eight hours per day, over a five-day period. A part-time member of staff will work reduced hours such as 24 hours over three days.

In hospitality, hotels, and events, employees may be required to work in shift patterns, including evenings and weekends, and will sometimes work longer hours compared to the traditional working week. There are different legal requirements across the world in terms of maximum hours that can be worked, and in some countries there is an opt-out of this to work longer.

In European law, the EU's Working Time Directive (2003) requires member states to limit working hours to 48 per week. The Directive states that workers should have 11 hours rest-time between shifts and at least 20 days paid annual leave. Employees can opt out of the Working Time Directive, which is common within hospitality, hotels, and events.

4.1.2 Minimum Legal Wage

Those employed under permanent contracts are usually legally entitled to payment of the legal minimum wage (although this does not always apply to hospitality in the US where there is a widespread tipping culture which compensates for lower wages). Employees should not be expected to start their shift early or clean up for example after the shift has ended as this is classed as free labour meaning the minimum wage requirement is not met. There may be overtime payments in place, or in other instances time in lieu is given in exchange and the employee can take time off later to compensate. In other countries, there will be provision to opt out of working-hour restrictions such as Working Time Regulations in Europe and to work in excess of required hours, potentially without any recompense.

4.1.3 Annual Leave

A permanent contract will specify the number of days allowed for annual leave. This is typically 20–28 days in European countries. In the US the average number of vacation days is around ten days, and there is no legal requirement surrounding paid vacation time. Different organisations globally will provide different annual leave entitlements, which may or may not include public holidays, cultural, or religious days.

Some firms will offer additional special days such as birthdays off work, or additional days as a reward for long service.

As service industries are often seasonal and demand is variable, a request to take leave may be rejected, especially during busy periods, or when other staff are on leave. Some firms will also require employees to take leave during quiet periods.

Annual leave is often a health and safety requirement to ensure employees have sufficient rest periods and a legal requirement. If holiday entitlement is not used, some organisations will allow for leave to be 'rolled over' to the next year, whilst in others, employees will lose this time off if it is not used. There may also be an option to buy additional leave, resulting in a deduction from wages.

There may be restrictions in how many days can be taken such as two working weeks, and in exceptional circumstances, such as a honeymoon, three weeks may be granted.

Those who are on maternity or paternity leave will still accrue annual leave.

4.1.4 Maternity/Paternity Leave

Some countries offer statutory paid leave for new parents which may be gender dependent. Maternity leave is for the mother, and paternity is for the father to promote gender equality as fathers take on the responsibility of childcare.

The US is the only country out of the 100 member-countries of the Organisation for Economic Co-operation and Development (OECD) which does not offer paid leave for new parents.

Maternity leave is typically given to a mother after childbirth, for recovery and to bond with their baby. Depending on country and the employer, this will include some paid and unpaid time off and can also be used for adoption or extended to those who suffer baby loss. Maternity leave can be for a few weeks, up to nine months, or one year. Payment may be in full, or partial by the employer, or paid for by the government.

Paternity leave is time off work for fathers or partners after the birth (or adoption) of their child to support the mother and to care for their baby. Paternity leave is generally shorter than maternity leave. Payment also depends on government rules or organisational policy.

In some instances, fathers can share leave with the mother, whilst in other scenarios only maternity leave can be taken and paid leave is not always offered.

4.1.5 Redundancy

Redundancy or severance pay is compensation offered to employees whose contract is terminated through no fault of their own. This is usually due to economic uncertainties or downturn of the company, or a company downsizing. Rights to redundancy pay will normally also be outlined, which may typically be one week's pay for every year of service, but the laws vary significantly between countries. Many countries will also cap the maximum payout and might dispute how many years' service has been completed.

Redundancy can be voluntary or mandatory.

Voluntary redundancy or voluntary severance is when the employee has a choice to leave the company in exchange for a redundancy payout package. The payout is generally more generous to encourage individuals to volunteer to leave, and payout is dependent on length of service and affordability. An employee can then leave on their own terms, such as opting for early retirement or may seek employment elsewhere.

Mandatory redundancy is when the decision to make someone redundant is made by the employer. The decision might be based on skill set or performance measures. It is not based on 'last in, first out' as commonly thought. A severance package will also apply.

In either instance of redundancy, the employer will have procedures to follow and may legally be required to consult with the workforce or with unions to negotiate severance deals, procedures, and time frames.

In the UK, employees are entitled to redundancy pay if they have been employed by the company longer than two years. Many employers will pay one and a half months' pay, per year of service. An Employment Rights Bill (2025) makes it a legal requirement for companies to consult with employees if 20 or more redundancies are proposed across the organisation.

In the US, there are no federal laws governing redundancy pay and instead there is an agreement between the employer and employee. At the time of writing, eight states have laws that stipulate severance pay but employers are not obligated to offer this (but it must be paid if promised).

In Germany, redundancy is paid if stated in the contract of employment. Typically, two weeks' salary, per year of service is paid, but there is no legal requirement here.

In Canada under the Canada Labour Code, redundancy is paid if a person has been employed in the company for longer than 12 months and is then entitled to two days' pay, per year of service.

In Japan, the law is protective of employees and whilst there is no specific requirement, organisations may offer generous severance packages for employees who volunteer for redundancy, which is typically one month's pay for the first year of service and a further one month per two years' service after that.

In Australia, the National Employment Standards governs redundancy pay entitlements. Severance pay is generally four weeks' pay when the employee has been employed between one and two years, increasing to one to two weeks' pay for each year of service after that.

China generally pays one month's salary per year of service when the employee has been employed for more than one year (half for six months' employment).

4.2 Zero-Hour Contracts

Zero-Hour Contracts are also known as casual work, piece work, on-call, and hourly-paid work. Generally, there is no specific legal definition of zero-hours. The use of Zero-Hour Contracts arose in the 1990s and they are increasingly used by many employers.

A Zero-Hour Contract of employment is where the average hours of work varies from zero hours to 20 hours per week and staff work when hours are made available by the employer. There is no guarantee that hours will be available, and staff are not obligated to accept hours.

Hospitality, hotel, and event industries, alongside health care, are the largest users of Zero-Hour Contracts within the UK, but these contracts are widely used across Europe.

Businesses in hospitality, hotels, and events often use Zero-Hour Contracts as they provide flexibility to increase or decrease staffing in accordance with fluctuating business demands. This is especially useful where hotels and events are seasonal, such as coastal resort hotels and summer festival events. Zero-hours can therefore lead to cost savings whereby staff are paid for hours worked and staffing numbers can quickly be increased or decreased as reservations or events are confirmed.

Zero-hours also provides flexibility for staff, as they are not obligated to accept hours, enabling staff members to work when it suits them, and can fit flexibly around their other commitments such as childcare or study.

A university student may choose to work in a restaurant in their university town, and work at their home branch during vacation periods, and decline hours when assignment deadlines are due, for example. Likewise, someone who already has a job, can utilise a Zero-Hour Contract in a second job and supplement their salary.

Zero-hours lead to an increased administrative burden, given the number of employees under these types of contracts and their varying hours worked causing payroll differences.

As staff are not guaranteed hours and might not work on a regular basis, service standards can suffer because of inconsistent exposure to the workplace, and inconsistencies in training – especially where changes or updates to procedures occur.

Also, zero-hour staff may not feel part of the organisation due to these factors, and due to irregular pay, may not feel as motivated as employees who are on standard contracts.

There are also concerns raised by government, unions, the media, and Human Resources professionals as to the exploitation of workers under this type of contract. There are cases where workers are left without hours, for example, and less favourable rights exist in comparison to permanent contracts of employment. As staff are not guaranteed hours, they may consistently get zero hours week after week leading to financial difficulties, and may not be able to secure loans, credit cards, or mortgages.

Staff on these 'unguaranteed' contracts are entitled to the minimum wage and holiday pay in countries that require them, but in the UK specifically, zero-hour staff are not entitled to sickness pay, maternity or paternity leave, or redundancy pay.

Such contracts can lead some events venues, restaurants, and hotels to threaten staff that if they do not work a certain shift, such as Christmas Day or New Year's Eve, they will not be offered further shifts, which heightens concerns as to employers manipulating staff employed under this type of contract, leaving staff in fear of turning down work or being off sick. Some employers may also make the contracts challenging by not communicating when shifts are available, or cancelling shifts at short notice, or sending staff home early, reducing hours and pay.

Being on standby and waiting for shifts to be offered may also make it difficult for staff to make plans or seek other employment for fear of turning down shifts for financial reasons and in terms of not being offered further shifts. Therefore, zero-hours makes it difficult to search for alternative employment, attend interviews, attend to studies, or commit to social events, causing issues with work–life balance.

Numerous venues have resorted to offering fixed-hours contracts instead, thus guaranteeing their staff set hours each week. But this is not suitable for all those who need a flexible contract that does not commit them to work fixed hours each week.

Whilst the UK, one of the core users of this type of contract, prepares the Employment Rights Bill, government is planning to ban zero-hours in order to improve the rights of workers. Whilst this is a positive move, this could be costly for industry and staff, whereby flexibility, cost savings, and economic uncertainties continue. It may be that employees will still be able to opt to remain on this type of contract. It is to be seen whether employment rights will improve, and if staff will be offered the same rights as those employed under permanent contracts of employment.

AUTHOR'S VOICE

I have been employed on Zero-Hour Contracts for several years for different reasons. I can see both the benefits and the issues associated with them, having experienced zero-hours as my only source of income, alongside supplementing my permanent contract with zero-hours work.

When I entered academia to teach hospitality, I was employed under zero-hours. This was worth the risk due to a career change from working in hospitality to a career in education. However, during this period, I had no set income and was unable to rent a property privately. At 30 years of age, having rented since I was 18, I needed to ask my parents to be guarantors of the rent.

As I had an unstable income, I opted to seek work with the local football stadium, and I was also managing weddings at weekends for an outside caterer. Both jobs enabled me to supplement my salary and pay bills, as well as afford holidays and a social life.

In recent years, I have been employed full time but with increasing mortgage rates, alongside a cost-of-living crisis in the UK, I have once again gained secondary employment on a zero-hour basis.

I now have secondary employment as a zero-hour employee as Events Duty Manager for the council. The job fits around my full-time career, my social life, and other commitments. This benefits me in multiple ways: firstly, by exposing me to a range of events helping me to maintain subject currency for my role in education, secondly it is work I enjoy doing, and thirdly, I earn additional income on a flexible basis.

To better manage Zero-Hour Contracts, fixed hours can be offered for those who need guaranteed hours, alongside putting into place policies and guidance as to notice periods, when work is available, and shift cancellations. Where feasible, an online system for shifts and payroll is helpful so that shifts are automatically released online, and staff can claim these, without managers and staff having to exchange emails confirming shifts. Emails can take time, be misconstrued, or missed, and shifts not claimed. Also, staff might feel uncomfortable to drop shifts by email or in-person, so it can be helpful to have an online system to drop shifts.

Alternatively, an email at the beginning of the month outlining the next months' shifts can be sent, but employers should be careful how this is worded and not to threaten staff if shifts are not claimed. This can be considered as manipulative, despite being part of the business needs to fill these hours and should be written more constructively and fairly.

Notice of shift cancellation for both parties should be perhaps 24–48 hours minimum to allow for someone else to claim the shift or for cover to be arranged, and to give employees notice should they need to make arrangements such as finding childcare. Some businesses may cancel shifts one or two hours beforehand which is unreasonable notice.

Ideally, if a person is on shift and gets sent home, they should be paid for a minimum number of hours or for the entire shift, even if operations are quiet.

A complete ban on zero-hours may not be feasible for workers or employers, but reasonable adjustments can be made to ensure both parties are happy with the contract.

INDUSTRY VOICE

Tim Claydon, Catering Manager, sports stadia

As the concourse and bars' manager for 26 bars, I had over a hundred members of staff every match.

On the payroll, we had about 170 all on Zero-Hour Contracts. Whilst there are numerous arguments for and against using zero-hours, if you treat staff well and are honest with them, they respect these constraints.

Little extras at Christmas and on public holidays when working, such as sweets/candy on arrival, cakes, or helping celebrate milestones such as birthdays or weddings, all demonstrate a manager who cares. This really does make a difference. The sickness and absence records are much lower than for other colleagues across other sites.

In addition, although the staff were on Zero-Hour contracts, they are paid above minimum wage to compensate for the infrequent hours that are inherent in working match days at a sports stadium.

4.3 Agency Workers

Sometimes, an employer might not be able to find enough staff, for instance during religious or other cultural celebrations where there are big events, and the number of attendees is high. In such instances, it may be necessary to use a staffing agency to supply temporary staff to cover one-off events. These temporary workers will be appointed by the staffing agency but at a higher cost than employing staff directly within the hotel or events venue.

The staffing agency will pay the staff but will charge a fee to the venue which means wage costs would be significantly higher than if employing staff directly.

Staffing agencies will often provide transport in situations where large numbers of temporary staff are required. This is a good idea because it provides staff with free transport, guarantees they will attend, and ensures they will arrive on time.

When deciding on a staffing agency, care needs to be taken to ensure the staff are being paid a fair wage, and their rights are protected.

There are also recruitment agencies that can provide permanent or temporary staff and may shortlist and conduct interviews on behalf of the restaurant, hotel, or event venue. If subsequently employed, the recruitment agent will charge a fee for their finding and selection services. The fee can be an agreed percentage of the annual or average monthly wage for this recruited staff member, which could also be referred to as commission in exchange for the agency's services.

INDUSTRY VOICE

Dr Philip Berners, Associate Professor in Events Management

I have often needed to use agencies to supply me with temporary staff – usually, for large-scale events where I didn't have enough of my own staff.

Always use an agency which is well known in the industry and has a good reputation for supplying quality staff. You wouldn't want an agency to send staff who are disinterested, untrained, scruffy, impolite, or lazy.

Remember, the staff reflect you at your event or hotel. They also reflect the agency who supplies them to you. If the agency doesn't care about the quality of staff they send, don't use that agency!

At one event I organised, the agency staff all left their stations and went on the dancefloor to join the fun! After that occasion, I insisted all agencies must send employment managers to oversee their staff and sign them in and out. After all, the staff weren't employed by me, so I had no jurisdiction over them.

4.4 Casual Work

Casual work is less formal than a Zero-Hour Contract and there may not even be a specific contract in place. Casual work offers flexibility but is less defined and can be for a one-off project without any expectations for future work. In casual work, there are no set hours, and work may be less frequent than on zero-hours – there is no guarantee of work being available, but it is offered when the organisation needs staff.

Casual staff (casuals) are sometimes paid in cash, which is illegal in the UK if taxes are not declared when required. Nevertheless, paying casual staff in cash does happen in industries where casuals are necessary, such as the events industry.

Casual staff, like contractors or self-employed individuals such as freelancers (see Section 4.6), may invoice for their payment and file their own tax returns. Otherwise, the organisation can pay tax on their behalf to be legally compliant.

4.5 Flexible Working

Flexible working enables employees to determine their own working hours and even the days they work in the workplace or remotely from home where feasible.

4.5.1 Flexitime

The employee starts and finishes work to their own schedule, within reason, for example around school times, arriving later to the office and going home later, or arriving earlier in the morning and finishing early. This type of flexible arrangement will be agreed and align with business needs.

4.5.2 Compressed Hours

The employee works full-time hours over fewer days, so if working a 40-hour week they may work those hours over four days instead of five, and ten-hour days rather than eight. This is helpful for someone who has other commitments such as caring for a dependant or who would rather work longer hours over fewer days for a longer rest period. This leads to better work–life balance whilst still meeting contractual working hours. Employees may be more motivated, productive, and efficient as a result. Working fewer days also provides the employee with cost savings when commuting.

Offering flexible working and compressed hours may lead to employment and retention of a talented workforce in a competitive market.

Employees can request an amendment to their working hours to flexible working and this should be offered to all eligible employees and should be assessed to ensure business needs can still be met and policies amended to reflect different work patterns. However, the employer maintains the decision and has the right to reject a request on reasonable and justified grounds.

If the compressed hours option is taken, working longer hours may result in a team that experiences burnout and impact negatively on well-being, increasing sickness days, absenteeism, errors, and accidents.

4.5.3 Job Share

Two or more people share a full-time role, for example two people work 2.5 days each, or one works three days and the other works two days, normally opposite days to one another, or maybe with overlap for handover and communication purposes. Job-sharing is a contemporary working arrangement whereby flexible working is made available to help individuals balance work and personal life.

A single job role will be split into two contracts, allowing individuals to work within what was once a single job role. This enables more bespoke working hours to fit around commitments such as childcare.

The job-share arrangement may require individuals to work across different projects, whether at the same time or opposing hours. This is especially useful where standard office hours apply, for example in sales roles, finance, or other administrative roles within hospitality. It may not always be feasible in the service industries such as hotels and events.

4.5.4 Working From Home (WFH)

Working remotely away from the place of employment, WFH is another form of flexible working that has grown in popularity since the Coronavirus (COVID-19) pandemic in 2020/2021. Whilst working from home is not new, during the pandemic many businesses were forced to close, and employees were unable to work in shared workplaces to reduce the spread of the disease. This led to many employees adjusting to a pattern of WFH, with varying levels of success.

During the period of the pandemic, many firms recognised that employees could be trusted to work away from the workplace, leading to some employers making this a permanent arrangement. Some even closed offices, leading to cost savings.

This enhanced work–life balance for many, and contracts were revised to enable individuals to remain working from home, whilst others opted for a partial or complete return to the workplace.

Not only the needs of the business, but the requirements of employees should be considered. Some prefer to be in a work environment away from domestic distractions, and some enjoy the social and communication factors of the workplace.

4.5.5 Hybrid Working

This involves remote working from home blended with time in the workplace, which may be specific set days or a flexible arrangement. Hybrid working requires a certain number of days in the normal place of work, compared to home, for example.

4.5.6 Four-day Working Week

The four-day working week has been trialled across multiple sectors and across the world, with some businesses choosing this structure due to perceived benefits such as higher productivity when staff are well rested.

The four-day working week is widely accepted as a 20 per cent reduction in working hours, for the same pay, with employees working four days out of five. But, unlike compressed hours, the employee still only works their standard daily hours, for example they may work eight hours a day, over four days, resulting in a 32-hour working week, as opposed to 40 hours.

Many organisations suggest they have adopted, or intend to adopt, the four-day working week. However, they are in fact adopting compressed hours, and employees are working the same hours over fewer days, resulting in four longer working days, rather than experiencing a 20 per cent reduction in working hours. Both provide a better work–life balance and can enhance employee productivity, commitment, and loyalty.

The concept behind the four-day working week is that staff have a better work–life balance, have more time for family and other commitments, and have three days off per week. Therefore, they are deemed to be more rested, happier, and more productive at work. Employee welfare is boosted, and staff are less likely to suffer from burnout, stress, or illness.

In turn, it should lead to higher employee retention, less absence, and higher morale due to staff feeling more valued. A people-centric organisation that offers this flexibility may attract higher quality recruits and boost company reputation by publicising their corporate ethics and values.

However, many organisations consider the four-day working week reduces productivity. For some businesses, such as hospitality, hotels, and events which operate 24 hours a day, seven days a week, 365 days a year, the four-day working week is not feasible and could lead to staffing shortages and a rising wage bill to cover the additional day with more staff.

A rise in customer dissatisfaction might be experienced as the response to complaints, and enquiries could take longer to address when working days are reduced. It might also result in inconsistent service, causing a rise in complaints. Furthermore, expecting staff to do the same amount of work in fewer hours may cause pressure and increase workplace stress and exhaustion.

INDUSTRY VOICE

Sophie Linin, Deputy Head of Events, Royal Museums Greenwich

Flexible working for hospitality staff can be challenging when so much of what hospitality staff do is customer-facing. An organisation should try to establish a case-by-case basis for flexible working, which works within whatever guidelines the organisation has around this topic.

For new hires, it is best to be honest throughout the recruitment about the opportunity for flexible working so that people are aware of what the options may or may not be. Speak openly with your staff member about why they feel that they need flexible working, what their aims are, and what they need to achieve out of the arrangement. Then, compare this with the job needs.

There is a range of options for flexible working, and you can usually agree something. It may be that you can offer later starts, earlier finishes, four-day weeks, job shares, or remote working. Whatever you agree, it is key to ensure the agreement is formalised in some way, even in an email, and can be referred to at a later stage.

4.6 Freelancers, Contractors, and Consultants

These types of workers are self-employed, or they are with other companies whose services are being used.

Freelancers are specialists in their field of expertise because they get jobs and business due to their specialism, reputation, and trustworthiness. Services include marketing or website design, and many technical and production managers for events are freelance as they get called to provide their services from event to event.

INDUSTRY VOICE

Dr Philip Berners, Associate Professor in Events Management

Freelancing is an excellent and appropriate structure for the events industry where venue managers and other organisers of events have a fluctuating or pulsating need for specialist services.

Just about every day, I was working alongside freelancers. Sometimes, they were contracted by the client or the client's representatives such as technicians or security. Other times, I contracted freelancers myself to help with areas where I am not a specialist – again, technicians or security are examples.

Over time, working in an industry, you get to know freelance specialists, which is important because you need to call in the support from people who you know, trust, and get on with.

Contractors usually work for an organisation for a fixed period, for example a catering contract at a sports stadium bidding to win the contract to operate food and drink services. The fixed period might be for a one-off event, or it could be a longer contract over three, five, or ten years, say, providing specialist services which the venue cannot. Examples of 'contract catering' include *Levy Restaurants UK* at The O2 London Arena; and *Sodexo Live!* at the Vancouver Convention Centre.

Contractors may sub-contract their services to another provider, such as a cleaning contract, then find other self-employed cleaners to provide office cleaning or housekeeping services on their behalf.

After the contracted period expires, the venue can decide to extend the contract, source a different provider, or operate those services themselves 'in-house'.

Consultants provide specialist skills to advise and support business growth and development – providing guidance, tools, and information to organisations on how to improve sales, customer service, social media strategy, competitive positioning, or branding as examples.

Generally, an organisation will only utilise consultants who have extensive industry experience and expertise. The individual consultant will be self-employed or might be working for a consultancy firm.

The consultancy period for a project would be variable depending on business needs but can be costly, which often determines the time frame. As the individual is often paid day-by-day, costs tend to be higher to mitigate the risk of not securing regular work and due to use of their expertise.

Table 4.1 provides a summary of the basic employment terms and rights for each type of contract. Employment rights vary from country to country, and the particular contract issued by the employer.

Table 4.1 Summary of Different Contracts of Employment

Contract Type	Description
Full time or Part time	Permanent ongoing employment until given notice – usually entitled to full legal rights such as minimum wage, holiday pay, redundancy, maternity/paternity leave, and sickness leave in some countries.
Temporary/Temp	No specified duration of employment given; an employee may be made permanent at any time. Rights are based on length of service and will vary country to country. The period of work may have an unspecified finish date.
Fixed Term	Specified duration of employment, e.g. 6 months for an event or maternity cover. Contract is not renewable and redundancy rights may be waived. Same rights as permanent employees in terms of pay, pension, and holiday pay.
Zero-Hour Contract (Also known as casual work, hourly paid, piece work, or on-call)	Staff are not obligated to accept hours and can work elsewhere; employers do not have to guarantee work. Offers flexibility to both parties. Entitled to the minimum wage and paid holiday based on average hours worked. Not entitled to sickness pay, redundancy, or paternity/maternity pay.
Compressed hours	Full-time hours worked over fewer days, for example a 40-hour work week over five days may be compressed into four days, working ten-hour days rather than eight hours per day to make up the hours.

Contract Type	Description
Four-day working week	Employed to work four days per week, this usually results in a 20 per cent reduction in working hours for the same pay, with the intention of a more rested employee who will be more productive during the workday due to a better work–life balance.
Annual Hours	A fixed number of hours worked over the year, often with varied work patterns over the year.
Flexitime	Flexibility over completion of work hours, e.g. late start/late finish or making up hours on another day.
Job Share	When two or more employees share a job role, the work, and working hours e.g. 20-hours per week, each.
Agency	Hire of temporary casual staff via an agency. The company pays the agency for the employee's hours. After a period of continuous employment in some countries, some agency workers get the same terms and conditions as permanent staff.
Freelancers, Consultants, and Contractors	Self-employed or working for another company; may not be entitled to the same rights, other than Health and Safety. Freelancers provide specialist skills whilst consultants work on projects or provide support and advice. Contractors are often used for services such as technical production, security fences at events, security or stewarding, laundry and linen services, florists, caterers, or IT services/systems.

Chapter 5

Onboarding, Training, and Development

Edward Gallier

5.0 Introduction

This chapter provides practical guidance in the field of learning and development, a specialist area of the Human Resources function. Learning and Development (L&D) is responsible for developing newly recruited team members to full potential and drives retention and stability of a highly performing team.

The chapter covers areas of talent management, employee onboarding, learning and development, leadership, learning styles, development of managers, qualifications, and transferable skills.

In a competitive job market, useful learning and development opportunities within any organisation, large or small, will contribute to a reputation as an employer of choice. Learning and development should be seen as an investment in the team and in building a stronger and more consistent product offer rather than a direct cost at the point of delivery.

5.1 Talent Management

Talent management is key for hospitality. It is a people-management function that looks at the ways a company hires and inducts employees, keeps them happy, productive, and develops their skills. Numerous studies show the relationship

DOI: 10.4324/9781003469803-6

between talent management and a company's performance, especially in hospitality when so much depends on the 'human factor'. A strong talent management strategy implemented well, will have a positive business impact.

But what should we focus on in talent management? This is outlined in this section:

5.1.1 Finding and Hiring the Right People

Talent management and the influence of learning and development starts before an employee joins an organisation. It is important that the L&D function has an influence on the process of finding and hiring the right people: finding the right person who can thrive in the right job is key to organisational success. L&D should have an influence on future hires. An example of this is the job description document (see Section 2.4).

A job description should contain information about the company's vision, mission, and values, painting the picture of the company's personality and direction. There should be a summary of the job role to help the candidate and recruiter decide if the applicant is a good fit.

Different companies may use the same job title for different roles, so this stops any overselling of a job role or misunderstandings. The main tasks should be outlined to paint a picture of an average week or month.

Key to development is the person specification (see Section 2.5) within the job description. This should outline the ideal candidate for the job in terms of knowledge, skills, and behaviours. It is important when crafting the person specification, that an organisation does not veer into bias or discriminatory descriptions that would limit the opportunity for the right candidate to be recruited for the right role. Most importantly, the recruitment process must not fall foul of national legislation. Discrimination in the workplace and especially in recruitment has both a financial cost and a reputational cost to any business.

Measurable performance indicators should be included. These help the candidate to understand the impact of their job role.

A list of ongoing learning should be included to help a candidate understand the learning and development journey they will embark on during their probationary period and induction. This list should also include development opportunities post-probation which, along with describing the company's approach to learning and development and outlining future career paths, can be a positive selling tool when the candidate compares similar job roles they are applying for at the same time.

5.1.2 Managing and Rewarding Performance

A highly performing and productive employee is a desirable business objective. To be able to manage and reward an employee, performance goals need to be set. This could already have been done in the job description under 'measurable performance'.

Setting regular performance goals for the short and medium term is an important way to help an employee's work encompass stretching and motivation to achieve set goals. It can be useful to follow the SMART acronym: Specific, Measurable, Attainable (or Achievable), Relevant, and Timebound.

> **Specific:** What do you want to achieve? What is the task or goal?
>
> **Measurable:** How will success be measured; what does success look like? Will you evaluate it, and what will the frequency of check-ins be?
>
> **Attainable:** Are all the necessary skills and resources in place to achieve this goal? If not, can this be rectified?
>
> **Relevant:** Is this goal in line with the other goals for the team or company?
>
> **Timebound:** What is the time frame you have for achieving this goal?

Each goal should contain the five elements of SMART. It is not correct to have one goal for each area of SMART.

The SMART acronym helps to structure a goal which will deliver performance and reward for the individual and the company. All goals should be linked to company or departmental objectives, an employee's review, and any developmental conversations that have been held. This ensures all goals are aligned to personal and business needs and there is no conflict between these. Over-promising and setting goals that are not aligned to personal and business objectives can lead to conflict and disagreements and will lower motivation and result in a break in the trust relationship between manager and employee.

It is important with goal-setting, that regular milestones or review dates are built into the process to track performance, rather than just the completion date. If the goal is running behind schedule or becomes a challenge, this can be identified as soon as possible, and corrective action taken, which is better than missing a goal and demotivating the employee.

Rewarding goal achievement and performance can take many forms. These can be financial, but should not be limited to financial rewards.

It is important to identify the distinction between recognition and reward. Recognition of good performance and goal achievement could take the form of a face-to-face thank you, an online post, or handshake. The power of recognition should not be overlooked because of the relationship between manager and employee. The power of recognition shows the position power a manager holds in relation to employees. A word of thanks from a manager can have a higher impact and create a feeling of worth greater than you would expect – especially if there is a productive and truthful relationship between manager and employee.

Rewards can be used to manage performance and recognise achievement. This could take the form of financial or non-financial reward, a gift, or a prize. When using rewards, it is important that the company is transparent and shares in advance the rewards that could be awarded for performance or goal achievement.

To provide rewards in advance of results could be construed as bribery, so rewards should be given after work has been performed or goals are achieved.

When designing rewards, it is important that the opportunity to be rewarded is equally available – there are no favourites, and no unintentional unconscious bias. If the reward has a value, it is important at the time of design to consider any tax implications over a tax year for an employee who may receive multiple rewards. The process of setting up a reward and any tax implications can be a manual process but there are several reward and tracking apps available. An example is *workstars.com*

INDUSTRY VOICE

Dr Philip Berners, Associate Professor in Events Management

I am not a true fan of rewards to motivate staff. In my experience, rewards can demotivate other members of the team if the same staff keep receiving rewards time after time.

There may be reasons why a member of staff is not or cannot achieve rewards – maybe they are scheduled to work quiet shifts, or they are part time, or they are not customer facing. Some employees simply are not motivated by rewards but can be demotivated if someone else is getting something they are not.

Rewards do work if all employees are fully included and can achieve them. For this reason, I feel recognition and reward should be individual – not group, team, or departmental rewards – so that each employee has their own goals and rewards package built into their job.

5.1.3 Tailoring the Employee Experience

Post-pandemic since 2021, there has been a paradigm shift in what employees require from their job role. It can be observed that employees require a greater balance between their work and private life. It can also be seen that individuals demand richer experiences in their private life and at the same time can demand from their employers a richer and more engaging time at work.

Fulfilling only the main task of the role is no longer motivational to an employee. During their time at work, it is more important for them to feel part of their working team and their employer organisation. The need to feel part of the brand and engaged with the employer can manifest itself in work-based voluntary work, charity fundraising, community work – and in the learning and development field, the need for a personalised experience from the learning offering.

Regular communication is the heart of any tailored employee experience and should be the priority of a manager. Some managers find it difficult to focus on a rich conversation and often spend time talking about an employee's social activities and days off. Whilst such conversation is important to understand the wider life and personality of an employee and should not be overlooked, it is also important to lead a good and regular developmental discussion focused on balancing the needs of the employee and the business.

A useful tool for this discussion includes facilitation cards: there are many of these products available such as sets of cards produced by *atmybest.com*. The advantage of these cards is that the catalytic questions that are posed are great conversation starters.

One of the structured outcomes of these regular conversations would be a personal development plan (PDP) for the team member. A PDP should be a formal and documented record that can be referred to at any later time. It should be a working document rather than a document which is filed away and only reviewed annually. A PDP should contain the following:

Development objectives which have been identified to enable employees to meet the learning and development needs identified at the skills analysis stage.

Priorities identified and whether the development objective is:

- Critical to the employee's current role
- Beneficial but non-critical to the employee's current role

- Critical to their progression into a future role
- Beneficial but non-critical to progression into a future role

Activities that can constitute learning or development and enable an employee to achieve development objectives, for example formal training, on-the-job training, work-shadowing another colleague.

Support or resources needed to help the team member achieve development objectives. Typically, this would involve support from a manager, the department, or colleagues, to enable an employee to undertake a learning or development activity, such as allowing time away from the business for an activity, or funding to enable it. In a chain of properties this information is fed into Group Human Resources department, so if a course is not already listed on the learning and development plan, an employee may request it.

Target and actual dates for when it is intended to achieve the development objectives, followed by the date this has been achieved. Data in these columns is particularly useful when the PDP is reviewed as it will enable managers and the employee to identify any factors that may have prevented the target from being achieved and to identify contingencies to prevent this from occurring in future.

Review dates to identify when progress towards targets will be reviewed. Target completion dates should all be within the next six months.

A Personal Development Plan can be structured as simply as a grid within a paper document but there are more sophisticated online tools and app-based tools which encourage regular communication and engagement between the manager and employee.

5.1.4 Optimising Workforce Planning and Strategy

Workforce planning is an opportunity for the learning and development function to show that it is not siloed but engaged in and linked to business operations. An effective workforce strategy is built around the company's strategy and direction. It should be viewed as a core business process which allows the business to evolve in a planned way rather than dealing with unforeseen or unplanned change. In a fast-paced sector where tastes and trends of customers can often dictate the products and services a company offers, the company needs data at hand to make the changes in a planned way.

Workforce planning falls into two types of activities: hard, and soft. Hard workforce planning is based around the use of data. For example, the number of people employed and the skills, knowledge, and behaviours they hold, and the job roles they undertake in which departments, and the impact that those roles and departments have on revenue and profit, and how these change over time.

The aim of workforce planning is to ensure the organisation has the right number of people to deliver the products and services they offer, at the right time, in the right place, with the aim of always having the best people in the most important and critical roles.

Soft workforce planning can be referred to as more strategic. It is about planning in advance a company strategy, and within the strategy business information can be assessed. This is where learning and development can play its part. The learning and development function should be able to provide data on the skills, knowledge, and behaviours held by each employee. It is important that data also shows future aspirational roles for each employee and the learning and development initiatives or experiences they are planning to gain to get them to that aspirational role. This data can be used to identify any workforce gaps when planning the future human resource needs of the business.

The process below provides a basic insight into this workforce planning process:

1. Assess the current workforce position
2. Establish future workforce needs
3. Identify any gap between current position and future needs
4. Identify actions and initiatives to support change
5. Consider the impact of the process on payroll and other learning costs such as learning design and delivery

All learning should take place in paid worktime to show the commitment to the change from the business. This is most important for employees who earn around the minimum wage threshold. Any learning delivery of any type, face-to-face or online, that takes place outside worktime is still considered as work and may reduce the hour rate earner by the employee below minimum threshold set by governments.

6. Communicate and gain buy-in from stakeholders
7. Implement the change plan which will include learning and development interventions to modify employee skills, knowledge, and behaviours for future
8. Monitor progress against established timelines
9. Maintain communication around progress and achievements

INDUSTRY VOICE

Paula Musson, Assistant Group HR Manager, Leonardo Hotels

I had two great candidates at the final stage of the interview process, which posed a real dilemma of who to make an offer to. Both candidates had great experience and knowledge within the industry, just different personalities.

I offered to one candidate and had to reject the second. I felt that I really needed to spend time giving feedback to the unsuccessful candidate and keeping them warm.

The first candidate accepted the offer; however, they did not start. I was able to go back to the second candidate and have a discussion on where they currently were in their employment journey. It was only though the time spent keeping the candidate warm and building a relationship that allowed me to do this. This candidate accepted, started, and has continued to grow with us.

Always make sure you spend time with candidates who you are going to reject: you never know when they may be a candidate again.

5.2 Employee Induction (Onboarding)

An employee induction, also known as onboarding, should be a scheduled opportunity to create a positive first impression of a company. It is the employer's opportunity to confirm in the mind of a new hire that they have made the right choice. In an employment marketplace where there are more job roles than available workforce, jobseekers hold the power. This can be overlooked by a complacent employer. Research demonstrates that an effective and timely induction significantly impacts successful integration and retention of employees.

The benefits for employers include reduced staff turnover, increased employee stability, and reduced absenteeism. By engaging early with new hires, they become committed to the organisation, new colleagues, and the job role sooner. Remember, to start a new job with new colleagues and new surroundings is stressful, so to onboard and embed that person ensures they feel comfortable with the move they have made.

For the new employee, a good induction enables them to understand the company sooner, their role and contribution in the company, and how the company wants them to work. It is an opportunity to meet new colleagues who may be starting at the same time and learn from established colleagues through mentoring and training to get up to speed quickly.

It is worth highlighting that most new hires will find their new job role using a website or app. Once they have been interviewed and been selected for a job role by the employer, they may have accepted based on the interview and selection process and data they have found online. It is a mutual agreement to take the offered job role.

What should be remembered is that the same website or app that highlighted the firm's job, will not know that the individual has been appointed and has started the new job role. This means the new hire may still be receiving similar job offers from the app. It is in the company's interest to integrate and settle a new hire as soon as possible. This urgent focus on induction also has a positive effect on employee turnover, absenteeism, and employer brand.

INDUSTRY VOICE

Emily Timbrell, Head of Learning and Culture, Nobu Hotel London

Working in such a transient industry where turnover tends to be high, it is crucial that we engage new starters at the beginning of their employment with us. Recruits, particularly in line-level roles, may have had multiple job offers when they accept our offer, and we need to offer something that shows we stand out.

Too often, the onboarding process refers to a training programme that is run by the Human Resources function sharing information about the property, employment, health and safety, etc. Whilst this is valuable, the programme must form part of the onboarding process and not itself be the 'onboarding'.

We like to define onboarding as a three-month process, an opportunity for us as employers to provide the recruit with the necessary information, training, and resources to promote their success in the workplace, whilst enabling the recruit to explore, learn, and engage with their new workplace.

A new recruit's onboarding plan should go together with the same timeline as the new starter probationary review so that by the time the probation review is due, the employee has been provided with the necessary skills development to set them up for success.

Induction or onboarding should not be a single action or course. The process should be a planned and systematic process taking place over an extended period. A useful measure of time and content of the induction would be, 'What can be learnt and assessed within the new hire's probationary period?' This period in general could be around three months. The period is sometimes longer for a management role.

Using the period of induction as a guide ensures that the probation period has a structure and specific learning outcome. A well-executed induction supports the employer brand that was described during the recruitment process. An employer that is seen as delivering promises made at recruitment will be valued by the new hire.

When structuring an induction, it is important to consider that what is important to an employer, is not always the same for the new hire. The induction provides an opportunity for the employer to highlight and share information and company values, culture, and direction. Just as important on a personal level for the new hire, would be changing rooms, break rooms, restrooms, uniform, and wage payment.

The induction process would often be outlined and produced by the Human Resources and Learning and Development functions in conjunction with business operations, made up of several integrated elements.

New hires need to understand the company, culture and values, its people, and just as importantly, what is expected of them in their role. It is important that when it comes to the delivery of induction, managers are involved and not just Human Resources. Involving line-managers in the delivery of induction gives the opportunity to meet new hires, influence their understanding, and start to build rapport and trust.

INDUSTRY VOICE

Sophie Linin, Deputy Head of Events, Royal Museums Greenwich, © National Maritime Museum

I try to implement a thorough induction programme that lasts at least two weeks. I break down elements of the job description into separate parts and book meetings for the new hire with different people to different elements. This allows them to begin forging a wide range of working relationships and understand the team dynamic alongside learning their role. I also try to involve other departments in this training, so they can build wider connections.

Don't forget to book them some downtime during the induction though! They will need time to re-read any notes, arrange their email folders, set up their desk, and digest what they are learning.

Once the induction programme is completed, have a meeting to discuss each section and check how comfortable they are with each area.

Don't expect them to be immediately able to do their job at 100 per cent; you will need to give them work in piecemeal fashion to build their workload.

When planning the delivery of induction, a blended approach should be considered. To make the induction flexible and accessible, a mix of delivery styles should be considered such as online learning, webinar, classroom, podcast, documents to read, mentoring, and quizzes as examples. A quiz demonstrates the inductee's learning.

An employer may consider starting the induction process prior to the new hire starting employment. This provides an opportunity to stay in touch with the individual to 'keep them warm' (engaged) during the time between accepting the job offer and the start date. This could be early access to company information, the completion of onboarding paperwork, video resources, issue of the staff handbook, and any other useful information.

When hiring employees around the minimum wage threshold, it is important to make clear that any issued tasks are voluntary and not critical to be completed, to gain the job role. Mandatory tasks should not be issued, or job-critical learning or quizzes, unless you are willing to pay the new hire for their time taken to complete the tasks so earnings do not fall below minimum wage levels when taking this time into consideration.

A checklist should then be used to monitor progress of induction for employers, Human Resources, and the employee to refer to. This can be used if a dispute occurs to demonstrate what information has been provided, or to identify what training and information still needs to be delivered. Managers (or Human Resources) and the new starter should sign and date each activity to ensure induction is completed in full.

JENNIFER KAYE'S VOICE

Induction plays a vital role in staff retention, and if lacking, can lead to staff members leaving within the first few weeks of employment.

This may be due to lack of understanding of what the job role entails, and if training is lacking, feeling incompetent and frustrated at not being able to perform confidently within the job role. This will result in loss of productivity and low morale, and even poor integration into the team.

A team member can have their probation extended, or further training or support offered and if they still fail to perform, or the organisation fails to support development, ultimately a new starter may then leave through dismissal through failed probation, performance management measures, or resignation.

This will have a detrimental impact on the individual's employment record due to the short employment period, and reputational damage to the employer where service may suffer. In addition, remaining team members must fulfil the duties of the absent person, further impacting morale.

If the new employee leaves, this will mean further skills shortages, wasted time for the inducting manager and recruiter, wasted recruitment fees and time, and the recruitment process will need to begin again.

When thinking what to include in the induction process consider:

Before day one

- Joining instructions, access codes, or login details to essential portals
- Evidence of the legal right to work
- New-starter details
- Company conditions of employment
- Code of conduct

From day one (but not as one course or workshop as this could overwhelm):

- Company advertising or media to understand the brand/product from the customer point of view

- Health and safety information
- Health and safety policy and accident reporting
- Workplace compliance
- Emergency exits and evacuation procedures
- First aid and mental health first aid contacts
- Security procedures
- Any required security passes and keys to ensure they can complete their job role
- Confidentiality
- Mandatory training as the employer sees as appropriate, but should include data protection, bribery, modern slavery and human trafficking, child sexual exploitation
- Property map or guided tour
- Telephone and computer system information
- IT systems, logins, and passwords
- Car parking and transport benefits
- Hours of business within different departments or units
- Remote/flexible working tools and access to work systems, including relevant file-sharing and communication tools
- Company information
- Company background
- Company strategy
- Culture and values
- Mission statement
- Brand
- Organisation structure – local, regional, global
- Products and services offered
- Any quality systems and awards which have standards that need maintaining
- Customer/guest care policy
- Benefits and policies
- Pay date and method
- Tax and national insurance

- Pension schemes
- Expense claims
- Working time, including hours
- Break periods
- Holidays and other leave entitlements
- Probationary period
- Diversity, Equity, and Inclusion policy
- Well-being policy including absence/sickness.
- Internet, email, and social media protocols
- Performance management
- Disciplinary procedure
- Grievance procedure
- Role-specific information
- Clear outline of the job/role requirements
- Introduction to the team and ways of working
- Meeting with key/senior employees
- Learning and development
- Regular coffee chats and reviews during the induction period (probationary period)
- Development opportunities and future aspiration roles
- Personal Development Plan

When structuring the induction it should be remembered:

- Not to give too much information too soon, especially on the first day (information overload)
- Not to use the same presentations or content for all employee groups/levels. Information should be level appropriate
- Human Resources should not deliver solely: it should be a shared process
- Do not create unreasonable expectations for the new hire or for the company by overselling the job
- Do not focus only on administration and policy which is important to the company, but not engaging for the new hire

Remember during the induction process and at the conclusion of the induction, to evaluate the process and content with the new hire. This could be coffee chats and reviews as part of the induction process, or a separate process. This data will be invaluable when editing and modifying the process in future.

INDUSTRY VOICE

Loredana Burdulea, Cluster HR Manager, Leonardo Hotels

An effective induction programme is critical to setting up new employees for success. At Leonardo Hotels, we have found that the first few days are key to embedding not only essential job knowledge but the company culture and values.

Our induction process varies slightly by hotel brand, but it always follows a blended approach. The new recruits engage in online training via *GROW* online, face-to-face sessions with HR, Heads of Department, and *NEW* Team Coaches, along with continuous reminders through *LEAPP* chats. The programme is designed to be completed within three months, ensuring that non-management employees complete before the end of their probationary period.

Our induction programme incorporates the *BELONG* induction workbooks, offering the opportunity for every new hire to compile a profile to learn about their primary colour energy. This concept follows in other areas of induction and guest care training. It has become cultural. This understanding helps team members better engage with colleagues and guests, enhancing service interactions. For example, once an employee knows their colour energy, they can apply this knowledge by 'guessing' the colour energy of guests. Additionally, the new recruits receive training on essential manual handling techniques to ensure they carry out their roles safely and effectively, reducing the risk of injury during their daily tasks.

By creating a structured and engaging induction process, we aim to reduce the uncertainty that often comes with starting a new role. Feedback from employees shows that this blend of structured learning, practical experience, and peer interaction boosts confidence and helps them feel part of the team faster.

By emphasising early support and engagement, we have seen stronger retention rates and a quicker transition into full productivity.

5.3 Learning & Development

Employee Learning & Development (L&D) opportunities should not be taken for granted in the workplace. L&D requires an investment by the employer and delivers positive people outcomes.

A planned L&D offering from an employer should be part of a wider Employee Value Proposition (EVP). An EVP can be described as a bespoke set of value-added benefits offered by an employer to their employees in return for their skills, experience, commitment, and hard work for the organisation. Overall, this could be items such as pay and other remuneration, benefits, rewards, career and learning development, and work–life balance, as well as an outline of values, mission, social purpose, and culture.

The EVP shares the bespoke benefits an employee can expect from the company. It demonstrates why a company is the right place for an employee to thrive. The EVP plays a key role in attracting, engaging, and retaining talent and building the employer brand in what is always a competitive employment sector.

Workplace learning delivers several strategic benefits to the company. The provision of any L&D must get buy-in from the senior management team and be linked to the company's business objectives to show the employee is able to contribute to the delivery of these objectives:

- Develop an internal talent pipeline
- Increase service standards and guest ratings
- Become an attraction tool as part of an EVP
- Help ensure stable and consistent growth
- Act as a talent retention tool
- Be core to new product development

L&D can contribute to business success at many levels, as shown here:

Level 1 – Frontline Operational Team Development

- Technical job skills and knowledge
- Brand and standards
- Critical health, safety, and risk training
- Guest care training
- Well-being and lifestyle training

Level 2 – Supervisory and Early Management Development

- Team development and motivation
- Communication
- People planning and rota
- Problem-solving
- Conflict management

Level 3 – Management Development

- Core leadership and management competency development
- Team well-being
- Health, safety, and risk management

Level 4 – Senior Leadership Development

- Business planning
- Employment law
- Well-being in the workplace

Look for a framework of development that meets your needs. The Institute of Hospitality (IoH) offers the 'Five Pillars of Learning' which is a good start. They are broad and offer ideas for team development that can be applied to Level 2 and above from the model shown.

The IoH Five Pillars of Learning

1. Business

   Includes: Finance; human resources; sales and marketing; operating models; vision and mission; business strategy; competitors; analysis of management information; contingency planning; the technology supporting the delivery of products; environmental; and legislative and social responsibilities.

2. Customer/Guest

   Includes: Determining the customer service journey; impact of service failure on hospitality; customer feedback as a competitive tool; implementing and evaluating hospitality marketing and sales strategies; understanding what it means to champion the business and maintain comprehensive product/ service; brand, and market knowledge.

3. Leadership

   Includes: Management and leadership styles; diversity and inclusion; a culture that demonstrates social inclusion; and an understanding of how to lead the implementation of change.

4. Self-Care

   Includes: Mental health; physical health; personal effectiveness; managing self; emotional intelligence; work and business culture; and conscious leadership.

5. Team

   Includes: Creating a people strategy; communicating and engaging with people and teams; management of team recruitment; learning and development; and retention.

For most businesses, the service and hospitality standards, and how these are delivered and measured, is a business imperative. These standards and processes, known as 'Standards of Operational Procedure' or 'Standards of Performance' (both, SOPs) have often been developed over some time and are integral to a brand and the expectations of the guest. It could be called the brand DNA.

When planning a learning intervention, especially at a frontline service level or guest care, it is important to be familiar with the brand SOPs. It can be tempting as a new manager or new in role to spend time being creative and wanting to 'make your mark' by setting new standards and processes and training the team. It is important to understand what standards form part of the SOP and which do not.

Usually, SOPs should not be modified without prior approval from senior managers or the SOP owner. This is paramount within a franchised brand operation. There is a risk of putting in a lot of effort designing and implementing standards that have a negative impact on the business operation and your reputation. Know what needs training and to what standard.

Once aware of the SOPs, it should next be understood what the priorities are for training and who needs to be trained. This can be established by a Training Needs Analysis (TNA). A TNA should focus on objective data and observations rather than subjective views, to ensure a fair and transparent TNA as a base for learning.

A TNA is an assessment for a department or an individual to identify the gap between current skills, knowledge, and behaviours required and where the individual or department currently is. The TNA helps prioritise the required development areas, dependent on team, guest, and business impact.

Knowing what training needs to be delivered is only part of the picture. L&D should be thought of as a language. If the training is not being easily received and retained by those learning, its effectiveness and return on investment will be diminished. A range of training methods should be considered which work across the team, budget, time frame, and culture of the company.

Who to deliver the training

External training providers – These bring external content and delivery focus. They are flexible individuals, often self-employed, with skills, knowledge, and experience. No long-term commitments, paid per training session delivered. Always seek recommendations from trusted sources and testimonials.

Internal subject matter experts (SME) – Do not overlook the wealth of knowledge that sits within the department or business. Experienced managers can be a great source of brand-specific training. They have great experience of business processes and can share their experience and network with the learner. Some subject-knowledge experts may need support in building learning delivery skills so that **their** interventions are most effective. Be aware that this is not their core role so scheduling could be an issue and learning sessions should be planned.

Internal trainers – These delivery specialists are based in the business and would design and deliver learning on a full-time or part-time basis. Working with these specialists could save external trainer charges. They have more schedule time available than an SME, and are brand aware. These trainers may also have been accredited to deliver externally written training programmes.

How to deliver training

Face-to-face delivery – where learners attend a workshop at a venue often in the workplace. They learn as part of a group with the trainer or facilitator. When considering using this delivery style, establish what benefits it would bring you: Is there need for a shared learning experience, a live discussion, hands-on practice, or group work? Is the networking element of the workshop important? This training delivery is popular and effective but needs to consider the payroll cost of the training, the cost of the facilitator, the availability of the facilitator and the learners, any travel or accommodation costs, and refreshments provided.

Coaching – a useful, one-to-one, focused style of standalone learning delivery or as follow-up to a learning intervention. Coaching an employee provides them with the opportunity to learn from themselves under the guidance of another. It is a chance to experience different and multiple approaches to a challenge or to make a change in behaviour that may not be working for them.

Webinar delivery – has become popular in recent years and can be a complementary partner to traditional face-to-face delivery. Webinars are ideal when there is need to share an idea or information to a group in different locations or at a range of times. The costs associated with face-to-face delivery are reduced with a webinar. Look for specific webinar learning applications which offer several engagement tools, quizzes, and breakout-rooms to maintain engagement and ensure the learning is retained post-learning session.

Online/web-based delivery – many learning providers offer online web-based learning solutions. They usually charge per course or per learner and offer flexible options, are available 24/7 to learners, and the content is consistent for each learner. Tracking of learning completion is easier. This method is often used for certified learning or compliance training, such as food safety or health and safety.

Artificial Intelligence (AI) learning – is often scenario based. It is an opportunity to learn through an experiential interaction with an AI-generated person and gain real-time feedback. This delivery method is useful for learning skills that are behaviourally sensitive, such as a grievance hearing, disciplinary, or appraisal. Learners can practise in a safe, controlled environment, receive a score for their completion, and then hone their skill by revisiting the exercise and working on low scoring areas.

Learning Management System (LMS) – are a brand or business-specific option similar to online/web-based learning. These are cloud hosted and available to learners 24/7. This total-system approach holds all learning content within the system or created via a publishing tool, along with individual learning records. This combined platform is useful for managers to track learning engagement and completion, along with planning learning needs.

Once training has been delivered, it is important to establish the impact of the learning. *Kirkpatrick's* levels provide a framework to achieve this, which is more than just a measure of how much the training was enjoyed on the day.

5.4 Multiskilled Employee Base and Employee Deployment

A multiskilled employee is someone who can learn and perform different tasks or roles in a department or across the business, rather than just in one area.

Multiskilling can take several forms:

- Vertical Multiskilling, or Upward Multiskilling, or Job Enlargement, involving developing additional skills and knowledge at the same level
- Horizontal Multiskilling, or Job Rotation, involving developing skills and knowledge across different job roles
- Depth Multiskilling, or Skill Expansion, involving developing a deeper level of knowledge in a specific area and still maintaining a broader skill and knowledge base

Examples of this approach could be:

- A front-desk team member to also work in the conference department
- A housekeeping team member to also work in breakfast service
- A restaurant team member to also work in events
- A table attendant who also works in the bar
- A chef who works across several kitchen sections
- A head of department also being a duty manager

Multiskilled employees within a whole business or within a department brings several business benefits to consider. However, it can cause resistance to the concept of multiskilling as it can be seen as a trade-off between a specialist who has depth of knowledge and skill, or a generalist who has a broad appreciation of skills and knowledge across a number of fields but may lack the depth of specialist knowledge.

In such a dynamic sector, no single approach is correct, so the use of a multiskilled team in different situations should be considered, dependent on goals and desired outcomes.

INDUSTRY VOICE

Dr Philip Berners, Associate Professor in Events Management

It is important not to impose multiskilling or cross-training on staff. They need to agree with it, and it should be presented in a way that brings their buy-in. Explaining the benefits to the business and the benefit to the employee is essential. They need to understand why they should train in another area of the business which they have not chosen. If they understand it will protect their job and provide them with more skills and knowledge, they are likely to accept it. But people dislike change and in some cases are fearful of working in an area they do not know and might not like.

If an employee is resistant and does not embrace multiskilling, they should never be forced. After all, a waiter might have chosen to be a waiter, but did not elect to be a chef, receptionist, or cleaner.

Benefits of a Multiskilled Workforce

- Motivational – the opportunity to work across several roles could be an exciting prospect for a team member still wanting to explore different career options. It keeps work interesting and adds variety.
- Teamwork and reliance – working with a wider number of team members develops a wider appreciation of each role, complexities, and challenges, and will increase communication and the understanding of impacts between departments or roles, and less silo (independent) working.
- Reduces a 'not my job' culture – if an employee is multiskilled to work in several roles, they are more likely to accept a guest request that requires multi-department cooperation to make it happen.
- Increased flexible workforce – in periods of lower levels of business or when there may be job vacancies, multiskilling makes it easier for the workforce to move into roles that need to be covered as priority.
- Wider recruitment opportunities – having multiskilled roles is appealing for employees and offers roles to those who may not have considered a job in another area of the business. Multiskilling enables them to develop a wider understanding of the business and consider specialising.
- Payroll flexibility and a variety of shifts available – having a multiskilled employee base brings more deployment opportunities for the team. This could, if needed, reduce the total number of employees required in the business and/or offer longer shifts to employees being paid by the hour as they can work across two roles during a straight shift, or take extra shifts to fill staffing gaps and supplement their pay.
- Develops a broad base of skills, knowledge, and behaviours.

Drawbacks of a Multiskilled Workforce

- Reduction in specialists – if team members are multiskilled they may not have the time or experience to specialise in one field. The application of multiskilled roles works best within a blend of specialist and multiskilled roles.
- Lack of opportunity to develop specialist and deep skills and knowledge in a particular field – the lack of deeper knowledge and skill-learning in a role may be seen as devaluing. Some roles may not suit a multiskilled approach and can hinder recruitment.

- Service quality and customer satisfaction could slide if employees do not have pride in their job because they are being shifted around to other areas of the business. This is exacerbated if training is not robust or is variable according to which department does the training.

To make multiskilling a successful tool in the people management kit, consider:

Learning Plans – to develop a multiskilled team member, the learning of a wider range of knowledge, skills, and required behaviours should be a systematic process that can be recorded and tracked for the employer and the employee. It is important for both parties to be aware of the developed capabilities an employee has so that they are deployed correctly rather than pulled into roles they have not received adequate training to deliver.

Job Skills Checklists – to outline what a job role entails from the number and type of tasks within that role. As an employee develops and has been observed delivering the task, it can be checked off the list as complete. This is a useful tracking tool and is motivational to the multiskilled employee. The checklist could also be used to highlight what will not be learnt by the employee if they are in a wider multiskilled role, rather than a specialist holding just this single role.

Job Coaches – to build confidence and skill from a more experienced employee, possibly an expert in a specific job role who is keen and able to share their experience with the multiskilling employee. The coach can be valuable assistance to a line manager who may not always be on hand to support the development of multiskilling a team member. Consider the formal development of coaching skills for the job coach to make this role attractive to team members and an additional development pathway.

Feedback and Review Opportunities – as with any role, but particularly when the team member will be working with multiple colleagues, roles, and departments. Regular communication is important to surface any concerns from either party early, as well as recognise progress.

Being Open at Recruitment – a multiskilled role is not appropriate for everyone. When adverting such roles, be clear what the role is and the expectations of the role to avoid confusion later.

A Future Opportunity to Specialise – to use multiskilled junior roles as a pathway to specialist roles. This can be useful when promoting a multiskilled role, if appropriate.

INDUSTRY VOICE

Julie Norris, Cluster HR Manager, Leonardo Hotels

There are several benefits of having a multiskilled workforce, including employee development.

Being able to work across different departments gives the team a broader knowledge of multiple areas within the hotel, this develops them to become hands-on and effective supervisors and managers. It gives the team a varied roster, which helps with their work–life balance as they can work in multiple areas on different shifts and days.

It also gives us, as an employer, flexibility when we have employees on annual leave or on sickness leave, taking the pressure off the team and the hotel.

This is also an effective way to manage payroll costs across the business.

5.5 Leadership Styles and Employee Development

Can leadership be learnt? Of course, it can. Some people are lucky enough to have a predisposition to leadership, but of course it can be developed by an individual. Leadership ability is a trait that will set a great manager apart from a good manager.

Leadership has many styles; some are listed here:

- Laissez-faire – a hands-off approach
- Servant leadership – an employee-centric approach
- Coaching – a professional development focus
- Transactional leadership – a rewards and incentives base
- Transformational leadership – a focus on change and growth
- Autocratic – a top-down control approach
- Democratic – a team-based input approach
- Bureaucratic – a rules and policy-based approach
- Charismatic – a personality and energy-led style

Which style is correct? Well, they all are: in the right situation. The most effective leader is one who has a flexible and adaptable approach; they can flex. They can dynamically read the situation and think about the impact they are looking for and the people involved in the situation. Then, adopt their style to meet the needs presented. We could call this, Situational Leadership.

Dr Ken Blanchard has published widely on a deeper theory of Situational Leadership.

Focus should be to look for opportunities to raise your level of self-awareness, emotional intelligence, and therefore leadership skills and approaches, by seeking opportunities for:

- Self-reflection
- Learning from mentors
- Gaining stretching experiences
- Actively practise leadership styles and assessing outcomes in different situations

Behaviours of a leader can be applied by delivering coaching and mentoring, and listening to and hearing feedback from the people you lead.

INDUSTRY VOICE

Lucy Potts, Hotel Manager, Leonardo Hotels

Being at entry level position in my first hospitality role 16 years ago, I was told, 'Treat the customer as if they are stupid and you'll do fine.'

I didn't receive training where things were explained but I was thrown in at the deep end, and instead of nurturing me, I was reprimanded if I did something incorrectly as I had been shown just once. What does that instil? It says it is not okay to make mistakes, our customers are not important, and you are replaceable. I didn't stay long in that role.

Fast forward to now, where I have grown and been promoted through a well-established internal management scheme, been allowed to ask those questions, had time spent on my development, and had fantastic mentors who had been in my position.

If you don't develop your people and spend your time on them and understand what makes them tick, you aren't a leader. A leader builds their pipeline and does themselves out of a job. Leadership is not an exercise; it is a respected rite of passage that you are only ready for when you have your nurtured team behind you and believing in you.

5.6 Learning Styles

The delivery of any learning intervention, whether it is a short piece of department skills training or an off-job workshop, should be seen as a form of communication. It is the facilitator sharing knowledge, skills, and appropriate situation behaviours with a team or a group of people who will take something into their job role.

Like any form of communication, if the message is lost or cannot be understood it is time wasted or, worse, it risks confusion and misunderstanding. The design of the message being sent and received by participants needs to be 'sticky', in that it is memorable and can be applied in the workplace.

To ensure 'stickiness', a level of understanding of Learning Styles is useful. Learning styles are a range of theories that consider the ways individuals learn or absorb information. People learn differently. It is not about categorising individuals, but understanding that, as the facilitator, there needs to be focus on flexing across all or as many styles as possible within a learning session to maximise the stickiness.

A useful way to describe learning styles, is the use of the acronym VARK, developed by Neil Fleming:

- Visual learning – people learn by seeing, watching, or being shown a demonstration
- Auditory learning – people learn by hearing or being told
- Reading or writing learning – people learn by the written word or visuals
- Kinaesthetic learning – people learn by touching and feeling, such as being shown a demonstration, then practising it themselves to learn from it

Another learning model applicable in the workplace is [Edgar] Dale's Cone of Experience. The Cone is a visual analogy of abstract learning and more concrete experiences that involve the senses (seeing, hearing, tasting, touching, feeling). This can be used when designing training and development activities to aid learning. A range of media are available to assist training, all with different outcomes.

For example, when launching a new menu, coffee, or IT system, employees will be more likely to remember these changes through concrete experiences: if they can taste the food, sample the coffee, and test a new system, in comparison to seeing pictures, manuals, or being told about the changes. The latter are more abstract experiences.

An outline of Dale's Cone of Experience is given in Figure 5.1.

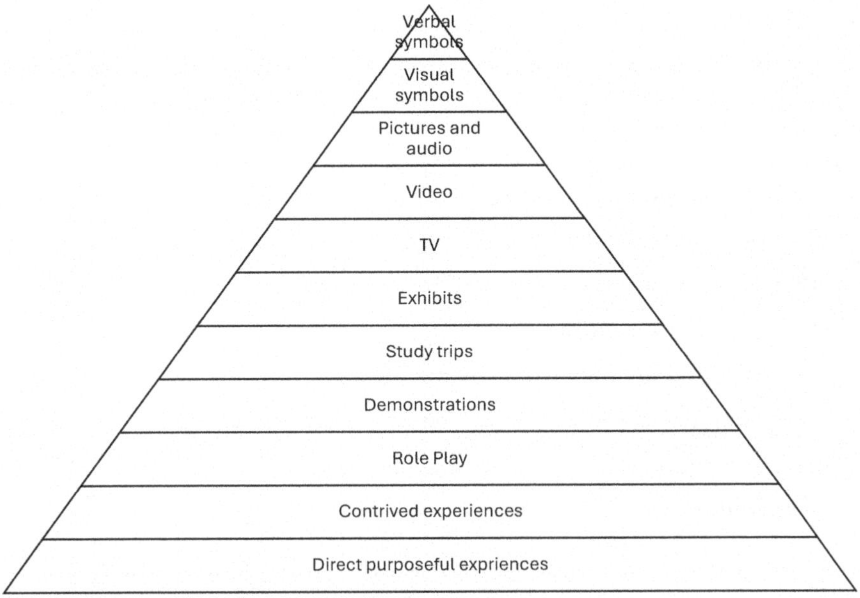

Figure 5.1 Dale's Cone of Experience
Adapted from Dale, E. (1970) 'A Truncated Section of the Cone of Experience' *Theory Into Practice*, Apr., 1970, Vol. 9, No. 2. P.p. 96–100.

INDUSTRY VOICE

Holly Marston, Learning & Development Manager, Leonardo Hotels

I enjoyed school for the social aspect rather than the learning side. But, as I branched into the working world, I found myself wanting to learn, develop, and understand, not just my job but others in the hotel and how they fitted-in with each other.

I was learning by doing (kinaesthetic) and suddenly, I couldn't get enough. This led me to look at learning styles and how people have a preference to how they learn.

When I design or deliver training, I always look at a blended learning approach so there is something for everyone on the course. I also include learning style awareness in our training with the Heads of Department and team coaches, so they are mindful they don't just default to their preference but include a range of styles within the training or support they are providing.

5.7 Management Development

Managers are leaders of the team and resources. To be most effective and drive company success, a development structure is useful because a manager's role is varied and could involve:

- Managing business operations
- Appointing human and capital resources
- Strong communication information to all parties
- Dealing with team conflict
- The health and well-being of team members
- Controlling the learning, growth, and assessment of the team
- Implementing business strategies and policies
- Being future focused

The biggest factors that influence the effectiveness of managers are their leadership style, people skills, and the network they build around them to support, coach, and advise them. It is useful, therefore, to determine the competencies a business deems important for their managers, so the progress in their development can be tracked. Progress in developing these competencies plays its part in a manager's review.

Examples of management competencies:

Teamwork – How do you support the team? Are you working co-operatively and contributing to team activities? Are you displaying the company vision, mission, and values? Do you lead by example? How are you helping the team achieve their goals and objectives? Are you embedding a positive culture within the team whilst promoting values and challenging poor behaviours?

Operational Excellence – How do you feel you are performing in your role? How do you achieve excellence in your role? How accurate, process driven, and organised are you? How do you demonstrate excellence in customer service (review *booking.com* scores or other KPIs)? What is the learning and development culture like within your team?

Problem Solving and Innovation – How do you resolve issues and get to the root of the problem/cause? Do you generate ideas which will improve the performance of your department/hotel/ office? How do you implement these? How do you resolve any conflict or difference of opinion with your peers and team?

Business Awareness – How do you keep up to date with business performance? How focused are you on delivering business goals and understanding the part you play in the business? How much is your department contributing to overall success? Are you achieving agreed KPI targets? How do you communicate business performance within your department/area and to your team?

Communication and Influence – How well do you communicate with your manager, your peers, and your team? What structured communication do you use with your team on a daily/weekly/monthly basis? How effective are the communication methods that are used in your team? What engagement activities have you initiated in the past year? How do you influence key stakeholders?

INDUSTRY VOICE

Dr Philip Berners, Associate Professor in Events Management

My research into how event organisers learn to do their job, led to the realisation that people need to recognise the value of creating their 'self-learning environment'.

Most people learn from experience but are not always conscious of what to learn and from where to learn. When organisers recognise that they can learn from their own working environment, they will search for learning opportunities.

An example is an event organiser at a venue who will learn from their clients. But when an international client books the venue, say an American client, here is an opportunity to learn how Americans organise their events and what standards they expect. But it requires the realisation of the value of creating that environment for self-learning.

Ideally, the events industry should be leading this concept, but it is up to the individual organiser – many of whom will not recognise the need to create their environment of self-learning. Of course, managers could lead employees to recognise the need for self-learning – if managers themselves recognise the need!

5.8 Qualifications

Hospitality can sometimes garner the reputation for poor working conditions, low reward, and low remuneration. These reputations are not limited to the hospitality sector. As with all sectors, it is important for jobseekers to be discerning and undertake their research when looking for employment.

A good employer will always have their eye on employee development, and the ultimate of this is formal and recognised qualifications. It should be the aim of a good employer to play their part in professionalising their workforce with recognised qualifications.

There are a wide range of qualifications for developing a team; some are hospitality specific and others more general development.

Institute of Leadership and Management (ILM)

The ILM offers a suite of leadership and management qualifications to enable learners to develop the skills, knowledge, and personal abilities to succeed as a manager at several levels. The qualifications are awarded by The City and Guilds of London Institute.

These qualifications are delivered by accredited ILM partners. Units can be completed individually or accrued to create a certificate. The units can be useful to include within in-house learning to enhance learning programmes.

Examples of ILM qualifications include:

- Level 2: Team Leader / Supervisors
- Level 3: Junior Managers
- Level 4/5: Middle Managers
- Level 6/7 Senior Managers, Directors and CEO level

National Apprenticeships (in the UK)

Apprenticeships are a useful tool to recruit new team members; they can also be used to develop existing team members for future roles.

An apprenticeship must include on-the-job and off-the-job training that lasts at least twelve months. As an apprentice, a team member should spend 80 per cent of their time on the job, learning and gaining experience, and 20 per cent off-the-job training which currently is around six hours. This off-job training may be at the workplace, or employees could attend a college or gain support from the wide range of accredited training providers delivering apprenticeships.

A key consideration for large employers is that the cost of the apprenticeship learner could be covered by their apprenticeship levy. This levy means the cost of learning would not generate an invoice. Smaller businesses could take advantage of levy gifting to cover the cost of the learning from a lager employer. They could also use a levy broker such as *Coop Levy Share*.

Institute of Hospitality (IoH)

The global institute for the hospitality sector offers several opportunities to develop team members. The Institute offers a range of membership types including graduate, associate, member, and fellow. Through the Confederation of Tourism and Hospitality (CTH), qualifications developed by the Institute can be accessed. These look at essentials of management, business planning, consumer management, business marketing, and sales.

- CTH (IoH) Level 3 Diploma in Hospitality Management
- CTH (IoH) Level 4 Diploma in Advanced Hospitality Management

The Hospitality Professionals Association (HOSPA)

HOSPA is the association for the hospitality sector that helps develop specialist leaders. They run several qualifications for management roles, which include:

- Finance management
- Revenue management
- Asset management
- IT leadership
- Commercial restaurant management
- Hospitality marketing

Wine & Spirit Education Trust (WSET)

WSET offers qualifications which are designed for employees at the beginning of their career, as well as experienced professionals. WSET is an awarding body that develops and delivers qualifications and courses in wines and spirits. Learning is accessed online and through accredited face-to-face trainers. Courses include:

Beer

- Level 1 Award in Beer
- Level 2 Award in Beer

Sake

- Level 1 Award in Sake
- Level 2 Award in Sake
- Level 3 Award in Sake

Spirits

- Level 1 Award in Spirits
- Level 2 Award in Spirits
- Level 3 Award in Spirits

Wines

- Level 1 Award in Wines
- Level 2 Award in Wines
- Level 3 Award in Wines
- Level 4 Diploma in Wines

INDUSTRY VOICE

Edward Gallier, Head of Learning & Development, Leonardo Hotels

Within our programmes, I decided to include units from the Institute of Leadership and Management (ILM) in the content design that carry unit credits for an ILM certificate.

The drive to include the units is to give an external input and develop out-of-sector knowledge in the programme. The qualification can increase interest in taking part in the programme and is an external recognition for learners. Organisations of any size can benefit from the tutors of the licensed provider's input in delivery in time, skill, and knowledge.

5.9 Transferable Skills

A transferable skill is a skill, knowledge, or ability that can be used in several situations and roles: not job-role-specific. Transferable skills are not just theoretical skills, they are practical and can be used in the workplace.

The development of transferable skills in the workplace can be a useful strategy to create a workforce that holds a variety of skills which helps them and the business flex and easily adapt when:

- Career opportunities arise helping to retain team members
- Gives confidence about the future
- A robust team that can cope with change

Skills to build within the team:

1. Communication – active listening, written, and verbal communication, confidence, presence
2. Dependability – punctuality, work ethic, meeting deadlines, honesty
3. Teamwork – rapport and relationship building, collaboration, self-awareness, conflict resolution
4. Organisation – time management, attention to detail, analytical thinking, prioritisation
5. Adaptability – creativity, positive attitude, energy, flexibility
6. Leadership – delegation, interpersonal skills, team-building, risk-taking, goal-setting
7. Decision-making – problem-solving, critical thinking, analytical skills
8. Empathy – listening skills, mediation
9. Initiative – self-motivation, high achiever, goal setting
10. Technology literacy – troubleshooting, programming skills, point of sale software (POS), customer relationship management software (CRM), productivity software

Bibliography

Dale, E. (1970). 'A Truncated Section of the Cone of Experience', *Theory Into Practice*, 9(2), pp. 96–100.

Chapter 6

Performance Management

Sophie Linin

6.0 Introduction

Performance management is an intrinsic element of most jobs, and certainly of every managerial role. This chapter aims to demystify the processes that encompass performance management, detailing not only why they are important but how they can be used as a support, as a calendar system, and as a development tool for individuals, teams, and the entire organisation.

This book has thus far discussed the Recruitment and Selection process, Induction, and Training and Development. Performance Management assumes those processes have been carried out successfully, and that the employee who exhibits the necessary skills and experience to carry out the role has been appointed and is willing to succeed.

6.1 The Uniqueness of Hospitality

Often unfairly maligned as a stop-gap career – the job one does, perhaps whilst studying – the hospitality sectors are in fact part of hugely commercial and successful industries. The sectors bring in tens of billions in revenue whilst being one of the largest employers, with millions of people working within the sectors.

DOI: 10.4324/9781003469803-7

Regardless of the area in which an employee works, the hospitality, hotels, and events sectors encourage a fully dedicated workforce. There are fearless individuals pushing boundaries and doing things never done before; competent strategists; skilled networkers; and back-of-house heroes without whom entire organisations would collapse.

Despite recent challenges from a global pandemic, economic inflation, Brexit, terrorism activity, and cost of living crises, the hospitality sector continues to flourish. This is attributable to its incredibly resourceful and resilient force of workers.

The hospitality industry is becoming more people focussed, recognising the importance of staff and the role they play to achieve the success of the organisation. Managing staff performance, therefore, is key to enhancing their performance and productivity, retaining staff, maintaining high quality and standards for customer delight, and achieving company objectives.

Hospitality, hotels, and events are primarily empathetic industries. People find themselves working in these sectors because they genuinely enjoy serving others, delighting people, helping or enhancing the experiences of their fellow humans. Employees are often naturally invested in the product and the business objective, which aligns them with company goals from the outset. This can make managing them easier.

There is no 'one size fits all' approach to managing the performance of those working in hospitality. As a service industry, often the financial renumeration is limited. Many workers are operating on hourly wages, perhaps on Zero-Hour Contracts. Others will be on highly lucrative commission-based financial renumeration packages. Some are working the traditional nine-to-five day, whilst others work until the early morning hours. Many hospitality staff work 60-hour weeks, yet others manage flexible working patterns and job-shares. The approach a manager takes to each of these groups or individuals is therefore likely to differ. This is what makes managing employees in this sector challenging, but hugely rewarding when carried out successfully.

A common frustration from hospitality employees is the constant busy-ness and the feeling that there are never enough staff. A manager needs to be ready to step in and assist when needed, as well as offer support from a distance. The managers who excel within hospitality have often worked their way from entry level positions, so they understand how each element works and are able to communicate effectively with people at all levels.

Many hospitality workers are used to working independently and might resent too much interference. There is a general preference from those in hospitality to complete tasks themselves, so it is 'done properly'. This can lead to challenges around delegating responsibilities and setting boundaries. Whilst employees might want to take on more responsibility, the job role they are working in may not allow for it.

Employees can move easily from role to role and business to business within the hospitality sector due to the transferable nature of their skills, making employee retention a struggle, and recruitment an almost constant process.

Clearly, hospitality needs a nuanced managerial approach and requires thought and care when addressing different needs and requirements. Whilst performance management is applicable for all sectors, adjustments may be necessary for hospitality workers.

6.2 Management and Imposter Syndrome

People advance into managerial roles in a range of ways. Many individuals are promoted into a managerial position within their current organisation, bringing with them a thorough understanding of the company, the ethos and values of the team, and knowledge of who is performing what functions and how well.

Being promoted into management in this way typically brings one major challenge: familiarity and (to a degree) overfamiliarity with the new reports who were one's peers, creating tensions around the perception that 'you used to be one of us and now you are one of them'. This is particularly common within hospitality, where an individual begins in a front-of-house, customer-facing position, and gets promoted to a team leader or office position with authority over those performing their previous role.

It may be that a manager is new into the role, or in a company they have worked in for some time and are in a position where they have hiring responsibilities. This means potentially engaging with recruitment, job description creation, and inductions for the first time.

Others may join a new company in a managerial role and must get to grips with their own position's tasks and requirements, as well as the company objectives, alongside fostering new relationships with their reports and trying to evaluate their successes and their challenges. It is common to feel insecure whilst settling into a new role with greater responsibility, trying to appear confident and assured, yet learning the new environment at the same time.

AUTHOR'S VOICE

When I was struggling with the dichotomy of remaining popular and getting the work done, I was told by an experienced manager that 'managing people is not about being on everyone's Christmas card list, it is about achieving your objectives by getting the best out of people in your team. Be fair but be in charge.'

Whichever way you become a manager, and regardless of the scenario you find yourself in, having a tried, tested, and reliable performance management mindset will serve not only to quieten the 'imposter syndrome' voice in your head, but will enable the rapid development of strong manager–report relationships. This will allow you to achieve your own role objectives and in turn contribute to the success of the organisation.

6.3 Performance Management, Setting Expectations, and the Job Description

Establishing employee needs and expectations, alongside communicating the needs and expectations of the business, are imperative for a manager or for Human Resources. Performance management includes assessing how an individual is performing within their role, whilst considering future support, training, or progression needs in alignment with the scope of their role within the organisation.

When performance managing a new employee, the employee will be supported during the induction period, providing an overview of their department, team, managers, their role and responsibilities, alongside health and safety and other requirements of the business.

Once settled into the role, a manager will establish how confident the individual is in terms of fulfilling the duties and responsibilities within their job description and competency.

This is a good opportunity to enquire about an employee's career history, beyond what has been gleaned at interview. Information can be gathered on where they have worked, what roles they have filled, why the current company was joined, and what skills they have that are not currently being utilised.

It is also an opportunity to find out what they feel works well within the team and the organisation, what challenges they face, and what they wish might be different. This is a fact-finding mission, an opportunity to develop a coherent understanding of the person and how they best fit within the department.

When managing performance for those who have been in the role for some time, the job description will still be referred to and a discussion held as to each point within the description to establish growing skills, knowledge, and ability within the role.

Here are some questions that a manager might ask when assessing performance in line with the requirements of the job as per the job description:

- Do you feel that your job description is accurate?
- Does your job description align with what you feel you are doing daily?
- Do you think there is there anything missing from your job description?
- Is there anything in the job description that you don't do?
- Where do you feel most confident?
- Are there any duties or responsibilities you feel unsure about?
- What excites you or inspires you within your role?
- What new things would you like to learn?

If confidence, skills, or competency is lacking, further training should be offered, mentoring or further support could be provided, or it could be that the job description needs updating in line with current tasks and responsibilities because the way of working might have changed over time.

This is not the time for decisions to be made. A few small things may be immediately resolved, bringing important and welcome changes. However, caution is recommended before making significant changes until a solid understanding is reached of all potential causes and effects of any changes on the existing team or department dynamic.

There is often a reason why certain things are set up and work is completed in a particular way, even if it is not immediately apparent. Instead, it could be a hangover from other members of staff who no longer work in the organisation.

The aim of the performance management process at this stage is to establish a clearer picture of individual employees and how they relate to their job role. When managing multiple staff, this will also provide an understanding of how the team dynamics work, give an indication of who the high performers are, and who may be struggling, as well as early signs of any potential conflicts.

6.4 Personality Traits and Performance Management

When managing performance, it is worth keeping in mind the different personality types of people within the team. Multiple books and articles have been written, research conducted, and many tests devised to assess personality and to help identify workplace team dynamics (Myers Briggs, Belbin, and Insights are all in regular use). These models help when dealing with the psychological make-up of teams, but to keep it to a basic level, these tests can help determine how team members' needs can be met and how these dynamics can influence productivity, decision-making, or conflict.

Some team members who are quieter, more introverted, and reflective may need agendas in advance of meetings to plan their thoughts. They might have valid points to make but are reluctant to speak when the louder, more extrovert individuals dominate discussions.

Consider how to best manage those who just want to get on and do things, but sometimes need holding back, or support those who need closer supervision and guidance. Consider how to help creatives find a valid place in the team to utilise their skills, and conversely how to maximise the skills of those who tend to be more perfectionist and pay attention to detail compared to those who do not.

Think about these traits and identify team member skills and aptitude and who they are and how to manage these individuals. This might require speaking to individuals to best establish their needs and what would work best for them. The Human Resources department or manager can help to identify training in this area to support manager skill set.

6.5 Expectations within the Team

This is an opportunity to clarify expectations as a manager. If employees are expected to be at their desks for 9 a.m., if it is preferred for them to take a full-hour lunch break away from their desk/department/job, or if there are expectations about how people behave in the workplace, now is the time to inform people.

By setting clear expectations of people, Human Resources and managers are less likely to have to deal with difficult conversations at a later stage.

With hospitality staff, it is common for people to be working within a team with different hours, different contracts, and different financial and rewards packages. It is important to establish clarity about what is expected of each person in a way that aligns with their specific role and responsibilities. Whilst it could be acceptable for a member of the sales team to work remotely two days a week, this option would not be available to operational staff members.

AUTHOR'S VOICE

When managing remote workers, it is important to establish any additional guidelines for remote working. As an example, when working entirely remotely during the pandemic, I reached out to my reports between 9 and 10 a.m. to check in and see if they needed anything specific from me that day.

This established a rapport each day with employees, reminding them that I was available for support, as well as making sure they were online and responsive. This became less necessary as time went on and we all became accustomed to remote working, but I am clear with my team now that I expect someone to be onsite to manage the sales phone every day and that everyone should be on site three days a week.

I also host monthly whole-team meetings which everyone must attend in person.

The use of internal messaging systems such as *Jabber, Microsoft Teams,* or *WhatsApp* can help foster a sense of 'team' for remote workers. Keep the messages light but do not let them descend into rudeness.

6.6 Expectations within the Company

A line manager is responsible for direct reports (and their direct reports). This means aligning reports with an individual manager's expectations, as well as any company-wide expectations, for example around language, email decorum, call scripts, or hybrid working, for which Human Resources will normally have policies or protocols. These policies, protocols, or standard operating procedures (SOPs) help shape performance management.

It is also a manager's job to ensure that the department is running in the most streamlined, successful, and profitable manner. It is necessary for the manager to understand how the organisation works to be able to achieve this. For junior managers this may feel less important, but knowing how and who to escalate things to which are beyond remit and experience is invaluable. A manager will need to have a fully comprehensive overview of each person's role and responsibilities and understand how they factor into the bigger picture and how their role fits into the scope of the organisation.

A manager would, therefore, need to be honest with the staff they line manage as to the goals they themselves have been set, as well as individual and team goals/

objectives. The transparency will help staff to understand their role in achieving those goals and view themselves as an active participant. This helps ensure commitment from individuals and teams to achieve strategic goals.

6.7 Performance Management and Probationary Periods

It is standard for most roles to have a probationary period which acts as a trial for both employee and organisation. Whilst not a legal requirement, this is commonly a three-month or six-month period, although it can be as long as a year, or as short as one month. A probation period could also be extended if more time is need for the employee to settle, or to provide more training for the role to see if it helps with performance.

The employee and the role might not be a good fit for one another, or it may be that the employee is not able to fulfil the duties of the role for which they were employed. Thus, probation allows for shorter notice periods for both the organisation and employee to provide, without affecting employee statutory rights.

Some companies might withhold certain employee benefits like private medical insurance until an employee has passed their probation. Sometimes holiday allowances are limited during probation or are increased once successfully completed.

Probationary periods are also often used for recently promoted employees as an opportunity to provide additional support for individuals as they adapt to their new responsibilities.

Managers can find it challenging with new starters and it is easy to understand why. The time required to train new employees, the added pressure on team members while the new person gets up to speed, the increased likelihood of mistakes, the increased number of questions, and the need for regular check-ins – all these can create additional strain.

However, it is often overlooked just how valuable a fresh pair of eyes can be. A manager can explore this with new employees during the job description alignment. New starters are in a unique position to be able to identify negative attitudes that have become embedded and normalised within the company. They can ask questions that challenge the typical mindset of 'Well, this is how it has always been done', and they can approach even the mundane tasks with creativity and innovation. This fresh perspective can be invaluable, even to the most experienced team members.

An example probationary review document is noted in Table 6.1 as contributed by Leonardo Hotels.

Table 6.1 Industry Example Probationary Review Document, provided by Edward Gallier, Leonardo Hotels

<table>
<tr><td colspan="2">Congratulations on reaching your first 30 days with us. You will have been working hard on learning about the Company and your role so you will have lots to discuss during this review. This review meeting is an opportunity to discuss your progress and performance to date with a view to you successfully completing your probationary period. This review should be an open and honest conversation with regards to any issues that either party may wish to disclose, with this form being used to structure the meeting and to document agreed future actions and comments.</td></tr>
<tr><td>Employee Name:</td><td>Line Manager name:</td></tr>
<tr><td>Job Title:</td><td>Department:</td></tr>
<tr><td>Start date:</td><td>Date of this review:</td></tr>
<tr><td colspan="2">Settling in:
1. How have you found working for the company during your first few weeks?
2. Manager's feedback:
Discussion points: relationship with buddy; induction; check understanding of vision and values; housekeeping items such as locker, uniform, employee facilities, name badge; equipment required and relevant logins; awareness of company benefits; knowing where to go to for help and support.</td></tr>
<tr><td colspan="2">Learning and development:
1. Have you completed your online training?
2. What additional training have you had?
3. What additional training do you require?
4. Manager's feedback:
Discussion points: Check training completion and progress. Set a target for the next review with regards to what should be completed and when. Outline time frames. Discuss any barriers to completing learning and how these can be overcome.</td></tr>
<tr><td colspan="2">Team and communication:
1. How have you settled in with the team?
2. What do you like about communication within the team and company? What concerns do you have? Is there anything that could be improved or support that is needed?
3. Manager's feedback:
Discussion points: Feedback on teamwork; communication channels being used, feedback on any concerns.</td></tr>
</table>

(Continued)

Table 6.1 (Continued)

<table>
<tr><td colspan="2">General:
1. Overall, how are you feeling about your time in the company so far? Is there anything else you would like to bring up or discuss at your review?
2. Manager's feedback:
Discussion points: Timekeeping, attendance, appearance, conduct, H&S, communication skills, any concerns that would affect the passing of probation. If concerns, detail what action to be taken to ensure things are improved including timescales.</td></tr>
<tr><td colspan="2">Summary:</td></tr>
<tr><td>What is going well?</td><td>What are the improvements needed?</td></tr>
<tr><td colspan="2">Agreed actions to be completed and date:</td></tr>
<tr><td colspan="2">Employee signature: Date:
Manager signature: Date:
Once completed, this form should be forwarded to HR for filing and a copy retained by both employee and line manager to review.</td></tr>
</table>

6.7.1 Benefits of the Probationary Period – for the Manager

The probationary period provides the opportunity for a more in-depth evaluation of an employee than the recruitment process allows. While a candidate might have demonstrated all the prerequisite qualifications during the recruitment and selection process, it may become clear once they start the job and complete their training that they are taking longer to settle in than was hoped or expected. It might be they are finding the work they are being asked to do particularly challenging due to a lack of requisite skills, lack of confidence in themselves, a more intensive regime than they are used to; all of which can be dealt with by effective management.

This period of probation can be utilised to offer extra support or training where needed, or to be clearer about what the organisation is expecting from an individual. Probation can be extended to give employees an opportunity to improve. Once all options have been exhausted, termination can be pursued more swiftly, allowing the process of recruitment to begin again.

Probation is an opportunity to monitor performance, and if there are any skills gaps, further training and support can be provided. Probation can also be extended until performance is satisfactory and employment made permanent. If the individual still fails to perform, once all options such as training and mentoring have been considered, and probation having been extended, at this point an organisation may terminate the contract and release the employee.

6.7.2 Benefits of the Probationary Period – for the Employee

On paper, a job may seem to align with someone's expectations; in reality, an organisation or job role may not meet these needs or preferences. Hospitality, hotels, and events offer a wide range of careers and companies, each working at different paces and with different expectations.

The probationary period allows an individual the time to evaluate whether the job description, team dynamics, and company culture are suited to them. If they do not align with what the individual was expecting, or what they are looking for, it allows the opportunity for them to step away from the role with minimal impact and, if handled sensitively, with little lasting damage to their self-esteem and a clearer idea of what they do want to pursue.

If an employee feels further support or training is needed, the individual should request this from line management. Initially, they may feel out of their depth, may struggle to fulfil the role, and feel deflated. Many employees leave within the first few weeks of employment in hospitality, hotels, and events – partially due to the transience of the sector which means if they are not happy, they will try somewhere else. If additional support and training is given in the initial employment period, alongside effective induction, it will boost the employee's skill set and confidence within the role. This will help retain new recruits. If probation is extended, it provides additional opportunities for individuals to learn on the job and develop their skills.

6.7.3 Ensuring Successful Probation

It is important to recognise that it takes time for people to understand their role, their place within an organisation, what is expected of them, and then to begin performing at the required level. Different people learn at different speeds. Some will find it easy to pick up a phone and answer enquiries on day one but may struggle getting to grips with a new Customer Relationship Management system, for example. Others might struggle to complete any tasks until they have a thorough understanding of all elements of the role and how they all align, and how all the pieces of the puzzle fit.

AUTHOR'S VOICE

In my current role, I speak regularly with new staff members about the journey they are taking. I explain that it will likely take three months for them to completely understand their role, what they are expected to do daily and weekly, and what their specific purpose is.

It will take a further three months to see how their role fits within the wider organisation, how it all pieces together, and what their contribution looks like in the wider scheme of things. That takes them up to the end of their six-month probationary period which, hopefully, they pass. At that point, it is then another six months of further development, fine tuning, and experience.

At various points they will likely be plagued by imposter syndrome, have successes and failures, and question whether they know anything at all. This is where skills as a line manager should come to the fore, by listening, motivating, and encouraging staff members to develop the confidence to be the high-performing employee they are capable of being.

By the one-year point, I can expect they will finally be confident that they know what they are doing, and with this newfound confidence, they can then begin to evaluate themselves, look to streamline processes, make better decisions, and begin to excel in their role.

Having regular check-ins during the probationary period benefits both the manager and employee. A well-structured induction and training programme from day one, involving all members of the team who the new hire will be interacting with, and integrating them into the broader organisation, helps them understand their role, forge positive working relationships, and gradually become less dependent on their manager.

Being available to answer their questions, no matter how trivial they may seem, will boost their confidence, and encourage them to take initiative. This approach fosters a smooth transition and sets the foundation for long-term success.

Explaining this at an early stage and assuring them of manager support all the way, alleviates much of the stress that comes from staff who lack confidence in their ability to do their job role or in their skill set, and not feel judged by others stemming from internal pressure to succeed immediately.

The manager's role is to develop people to be high performers, not to just help them scrape through. A manager, or Human Resources, can set small, agile goals which allow them to feel they are succeeding; provide gentle feedback that steers them in the right direction; and encourage those sparks of creativity that often come with an outsider's perspective.

6.8 Setting Goals and Objectives

Hospitality industries primarily have a commercial focus and will commonly measure performance of staff members against financial targets. This is a valid form of motivation and of performance measurement: for example, assessing how well a salesperson is performing based on how often they hit or exceed their financial targets. This could be the events team and how many weddings have been confirmed, and revenue versus the number of weddings, and projected revenue set by the manager as a target. A manager may want to increase spend per head in a restaurant, for example, to increase profits, and therefore sets the team or individual's KPIs such as upselling of premium drinks, or selling a certain number of side orders or desserts.

However, this approach can be a too simplistic way of looking at targets and goals when applied to all hospitality, hotel, or events workers. Financial targets are typically set by senior management and might not consider other aspects of hospitality workers' roles. For example, when setting goals for operations team members or for those working in marketing, financial targets might not be relevant, or constructive, but other quantitative measurements are.

Key performance indicators (KPIs) are quantifiable measurements over time. They enable managers to set goals across a range of different job functions. When setting KPIs, a manager will look at what needs to be reported each week or month, assess changes that have taken place month on month and year on year, and set goals around the improvement of these.

INDUSTRY VOICE

Dr Philip Berners, Associate Professor in Events Management

Objectives tend to be financial because most organisations realise the need to be profitable so they can continue and can grow. This makes the financial objectives – revenue, costs, profit – the priority objectives. And they are easy to measure because the accounts show if the goals have been achieved.

But there are other objectives to consider which are harder to measure. Client satisfaction is one. Customer satisfaction is another. Then, there is the level of staff retention.

Whatever the objective, remember they need to be measurable. Client satisfaction can be measured by how many clients return to give you repeat business. Customer satisfaction can be measured by surveys to guests to measure how many were delighted. Staff retention can be measured by how many staff stay for a certain length of time and how many leave within a certain length of time – this can be measured for the organisation or each department.

For me, the priority objective is safety. This is higher than profit. Think about it – if somebody gets hurt or injured at your hotel or event, this harms your reputation (impacting profit), or you might have to give refunds (impacting profit), or you might be sued for compensation (impacting profit). So, how can profit be a higher priority than safety?

The Safety Objective is the easiest to measure. It is zero. Zero people hurt; zero people injured. It never changes.

Many organisations follow the rule that goals should be SMART (Specific, Measurable, Achievable, Realistic, and Timely). This could include KPIs and targets. SMART goals require careful consideration to ensure they meet the criteria. Avoid vague, unattainable, or immeasurable targets such as 'Sell more audiovisual equipment'. Instead, use more precise goals like: 'Increase audiovisual equipment hires from 45 per cent to 50 per cent by the end of the year.' The difference between the two is significant. The first is non-specific and unlikely to motivate an employee, as it could leave them confused and overwhelmed by the expectation. The second is focused and should be accompanied by either a manager-set plan of action or an understanding that the employee knows how to achieve the goal.

Goals without plans of action are unlikely to be achieved. People cannot simply 'be better'. Managers must ensure their reports have all the necessary training, skills, and knowledge, and are provided with assistance or guidance needed to achieve their goals.

6.9 Staff Motivation

A manager should identify what makes employees motivated and inspired to work. Why they get up and go to work in the morning; what they enjoy about their day and what they find difficult or boring; how they operate within the team and who brings out the best in them; and how best they might be motivated and inspired.

When looking at motivating staff members, it should be determined what the organisation needs from them: is it to make more money; to work better within the team; to encourage team members to be more creative; or to help individuals manage their time better and be more productive?

Establishing the goal will allow Human Resources and managers to better assess how to drive employee motivation to reach end goals.

Appraisals can then be used, as well as one-to-one meetings, to understand what drives staff motivation, their skills, competencies, aspirations, training needs, and the resources needed to inspire staff to achieve their fullest potential in delivering organisational, team, and individual goals.

Strong, positive leadership itself will motivate staff. People who respect their leaders and feel respected by their leaders in turn, who understand the company ethos and who believe in what they are doing, are far more likely to invest more energy into their work. Being included in company strategy, receiving recognition in organisation-wide meetings, sharing successes across company-wide memoranda, and being involved in decision-making can better embed staff members into building the success of the organisation.

However, a weak manager can result in team members experiencing frustration within the workplace, cause productivity issues, potentially cause conflict, and lead to staff leaving the company.

AUTHOR'S VOICE

I share my own department strategy with my team, involving them in major decisions or explaining why I have come to a particular conclusion. I offer the opportunity for people to see firsthand the wider factors that I am including in any strategic plan, as well as listening to and addressing any concerns they may have and taking the time to reassure them.

I want my team to be behind everything we do, supporting it and engaged in its success. Rewards will then be offered in recognition of achievements, their hard work, and commitment.

6.10 One-to-One Meetings

One-to-one meetings (or one-on-ones, also written as 1:1) are regular 'catch-ups' with team members and are the mainstay of performance management, an opportunity to check in: nothing more and nothing less.

A *Gallup-Healthways* study of 38,000 workers in 2018 concluded that team members are much more motivated to perform outstanding work and are generally more engaged when managers provide weekly versus annual feedback.

Here is where managerial flair will come into play. Some will be familiar with the terms 'micromanaging' where a manager prefers to monitor their reports and their work in detail, and 'macro-managing' where a manager is hands off and prefers to look at the bigger picture. In most cases, the reality is far more nuanced.

There are managers who maintain boundaries with their reports, only discussing work. There are managers who are friends, family even, to their reports, open to discussing anything and everything. There are managers who shout; others who never raise their voice, who say everything they need with a '*Hmm*' or a raised eyebrow.

Yet, they should all carry out 1:1s.

Google Project Oxygen confirmed that managers who have regular 1:1s with their reports tend to score higher in performance than managers who do not. So, it really is a win-win.

One-to-ones should be held somewhere private. Many organisations have onsite meeting rooms which can be used. It may be that it is better to go to a nearby cafe or restaurant to make it more informal and relaxed and to help establish rapport and trust. Ideally, the manager should be the one who gets (and buys) the coffee at such meetings. It is a humble act and shows respect for the other person.

One-to-ones can be held via videoconferencing if both parties are somewhere where they can speak freely, comfortably, and confidentially. If it is anticipated to be a difficult conversation, an in-person meeting should be conducted in a private room to allow clarity and openness, as well as to keep confidentiality where matters may be sensitive or private.

6.10.1 Length and Frequency of One-to-One Meetings

A one-to-one meeting should be as long as it needs to be, but usually lasting 30 minutes to one hour.

If there is nothing to discuss and everything is going well, or the manager has no new directives to give, and the employee has no queries or questions to resolve, the meeting will be quicker. In which case, the session is an opportunity for employees to update their manager on their projects/work, advise of any potential challenges that may require the manager's attention in the future, but which they currently feel capable of managing. The manager may also need to provide staff with general updates on wider organisational updates.

However, it might be that a team member needs to discuss something specific. The benefit of a one-to-one is that the employee knows when they are going to be speaking with their manager, they can plan what they will say and arrive knowing what they need help with. A manager is there to listen, mentor, and assist.

A one-to-one meeting can be more beneficial than an annual appraisal as it enables managers and their direct reports to form a more familiar professional relationship, talk about more time-bound issues or questions, and helps identify support needs early on.

This ensures issues and concerns are addressed in a timely fashion.

Truly, a one-to-one should be conducted as often as the manager or employee needs them. A common mistake of first-time managers is to manage an individual how they (the first-time manager) would like to be managed. If the manager themselves has had a manager who was too demanding, or too evasive, then seek to be the opposite.

AUTHOR'S VOICE

When I first became a manager, I was managing people who had formerly been my peers. I struggled to make the adjustment, thinking that I knew them very well as people and therefore knew how they should be managed. I did not. I made some errors and found that I needed to go back to the basics, realign boundaries and expectations, and change my methods. As a manager, you need to be agile; if you have many different people in your team, you cannot operate a one size fits all approach.

Ask in the first meeting, how do you like to be managed? How do you want me to present feedback to you, good and not so good? Many people will know exactly what they want from a manager, and it can then be provided quite easily. However, a practised manager will know he should manage someone how they need to be managed. If someone says they do not like being micromanaged, but they then begin to make mistakes, they will need to be monitored more closely. When someone says they prefer not to be given deadlines, this does not mean they should never be given deadlines.

I have worked with people who said they did not need weekly 1:1s. I knew, however, that they would grab me for five minutes every few days with a question about something or other. This was fine for me at the time, as I tried to be visibly available as much as possible for these opportunities and I am confident in pushing back when I am unavailable, instead requesting that they book something in my calendar. Other managers might simply not have the time for these brief interruptions or will feel uncomfortable with pushing back. In this case, a 1:1 should be implemented weekly under the clear understanding that this is when things that do not have an immediate impact or operational effect should be flagged and discussed.

I have worked with people who preferred a regular meeting appointment in the diary, at the same time every week, and they always had something to say, an update on one thing or another, or a query they just wanted to brainstorm with me. With hospitality workers, you might be managing someone who only works a few days each week and therefore a weekly 1:1 will be unnecessary. A 1:1 is needed only every fortnight in this scenario. Some hospitality workers have more repetitive, unchanging jobs and are less likely to be dealing with regular challenges; it may be more appropriate to have a monthly 1:1 in this case.

6.10.2 Discussion in the One-to-One Meeting

Anything can be discussed during a one-to-one, but it may be useful to use a framework such as:

- How are you?
- What are you working on?
- How can I help you?
- Can you update me on [task] I gave you last time?
- I would like you to work on [task].

It is helpful to ask and expect employees to arrive with a coherent list of things they are ready to discuss, to ensure the meeting stays purposeful. It could be that the purpose of the one-to-one is for the manager to provide updates on their own work and how it might impact the employee. If this is the case, preparations should be made to communicate what information is needed and can be shared, and to answer any questions the employee may have.

Many questions are straightforward and should be answered clearly by the manager, with a check or summary at the end to confirm the employee has understood the response. In some cases, it could be beneficial for the employee not to have their questions answered. A coaching approach, using prompts to let them think for themselves and produce a plan of action themselves can be more conducive. An employee will have to use their understanding of the topic, the process, or the organisation to devise a solution, and the critical thinking will better serve them for future challenges.

For example, if someone asks:

- How do I respond to [client] when they have asked about [situation]?

A manager could answer:

- What do you know about [situation]?
- What do you think you could you say to them?
- What would you want to say them?
- What do they need to know about [situation]?
- What have you tried so far?
- What else do you think you might try?
- What support do you feel you need from me?

By encouraging the employee to think about the question, the manager can encourage independence and autonomy within the workplace and prepare the individual to work without relying on their manager (which is the goal of any successful manager).

This approach develops confidence and satisfaction from the employee solving the problem themselves. An employee might know the answer already, and just want to run it past their manager to check. Or they may not know the answer at all, in which case this will indicate further training is needed. It could be that the question is new to the manager also, and the manager will then need to understand more about the client and the situation to be able to best assist the employee.

By responding in this way, the manager is also encouraging the team to find solutions rather than live with problems.

AUTHOR'S VOICE

My team knows they will get a better and quicker response if they come to me with 'This has happened – we were thinking about doing [solution] or [alternative solution]', rather than just 'A problem has arisen,– what do we do?' I want my team to be constantly making assessments of situations, risk-assessing in advance, judging changes in the moment, and responding accordingly.

This is vital for those working in events, where the manager will not always be on site and individuals need to have confidence in their own decision-making skills. Getting people into the habit of thinking for themselves early is going to stand them in far better stead than simply answering every question for them.

Listening skills are important because managers are constantly multitasking and dealing with numerous people and employees can act as the manager's eyes and ears. When suggesting there is a problem, a manager should listen, and listen to concerns and suggestions employees make. Even when they are saying something is going well, listen.

If an employee is complaining about a colleague, the manager should listen. Not everything being said will be valid due to emotion and the opinion of the storyteller, but the employee has a concern and might need support. It can tell a lot about the person complaining – not only are the words being said vital, but how they say them is a big indicator of other aspects of their job performance. How confident is the person feeling? How motivated are they? What are their relationships with colleagues? Why do they act the way they do?

The simplest act, that of listening to another person, can change a view of them and can further transform how the manager treats them and how to manage them.

6.10.3 Annual, Biannual or Monthly One-to-One Meetings

One-to-ones are an excellent opportunity for a general catch-up, but they rarely afford the time or opportunity to delve deeper into certain areas. They are not designed to. Where 1:1s are operational or tactical meetings, annual or biannual meetings are more strategic in nature. Development opportunities, training, and wider areas of discussion are better suited to the latter where time can be allotted to add greater focus and more depth to conversations.

Different organisations will have different recommendations, and different hospitality businesses will have varied needs. But longer meetings can also be within smaller sub-teams, the whole department, or with another relevant department, depending on how the business is set up, for example a weekly or fortnightly sales meeting, a monthly joint sales and operations meeting, and a quarterly departmental meeting.

Each will have a different focus and whilst many focus on the performance management of individuals, it is important to ensure that the team, sub-team, and departments are working together coherently and functioning successfully as one.

6.11 Performance Reviews/Appraisals

In almost every company, performance reviews are the mainstay of the performance management calendar. Often done annually and consisting of a focused and objective assessment of the individual's performance over the past year, measurement against KPIs (targets or goals), and setting new goals to achieve over the forthcoming year. This annual appraisal meeting is usually held between the employee and their line manager.

An employee should be notified of their appraisal in good time, for example a week in advance, and both parties will complete a standard form designed by human resources prior to the meeting to analyse performance against set criteria relative to the job role. This is usually against key performance criteria with spaces for notes and a Likert scale to rate performance levels.

The appraisal should be a two-way meeting with both the employee and their manager having an opportunity to discuss strengths and areas for development, any training needs, future aspirations or progression, and any issues or feedback the employee may wish to discuss. Both parties will discuss perceptions of performance, using examples of work and even the job description to refer to.

Many businesses have bonus structures that align with an individual's performance against their objectives. For example, a well-performing employee may receive an annual bonus higher than that of lesser-performing employees or a salary increase relative to their demonstrable efforts. An appraisal may also determine other rewards and recognition the employee receives which will further enhance their motivation and productivity performance.

A positive appraisal will have a positive effect on any bonus; a negative appraisal and the employee not only feels unsuccessful in their role but potentially misses a financial incentive or reward. Understandably, these are highly stressful periods for the employee, but they are also challenging periods for managers.

Those who manage multiple employees often conduct staff appraisals within the same period, as dictated by the company. It requires some administration, is time consuming, and the conversations can be intense and emotionally charged. However, appraisals are immensely valuable and can be enjoyable and rewarding for manager and employee, alike.

Table 6.2 Industry Example Appraisal Form provided by Edward Gallier, Leonardo Hotels

<table>
<tr><td colspan="3">Name:</td></tr>
<tr><td colspan="2">Job Title:</td><td>Department:</td></tr>
<tr><td>Employment Start Date:</td><td>Date of this Review:</td><td>Date of next Review:</td></tr>
<tr><td colspan="3">You will be assessed against the company's core competencies with the following ratings being used throughout the process:</td></tr>
<tr><td>Competency Rating</td><td colspan="2">Definition</td></tr>
<tr><td>Role Model</td><td colspan="2">consistently exceeds expectations – could develop others in this area</td></tr>
<tr><td>Performing well</td><td colspan="2">consistently shows a good level of competence</td></tr>
<tr><td>Getting There</td><td colspan="2">some competence, needs further development</td></tr>
<tr><td>Under Performer</td><td colspan="2">not meeting the required standard</td></tr>
<tr><td colspan="3">What were your successes over the last year?</td></tr>
<tr><td colspan="3">What were your challenges over the past year?</td></tr>
<tr><td colspan="3">What objectives have been achieved from the last review meeting?</td></tr>
<tr><td colspan="3">Which have you not managed to address and why?</td></tr>
<tr><td colspan="3">How do you know you are completing your job role to a good standard and meeting the brand standards and procedures? Examples.</td></tr>
<tr><td colspan="3">What skills and knowledge would you like to develop to perform your job competently? Examples.</td></tr>
<tr><td colspan="3">List the Learning you have completed (face-to-face, online, webinars and self- learning) in the last 12 months.</td></tr>
</table>

What development would you like to look at in the coming year to get you to your next goal?	
Have you received any guest feedback or online reviews?	
	Comments
Timekeeping	
Attendance	
Appearance	
Conduct	
Communication Skills	
Health & Safety Awareness	
Attitude to Co-workers	
Attitude towards Team Leaders/Managers	
The future/career planning 1. What are your career aspirations? 2. What would be your desired next role? 3. What do you see as a time frame for achieving this?	
Objectives for the next review. 1. XX 2. XX 3. XX 4. XX 5. XX	
Overall comments from employee:	

(Continued)

Table 6.2 (Continued)

Additional Comments/Feedback from your Manager:	
Signed (Employee):	Date:
Signed (Manager):	Date:
Signed (HR Manager/Officer):	Date:
Please ensure that a copy of this performance review is retained on the employee's file.	

6.11.1 Making Appraisals Easier

The main challenge with appraisals comes when the manager or employee is not adequately prepared for the review. There should be no surprises at an annual review. Regular check-ins, as discussed earlier in this chapter, will allow for plenty of thoughtful feedback throughout the year. No employee should go into an appraisal to be shocked by negative feedback on their work and come out confused. It is the job of the manager to have flagged any performance issues early, assessed any risks of not hitting targets, and attempted where possible to resolve issues before reaching the date of the appraisal.

Managers should enter the appraisal with an idea of future objectives, targets, and KPIs, but without a rigidly fixed agenda. They should have feedback from peers (discussed further in Section 6.11.3) and examples of issues that either need to be discussed or are demonstrative of excellent performance. It should feel like a conversation, not a lecture. Feedback from the individual (appraisee) to the manager (appraiser) is as important and welcome as feedback from the manager to the report.

6.11.2 Traditional Appraisals

Traditionally, appraisals are completed annually and follow a robust if strict template (almost always provided by the company or Human Resources) to measure employees against goals that were set for them on joining the company or their previous appraisal.

This may be referred to as a one-to-one, individual, or Management By Objectives appraisal (MBO).

Positive and negative feedback on certain incidents throughout the past year are discussed and an assessment is made of how well an employee is performing and what learning or development might need to be provided to offer them further support or assistance in achieving their goals. Then, new goals are set and agreed for the forthcoming year.

This format provides a consistent record of an employee's performance over their years with the company and is generalised, so works successfully with a high number of employees. It requires minimal additional output from the manager or employee to complete and allows for a straightforward comparative analysis between multiple team members, particularly across different teams.

However, the use of a template can lack opportunity for nuance and creativity, the chance of bias based on an employee's relationship with their manager is increased, and there can be little in the way of that essential human touch.

JENNIFER KAYE'S VOICE

When working as a reservations agent my manager sent me an appraisal form to complete the week before my scheduled annual appraisal. I scored myself as to how I felt I had performed, and my manager did the same.

We met the following week and had an open discussion outlining my strengths and areas for development. Progress towards my targets was discussed, including answering client phone calls within one minute, call waiting times, number of reservations made, and hotels and event venues I had visited over the year ('familiarisation trips' or 'fam trips'). My manager also played some call recordings to analyse my customer service skills.

I had met all my targets and received an annual bonus during the summer company celebration.

However, one of the call recordings identified issues concerning a difficult conversation with a hotel receptionist when trying to make reservations for night workers. They would check-in at 10 a.m. and check-out late-afternoon so the room could be sold again to other guests in the evening.

But the receptionist did not understand the reservations due to numerous and varied requirements of each guest and unusual check-in time. This resulted in the receptionist shouting and swearing at me. I remained calm, asking if she wanted me to call back or email the reservations, or if she wanted to talk to my manager. I had asked her to stop shouting and swearing. She continued to be abusive. I eventually insulted her and said how rude she was being.

During the appraisal, my manager advised me that I should have said I would terminate the call if she continued to shout and swear. This was good advice, and I was a little embarrassed, but it was helpful information.

During the appraisal, I asked if I could get training in complaint handling, and my manager arranged for me to shadow calls and emails with clients until I was confident in processes and able to cover complaint handling when my manager was off duty.

6.11.3 360-Degree Appraisals

The 360-appraisal style of performance review is becoming more common and offers a more holistic approach than the traditional review. Originally designed to be a more coherent way for organisations to assess managerial positions, it is now used for employees at all levels and involves gathering feedback from colleagues, managers, clients, and reports, to offer a fully rounded (360-degree) view of how someone is performing. This is particularly successful for hospitality roles where much of an employee's work is with external clients, suppliers, guests, internal teams, and other people outside the organisation.

A 360 appraisal involves asking peers, managers/supervisors, customers, and even suppliers, for example, for feedback on individuals. This provides a more extensive review of employee performance.

Client feedback may come from customer comment cards, email feedback, *Tripadvisor* reviews, and complaints, for example. With peers, it is questionable as to whether they are suitably qualified to judge a colleague's performance. Peers who are friends may be generous with feedback, whereas others may be over-critical. The 360 approach also takes time and resources to compile so is not always the most effective approach.

A document or email folder for storing copies of emails with feedback, notes, and examples of specific incidents or other relevant information is useful to refer to and will help a manager's memory when discussing performance.

360-degree reviews benefit from including factors that are qualitative rather than quantitative examples which fall outside the SMART goals rule: factors such as working with others, communication skills, and leadership qualities – collectively known as 'soft skills'. It allows employees to see things from an unfamiliar perspective (somebody else's perspective), focusing on the 'how' rather than the 'what', and increases self-awareness to encourage better or corrected behaviours.

Individuals who provide feedback to the 360 approach should be anonymous where feasible. The anonymity allows people to be honest with feedback, and for managers to gain an insight into how a report handles situations and clients when the manager is not directly involved.

As previously stated, the 360-approach does take time to collate the feedback from other parties and it could be argued that those parties are not qualified or sufficiently objective to provide fair feedback. Some colleagues may provide biased feedback, especially if they are friends with the appraisee (or not).

The challenges of the 360-degree appraisal include employees taking feedback personally. It is key to ensure the questions are objectively phrased, and feedback is delivered sensitively by the manager.

Examples of good 360-degree appraisal questions:

- In what ways does [name] inspire and motivate others to achieve their best?
- Provide a specific example of how [name] could improve their communication style with clients.
- Provide a specific example of how [name] identified and addressed a potential problem before it escalated.
- What would you say are [name's] strengths?
- What would you say [name] could improve?
- What three words would you use to describe [name]?

There is no need in the appraisal to dictate the exact words someone has written in their feedback – this could entice the appraisee to calculate who said what, and potentially cause mistrust or division within the team. Instead, feedback from other parties should be collated into a single anonymised document.

The idea of this style of performance management is to help the employee be more confident, more self-aware, and more receptive to change.

6.11.4 Management by Objectives and Continuous Performance Management

Management by objectives is a style of appraisal which focuses less on feedback but more on goal and objective setting. Specifically, this emphasises setting SMART objectives for employees. First the SMART goals are set, then monitored via regular check-ins with the opportunity for small amends and feedback, before evaluating the employee against their objectives and providing reward or incentive.

This aligns with continuous performance management (CPM), which is a quarterly detailed appraisal covering four key areas outlined in Figure 6.1.

CPM offers the opportunity to look not only at how the person is currently performing in their role, managing against SMART agile goals which are moveable and amendable as needs require, but also to monitor their well-being and their career and personal development.

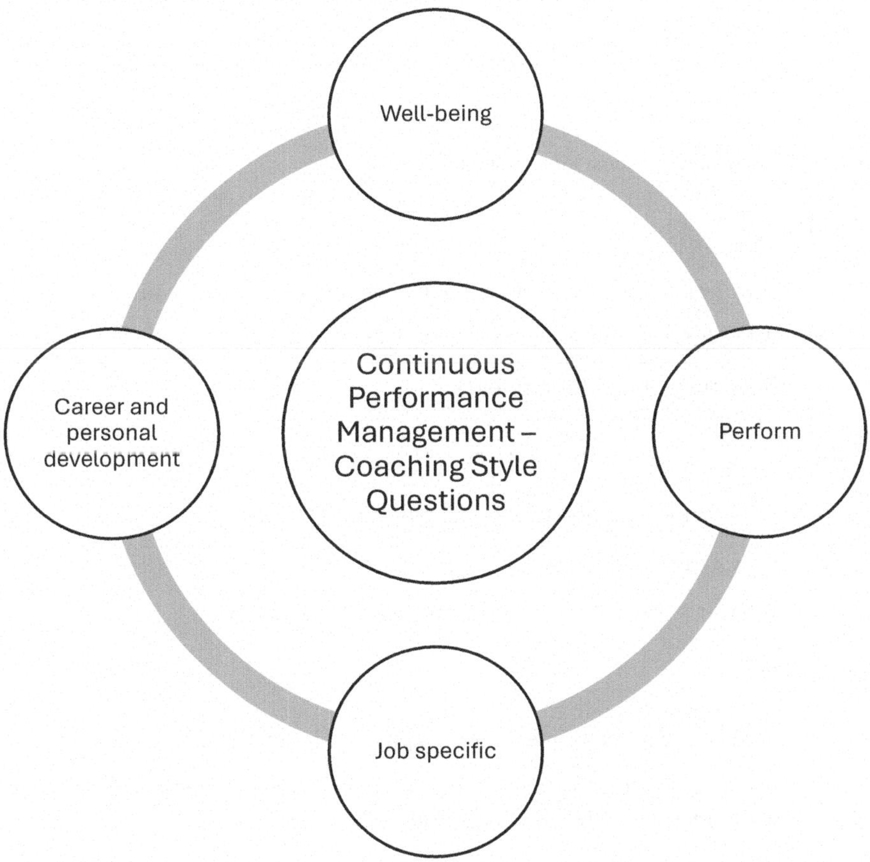

Figure 6.1 Continuous Performance Management Model

SOPHIE LININ'S VOICE

I regularly speak with my reports during these sessions about their ambitions for the future, within the company or not, and what we can do to better prepare them to achieve their goals. It also allows for time to discuss how the person is feeling, either professionally or personally. Many work problems are symptomatic of personal struggles, and I value the opportunity to understand and offer support with issues outside the work environment.

Within the CPM format of my current organisation, generic questions or prompts are provided under a series of headings, which allows the manager to select the most relevant questions for their report but without it feeling too targeted or direct for the employee. These are open-ended questions which invite conversation and encourage reports to think about solutions, promoting a proactive approach to dealing with obstacles.

Here are examples of questions to ask:

Well-being

- How much are you enjoying your work and role in the team?
- What kind of environment enables you to flourish?
- How are you handling setbacks?

Perform

- What achievements do you feel particularly proud of?
- How can we challenge you?
- What is getting in the way of improved performance?

Job Specific

- What do you need to feel more supported by the team?
- Are you aware of how your role and the team's purpose fits into the wider picture within the organisation?
- What skills, expertise, or behaviours do you feel you need to develop to be successful in your role?

Career and personal development

- What happens on a good/bad day at work?
- What would you like to do more of, that you care about or enjoy?
- What is your career or life aspiration? What would you like to do next?

Questions such as these enable free-flowing conversation outside the traditional 1:1 format, with the aim of enabling managers to gain insight into how best to motivate and provide feedback to their team on a day-to-day basis by establishing what makes the employee tick.

6.12 Promotion and Progression

The joy in managing people comes from being able to see people learn and develop – to progress. Hopefully, opportunities arise to provide rewarding development opportunities and ultimately promotion or progression to higher levels. Promotions usually involve at least one of the following: a salary increase, a job title change, or increased responsibilities. The best promotions involve all three.

Promotions should come when a person has successfully carried out all elements of their current role and is prepared (and wants) to achieve (and learn) more.

The worst mistake is to promote someone who is already struggling with their tasks, or advancing someone from a role where they were successful, into a new role for which they are not well suited. This can lead to frustration for an employee and setbacks for an organisation.

This is prone to happen in hospitality, hotel, and event roles where staff shortages encourage quick but unsuitable promotions without adequate training ('over-promotion'). It is important to ensure all staff, at whatever level, have the necessary training and experience to take on a new role.

INDUSTRY VOICE

Dr Philip Berners, Associate Professor in Events Management

Over-promotion is where a person is promoted to a position above their capability, training, qualifications, or experience. It occurs when a staffing gap requires filling, usually urgently. This means an employee receives promotion purely because they are there and it is convenient, not because they have earned it, demonstrated they can do it, or are capable of undertaking it.

For the promoted employee, the additional responsibilities coupled with an inbuilt feeling that they are not doing the job well is stressful and can cause burnout.

For the team, it can cause resentment to be led by somebody who they feel shouldn't be in the role or shouldn't have been promoted to do it.

For clients, customers, and guests, it causes complaints when the over-promoted employee is not capable to make decisions or resolve problems.

Ideally, an employee should be made ready for promotion by demonstrating they are competent in meeting the requirements at the next level. The next level requirements will be known from the job description, so if the employee is ready, promote them!

The best way to assess an employee for promotional opportunities is to conduct a thorough job description evaluation. Are they confidently and capably completing all elements of their current job description without assistance from managers or others? Are there things they are doing that are currently outside their job description, and perhaps above their pay grade? Are they stepping into managerial responsibilities, leading teams or projects, or taking on tasks that support your own work, or other leaders within the organisation? Do they want to step into a managerial role?

In some roles it is possible to progress in a career without managerial duties; this is less likely within hospitality, hotels, and events due to the way the sectors work and grow, and not everyone wants to be a manager. Some employees are comfortable where they are and do not want to advance – this applies to students, parents, part-time staff, and carers. Human Resources and managers could consider delegating additional responsibilities to the employee and monitoring how they cope with them. This will give a clearer idea of their readiness for promotion.

In certain situations, it may be suitable to conduct a formal interview process, particularly if there is only one position available and multiple team members who could potentially fill it. This can feel risky for managers, as there is the potential of disrupting and demotivating current team members if they are not given the promotion.

The key is honesty; being upfront with the team about the role on offer, what it entails, as well as any additional hours expected or pay increases. Be clear that one role is available, and the interviews will be conducted fairly and objectively, and in line with any company policies concerning recruitment, equality, and diversity. The position can be advertised externally to widen the catchment, so it could be that no internal staff member gets the promotion – but if they do, they were truly the best fit.

Being specific about what traits and qualities are required of the successful candidate and outlining the expectations of the role to those looking to apply, allows honesty and clarity of feedback to unsuccessful candidates. Being honest about the rationale why an employee was unsuccessful presents the opportunity to discuss future development prospects to enable them to be better prepared for future promotion openings. Transparency supports their growth and encourages a clearer pathway to success.

An organisation that promotes employees internally should further support the employee in their new role as a new starter – it is a new job – with an induction programme and access to a manager (or Human Resources where relevant) for queries. They will be as keen to succeed as the firm is; a manager should not allow inadequate support to be the reason for their confidence in their abilities to fail.

6.13 Grievances and Disciplinaries

Sometimes, things do not work out as expected. People may struggle with certain tasks and be unable to carry them out in the way the organisation expects. Individuals do not get on with everyone, and conflict arises. Somebody could expect something which a manager or the company are unable to provide. Whatever it is, managers and Human Resources might find themselves in a situation where a resolution needs to be found. Every manager faces this at some point, and it is common to feel failure as a manager. This is not the case and is an important moment to take a breath and problem-solve, something that hospitality has undoubtedly prepared employees for many times before.

The purpose of grievance and disciplinary procedures is to act early and resolve a situation; to contain it.

Start at the beginning

Look at what the catalyst is. What has happened? When did the problem arise? Has it been broached casually in a 1:1, then formally in an appraisal? Has there been any progress; has nothing happened at all; or has the situation got worse?

It is helpful to create a log that records the times something has happened, any opportunities there have been to address it, any outcomes that were agreed, any previous resolutions, or any future fears. This allows the manager and Human Resources to assess the trajectory of a problem with the person or people involved, but also provides a record should the situation head into a formal disciplinary process.

Problems do not always arrive unexpectedly. There are often small niggles that escalate over time into something larger and more damaging. By having a comprehensive calendar of check-ins, as discussed earlier in this chapter, there will be plenty of opportunities to broach difficult situations in a less formal context.

Broach the subject

Flag something first in a 1:1, start with a question – 'I've noticed that [problem] is happening. Can you tell me more about it?' or 'I feel that you are struggling with [problem]. Is there any support I can provide to help you with this?'

By asking questions, the manager is inviting the individual to share issues, to share their side of the story, or to open up about how they are feeling. Inviting the individual to suggest potential resolutions, or recommendations on how to progress is also useful. By addressing it in this way, the manager and employee can have an open conversation and offer any support as needed.

The manager could also set flexible deadlines for a resolution or be alerted to any future risks which need to be monitored more closely. Sometimes, the employee is not aware of the problem, in which case they have been alerted to something and are now able to self-reflect and hopefully self-correct.

The manager, or Human Resources, needs to be mindful of what is said in these situations. Something said, even as a throwaway remark, could be used at later stages with damaging consequences to managers, Human Resources, and the company. If the manager feels unsure about how best to approach the issue, it is advisable to engage with Human Resources as early as possible to get the support needed and receive advice on the best course of action.

Raise it formally

If resolution has not worked, the situation will need to be raised formally, either in the next appraisal or in a specific meeting to address the issue. This is the time for facts. The log of situations, conversations, or issues is used to discuss the various times a situation has occurred, any extenuating circumstances around each incident, and any resolutions previously agreed which have not worked.

The manager, or Human Resources, must be clear and precise in conversations outlining issues, with the use of facts and statistics rather than thoughts and feelings. It is important to be specific about the impact the issue is having, either on the employee, the manager, or on the wider team or organisation. At the end of this meeting, clear resolutions should be stated with deadlines (SMART goals). Consequences should also be outlined, should the resolution be unsuccessful.

The clearer and more factual the manager can be, the easier it is for both the manager and the employee. Conversations should be timely and concise. Avoidance is unhelpful. The longer it is left to have a difficult conversation, the more difficult it becomes. Both the manager and the employee want resolution because if it does not happen, the situation escalates, moves beyond control, and could end with dismissal.

6.13.1 Resolution

Resolutions will be different depending on the scenario. If someone is not hitting deadlines, it needs to be established whether they can complete the task or role at all within those time frames, or if the deadlines are unrealistic. It might be necessary to deprioritise other tasks so the employee can meet more prioritised deadlines. If there is an employee creating conflict, it will be necessary for them to act differently in a work environment. Mediation between two individuals may be required or wider team boundaries and ground rules need to be set. If someone is failing to hit targets, they might benefit from further training and skill set enhancement, or better motivation.

A thorough understanding of the employee and the problem itself, will determine and enable agreement on a way forward that works for everyone. It could be that the employee is not happy in their role, or they are experiencing personal challenges – that the problem is symptomatic of a wider problem of which the manager was unaware.

There are actions that a manager, or Human Resources, can take to resolve the problem. It is important to be open for possibilities and recognise there may be need for compromise.

6.13.2 Escalation

Often, a single manager is unable to resolve a situation. Line managers are sometimes too close to the situation to see a clear way through. Human Resources departments are there to support and assist managers, ensure legal and internal policies are followed, as well as provide support for the employee. It could be that HR are already involved – perhaps the employee has engaged with them, or the manager who needed guidance. It may be that the manager has involved HR following earlier attempts at resolution which were unsuccessful.

Formal grievances and disciplinaries will then be raised to follow each organisation's protocol, but they usually involve someone from outside the department to objectively assess the situation. There is also potential for union representatives to support the employee during the grievance or disciplinary meeting, or 'hearing'.

A manager may be given a resolution at the end of the process which they are not happy with; it is their responsibility to comply. The employee may be given a resolution they are not happy with; again, at this point it is their responsibility to comply. A formal warning is issued for incidents when an employee has breached policies, standards, or expected behaviours. If no resolution can be found and no way to continue, dismissal or resignation is the only foreseeable outcome.

6.13.3 Dismissal

Dismissals come with a clear business need. The employee is demonstrably failing in their role in some way, despite attempts to resolve issues. On occasion, there is a clear catalyst, for example theft, which immediately breaches the employee's contract and dismissal is the only way forward in response to gross misconduct. Generally, dismissal is the final part of an extensive disciplinary process which has followed all legal processes and company policy.

The Human Resources team will be involved at the stage of dismissal and in full support of the decision and be able to lead or assist throughout this end stage by giving clear guidance on what to say, how to make it easier, and what the next steps are.

Here follows an overview of factors to consider:

When in the position of dismissing an employee, it is important to be clear and concise in all communication. Managers and Human Resources must be prepared to answer questions about why, have the data and reasons ready to be explained, and to be prepared for the employee to be distressed or upset. The employee might request a 'final opportunity' but opportunities for change would already have been explored, so an organisation can clearly demonstrate those opportunities have come and gone.

Clear decisions should have been made as to whether the employee is being dismissed immediately: to go to their area of work to collect their items and leave the premises. They may be expected to work until the end of the day or month, or to work a notice period. If the former, it is recommended to have the conversation with the employee outside normal work hours to minimise impact on other team members.

The next steps will need to be explained to the employee so they know what they need to do, and financial impacts discussed – when they will be paid and to what date, and any remaining annual leave, and pension implications. The process for appeal or wrongful dismissal claims should be outlined with Human Resources present for support and guidance.

It could be necessary for the dismissed employee to handover any live events or current clients, information on reservations, ongoing guest enquiries, or other operational concerns.

Some organisations will implement gardening leave which means the employee leaves immediately after resignation or dismissal but continues to receive pay and contractual benefits until the end of their contract. It is usually implemented to prevent the former employee access to commercially sensitive information which they could damage or pass to a competitor. This type of harm can take the form of database leaks, taking company clients with them, or financial administration risks. If gardening leave is not implemented, a manager and Human Resources should have a comprehensive understanding of any current tasks or events the employee was working on and put in place a suitable handover of any information and client liaison.

Not everyone is suited to every role or company. It is possible the individual would thrive in a different company, or in a different role. A manager and the Human Resources department's primary responsibility is to protect the company and the team, and any decision made should be the result of a robust assessment process.

Once the decision has been taken and the employee informed, the decision will need to be shared with the wider team. This will discourage gossip and sharing of misinformation. The manager will need to be clear and honest with other employees without sharing confidential information.

It should be explained that following a disciplinary process, [name] is no longer employed with the company. The impacts the decision will have on the team should be outlined, for example increased workloads or recruitment processes. The team may have questions around other people's potential for dismissal; people should be reassured that the decision was made following an extensive process where a range of resolutions were sought but were unsuccessful, leading to the eventual dismissal.

INDUSTRY VOICE

Philip Berners, Associate Professor in Events Management

For me, dismissing an employee is a tragedy. It is also a failure of management.

Usually, I will put great effort into turning a problem employee to good – I treat it as an exercise of good leadership to resolve the issue and retain the employee. Solutions can be found if I work with the employee to find them.

Not every employee can be retained, however. Gross misconduct such as theft is a dismissible act.

Gross misconduct aside, then, I always consider that if the employee was recruited into the company, they should be retained. Otherwise, there is something not right with the recruitment and selection process – in which case it needs reviewing.

I have often found that the extra effort put into a problem employee, makes that person an excellent employee.

Chapter 7

Reward Management

Dr Mostafa Marghany and Nirmeen Elmohandes

7.0 Introduction

The key to Human Resources practices, especially in the dynamic world of hospitality, hotel, and events, is reward management. This chapter provides an understanding of the nature and purpose of reward management, and the types of rewards available, alongside motivational theories which underpin practices.

Reward management is fundamentally concerned with creating and implementing plans to recognise and compensate staff members consistently and fairly.

This process assists in retaining personnel, inspires employees to reach greater performance standards, and harmonises their aspirations with those of the company.

7.1 Role and Purpose of Reward Management

In the hospitality, hotel, and event sectors where talent acquisition, motivation, and staff retention are paramount, reward management is one of the most important functions within human resource management. Rewards play a vital role in driving employee performance, satisfaction, increased productivity, and overall organisational success.

DOI: 10.4324/9781003469803-8

Reward management is the development, implementation, and maintenance of a system that motivates and retains the workforce and entices new talented recruits into the business.

Through rewarding good performance, employees feel valued and appreciated for their contributions, resulting in a working environment from which both the employer and the employee benefit.

7.2 Types of Reward

'Total reward management' is a strategy which combines all compensation, benefits, and rewards provided to employees, and should complement organisational culture, values, and objectives. Through total reward management, a business can enhance staff loyalty and productivity.

Total reward management is a concept that contains both financial and non-financial rewards of which both play an equal role in influencing the behaviour and performance of the workforce.

In terms of financial and non-financial rewards being two main types of reward, financial is generally referred to as an extrinsic or tangible reward, and non-financial refers to an intrinsic or intangible reward.

7.2.1 Extrinsic Rewards

Extrinsic rewards tend to be physical and hold some sort of monetary value such as salary and bonuses. These could be considered as transactional rewards. Financial rewards equate to total remuneration.

Financial rewards are the most direct form of compensation, offering monetary benefits to employees for their performance. These rewards are primary in nature, as they help fulfil the basic needs of the employee and are considered the prime motivator in most cases.

Base salary/pay and pay rises

Financial rewards include base salary or pay. Basic pay is the expected salary or wages an employee receives for doing their job. It is essential in forming the base of an employee's total compensation package; thus, it ensures an employee's ability to meet their daily financial needs.

For example, a front-desk manager at a large hotel would earn a base salary that is competitive and commensurate with the duties, experience, and complexity of the work. This base salary ensures financial stability, attracting competent professionals to the job. Pay is generally higher for jobs that involve more responsibility or risk.

Contingent pay

An organisation might also offer an annual salary increase in line with meeting targets or increased experience, and this may be adapted according to employee efforts. An employee who has consistently excelled in their role and exceeded expectations may get a higher salary increase than an employee who simply meets targets and fulfils their basic duties.

Bonuses

Bonuses are additional payments to employees based on performance or when a particular set of organisational goals have been achieved. They are strong incentives that encourage the employees to go beyond expectation.

For example, an event coordinator may get an additional payment as a performance bonus for effectively handling a high-profile event. The rationale behind this award is not only in appreciation for hard work and dedication, but to induce effort in performing similar work in future.

Profit sharing

Profit sharing designates a proportion of a company's profits to its employees. Such a reward aligns the employees' interest with the company's financial success, which helps them to feel ownership and dedication.

Commission

Commission is another method often used in sales-based roles; it is a percentage of what a worker sells. This is another way performance can be directly linked to remuneration.

Salespeople in a convention centre can be paid a commission for booking events, so they are always proactively looking for and soliciting new business prospects.

Pension

A pension is an indirect financial reward that contributes to security in retirement by covering the future cost of living. An employer, private, or government scheme can be used. An employer will add a percentage of the employee's salary into a pension, to which the employee may also contribute, and builds the 'pension pot' over their period of employment.

Holiday leave

Many countries have a legal minimum number of days for annual leave (or vacation leave) which forms part of health and safety and employee well-being. An organisation might enhance the legal minimum number of vacation days based on length of service; and may offer additional days for celebrations. This off-time serves as a means of revitalisation; it is an essential factor in sustainability in prevention of burnout without a slump in productivity. Adequate Paid Time Off (PTO) is one of the most important contributors to well-being among employees and can increase loyalty and decrease turnover. Offering employees a paid leave of absence enables staff to recuperate and return to work re-energised.

Bereavement, compassionate leave, or parental leave

Whilst this might not be a legal requirement, an organisation may offer paid discretionary leave for bereavement, emergencies, or to care for others. Bereavement and compassionate leave are normally discretionary and can be three to five days, or longer depending on the situation. This may be paid or unpaid. Parental leave could be given for new parents, time off for school activities or other educational or medical appointments for children. Maternity and paternity leave is offered for new parents, as discussed in Chapter 4.

Health benefits

The health package includes both medical and dental benefits, as well as vision insurance. These benefit the employee, ensuring they and their families have access to health and well-being services.

A business might extend its employee benefits to include total health coverage which takes care of all types of medical services and therefore produces complete satisfaction and loyalty in employees. This could further translate into good productivity and less absence from work.

7.2.2 Intrinsic Rewards

Intrinsic rewards are aligned with internal feelings of satisfaction; psychological rewards come from doing meaningful work and being recognised for good performance. This can be through praise, recognition, and learning and development, as well as the job itself and can be utilised as relational rewards.

Non-financial rewards have such intangible benefits that satisfy the psychological and emotional needs of an employee. These, from the points of view of long-term motivation and job satisfaction, provide recognition and a sense of having achieved something worthwhile.

Recognition programmes

Rewards and recognition programmes acknowledge even the minor efforts put in by employees; this may include awards such as employee of the month, or public recommendations, for example from *Tripadvisor* or customer comment cards, or just a simple thank you by customers or managers.

An 'Employee of the Month' programme is when exemplary employees are given recognition in front of their peers and may be awarded a certificate or a small gift. Public recognition of this nature will have positive effects on morale and will act as an impetus for others to achieve the same.

Training and development

Workers respond to opportunities for employee development and the growth of their career. Employees find importance in training, seminars, and opportunities for promotion.

Training programmes provided by a company can involve new skills necessary for promotion to the next level in the firm. Any such opportunities extended to employees will increase their loyalty towards the company, reducing the level of staff turnover.

Training and development form part of performance management, discussed in Chapter 6. Training and development demonstrate a firm's commitment to employee development, which enhances skills and employability.

Training may be requested by the employee to enhance skills, confidence, and productivity, for example training in complaint handling, making coffees or cocktails, or shadowing someone in another department or cross-departmental training to help multi-skilled employees.

Training can also address performance issues identified during one-to-ones with team members or as identified during the annual appraisal. Any training redevelopment will enhance skill set and employee confidence, and improve operations. This can also lead to staff retention as staff feel valued.

Training may be classroom based, online training (such as food safety or fire safety training); demonstrations, shadowing, or discussions with peers and managers, or case studies are examples.

Organisations might offer short training courses off site, such as alcohol licences, first aid courses, or cookery skills courses. A firm could offer to pay for supplementary qualifications, such as apprenticeships, accounting qualifications such as AAT, Chartered Institute of Personnel Development (CIPD) for HR professionals, marketing qualifications, degrees, or Masters qualifications.

Career development and progression

Employees can be incentivised by being offered opportunities to progress within the organisation. This includes a sideways promotion to another department, upwards progression into a supervisory or management role, or intercompany transfer to another location as examples.

This motivates staff, due to recognition of achievements and future potential. Staff recognition and investment in their career can help retain talented recruits where opportunities exist for relocation to other sites, internal progressions, and promotion.

Internal staff are often overlooked, and external candidates recruited due to other work experiences and skills which internal staff are perceived not to possess. This may alienate internal staff, leading to motivation issues, loss of productivity, and even staff leaving due to lack of opportunities for progression.

Work–Life balance initiatives

Employee programmes balancing personal and professional life are increasingly a concern, including flexible working hours, remote working options, and wellness programmes.

A hospitality company might offer flexible scheduling, job shares, remote working, hybrid working with time split between home and the workplace, or paid time off, thus meeting the personal commitments of employees.

Others may offer onsite wellness facilities—including a gym, doctor, dentist, fitness classes, or yoga for example. Mental health and well-being support such as employee assistance programmes offering counselling or cognitive behavioural therapies can be utilised. Some firms offer leave for menstruation, menopause, or mental health days. Initiatives such as these contribute to employee job satisfaction and reduce stress.

Additional annual leave for special events or birthdays may be granted, and facilities or financial support towards childcare, or additional days off for parental leave.

Other incentives include paid breaks, paid nap breaks, sleep pods, food and drink, hotel stays, or discounts at events, and meals and friends and family offers – many of these cross into extrinsic financial incentives.

Autonomy

Autonomy refers to the amount of control afforded to the employee in going about their performance. High levels of independence are bound to grant immeasurable motivation and satisfaction to employees. For example, an event organiser may be granted the freedom to design and execute events in the manner they envision, which will encourage creativity and innovation. Such levels of autonomy usually result in improved job satisfaction and stronger feelings of ownership over one's work.

Job enrichment

Job enrichment refers to the increase of responsibilities at a meaningful level which improves a job's interest and satisfaction for the jobholder.

A hotel, for example, can adopt a job enrichment programme in which the housekeeping personnel are trained in customer service and are given higher responsibilities, such as ensuring the needs and wants of clients are well attended. This will create a high-involvement situation and, hence, motivation among employees.

The various rewards can encourage a motivated, highly productive workforce. However, different people will assign different values or perceptions to different rewards. Therefore, whilst one reward will motivate one person, it may not the next. An organisation's rewards offering should therefore include numerous rewards or allow employees to choose their own where feasible.

JENNIFER KAYE'S VOICE

Rewards should have a high valence to those receiving them, valence refers to the value an individual assigns to a particular reward: the emotional value or perceived importance of rewards to individuals. A reward with high valence is seen as desirable to someone, for example some may be motivated by money and others by a sense of achievement.

Rewards with low valence are those which are perceived as little value to the individual such as a bottle of wine if they do not drink alcohol, or a day off where they would rather receive additional pay for working overtime.

The higher the valence the more motivating it is. This is often cited in Vroom's Expectancy Theory outlined in Section 7.6.3.

Regardless of which rewards a company offers to their employees, affordability should be considered, and rewards used which align with corporate values, alongside employee needs.

EDWARD GALLIER'S VOICE

Head of Learning & Development, Leonardo Hotels (UK & Ireland)

I remember when we first implemented the Employee of the Month award. To my surprise it was not universally appreciated, or so I thought. Some team members made fun of it. I was disappointed by this but a year later I found one of the certificates in pride of place pinned up on the Sous Chef's wall.

A reward and recognition programme can really help develop culture and show team members what behaviours and ideas the business appreciates from team members.

We should always remember, though: different team members and personalities will want the award delivered in different ways. Everyone wants to win, everyone wants the prize, but not everyone wants to wear a badge or have their photo on the employee noticeboard!

7.3 Combining Different Types of Reward

Truly effective reward management is the result of a balance in blending financial and non-financial benefits with intrinsic rewards into one mixture. This holistic approach ensures various aspects of employee motivation are addressed, resulting in higher overall satisfaction and performance.

Any hospitality or event organisation can develop a comprehensive reward system, including financial rewards (offering competitive salaries), non-financial rewards (free hotel stays, meals, or event tickets), and other benefits packages (such as comprehensive health benefits). This multifaceted approach to rewarding will help attract and retain talented human resources and motivate employees to harmonise personal goals with organisational ones.

JENNIFER KAYE'S VOICE

When I was working as a Reservations Agent, the organisation offered a variety of rewards.

Reservations agents were set performance targets to visit ten hotels and event venues each year on educational familiarisation trips. This enabled team members to become more familiar with preferred suppliers that paid commission when reservations were placed with them, helping to enhance company profits. The team enjoyed corporate dinners, drinks receptions, and events which also helped to build team dynamics when visiting venues. The visits improved product and service knowledge, enabling agents to make more informed recommendations to clients, which improved client satisfaction and increased revenue for the agency and the supplier.

I enjoyed my job, and intrinsic motivation and enjoyment of the job itself drove me to work hard and meet targets. If we met targets, the company offered bottles of wine as a monthly incentive. Wine neither motivated me nor caused dissatisfaction but the company was willing to provide flexibility when determining what rewards to provide.

After three years of service, I was given a long-service award which consisted of a choice of rewards that were a fixed selection, so I felt more satisfied knowing rewards were flexible depending on my personal preference.

I also wanted to improve my customer service skills, so my supervisor agreed to let me shadow her responding to email complaints. This taught me response times and processes, and, over time, I was responsible for fulfilling this role whilst she was on annual leave which made me feel trusted and I enjoyed being given responsibility.

The agency held Employee of the Year awards at their annual summer celebration which included barbecues, and they organised an annual Christmas party in a hotel. This further enhanced team cohesion and employees felt part of the company and socialised with management, which showcased company commitment and how employees were valued.

In addition, if team targets were met each year, the entire team was given an annual bonus which inspired us to work hard. During the financial crisis of 2008–2009 due to the economic downturn and reduced company profits, this bonus was not feasible. However, some individuals expected this reward as they no longer considered it a bonus, but an expectation. Rewards are not guaranteed and should align with the strategic needs of the business.

Therefore, the agency utilised a variety of extrinsic and intrinsic rewards and the benefits of these were multifaceted. Some rewards improved customer service, sales, commission, and reputation. Other rewards boosted team or individual motivation. Yet, other rewards improved team cohesion, all of which helped the company achieve its strategic goals. But it is important to recognise the different value individuals assign to rewards and help manage expectations, so rewards are consistently valued by employees.

To provide a wider variety of rewards, some organisations will use external rewards providers that negotiate rewards from a variety of suppliers such as cinemas, restaurants, hotels, gyms, and shops on behalf of subscribing organisations. The reward provider will provide an app or website which employees can access to select their own perks and benefits such as discounts, vouchers, and leisure activities. This may include firms such as *Red Letter Days* or *Perkbox* as examples, and an employer will pay for a subscription to access the rewards offered by the external rewards platform.

CASE STUDY: IMPLEMENTING A NEW REWARDS PROGRAMME TO BOOST STAFF MORALE

Contribution from Nirmeen Elmohandes, PhD Researcher, University of Debrecen, Hungary and Canterbury Christ Church University, UK

In a small Egyptian hotel, with 20 rooms and 15 workers, the hotel encountered challenges related to employee morale and staff turnover. The management pointed out three main areas to be addressed: working hours, recognition, and chances to grow.

A new rewards programme was introduced, including flexible scheduling, an Employee of the Month scheme with public recognition and bonuses, and free professional development courses.

The programme was communicated through meetings and handouts, with a feedback system in place for continual improvement.

In just three months, workers felt happier, fewer quit, and they liked their jobs more and got more done. They felt more important, which led to taking better care of guests and making them happier.

The management successfully enhanced motivation and loyalty by connecting the rewards and benefits with employee preferences.

7.4 Strategic Benefits of Rewards

The strategic benefits that accrue from a fair and equitable rewards system include:

Talent attraction and retention

One of the significant roles of reward management is to attract and retain the best employees. Nowadays, hospitality and events have turned into a very competitive business environment; to survive, organisations need to attract skilled and experienced professionals. Competitive reward packages include attractive salaries, bonuses, and many benefits that help an organisation appeal to potential employees.

The most important factor in rewards is retention of employees. High staff turnover is costly and disruptive. A well-structured reward system will minimise staff turnover by ensuring employees feel appreciated and compensated.

Increasing motivation and performance

Employees tend to be motivated to perform well through reward management. An act of developing rewards in line with organisational objectives encourages high performance in employees. For instance, performance-based bonuses and incentives explicitly map employee efforts to the rewards extended to them, thereby showing that effort and dedication are recognised and rewarded. This not only affects personal performance but contributes to the success of the organisation.

Reinforcing organisational culture and values

Reward management is an equally important dimension of the reinforcement of organisational culture and values. Rewards offered and the criteria for providing them send a signal about what the organisation values. For example, if one of the most important values is teamwork and cooperation, then rewards would be accorded to the team, but not for individual performance. This approach unites the culture wherein employees are in line with pursuing common goals.

MOSTAFA MARGHANY'S VOICE

At a well-known fast-food chain in North Africa, the management observed a decline in customer satisfaction during peak hours, which they traced back to low employee motivation.

A shift manager discovered through a survey that many employees desired more leisure time.

In response to this issue, the manager implemented a system of flexible scheduling and additional time-off as incentives for exceptional performance. Staff members who achieved their goals were given the option to select their own work schedules and increase extra days-off by finishing tasks in advance.

This approach promptly resulted in heightened staff morale and customer satisfaction. The manager ensured continuous success by regularly conducting one-on-one meetings to stay updated on the team's needs.

7.5 Ensuring Equity and Fairness

Another important objective of reward management is to ensure the distribution of rewards is fair and equitable. It is evident that if employees see rewards distributed equitably, they are more likely to be satisfied and motivated. This is brought about by the open criteria through which performances are evaluated and how the rewards are decided. Fair reward practices ensure trust between the workers and management, in which case, the working environment becomes positive and productive.

Rewards should also be fair and consistent, transparent, and equitable. All employees should be able to achieve the required objectives, key performance indicators (KPI's), or targets to be rewarded.

Each department may be subject to different rewards, for example a sales team selling conference spaces or hotel rooms might earn commission, whilst front-of-house staff may earn tips/gratuities, and back-of-house staff may receive higher wages to compensate for lack of commission or gratuities. Different rewards will itself create issues, so some restaurants or hotels distribute tips to back-of-house staff as well, for example.

Other staff can feel envious of those who achieve rewards or feel overlooked for rewards, and this can cause motivational issues and even conflict.

In addition, if an employee works hard but does not receive recognition, and another employee is less productive, the former might stop working as hard because they do not see how working hard is beneficial.

This aligns with what is known as Equity Theory.

7.5.1 Equity Theory

The concept of Equity Theory, introduced by John Stacey Adams in the 1960s, focuses on humans' subjective evaluations of fairness in how they are treated relative to others. Employees assess the equity of their benefits (outcomes) against their effort or qualifications (inputs) by comparing their own input/output ratio to that of others. If this proportion is viewed as unfavourable, employees develop a sense of unfairness in the distribution of rewards.

Equity Theory focuses on a vital element of motivation and job satisfaction, emphasising how the perception of fairness can influence morale and potentially affect performance. Although it merely addresses a specific aspect of the whole motivational process, its impact on workplace dynamics and employee satisfaction is significant. Managers should prioritise equity to maintain morale and prevent any dissatisfaction that will impact performance.

To have a deeper comprehension of Equity Theory, it is important to acknowledge the significance of clear and open communication, as well as fair compensation systems. These factors are essential in making employees feel appreciated and treated fairly, which in turn promotes a workforce that is more motivated and productive.

7.5.2 Compliance with Legal and Ethical Standards

Reward management goes further than setting appropriate remuneration packages to ensure that all rewards given are in line with legal and ethical standards. This includes compliance with labour laws, non-discrimination of employees in compensation, minimum wages, overtime pay, and such related other legislations. In turn, ethical consideration towards reward practices ensures that the package is fair, thus there is no risk-exposure for over-exploitation. This is crucial for litigation avoidance and upkeep of the organisational image.

7.6 Rewards and Motivation Theory

Knowing what motivates people is key to managing human resources, in recruiting talented employees, retaining employees, and boosting company image as a reputable employer. By understanding the key factors of motivation and their impact on work outcomes, Human Resources can establish better rules and practices.

Below, some of the prominent motivation theories are explored:

7.6.1 Maslow's Hierarchy of Needs

One of the most well-known theories is Maslow's Hierarchy of Needs, formulated in 1943. Maslow suggested people have needs in a certain order starting with the basics or lower order needs which are needed to live, and stipulated that higher order needs are not met until lower order needs are met.

Lower order needs are considered as physiological, safety, and social needs and the need for physical and social well-being. Once people have these, they try to meet higher needs: social belonging, esteem, and ultimately self-actualisation, which is seen as the top goal.

Maslow proposed that once a need is fulfilled, the next one becomes the focus. However, the need for self-actualisation (or self-fulfilment) is unique: it is a perpetual drive that can never be completely satisfied. Maslow portrayed humans as 'creatures of want', pushed by the urge to meet unfulfilled needs. The most urgent unmet need serves as the strongest motivator at any moment.

Psychological development takes place as individuals advance through various stages, although this process is not always sequential. Lower-level demands do not vanish completely; they may become inactive but can re-emerge as sources of motivation. The continuous interaction between requirements emphasises the ever-changing character of human motivation.

These needs have been applied to the workforce in Figure 7.1.

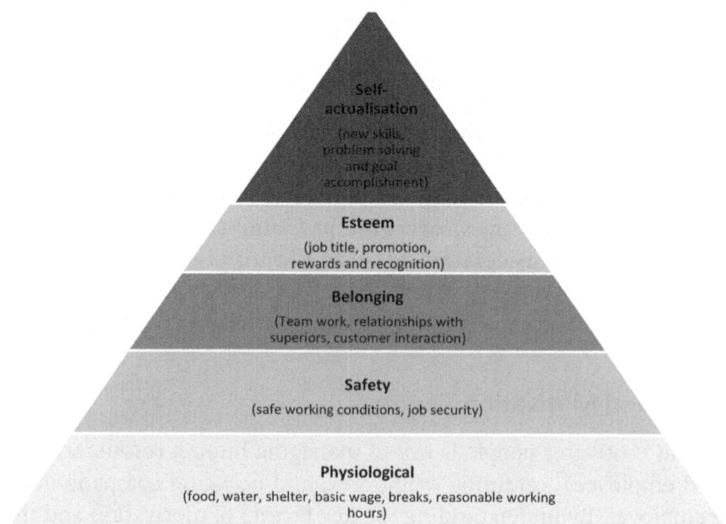

Figure 7.1 Maslow's Hierarchy of Needs in the Workplace
Contributed by Jennifer Kaye, adapted from Maslow.

7.6.2 Herzberg's Two Factor Theory

Herzberg's (1968) Two Factor Theory, also known as 'Motivation-Hygiene Theory', shares similarities to Maslow's Hierarchy of Needs whereby higher-level needs such as achievement and recognition motivate individuals. Herzberg identified two sets of needs following interviews with 203 engineers and accountants using the critical incident approach.

These needs are:

> 'Satisfiers' which relate to personal growth and the nature of work itself (job content) including desire for achievement, the level of engagement with the work, the sense of responsibility, and the potential for career progression.
>
> 'Hygiene' factors which are dissatisfiers such as pay and work conditions which are external to the job itself (job context). Hygiene variables relate to the workplace environment, including aspects such as salary and working conditions.
>
> The term 'hygiene' is derived from the medical context, referring to practices that prevent disease and maintain a clean and healthy environment. While hygiene elements do not provide satisfaction or motivation on their own, their primary purpose is to minimise job unhappiness. They have a minimal impact on positive job attitudes. For example, pay is not a satisfier, but if it is inadequate or perceived as inequitable, it can cause dissatisfaction. However, simply providing adequate pay does not result in lasting satisfaction.

The Two Factor Theory implies humans have basic biological needs and learned drives which identifies with Maslow's physiological and security needs and the need to secure regular work and pay.

Herzberg's theory revealed job security as the least important factor in his study, whereas today this may not be the case due to the increase in use of more precarious forms of employment such as Zero-Hour Contracts, especially in the hospitality, hotel, and events sectors as one of the largest users of this type of contract, and redundancies during economic downturn.

The 2020/21 global pandemic saw a rise in staff on furlough with earnings significantly reduced for some employees with others being made redundant, or for those on casual contracts receiving zero hours of work consistently over an extended period. This led to many employees leaving the industry for better job security and financial security in other sectors, such as retail, when the hospitality sectors were mostly closed.

See Figure 7.2 for a comparison between Maslow's Hierarchy and Herzberg's Two Factor theories, contributed by Jennifer Kaye.

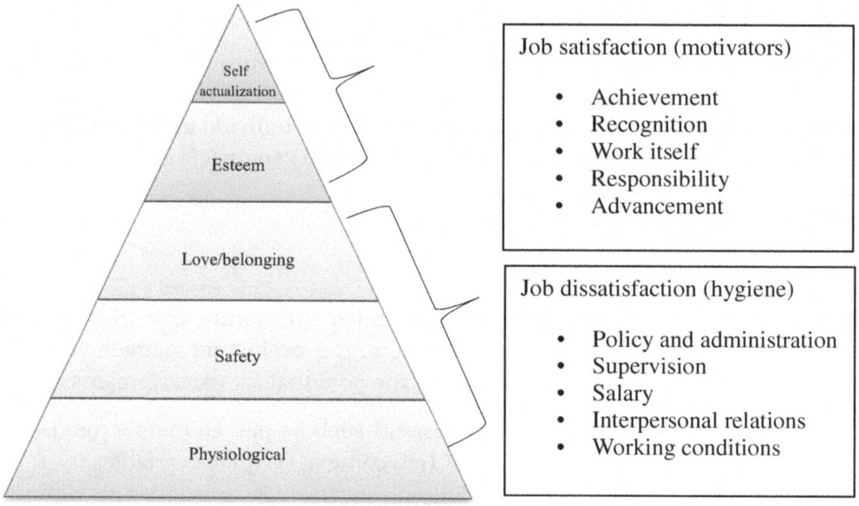

Figure 7.2 Comparison of Maslow's Hierarchy and Herzberg's Two Factor Theory

7.6.3 Expectancy Theory

Expectancy theory was created by Victor Vroom in 1964 and suggests that motivation is likely to be high when individuals have a clear understanding of what is required to get a reward, possess the belief that they can achieve it, and have the expectation that the reward will be valuable.

The theory has three dimensions: Expectancy, Instrumentality, and Valence.

- Expectancy is the likelihood that exerting effort will lead to the desired level of performance.
- Instrumentality is the belief that successful performance will result in rewards.
- Valence refers to the subjective worth of a reward, the value a person assigns to rewards, and other work-related outcomes.

The power of expectations can be influenced by previous encounters (reinforcement), but individuals frequently come across novel circumstances, such as changes in job responsibilities, payment, or working conditions imposed by management, where past experiences do not offer adequate guidance on the consequences of these changes. Under such conditions, motivation will be reduced.

If any of the dimensions are low, motivation will be low as per the formula that follows:

Motivation (M) equals the sum of Expectancy (E) x Instrumentality (I) x Valence (V)

$$M = E \times I \times V$$

Managers can put into place actions to enhance staff motivation in terms of expectancy:

- Identify expectations: identify the tasks and the standards for performance required to get rewards.
- Select competent workers with the right skill set and expertise.
- Plant the concept of self-efficacy: provide training and resources to ensure workers feel confident to perform the required tasks.
- Rewards to performance: ensure the promised rewards are directly linked to the performance and are seen as valuable by the employee.
- Clarify performance goals and support work efforts.
- Provide sufficient resources: employees should have the time, support, and tools to perform their tasks professionally.
- Constructive feedback: provide regular feedback to help employees stay on track and make necessary changes.

To improve valence, managers should:

- Identify individual needs.
- Adapt rewards to meet the needs of employees, providing choice and variety.

7.6.4 Goal Setting Theory

Developed by Edwin Locke in 1968, and republished by Locke and Latham (1979), Goal Setting Theory emphasises that motivation and performance are improved when employees are set challenging goals, and when they receive feedback on their performance.

Participation in the goal-setting process is important to protect promises on challenging targets. Goals must be clearly defined and be measurable, such as achieving a sales target for how many weddings should be booked into event spaces in the year; sales of the dish of the day; or room occupancy targets.

Explicit goals can be highly motivating and provide employees with clear direction within their work and clarify performance expectations. Feedback is vital in supporting motivation, specifically towards achieving progressively higher goals and can shape the desirable behaviours in employees to meet organisational performance standards, such as upselling and cross-selling skills, and increase profitability.

Goal Theory has considerably influenced performance and links reward management practices whereby employees are rewarded based on performance and achievement of goals.

However, the comprehensiveness of Goal Theory has been challenged. Individuals pursue different goals in diverse settings, challenging the notion that goals are always available and actively examined. This implies that goals can be influenced by external factors and may not always be consciously recognised. Furthermore, goals are only impactful when they are in harmony with the overall context in which they are pursued. Notwithstanding these criticisms, backing for Goal Theory has been provided by emphasising the significance of self-efficacy, which refers to an individual's belief in their capability to achieve objectives.

CASE STUDY: DEMONSTRATING REWARD EFFECTIVENESS

Contribution from Nirmeen Elmohandes, PhD Researcher, University of Debrecen, Hungary and Canterbury Christ Church University, UK

An Egyptian independent hotel with 20 rooms and 15 workers aimed to enhance employee engagement and business performance through effective reward practices. This included setting goals to work towards and varying the rewards they offered.

Management regularly reviewed and updated their reward arrangements to guarantee they motivated staff. This contained monetary bonuses, flexible scheduling, and professional development opportunities. Recognising the significance of consultation and change management, managers involved employees in developing and refining the reward system through regular meetings and feedback sessions.

The hotel presented an 'Employee of the Month' programme, offering public recognition and a bonus for outstanding performance. Employees who met performance targets could have more time for a better work–life balance. Professional development was promoted through courses and training programmes, helping employees to advance their career.

These strategies increased employee engagement, job satisfaction, and retention rates. Improved morale and motivation among staff translated to better customer service, higher guest satisfaction, and improved business performance.

Chapter 8

Employee Well-being, Equality, Diversity, and Inclusivity

DOI: 10.4324/9781003469803-9

Part 1: Staff Well-being

8.0 Introduction

This chapter is presented in two parts. The first part covers staff turnover, duty of care, health and safety, mental health and well-being, bullying, harassment and victimisation, sexual harassment, and compassionate leave. This first part will also raise awareness of the impact of the menopause on employee well-being, diversity and inclusion, and the role of Occupational Health in supporting employees.

Part Two of this chapter covers trans-inclusive practices.

Employee well-being enhances employee motivation and psychological contract with the firm, contributing towards staff retention.

8.1 Staff Turnover

Staff turnover is reported as 30 per cent in hospitality, with staff usually leaving within the first weeks of employment. This is attributed to unsocial working hours, low pay and benefits, and lack of career prospects. Other industries report around 15 per cent staff turnover. As the hospitality and events industry is heavily reliant on a transient workforce (students, young people, and migrant workers – and the ease of transferring to other jobs), employment within these sectors is often temporary whilst staff train for other careers or move to another country further impacting retention rates.

To calculate staff turnover rates:

- Calculate average number of employees
- Identify how many employees have left the organisation in a given period (a month or year)
- Divide the number of employees who have left the organisation by the average number of employees (then multiply by 100 for the percentage)

Example turnover calculation

36 staff members.
4 have left in the last year.

4 / 36 = 0.11
0.11*100 = 11% staff turnover

To calculate cost of staff turnover according to *indeed.com*:

(Hiring costs + onboarding costs + training costs) x (number of employees x annual turnover percentage) + lost productivity = annual cost of turnover.

Employee turnover can be reduced with strategies such as recognition, reward, progression investments in staff training and development, a better work–life balance, and investments in employee well-being.

This includes considering health, safety, and welfare of employees.

8.2 Health and Safety

All employees, volunteers, and managers have a legal responsibility to protect the health, safety and welfare of everyone on the premises. If an accident were to occur there could be devasting impacts on those affected, which could lead to lawsuits, fines, reputational damage, and even business closure.

It is necessary to report dangerous occurrences, prevent hazards, report slip or trip hazards, keep fire exits and emergency escape routes clear, use chemicals as directed, use gas and fire safely, wear protective clothing where needed, and follow guidance on any equipment and chemicals, and when manual handling, for example.

This is discussed in more depth in Chapter 12 on Employment Law. Under such laws mental health is also incorporated.

8.3 Mental Health in the Workplace

Mental health and well-being are protected under health and safety law, and employers have a legal responsibility to protect, not just physical health, but the mental health of employees. If an employee is exposed to bullying, harassment, victimisation, unrealistic workloads, or other pressures, this can result in burnout, stress, anxiety disorders, or other mental health concerns. Likewise, other factors in the employee's personal life will impact well-being, such as family relationships, health issues, drug and alcohol addiction, and financial concerns.

Such factors can lead to low productivity issues, accidents in the workplace, abusive behaviours, withdrawal from people, conflict, absenteeism, lateness, and staff retention issues.

Whilst some factors can be dealt with by performance management processes, such as adjustments to the work, free counselling, medical insurance, and compassionate leave, there are strategies employers can provide to protect their workers.

8.4 Well-being Support

Services an employer can adopt to support employees in terms of physical and mental well-being:

- Employee Assistance Programmes counselling by phone or online
- Mental Health First Aid Training to raise awareness and initial help in the workplace
- Discretionary time-off for well-being days
- Health insurance as a benefit
- Counselling services in-house or externally (paid for or discounted)
- Visual Display Unit (VDU) assessments to ensure desk stations are adaptable to prevent injury such as repetitive strain
- Eye test vouchers/medical cover for those who use computers in their work
- Gym memberships/gym access or discounts or other exercise programmes such as Yoga or walking groups
- Breaks for rest during workdays, regular breaks for those using screens, doing repetitive work or when standing for long periods, for example
- Generous annual leave entitlements and paid time off work for vacation, sick leave
- Birthdays off work
- Menstruation leave, with sick pay or discretionary days for those who experience severe symptoms which prevent them from carrying out their duties
- Food or drink provided during lunch break
- Healthy eating programmes or options on lunch break
- Flexible working patterns or remote working for a better work life balance
- Introducing the four-day working week, so staff are well rested, leading to higher productivity on workdays, working 20 per cent fewer hours for same pay
- Compressed hours working four days out of five, for example ten-hour days over four days
- Teambuilding activities such as sporting activities, cinema, or club nights
- Employee feedback forums to share ideas

- Rewards and recognition programmes, such as Employee of the Month, bonus, pay rises, discounted or free events/hotel stays/meals, insurance, progression
- Annual celebrations including team meals such as an annual barbecue or restaurant meal; can include activities or other festivities
- Offering qualifications and training to boost employability
- Clear policies on bullying and harassment
- Parental or adoption leave for new parents or for baby-loss
- Support for caregivers
- Prayer rooms
- Space to meditate or quiet rooms
- Charity days to undertake volunteering work

8.5 Compassionate Leave

Compassionate leave enables employees to take time from work in times of bereavement, for caring responsibilities, or other serious personal situations – giving employees space during times of personal crisis.

Compassionate leave can be paid or discretionary, a fixed number of days or flexible depending on the situation. Some organisations honour three to five working days, and additional days as discretionary, depending on the nature of the situation.

It may be that working hours need to be reduced, working schedules amended, or gradual return to workdays enabled.

8.6 The Role of the Occupational Health Team

The Occupational Health (OH) team (also known as the Wellness or Well-being team; Health and Well-being; Employee Support; or Health and Safety Team) is usual in larger organisations or sits with the Human Resources team. The role of the professionals in this team is to provide support to employees with work-based or personal problems.

A manager should refer an employee to OH, to provide support and guidance, and to identify the level or nature of support an employee should receive.

When meeting with an employee, the OH professional will discuss issues, make an assessment, write a report, and decide upon appropriate actions such as referrals to counselling, Cognitive Behavioural Therapy (CBT), time off work, adjustments to workhours, reduced workloads, or specific duties. OH recommendations will be communicated to managers to ensure support is put in place.

8.7 Menopause and Perimenopause

Menopause and perimenopause symptoms can have a detrimental impact on everyday life.

Perimenopause is when hormone levels start to change but menstruation is still ongoing. Menopause usually occurs between the ages of 45 and 55. Symptoms typically occur when over 40, but women as young as 20 or 30 can experience symptoms.

The menopause is typically when menstruation has stopped for over a year. Menopause is often referred to as 'the change'.

There are a range of symptoms that impact everyday work–life with some sources reporting

over 30 symptoms, some of which are difficult to determine the cause. Symptoms typically

include:

- Changes in the menstrual cycle
- Hot flushes and / or night sweats
- Headaches or dizziness
- Incontinence
- Weight gain
- Muscular and/or joint aches and pain
- Difficulty sleeping and feeling tired/lacking energy
- Depression, anxiety, and low mood
- Brain 229fog and issues with memory
- Low self-esteem and low self-confidence
- Panic attacks

Symptoms such as anxiety, low mood, and depression can result in difficulties focussing on work. Brain fog and poor concentration can lead to mistakes at work, delayed decision-making, forgetfulness, and feelings of frustration. Mental health can be affected, leading to some women leaving employment altogether.

According to Vankar (2024) as published on Statista.com, suicide rates among females in the United States is highest for those aged 45 to 64 and have increased in the last 20 years. In 2023, the highest suicide rates among women in England and Wales were in women aged 50 to 54 according to the Office of National Statistics (ONS, 2024). These statistics could be linked to symptoms associated with perimenopause and menopause which can have a detrimental impact on everyday life.

Whilst medical professionals can help by providing medications such as Hormone Replacement Therapy (HRT) and offering counselling services, hospitality organisations have a responsibility to support women in the workforce who are experiencing symptoms.

In 2024 the Equality and Human Rights Commission (EHRC) published workplace guidance for England, Scotland, and Wales. As symptoms are of a medical nature and can impact on ability to carry out day-to-day duties, these symptoms are considered as a disability and individuals are protected under equality law and health and safety, placing responsibility on employers to make reasonable adjustments. It is advisable to check legal requirements for the region where the organisation is based.

Many job roles within hospitality, hotels, and events involve working under pressure in customer-facing roles, long hours, working in various climates, and perhaps physical work. An individual experiencing menopausal symptoms may struggle to fulfil their role, leading to mistakes, confidence issues, and low self-esteem. Conflict might occur due to frustrated colleagues and managers not understanding why lower levels of productivity, absenteeism, mistakes, or memory issues are occurring.

This can lead to workplace frustration, conflict, sick days, disciplinaries, and staff retention issues. This is often due to lack of education and awareness as to how perimenopause and the menopause can impact individuals. Human Resources have the responsibility to educate the workforce and put supportive actions in place such as policies guiding managers how to respond to and support women going through 'the change'.

According to monopausefriendly.co.uk (2025), 75 per cent experience symptoms, 70 per cent experience stress, 35 per cent take leave due to symptoms, and 46 per cent do not disclose symptoms due to fear of negative perceptions. They also suggest 14 per cent of staff go part-time and 8 per cent do not apply for promotion as a result, due to loss of confidence and stress-related symptoms.

The Chartered Institute of Personnel and Development (CIPD) (2023) conducted a survey of 2,000 women aged 40 to 60 and found that 67 per cent of women's symptoms impacted them negatively at work, 53 per cent took sick days due to symptoms, 67 per cent felt hybrid and working from home would help in coping with symptoms, 17 per cent are thinking of leaving employment, and a further 6 per cent have left their job because of symptoms.

It is important to recognise that menopause, perimenopause, and menstruation are a health issue, and countries globally are increasingly recognising the impact it has on productivity and staff well-being. Reasonable adjustments will become commonplace as health is protected under equality and health and safety laws.

Due to lack of research and varying symptoms, it is difficult to provide specific support in the workplace, but support which may be offered includes:

- Policy to guide individuals and their managers on the support that is available
- Access to counselling services such as Cognitive Behavioural Therapies (CBT)
- Providing fans or air-conditioning
- Providing regular breaks
- Confidential and open communication with supportive managers
- Additional time to complete tasks
- Adjustments to workload or duties
- Adjustments to working hours or schedule
- Time-off for medical or therapy appointments
- Provision of sanitary products and toilets/restrooms
- Training and development for all to raise awareness and support

Menopause is becoming a more visible issue within the workplace and lawmakers and policy writers globally will inevitably respond to reasonable adjustments and support in the workplace to support employee well-being and to ensure compliance with the law.

8.8 Drug and Alcohol Addiction

The hospitality industry is a social work environment, where alcohol is consumed and, whilst illegal in many countries, drugs are commonplace.

INDUSTRY VOICE

Dr Philip Berners, Associate Professor in Events Management

I always say, 'Managing events is a social job, but the job is not to be social.' The job of organising events is much more than being social, even though the job happens in a social environment.

Events management is a serious job which requires planning, leadership, providing guidance, knowledge, experience, a range of skills, risk management, and communication. Yes, when the event is in full flow, the organiser does need to be social, polite, and friendly – but that is part of the job, not the job itself.

I do not drink alcohol at my events but when my clients want me to sit with them for a drink at some point when everything is flowing, I will clink glasses and take a sip 'to be social' but I never finish the drink. My view is that I am still at work and if something were to happen – an incident or some other issue which can happen through the de-rig until I finally leave the venue – I need to be clear-headed... and professional. That's my job.

Drug and alcohol consumption can lead to accidents, abusive behaviour, violence, antisocial behaviour, and impaired decision-making,

Celebrity chef, Gordon Ramsay discussed the problem with drug abuse in the ITV documentary '*Gordon Ramsay on Cocaine*' when he was asked to sprinkle cocaine on a souffle and had problems with patrons using drugs in restaurant toilets.

Drug and alcohol issues can stem from staff, guests, and clients, and preventive measures must be put in place to prevent illegal use of substances and intoxication.

Hospitality and entertainment venues can lose their trading licence if found not to prevent drug misuse on their premises. Venue design must take into consideration the use of open spaces where CCTV and staff can see dark corners and areas where drug dealing and misuse may take place, alongside security, and tactics such as placing ultraviolet lighting in toilets.

JENNIFER KAYE'S VOICE

When working as a Conference and Events Supervisor in a large hotel, there was white powder residue on toilet seats and cisterns, indicating drug use in the restrooms. My manager asked me to spray *WD40* onto these surfaces (a spray which can displace water, lubricate, and prevent corrosion). Once sprayed, if clients were to return and use those surfaces for drug-taking again it would dissolve the substances.

If employees are erratic, have unexplained absences, changes in behaviour, productivity issues, or are more accident prone, then it may indicate drug or alcohol addiction. This should be treated as misconduct and an investigation should be held by Human Resources.

Certain situations might determine the alcohol or drug abuse as gross misconduct and the contract of employment terminated following formal disciplinary procedures such as warnings and a final warning as detailed within the disciplinary policy.

8.9 Managing Violence, Abuse, Bullying, Harassment, and Victimisation

Workplace violence, aggression, shouting, swearing, sexual misconduct, bullying, harassment, or victimisation and other forms of abuse have a zero-tolerance approach in the workplace. Misconduct such as this should be considered as a formal warning, or gross misconduct depending on severity. Any form of abuse is unacceptable and must be addressed as soon as an issue is raised.

All organisations should have a no bullying and no harassment policy in place, alongside a grievance and disciplinary policy. This provides guidance for employees and managers as to the processes to follow, how to raise a grievance or complaint, and the time frames and processes which will be used to investigate it.

Bullying, harassment, and victimisation may stem from individual differences, conflict, hate crime, racial motives, and other prejudices, and can result in violence, verbal assault, or unwanted sexual behaviour for example, and be detrimental to physical and mental well-being.

8.9.1 Harassment, Bullying, and Victimisation

Sexual Harassment is when a person is subjected to unwanted sexual conduct that violates the individual's dignity and can be degrading, and offensive.

Flirting, sexual remarks or messages, touching and sexual assault, sexual jokes, exposing oneself, sexual images or videos are examples of sexual harassment and may include incidents that occur outside working hours.

Sexual harassment can be prevalent in any industry, but it is not just staff members who can be problematic, customers can also cause issues. Culture, social circles, and alcohol or drug use can escalate situations when customers visit hotels, events, restaurants, bars, and clubs. A bartender or waiting staff may be 'catcalled', verbally abused, or touched inappropriately, or worse. Employers must take proactive steps to prevent the risk of sexual harassment in the workplace and protect the workforce.

Most countries have a requirement for employers to take reasonable steps to prevent sexual harassment and to mitigate legal action and fines; incidents can also impact company reputation.

Bullying, harassment, and victimisation involve behaviour from others that is unwanted and harmful, but there are key differences between them:

> **Bullying** is repeated intentional harm or intimidation, whether physical, verbal, social, or online cyberbullying. Bullying is persistent over time with intention to harm someone. This can include insults, belittling, and false gossip.
>
> **Harassment** involves one-off or continuous verbal, written, or physical behaviour with the intent of causing harm or intimidation to someone because of a protected characteristic such as gender, race, sexual orientation, or religion. This includes sexual remarks, racist language, or physical assault as examples.
>
> **Victimisation** is often a result of the complainant reporting bullying, harassment, or discrimination and involves punishing or retaliating against them for reporting behaviours. This could involve derogatory comments, physical abuse, or damage to property, for example resulting from an employee reporting bullying to Human Resources.

CASE STUDY: BULLYING

Over a course of a year, a new employee was making derogatory remarks and spreading malicious rumours against a co-worker, suggesting they were better at the job, that they were more popular, and that their former employer was begging them to return.

After a few months of the co-worker suffering from panic, stress, and anxiety, Human Resources were informed, and the bullying and harassment policy was sent by email informing them of the process to raise a formal complaint against the individual.

An email detailing dates, times, incidents, and witnesses was sent to Human Resources as requested and a formal investigation took place with witnesses, the victim, and the employee interviewed as part of the process.

Human Resources led the investigation and during meetings a notetaker was present to capture key points so the report could be sent to both parties to check for accuracy. The Union supported the individual during the process to provide guidance and support in place of a supporting colleague or friend.

Human Resources then concluded the investigation, the new employee's probation was extended and eventually they were let go due to the numerous issues.

When an individual reports cases of bullying, harassment, or victimisation the grievance and disciplinary processes will be utilised.

8.10 Grievance and Disciplinary

Contribution from Penelope Lynn Ananiadis-McAravey, Business Owner, HR Consultant and Freelance Writer, HRAddict.com

Every company is entitled to satisfactory conduct and performance from their employees. Unfortunately, from time to time there is a shortfall. It is never good to ignore this, and so warning letters become a necessary intervention.

Once is it established what the essential information is that must be in the warning letter, a letter will be more conducive in serving its purpose.

A poorly written or absent letter may result in negative consequences for either party because the recipient of the initial warning letter failed to respond, for example due to communication errors from the employer.

8.10.1 Benefits of Employee Warning Letters

Employee warning letters are important because nobody wants to dismiss an employee. The employer has invested a substantial amount of time, energy, and resources in them. It is therefore a waste to short-circuit anyone's career, not to mention the disruption and trauma created before, during, and after their departure.

The main benefit of a warning letter is that it affords the greatest opportunity to recover from many potential losses. Here are a few of the other benefits:

It shows good management

Line managers are accountable for discipline and performance in accordance with company rules and standards. In situations of deviations or under-delivery, failing to act can be negligent and can look like a lack of management to the senior levels in the company. Issuing warnings when performance is not adequate, demonstrates commitment to the role.

It creates boundaries

Warnings give substance to company policies, rules, standards, and requirements. In some instances, employees might not take their obligations seriously without these policies and boundaries. Company performance, efficiency, and smooth operation would be at risk.

It demonstrates you care

At the heart of any warning letter is the desire by the employer to correct wrongdoing to benefit the company. This should be made extremely clear when issuing a warning letter. Goodwill will be preserved if giving warnings is approached honestly and with integrity.

It allows connection with employees

Warning letters go beyond being an important contractual record to safeguard the company and management. Warning letters give another opportunity to connect constructively with an employee on important work-related matters.

It demonstrates fairness

Warning letters reinforce how management is concerned with being fair and equal to all. The focus is on taking action to prevent future reoccurrence. The experience is not one of exacting punishment, but presenting an opportunity to learn, grow, and improve.

It establishes authority

Warning letters establish appropriate authority within the company. The role of line management is to set clear expectations on standards of behaviour and holding employees responsible.

8.10.2 What to Include in a Warning Letter

Each warning letter is unique. It should reflect not only the views of the writer, but the company's position on matters of misconduct or performance and incorporate the generally accepted organisational style for such letters.

It is therefore a good idea to review a few different company letter templates before drafting a warning letter.

To optimise the letter, a logical sequential flow is best. It is critical to incorporate the following elements into any employee warning letter:

1. Date the letter is being issued.
2. Employee reference details (such as their name, address, and employee number).
3. Letterheading confirming the letter is in fact a warning letter (final warnings should be noted as such).
4. Precise details of the employee's misconduct or poor performance, including times, dates, the nature of the misconduct or poor performance, the impact on the workplace, and future disciplinary actions that will follow if the misconduct is repeated, or performance does not improve.
5. The investigatory findings on the misconduct or poor performance, justifying the sanction of the warning letter.
6. Any items raised in aggravation or mitigation, such as prior warnings, financial, or other impact of the misconduct on the business. It is important to note that the employee's length of service and clean disciplinary records may be factors to consider.
7. Clarity of future behavioural expectations in terms of standards and requirements or reinforcement of rules to be followed. For poor performance, a Personal Improvement Plan (PIP) is warranted.
8. Duration that the warning will be in place on the employee's record, plus mandatory review periods and information on support that will be given to the employee.
9. Any appeal mechanisms that apply.
10. Signatures of management (and/or Human Resources) and the employee, plus any witnesses. Where an employee refuses to sign a warning letter, a witness is necessary to confirm the warning letter has been thoroughly explained, issued, and was received.

8.10.3 Tips for Writing a Warning Letter

The rule for issuing a warning related to misconduct or poor performance is that employees should never be surprised at the outcome if a turnaround or progress is not achieved. Justice is pivotal.

The objective is to construct an instructional warning letter that strikes the right balance in terms of gravity of the incident and motivation for improvement. Here are some tips to consider when drafting the letter:

1. **Be clear**

   It is important to specify the breach, whether it is a rule or company standard.

   The first paragraph of a warning letter should reference the nature of the misconduct or poor performance. This is done by setting out the findings from the incident investigation. All pertinent facts should be covered. This will vary according to the category of misconduct and the specific findings and circumstances linked to each case being dealt with.

   For example, in the case of an absenteeism matter, the letter will need to provide the number of days the employee was absent, including the dates, as well as what the company did to attempt to contact the employee during their absence.

2. **Substantiate the findings**

   It is essential to state why an employee would have clear knowledge and awareness of rules, standards, and requirements. At the least, they should have reasonable awareness, even at a common-sense level.

   In the case of absenteeism, for example, one might mention that the attendance rules are contained in the employee contract. There may also be other instructive references, such as induction orientation, staff manuals, general communication reminders, and the like. If previous counselling or warnings for a similar offence have been issued/communicated, these should be mentioned.

3. **Reinforce employee obligations**

   A warning letter should be direct in approach and articulate the employee's obligations to the company. Use evidence to highlight the company's previous discussions on the related topic, whether it be absenteeism, misconduct, or something other.

   For example, a letter for absenteeism could incorporate information about the company HR operational manual and when this was last reviewed with the employee.

4. **Highlight the consequences**

   Reinforcing the relevance and importance of a rule or standard within the workplace is helpful. The employee needs to put themselves in the perspective of the employer and reflect how what they have done affects the operational viability of the business and impacts others.

   Employees should appreciate that they have an inherent contractual duty to safeguard the employer's interests. Just as employers have a duty of care towards their employees, employees must strive to contribute to the performance and smooth operation of the business.

   Negative operational impact includes absenteeism, disrupting team activities, lowering productivity, causing customer delays, etc. Warning letters point to aggravating factors, especially if there has been a failure to respond to the company's prior corrective disciplinary efforts.

5. **Be consistent**

   It is important that the application of sanctions for various infringements must be consistently applied across all employees. The company should not dismiss one employee for a first offence of excessive and patterned absenteeism, for example, if the company has been through a progressive disciplinary approach with others.

6. **Be comprehensive**

   Reasons for issuing the warning letter, rather than taking other measures, should be offered. The assessed seriousness of the misconduct and its ramifications should be pointed out. It is important that the employee understands the rationale of the thinking and judgement which has gone into the decision to issue the letter, which provides the opportunity to show the company's mercy, if needed.

7. **Explain the objective**

   Stating the primary objective of issuing the warning letter is crucial and should include information about the disciplinary procedure and process. Explanations will help the employee to appreciate why the warning is an appropriate sanction under the circumstances.

8. **Emphasise what is essential**

   Once the letter has dealt with the misconduct, it needs to focus on the future. This means telling the employee directly what needs to change. What is being stipulated should be reasonable. This could be displayed in a bullet-point list showing what steps to take in future, or more comprehensive if it is a complex issue being addressed.

9. **Insist on employee ownership**

   Whilst management and Human Resources is there to support and encourage employees, it is their job to be compliant with the reasonable contractual demands of the employer. Employees should be reminded to take responsibility for their own actions to benefit the company.

10. **Remind the employee what is at stake**

    It is important to be clear on the immediate consequences of the warning letter. Explain clearly the next steps, and what the consequences are if things do not improve. The letter could also go into the issues the business will face if things do not change, and how this will affect the employee going forward.

8.11 Exit Interviews

Despite putting measures into place to protect the well-being of staff, and to retain them within the organisation, staff with inevitably leave for one reason or another. When an employee decides to leave the organisation, it is important to conduct exit interviews to identify why they are leaving.

This will help determine the effectiveness of recruitment and selection processes, and to determine workplace satisfaction in terms of teams, the role, superiors, training, pay, processes and systems, and other aspects.

Human Resources can then analyse this data to put systems into place to adjust to retain employees in the future to minimise impact on staff, managers, productivity, costs, and reputation.

Exit interviews are another tool for managers and Human Resources to discover the reasons employees decide to exit the organisation. Just as a hotel might conduct a debrief after lunch or dinner service, and an event has after-event evaluation, so an exit interview is a post-employee evaluation. It is a learning tool to understand why that employee has chosen to leave.

It is useful for a larger organisation to benchmark statistics against departments. For instance, if exit interviews reveal a problem in Housekeeping, and fewer employees over the same period have left from Reception, the manager can investigate and correct the situation which is causing employees to leave the firm.

8.12 Best Places to Work in Hospitality

There are several measures an employer can use to improve staff retention, engagement, productivity, and well-being. When staff are valued and investments are made in team members, it leads to positive employee relations, higher customer service, increased sales, increased profitability, positive reputation, and overall business growth.

Recognition can be gained as a good employer from organisations such as *The Times Top 100 Places to Work* and *Caterer Best Places to Work*. This can lead to an increase in applications from talented recruits, too. Hilton was named Number 1 by *Great Place to Work*, and Best Place to Work globally in 2023 by Fortune magazine and has been ranked highly in previous years.

Well-being initiatives help earn hospitality, hotel, and event organisations this title, alongside a strong emphasis of the importance of equality, diversity, and inclusion.

8.13 Equality, Diversity and Inclusivity

Often combined, it can be difficult to differentiate between equality, diversity, and inclusivity.

Equality in the workplace means providing the same – equal – opportunities and that people should be subjected to the same rights and be treated equally regardless of differences. Workplace examples include access to the same training, rewards, or progression as others, or the same salary, for example, for doing the same work regardless of ethnicity or gender.

There are numerous reports that suggest the gender pay gap is still commonplace, recognising that men are generally paid more than women. The causes are perhaps due to cultural differences, women taking time off work for childcare, and bias. Despite gender, individuals must be paid the same rate for the same work.

Diversity recognises individual differences such as gender, ethnicity, age, sexual orientation, disabilities, religion, and culture. Organisations will ask for this information when recruiting to demonstrate non-bias in recruitment and a diverse workplace culture. They may earn recognition and rewards for being an equal opportunities employer for doing so. Diversity ensures employers recognise and value these differences.

Inclusion helps ensure the differences are respected, valued, and supported and can contribute to the workplace. This may mean adjusting the application process such as application forms in braille; adjusting the workload, breaks, or place; providing additional support; flexible work patterns; celebrating religious holidays; or the provision of a prayer room, for example. This helps ensure employees feel respected and valued.

The recruitment process, onboarding process, training, performance management, rewards, progression, policies, and rules must be applicable to all, regardless of background, and changes may need to be made to ensure a fair and equitable workplace.

An employee's health, safety, and welfare must also be assured at work. Lawmakers globally will have health and safety laws to protect workers from physical or mental harm. Therefore, health and safety law, and mental health laws are enforceable in hospitality, hotels, and events by Human Resources and managers.

Bibliography

Vankar, P. (2024). *Female Suicide Rate in the U.S. from 2001 to 2021, by Age Group* Available from: https://www.statista.com/statistics/1114127/female-suicide-rate-in-the-us-by-age-group/

ONS. *Suicides in England and Wales: 2023 Registrations. Available from:* https://www.ons.gov.uk/peoplepopulationandcommunity/birthsdeathsandmarriages/deaths/bulletins/suicidesintheunitedkingdom/2023#:~:text=The%20suicide%20rate%20for%20females,rate%20for%20females%20since%201994/

Menopause Friendly UK. *Menopause at Work. Why It's Important.* Available from: https://menopausefriendly.co.uk/menopause-at-work/

CIPD. *Menopause in the Workplace.* Available from: https://www.cipd.org/uk/knowledge/reports/menopause-workplace-experiences/

Part 2: Creating Trans-Inclusive Workplaces

Zed Karoui and Alexandros Paraskevas

8.14 Introduction

In the contemporary business landscape, fostering an inclusive environment for all employees has become of paramount concern. This chapter, Part 2, focuses on the creation of trans-inclusive workplaces, an area of growing importance as organisations endeavour to embrace diversity in all its forms. The significance of this topic cannot be overstated, as transgender individuals often face unique challenges in professional settings that can significantly impact their well-being, job satisfaction, and career progression.

Diversity and inclusivity in the workplace, particularly concerning transgender employees, are not merely ethical imperatives but important factors in organisational success. A workplace that values and supports its transgender employees creates an environment where all individuals can thrive, contributing their full potential to the organisation.

This inclusivity extends beyond the immediate benefits to transgender individuals; it fosters a culture of respect, empathy, and openness that enhances the work experience for all employees.

Research indicates that 62 per cent of jobseekers would decline an offer from a company that does not prioritise an inclusive and diverse workplace culture. This statistic underscores the critical role that inclusivity plays in attracting top talent.

When employees feel genuinely cared for and can see the same care extended to their peers, they are more likely to remain with the company and recommend it to others, thereby improving retention rates and enhancing the organisation's reputation as an employer of choice.

Highly inclusive organisations achieve 2.3 times more cash flow per employee, 1.4 times more revenue, and are 120 per cent more likely to meet financial targets. Companies with greater diversity are 35 per cent more likely to outperform their competitors, fostering innovation through diverse perspectives and experiences. These statistics demonstrate how inclusivity is not just a matter of social responsibility but a driver of business success.

Companies that mirror the diversity of the world are better positioned to create inclusive products and connect authentically with broader audiences. This includes the LGBTQ+ community and individuals with disabilities. By fostering a trans-inclusive environment, companies can tap into new markets and perspectives, driving innovation and growth.

However, the road to true inclusion is not without obstacles. Approximately 60 per cent of transgender employees face workplace barriers, ranging from discrimination and harassment to lack of inclusive policies and inadequate health support. The impact is significant, with many transgender individuals experiencing higher rates of unemployment and underemployment, with 43 per cent of employers remaining reluctant to hire trans individuals.

This chapter aims to provide a comprehensive guide for organisations seeking to create truly trans-inclusive workplaces. It seeks to raise awareness about the challenges faced by transgender employees, offer actionable guidance for implementing inclusive practices, and emphasise the importance of supportive policies and workplace culture. By addressing these goals, this chapter equips organisations with the knowledge and tools necessary to create workplaces that are not only compliant with legal requirements but are genuinely inclusive and supportive of transgender employees. In doing so, organisations can harness the full potential of their diverse workforce, drive innovation, and contribute to a more equitable and inclusive society.

8.15 Understanding Transgender Issues in the Workplace

Transgender issues in the workplace require a clear understanding of key terms and concepts. The term 'transgender' refers to individuals whose gender identity differs from the sex they were assigned at birth. For instance, a transgender man is someone who was assigned female at birth but identifies and lives as a man.

It is crucial to note that being transgender is about gender identity, not sexual orientation.

Non-binary individuals are those whose gender identity does not fit within the traditional male–female binary, and they may identify as neither male nor female, as both, or as fluid between genders.

Gender identity refers to a person's deeply held sense of being male, female, a blend of both, or neither. This internal sense may or may not align with the sex assigned at birth.

Gender expression, on the other hand, relates to how individuals outwardly express their gender through behaviour, clothing, hairstyle, voice, or body characteristics. It is important to recognise that gender expression does not always directly correspond to gender identity.

For example, a transgender woman may express her gender through feminine clothing and hairstyles, while a non-binary person might choose an androgynous appearance that combines traditionally masculine and feminine elements.

Other relevant terms include cisgender, which describes individuals whose gender identity aligns with their sex assigned at birth; genderqueer, a non-binary identity that rejects or combines traditional concepts of male and female; and genderfluid, referring to individuals whose gender identity may change over time or depending on the situation.

Transgender employees often face significant challenges in the workplace. Discrimination and harassment are the most common experiences, ranging from overt hostility to more subtle forms of exclusion.

Misgendering, the act of referring to someone using a word, especially a pronoun or form of address, which does not correctly reflect their gender identity, can be particularly distressing. This can occur intentionally or accidentally, but is equally harmful. They also frequently experience bullying, which may include exclusion from team activities, public humiliation, or repeated microaggressions that undermine their sense of belonging.

Due to these ongoing concerns, 43 per cent of transgender individuals feel discouraged from seeking employment altogether, fearing the stigma attached to their gender identity. This stigma can lead to significant emotional and psychological strain, often compelling trans employees to hide their identity, which further limits their professional engagement and sense of belonging. This reluctance to come out can limit their professional engagement, as they may feel unable to participate fully in workplace activities or express themselves authentically. Many workplaces lack inclusive policies, such as gender-neutral dress codes or bathroom access that aligns with an individual's gender identity.

Many transgender employees face significant challenges in the workplace, including discrimination, harassment, and microaggressions. Due to these ongoing concerns, 43 per cent of transgender individuals feel discouraged from seeking employment altogether, fearing the stigma attached to their gender identity. This stigma can lead to a significant emotional and psychological strain, often compelling trans employees to hide their identity, which further limits their professional engagement and sense of belonging.

Transgender individuals often face systemic barriers in securing equitable employment opportunities. Research indicates that transgender employees often experience wage disparities, underemployment, and limited opportunities for advancement, which contribute to financial insecurity and hinder their career progression. They also have limited access to health benefits that cover gender-affirming treatments, and they report significant gaps in mental health support, with many healthcare plans lacking coverage for services sensitive to their unique needs. The absence of adequate mental health resources contributes to higher stress levels and can adversely impact productivity and overall well-being.

In the United Kingdom, several legal protections exist for transgender individuals in the workplace, although gaps remain. The Equality Act (2010) provides comprehensive protection against discrimination based on several protected characteristics, including gender reassignment. This means that transgender employees are legally protected from discrimination, harassment, and victimisation in the workplace. The Act covers various aspects of employment, including recruitment, employment terms, promotion, training, and dismissal.

The Gender Recognition Act (2004) allows transgender people to legally change their gender by applying for a Gender Recognition Certificate (GRC). However, the process has been criticised as intrusive and overly medicalised, requiring a medical diagnosis of gender dysphoria and evidence of living in the affirmed gender for two years. In 2018, the UK government launched a public consultation to explore reforms, but the September 2020 outcome made only minor adjustments, such as moving the process online and reducing the application fee from £140 to £5. The law remains binary (male/female) and does not recognise non-binary identities.

As part of the European Convention on Human Rights, UK employees can appeal to the European Court of Human Rights (ECHR) if their rights are violated. Although the UK is no longer in the EU, it remains part of the ECHR, which continues to offer protection against workplace discrimination.

Despite these protections, significant gaps remain. The narrow scope of 'gender reassignment' in the Equality Act (2010) may not adequately cover non-binary and gender-fluid individuals. There are also challenges in practical implementation, with inconsistent enforcement and lack of understanding within organisations. Workplace culture and unconscious bias continue to pose barriers, and fear of retaliation can prevent transgender employees from reporting discrimination or harassment.

8.16 Benefits of a Trans-Inclusive Workplace

Creating a trans-inclusive workplace offers significant benefits for both employees and organisations. These advantages extend beyond the immediate impact on transgender individuals, positively influencing overall workplace culture, productivity, and organisational success.

A supportive and inclusive environment substantially improves the wel=lbeing and engagement of transgender employees. When individuals feel accepted and valued for who they are, it reduces the chronic stress associated with hiding one's identity or facing discrimination. This reduction in stress leads to better mental health outcomes, increased job satisfaction, and higher levels of engagement.

A study by the Human Rights Campaign found that 46 per cent of LGBTQ+ workers remain closeted at work. In trans-inclusive workplaces, this percentage drops dramatically, allowing employees to be their authentic selves. This authenticity correlates with decreased anxiety and depression, leading to improved productivity and job performance.

Moreover, when transgender employees feel supported, they are more likely to remain with the company long term. This increased retention reduces the costs associated with frequent hiring and training and helps maintain institutional knowledge within the organisation.

The positive impact on employee well-being extends beyond transgender individuals, creating a ripple effect that enhances the overall work environment for all employees.

A culture of inclusion can also significantly reduce absenteeism. When employees feel valued and supported, they are less likely to take unnecessary time off work. This reduction in absenteeism not only improves productivity, but indicates a happier, more engaged workforce. The positive atmosphere created by an inclusive culture can also lead to improved employee morale, which in turn can boost overall job satisfaction and commitment to the organisation. Higher levels of engagement are directly linked to increased productivity, as engaged employees are more likely to be motivated, proactive, and invested in their role.

The benefits of a trans-inclusive workplace extend to long-term business growth. Companies that embrace diversity and create trans-friendly workplaces are often seen as forward-thinking and innovative. This reputation not only attracts top talent but enhances the company's standing as a leader in innovation. Employees take pride in working for companies known for their inclusive values, which can drive higher levels of innovation as employees feel more connected to the company's mission and goals.

Trans-inclusive policies significantly enhance a company's reputation, attracting diverse talent and building consumer loyalty. In today's competitive job market, companies with a reputation for inclusivity are more likely to attract and retain top talent. Younger generations place high value on diversity and social responsibility when choosing employers.

This enhanced reputation extends beyond recruitment. Companies known for their trans-inclusive practices often enjoy improved relationships with clients, partners, and the broader community. A study by Deloitte found that 57 per cent of consumers are more loyal to brands that commit to addressing social inequities in their actions.

Furthermore, trans-inclusive companies are better positioned to connect authentically with broader audiences, including LGBTQ+ communities and individuals with disabilities. This broader market reach can lead to increased business opportunities and revenue growth.

In the business-to-business context, many organisations, particularly those with strong corporate social responsibility (CSR) programmes, prefer to work with companies that reflect their own commitment to inclusivity. This can open doors to new partnerships and enhance existing relationships, leading to greater business opportunities. Trans-inclusive policies can thus become an asset in business negotiations and partnerships.

The reputation benefits of trans-inclusion also extend to investor relations. Many investors are increasingly interested in environmental, social, and governance (ESG) factors when making investment decisions. Companies with strong diversity and inclusion policies are often seen as lower-risk and more sustainable investments.

8.17 Creating Trans-Inclusive Workplaces: Core Strategies for Hospitality, Events, and Hotel Managers

Transgender inclusion in the hospitality, events, and hotel industries can be enhanced through various policies and practices that address the unique needs of transgender employees.

This involves developing comprehensive policies, providing accessible healthcare benefits, offering transition support, and fostering a culture of inclusivity.

8.17.1 Developing Inclusive Policies

A foundational aspect of a trans-inclusive workplace is the development of inclusive policies that explicitly support transgender employees.

Recruitment and hiring processes often present the first opportunity for organisations to demonstrate their commitment to trans-inclusion. These practices must be carefully designed to eliminate barriers and biases that transgender candidates might face during the application and interview process.

Organisations should review their entire recruitment pipeline, from job advertisements to onboarding procedures, ensuring that each step promotes inclusivity and respect for gender diversity.

For example, a hotel group can change its application process by redesigning its forms to allow candidates to indicate their gender identity beyond the traditional male/female binary. The company may also scrutinise its job postings to eliminate gendered language and actively promote opportunities through LGBTQ+ job boards to attract diverse candidates, including transgender applicants.

Anti-discrimination and harassment policies should specifically prohibit discrimination based on gender identity and expression, ensuring a zero-tolerance approach to harassment, misgendering, and deadnaming. Such policies must be clearly communicated to all employees and embedded into the organisation's code of conduct.

This approach could be taken by a leading conference centre that hosts major events, which could implement a comprehensive non-discrimination policy explicitly including gender identity and expression. This policy would ensure that transgender guests and employees are protected against bias or harassment during their stay or participation.

Similarly, a hotel chain could take this further by implementing a policy in which employees are encouraged to wear nametags that include their preferred name and pronouns (e.g. 'Sian (They/Them)'). The hotel's HR system would support this initiative by allowing transgender employees to use their chosen name and pronouns, regardless of their legal documents.

Traditional dress codes should be replaced with gender-neutral uniforms, allowing employees to dress in alignment with their gender identity.

Inclusive language policies are also crucial, promoting the use of correct pronouns and respectful language across all levels of the organisation.

With such policies, companies send a clear message that transgender employees are valued members of the workplace community, and that inclusivity is a core organisational value.

This could be implemented by restaurants, hotels, and venues through providing gender-neutral uniforms for all staff. Rather than maintaining separate uniforms for 'male' and 'female' staff, employees could choose attire that aligns with their gender identity. Such an approach would allow all employees to select uniforms that best suit them, reinforcing the organisation's commitment to inclusivity and respect for gender identity.

8.17.2 Providing Comprehensive Healthcare Benefits

Many transgender employees face significant challenges in accessing healthcare, particularly gender-affirming treatments. To address these needs, hospitality companies should offer health insurance plans that cover a range of gender-affirming services, including hormone replacement therapy, surgeries, and mental health support. Gender-affirming healthcare benefits are another critical component of trans-inclusive workplaces.

These policies should extend beyond traditional family definitions, allowing transgender employees to take leave for chosen family members and partners. The expansion of healthcare benefits and the coverage for gender-specific needs, demonstrates a commitment to the well-being of transgender employees and a positive contribution to their physical and mental health.

Hospitality organisations could offer comprehensive healthcare coverage plans within their employee benefits packages. Such provisions would ensure transgender employees are able to access necessary care without financial strain. These healthcare benefits would serve as a powerful marketing tool to attract the transgender community and encourage greater workforce participation. Through such initiatives, organisations would be able to position themselves as employers of choice for transgender individuals.

8.17.3 Transition Support and Resources

Transitioning employees often require additional resources, including confidentiality measures and personalised transition plans. Management should work with transitioning employees to develop a transition plan that outlines the desired timeline, communication preferences, and any required workplace adjustments. Confidentiality is essential throughout this process, as employees may wish to control the information shared with colleagues.

Flexible scheduling can also be beneficial, allowing employees to attend medical appointments or take time off as needed.

Counselling services tailored to the needs of transgender employees provide further support, helping individuals navigate the emotional and logistical challenges associated with transitioning. Through these resources, organisations offer a respectful and supportive environment that accommodates the unique needs of transitioning employees.

Hotels could implement HR policies that support transgender employees during their workplace transition, offering transition-related health coverage, and establishing support networks within the company. Such resources, when highlighted in recruitment efforts, would demonstrate a commitment to supporting transgender employees whilst strengthening the organisation's reputation for diversity, making it a more appealing workplace for candidates seeking an inclusive and supportive environment.

8.17.4 Fostering an Inclusive Culture

An inclusive culture is key to ensuring that trans-inclusive policies are not merely symbolic but are actively practised and respected throughout the organisation.

Mandatory training programmes on gender identity and inclusive practices should be implemented for all employees. These training sessions should cover topics such as respectful dialogue, pronoun usage, and allyship, equipping employees with the skills to support their transgender colleagues. Allyship is particularly important, as it encourages cisgender employees to advocate for transgender inclusivity, speak up against discrimination, and challenge biases when they occur.

The use of pronouns in email signatures, name badges, and during introductions should be normalised, creating an environment where correct pronoun usage is a fundamental aspect of everyday interaction. Such practices build a culture of respect and understanding, empowering all employees to contribute to a welcoming and inclusive workplace.

Leading event planners and hotel management organisations could establish regular training programmes for their staff on gender inclusivity. Such programmes would cover essential topics including the correct use of gender-neutral language, appropriate ways to address guests by their preferred names and pronouns, and the fundamental importance of non-discriminatory service. This comprehensive training would ensure all staff members are equipped to create and maintain an inclusive environment for both guests and colleagues.

8.17.5 Building an Inclusive Environment and Infrastructure

A workplace that genuinely supports transgender employees involves also building an environment and infrastructure that reflects inclusive values. Establishing gender-neutral facilities, fostering a supportive workplace culture, and promoting equal career advancement opportunities are essential strategies for creating an environment where transgender employees feel respected, safe, and encouraged to grow within the organisation.

8.17.6 Gender-neutral Facilities

Providing gender-neutral facilities is a fundamental aspect of building an inclusive workplace.

Transgender employees often face discomfort or discrimination when using gender-specific spaces, which can lead to feelings of exclusion and anxiety.

To address this, organisations should offer gender-neutral bathrooms, locker rooms, and other facilities that allow employees to use the spaces that align with their identity. These facilities should be as accessible and convenient as gendered options, and clearly marked with inclusive signage to signal that all employees are welcome.

These facilities should be as convenient and accessible as gendered options, not hidden in hard-to-reach areas of the building. Policies should allow transgender employees to use facilities that align with their gender identity, while providing private options for those who prefer them.

Hotel chains may demonstrate this commitment by ensuring all properties offer gender-neutral restrooms, particularly in common areas such as lobbies, meeting spaces, and restaurants. Such thoughtful facility planning ensures transgender guests and employees are not compelled to choose between male or female restrooms, thereby creating a more comfortable and secure environment for all users.

Signage and visual inclusivity play a significant role in creating a welcoming environment. Inclusive language and symbols throughout the workplace should be used, avoiding stereotypical gender icons.

For example, instead of using male and female figures to denote bathrooms, organisations might use icons that represent the facilities themselves, such as a toilet or basin icon. This approach not only supports transgender employees but benefits non-binary individuals and anyone who prefers more privacy.

When designing or renovating office spaces, organisations should consider creating more open and flexible environments that do not reinforce gender stereotypes. This might involve moving from traditionally gendered colour schemes or décor and opting for more neutral designs that are welcoming to all employees. Including visible symbols of inclusion, such as posters, signs, or flags that communicate trans-inclusivity can further enhance the workplace atmosphere.

For hotel companies with onsite staff accommodation, it is important to consider gender-neutral options for sleeping quarters. This ensures all employees, regardless of their gender identity, have comfortable and appropriate accommodation options during work-related travel or stays.

Wellness rooms and other shared spaces should be designed with inclusivity in mind. These areas should be accessible to all employees and designed in a way that does not assume or reinforce traditional gender roles or stereotypes.

Regular audits of workplace infrastructure will help ensure the physical environment continues to meet the needs of all employees, including transgender individuals. These audits should consider not only the existence of gender-neutral options but their accessibility, signage, and overall inclusivity.

8.17.7 Sustaining Workplace Inclusivity

Beyond physical facilities, workplace inclusivity encompasses the ways in which employees interact, collaborate, and support one another daily.

One effective way to cultivate this culture is through the establishment of Employee Resource Groups (ERGs) that specifically focus on LGBTQ+ issues. These groups provide transgender employees and allies with a dedicated space for community, peer support, and advocacy. ERGs allow employees to connect with colleagues who share similar experiences, discuss challenges, and work together to promote a more inclusive workplace. They also often collaborate with leadership and HR to suggest improvements, educate colleagues, and advocate for policies that support transgender and LGBTQ+ inclusion. When these groups are given a platform, they provide management with valuable perspectives that help shape a more informed and empathetic workplace inclusivity.

Several pioneering hotel groups have established ERGs comprised of transgender employees and their allies. Through these networks, these groups can provide vital support systems, coordinate awareness-raising events, and create safe spaces for meaningful dialogue about LGBTQ+ workplace matters. These ERGs demonstrate how structured support networks serve as cornerstones for building genuine workplace inclusion.

Celebrating LGBTQ+ events, such as Pride Month and Transgender Day of Visibility, is another significant way to reinforce inclusivity within the workplace.

Recognising these events not only demonstrates the organisation's commitment to inclusivity but offers educational opportunities for all employees to learn about transgender experiences and LGBTQ+ issues. Events like these can include workshops, panel discussions, or guest speakers, which help to raise awareness, debunk stereotypes, and foster understanding among colleagues.

This visible support sends a message to employees and external stakeholders, signalling that the organisation values diversity and is actively working towards a more inclusive culture. When organisations incorporate these celebrations into the annual calendar, they make inclusivity a recurring and integral part of the workplace experience.

Whether it is a hotel group, restaurant chain, or events venue, observing Transgender Day of Visibility is crucial to celebrate trans and non-binary individuals while raising awareness of the discrimination they face worldwide. This day shines a light on a population that is often ignored, marginalised, or victimised, providing an opportunity for trans and non-binary people to feel acknowledged through positive and realistic representation. Furthermore, Visibility Day offers allies a chance to learn how they can stand in solidarity with those who exist outside societal norms and often feel isolated.

Allyship also plays a key role in building an inclusive workplace culture. All employees, especially cisgender colleagues, should be actively encouraged to become allies by advocating for transgender rights, challenging biases, and supporting transgender coworkers. This can be achieved through allyship training, which equips employees with practical strategies for recognising and addressing microaggressions, responding to discrimination, and promoting respectful interactions. Encouraging employees to include their pronouns in email signatures, wear visible allyship symbols, or participate in LGBTQ+ discussions are practical ways to signal support and normalise inclusive practices. Furthermore, allyship enables employees to take an active role in creating a supportive work environment, empowers them to speak-out against discriminatory behaviours and fosters a culture of respect and solidarity.

8.17.8 Career Development and Leadership Pathways

Inclusive recruitment practices are essential for ensuring transgender employees have equitable access to career opportunities. Recruitment policies and practices should be reviewed to identify and eliminate any potential biases that may disadvantage transgender applicants. This might include using gender-neutral language in job descriptions, offering diversity training for hiring managers, and promoting the organisation's commitment to inclusivity during the recruitment process. Moreover, management can collaborate with LGBTQ+ advocacy groups and job boards that specialise in connecting diverse talent with inclusive employers. If inclusivity is prioritised from the initial stages of recruitment, organisations can attract a diverse workforce and signal their commitment to supporting transgender employees from the outset.

Transgender employees often face barriers to advancement due to discrimination, biases, or lack of support within traditional leadership structures. These challenges can prevent transgender individuals from accessing the same career development opportunities as their cisgender peers, limiting their potential for growth and professional success.

Robust mentorship programmes that connect transgender employees with experienced and supportive mentors can effectively counteract these obstacles. Mentors can offer guidance on overcoming workplace challenges, developing career goals, and building networks within the organisation. Such programmes foster a sense of belonging and support and empower transgender employees to pursue their professional aspirations with confidence.

Leadership training is another critical component of creating career development pathways that are accessible to transgender employees.

Future leaders should receive comprehensive training that integrates inclusivity and diversity as core themes. This training should include practical skills for supporting transgender employees, such as recognising and addressing microaggressions, facilitating respectful communication, and promoting a culture of allyship.

Leaders who are well-versed in inclusivity practices are better equipped to champion transgender employees, advocate for their advancement, and implement policies that remove barriers to growth.

With strong inclusive leadership, organisations can create a positive ripple effect throughout the workplace, normalising diversity and promoting an environment where all employees feel empowered to reach their potential.

Finally, the design of clear pathways to leadership for transgender employees, such as targeted leadership development programmes or sponsorship initiatives can provide them with additional support as they move into higher-level roles, help them build essential skills, expand their professional networks, and gain visibility within the organisation.

Hotel chains may develop targeted mentorship programmes specifically designed for LGBTQ+ employees, including transgender staff members. These structured initiatives can pair experienced mentors with employees to provide comprehensive career guidance, assist in navigating workplace challenges, and actively advocate for their professional advancement. Such programmes demonstrate how dedicated mentorship can foster both individual growth and organisational development.

8.18 Addressing Misconduct and Implementing Reporting Mechanisms

Clear policies must be in place that enforce a zero-tolerance approach to discrimination, provide accessible reporting channels, and empower employees through bystander intervention training. These steps are essential for maintaining an environment where all employees feel safe and supported, regardless of gender identity.

8.18.1 Zero Tolerance for Discrimination

As discussed earlier in this chapter, organisations should explicitly prohibit all forms of discrimination, including harassment, misgendering, and microaggressions, in their anti-discrimination policies.

These policies must be clearly communicated and accessible to all employees, leaving no ambiguity about the organisation's stance on unacceptable behaviours.

Clear expectations for respectful interactions can be set by defining and detailing behaviours such as misgendering and deadnaming.

More importantly, a zero-tolerance policy must be backed with prompt and decisive action. When incidents are reported, management should follow a structured investigation procedure to ensure all cases are handled consistently and thoroughly. The consequences for violating these policies should be well documented and visible, reinforcing the message that discrimination of any kind will not be tolerated.

8.18.2 Accessible Reporting Channels

Multiple reporting avenues should be available to safely report incidents of misconduct. These can include dedicated phone lines, online reporting platforms, and designated HR contacts who are specifically trained to handle sensitive issues related to gender identity.

Offering anonymous reporting options is particularly important for transgender employees, who may feel vulnerable or hesitant to report incidents openly due to fear of retaliation. Anonymous reporting provides a safer way for employees to voice concerns and can encourage more individuals to come forward with experiences of discrimination.

Once a report is submitted, follow-up is essential to ensure the issue is adequately addressed and that employees trust the process. The organisation should maintain transparency regarding how reports are investigated, while respecting confidentiality to protect all parties involved. Regular communication about the existence and accessibility of these reporting channels helps build trust and assures employees their concerns will be taken seriously.

8.18.3 Bystander Intervention

A bystander intervention training programme will equip all employees with the skills needed to recognise and respond to discrimination effectively.

Such training empowers employees to act when they witness harassment or microaggressions against their transgender colleagues. It can include practical exercises, such as role-playing scenarios, to help employees build confidence in addressing problematic behaviour in a way that is safe and constructive. It should emphasise the importance of allyship and the role each employee plays in upholding an inclusive culture. This training also serves as a proactive measure, reducing the likelihood of discriminatory behaviours by making it clear that such actions will not go unchallenged.

Regular analysis into the outcomes of investigations can reveal patterns or systemic issues within the organisation. This analysis can inform targeted interventions, such as additional training or updates to policies, to address recurring issues. Anonymised data on the number of incidents, the types of misconduct reported, and the actions taken can be shared with employees to demonstrate the organisation's commitment to addressing transphobic behaviour. Transparency in sharing these insights helps build a culture of accountability and demonstrates the organisation is actively working to prevent discrimination.

8.19 External Engagement and Community Support

Engaging with external stakeholders is a vital component of fostering a truly trans-inclusive workplace. This engagement extends the commitment to inclusivity beyond the organisation's walls, creating a broader impact to inform and reinforce the company's dedication to transgender rights and equality.

Partnerships with transgender advocacy organisations offer invaluable insights into best practices and current challenges faced by the transgender community. These collaborations can inform policy development, highlight areas for improvement, and ensure the approach to trans-inclusion remains relevant and effective. Joint initiatives such as training programmes, awareness campaigns, or community outreach events not only benefit from expert knowledge but demonstrate genuine commitment to supporting the transgender community beyond the workplace.

Trade unions play a significant role in shaping workplace policies and practices. Collaborating closely with unions to advocate for transgender rights and protections within collective bargaining agreements ensures transgender employees are supported across all levels of the organisation. This partnership can involve educating union representatives about transgender issues, including them in the development of trans-inclusive policies, and creating a united front in promoting trans-inclusion.

Diversifying the supply chain to include transgender-owned businesses is an effective way to extend support to the broader transgender community. This approach not only supports the economic empowerment of transgender individuals but brings fresh perspectives and innovations to business relationships. Setting targets for procurement from diverse suppliers and partnering with certification bodies that identify transgender-owned businesses can facilitate this process.

Corporate Social Responsibility (CSR) initiatives provide another avenue for engaging with external stakeholders on trans-inclusion. Incorporating support for transgender rights and advocacy as part of CSR strategies can involve providing financial support to transgender-focused charities, offering pro bono services to transgender advocacy groups, or sponsoring events that promote transgender visibility and rights.

Recognition from external bodies can significantly boost a company's reputation for inclusivity. Participating in and achieving high rankings in diversity indices and corporate equality ratings, such as the Human Rights Campaign's Corporate Equality Index, serves as a public endorsement of the company's commitment to LGBTQ+ rights. These accolades not only validate internal efforts but attract socially conscious consumers and investors.

Engagement with industry bodies and professional associations is crucial for promoting trans-inclusion at a sector-wide level. Taking a leadership role by advocating for trans-inclusive practices within specific industries, sharing best practices, and encouraging the development of industry-wide standards for trans-inclusion can have a far-reaching impact. This might involve participating in or initiating working groups focused on diversity and inclusion, contributing to industry publications on the topic, or speaking at industry events about the journey towards trans-inclusion.

Educational institutions represent key partners in building a pipeline of diverse talent. Collaborations could involve offering internships or mentoring programmes specifically for transgender students, sponsoring LGBTQ+ student groups, or participating in career fairs that focus on diversity and inclusion. These partnerships not only support transgender students but position the organisation as an employer of choice for diverse talent.

Building strong community relationships extends beyond formal partnerships. Companies can strengthen their connections with local communities by actively supporting LGBTQ+ causes and initiatives. This approach fosters goodwill and brand loyalty within the community while making a tangible difference in people's lives. Partnerships with local nonprofits and community organisations can further enhance the company's social impact, providing additional resources for transgender employees and the broader LGBTQ+ community.

Media engagement serves as a powerful tool for promoting trans-inclusion and shaping public perception. Utilising organisational platforms to raise awareness about transgender issues, share success stories of trans-inclusion in the workplace, and challenge negative stereotypes can contribute to broader societal change. This might involve proactive media outreach, thoughtful leadership articles, or social media campaigns that highlight the commitment to trans-inclusion.

Participation in policy development at local, national, or international levels is a crucial aspect of external engagement. This can involve contributing to public consultations on transgender rights, providing evidence to parliamentary committees, or actively lobbying for more inclusive legislation. Engagement in policy discussions can help companies shape a more inclusive legal and regulatory environment for transgender individuals. This advocacy role extends beyond mere participation and positions the company as a leader in social progress which can influence broader societal attitudes towards transgender inclusion.

All external engagement activities should be undertaken with sensitivity and in consultation with transgender employees and advocacy groups. Amplifying transgender voices rather than speaking over them, and always respecting the privacy and wishes of transgender employees when engaging in public-facing activities, ensures authentic and respectful engagement.

8.20 Measuring Success and Continuous Adaptation

Creating a trans-inclusive workplace is an ongoing commitment that requires consistent evaluation, adaptation, and improvement. Organisations can assess the effectiveness of their inclusivity initiatives and ensure they remain responsive to evolving needs with active feedback, regular policy reviews, and tracking of key metrics.

8.20.1 Gathering Feedback

Organisations should implement multiple feedback channels, such as anonymous surveys, focus groups, and one-to-one discussions, particularly with transgender employees. These methods provide a safe space for employees to share their experiences and perceptions of the workplace environment.

Regular surveys can assess overall employee satisfaction, while targeted feedback from transgender employees offers insights into specific challenges they may face and the effectiveness of current policies and support mechanisms.

Employee Resource Groups (ERGs), especially those focused on LGBTQ+ issues, can also play a central role in gathering feedback. They can act as intermediaries, communicating the concerns and suggestions of transgender employees to management, which helps bridge gaps between the workforce and decision-makers.

This ongoing dialogue ensures inclusivity efforts are grounded in the real experiences of employees, fostering a culture of continuous improvement.

8.20.2 Policy Review and Updates

As societal understanding of gender identity evolves, and as legal frameworks change, organisations must be proactive in adapting their policies. This process should involve consulting legal experts on LGBTQ+ rights and employment law, as well as seeking input from transgender employees and advocacy groups.

Policy reviews should extend beyond legal compliance, focusing on whether existing policies effectively support a truly inclusive culture. For example, staying informed on evolving terminology and best practices can guide adjustments to policies on pronoun usage, restroom access, and healthcare benefits. Periodic updates to inclusivity training content help ensure all employees are aware of current expectations and equipped to contribute to a supportive environment.

Regular policy evaluations demonstrate an organisation's flexibility and responsiveness to new developments, which is essential for fostering an environment that respects and supports transgender employees.

8.20.3 Tracking of Key Metrics

Metrics such as employee retention rates, satisfaction scores, and results from inclusivity surveys provide quantitative data on how well the organisation is supporting transgender employees.

For example, tracking retention rates specifically for transgender employees can reveal trends that may indicate either a supportive culture or areas needing improvement. Inclusivity surveys that assess employee perceptions of the workplace environment, including experiences with discrimination or support, can highlight potential gaps in policies or practices.

Monitoring of reports related to incidents of discrimination and how they are resolved can indicate the effectiveness of reporting mechanisms and disciplinary processes. When these metrics are analysed, organisations can identify patterns that may warrant additional training or adjustments to policies to ensure inclusivity efforts remain impactful and responsive to employee needs. More importantly, the combination of quantitative data with qualitative feedback provides a comprehensive perspective of the workplace environment and allows for a balanced approach to continuous improvement.

8.20.4 Continuous Adaptation

Beyond internal evaluations, organisations should engage in ongoing consultations with external experts and advocacy groups to stay informed on emerging best practices in transgender inclusion. This external input can provide fresh perspectives and ensure internal practices align with broader trends and advances in inclusivity.

Commitment from the leadership is paramount for sustaining this process. Senior leaders should model a commitment to ongoing learning, which may involve participating in advanced training, attending LGBTQ+ conferences, or advocating for transgender rights in public forums.

By integrating inclusivity metrics into performance evaluations for managers and executives, organisations reinforce that supporting a trans-inclusive environment is a shared responsibility across all levels of leadership. This approach promotes accountability but at the same time establishes inclusivity as an organisational priority.

8.21 Final Thoughts

This chapter has highlighted the complex nature of developing a trans-inclusive workplace, encompassing clear policies, supportive infrastructure, comprehensive training, and a genuine shift in workplace culture. Such a journey requires the firm commitment of every individual within the organisation, from senior leadership to new hires.

The benefits of fostering a trans-inclusive workplace are far-reaching. For transgender employees, it cultivates a sense of belonging, reduces stress and anxiety, and promotes better mental health and job satisfaction. For the organisation, it fosters a more positive and supportive work environment, boosts innovation and creativity, and enhances its reputation as a leader in diversity and inclusion.

Every organisation, regardless of size or industry, should take concrete steps towards this goal.

This begins with updating policies to ensure they explicitly prohibit discrimination based on gender identity and expression. These policies should include provisions for gender-affirming healthcare, inclusive restrooms and changing facilities, and flexible leave for transitioning employees. Mandatory training for all employees on gender identity, inclusive language, and allyship should become essential elements of in-house continual professional development. It is also important to foster allyship by encouraging all employees to be active allies to their transgender colleagues and create a culture where everyone feels empowered to speak-up against discrimination.

This is an ongoing journey that requires continuous learning, adaptation, and a genuine commitment to building a workplace where gender diversity is not just accepted but celebrated. With these principles, organisations respond to the needs of today and position themselves as adaptable and progressive entities ready to thrive in an increasingly diverse world. In doing so, they create spaces where every individual, regardless of their gender identity, feels safe, respected, and empowered to contribute their best.

Chapter 9

Global Human Resources and Managing International Teams

Sarah Powell

9.0 Introduction

This chapter explores practical examples and guidance on managing people of different nationalities in one location, as well as when Human Resources crosses borders and manages in a global context.

9.1 Managing in a Global Role

It is important to realise there is no one-size-fits-all when it comes to managing people. Whether it is in one venue, one country, or in a multinational organisation, there are many ways to motivate, engage, and manage teams.

Spend time with the team individually where possible, and in many cases stand back and observe. Do not be quick to judge their understanding, their self-presentation, their communication with their teams, and seek to understand individuals before becoming involved.

DOI: 10.4324/9781003469803-10

It can be considered extremely disrespectful to impose your ways of working and 'rules' without understanding the needs and motivations of others and it can be damaging to the reputation of Human Resources, the manager, and the business. Human Resources do not act without knowing the full implications and consequences of their actions on the workforce and this is amplified when working with global teams who hold different values and ways of working.

It can often be the case that Human Resources or a manager assumes they know everything about the people in their organisation, which may not be the reality. A manager should attempt to get to know their global team, to understand cultural and personal differences. It will help guide and steer those who work within the business and improve working relationships with teams all around the world if global differences are understood.

9.2 Cultural Lens

When managing people, bias – conscious and unconscious – comes to the forefront, as the way the world is experienced affects how we outwardly view and manage others. This lens through which the world is viewed, can be useful, but when working across countries it is essential to change and flex the shape of view as needed.

In certain cases, a shift is required as nationalities, countries, and cultures vary and at times feel alien compared to the way we 'usually' work. In many cases, it is believed that speaking the same language means the same way of managing, but this is not the case. The same language does not equal the same ways of working, motivations, or sense of belonging in the workforce.

9.3 Know the Team and Building Working Relationships

Human Resources plays a vital role in the culture of an organisation through its people. If a Human Resources professional takes the time to get to know and understand their workforce and their underlying and fundamental beliefs and values, there will not be a mismatch. In many cases this is crucial for the success of the business.

When time is spent observing, without judgement, it is time to seek understanding. There are many ways to get to know the teams, and when meeting face-to-face there are many steps which can be taken to ensure meetings are successful. These steps are outlined here:

Research prior: there are many books, online articles, etc. available regarding the specifics of the culture of many countries and managing different cultures in general. These can be used as a starting point for that initial meeting to start in the right way from the beginning.

AUTHOR'S VOICE

I have found many forums, websites, and online newsletters that you can subscribe to (often from the local government or tourist websites) that you can use for the countries where your teams are based. You don't want to overload yourself or also have biased or incorrect information and so the sources should be carefully chosen.

A weekly update email, though, can go a long way to keep up to date with developments abroad and how these could be affecting the teams.

Building strong working relationships cannot be the philosophy of out of sight out of mind and therefore information is key to knowing what is happening but more importantly how it is impacting the teams and what to do to support them. This can often be a message, a check-in, or a call if needed to let the teams know you are still there and available and that you care even from thousands of miles away.

Ask questions: do not be afraid to ask questions to aid and develop an understanding from others who work with global teams, but also from the global teams themselves. Being curious and asking about their culture, ways of working, hierarchies, and opinions help to cement respectful working relationships. This works both ways, so be prepared to help them understand how best to work with you, also.

Which other managers or teams within the business have direct experience working with the global teams: what is their advice? Take on board their feedback but be careful not to view things through their own personal bias or cultural lens; instead, listen for the facts as well as the do's and don'ts.

Observe: as previously mentioned, walking into different global areas of the organisation and implementing immediate change can work, but in the majority of cases railroading teams and forcing ways of working based on one's own perceived cultural lens can significantly damage the business and your own reputation as a Human Resources professional. Take time to observe behaviour, and working and communication styles, as well as leadership styles. Once this knowledge is gained, you can model how change, or ways of working, could be implemented successfully with the buy-in of the team. This saves time and energy, and the process is done respectfully and sustainably, meaning the change will continue as normal working practice.

Always be respectful: from the outset it is vital to show others that their culture is respected and, by working together, it will enhance the business and the individuals themselves.

No one should be made to feel ashamed of who they are or how they work and this is vital to remember as a Human Resources professional when working with others. Developing others and coaching them is part of the role, but it is essential not to want to change others to become more like us or our ways of working. A middle-ground must be found to ensure future success. This is done by working through the steps as discussed, as well as constant communication and reflection. A key, yet simple point of note when it comes to respecting teams – especially for a Human Resources professional – is how to address your teams. Employees may have names that seem difficult to pronounce; others have an English version of their name they are happy to be used. It is essential that whatever name anyone holds, the time is taken to learn how to pronounce the name correctly and understand the meaning their name may hold in some cultures, as this is something many are proud to have.

Build trust: this is something that is achieved over some time and is a long-term approach but starts from the first meeting. It is essential to consider the approach when meeting with teams. Research, seeking to understand, and observation are vital in building trusting working relationships. Trust is built through words and actions but also underlying factors that are not verbalised, such as the feeling of being supported, respected, and part of the team, as well as being included in the overall purpose of the organisation.

Immerse yourself: once you get to know the team, where possible start to build on this knowledge. This could be in the form of learning keywords and phrases, staying locally where possible on visits, respecting and recognising national days and holidays, etc. There are many ways to understand your teams more, and building cultural knowledge helps to flex and change your cultural lens. This knowledge will provide the best possible foundations with your teams to then go on to build very successful working relationships.

AUTHOR'S VOICE

When travelling to work with my teams in Botswana, I always try to learn one or two new words. These could be hello, goodbye, how are you, thank you – simple words that mean something to the teams.

I not only try to understand the word and its pronunciation but also other meanings the word could be used for to help me understand not only why it is said but also the meaning it holds for the local teams.

An example of this is the word 'rain' in Setswana which is *pula*. This is not only the word for rain but also the word for the local currency and to greet or bless someone.

Rain is so important in a dry country that naming the currency after this demonstrates how invaluable rain is to the whole country. Rain is therefore a blessing, and when Pula is said as a greeting, it means 'Let it rain.'

By asking these simple questions, you learn much more than just a word, you learn the meaning it holds and the part it plays in shaping the beliefs and values of your teams.

Understand values and beliefs: in many cases, culture plays a huge part in shaping the values and beliefs of the workforce and can often be what 'makes them tick'. For Human Resources to go against fundamental and deeply held cultural values can be a very challenging aspect to overcome and to recover from to build those strong, respectful working relationships.

Everything previously discussed will help you to understand what is important for the workforce and once this is understood it can be used to advantage in creating a highly engaged and motivated workforce. It is important to remember this works both ways and can be a useful exercise to hold conversations about what you believe in and why. By sharing, it can encourage others to do the same.

Beliefs are also critical to many cultures and can be deeply rooted. It is essential for Human Resources to understand and accommodate as much as possible especially around prayer times, religious holidays, and during periods of fasting. By having a level of understanding, which can come from research, as well as by asking team members, demonstrates support to teams and embeds an inclusive culture within the organisation.

Appropriate language and attire: it is essential to be mindful with language, but also body language when working alongside global teams and the clothes that they choose to wear. These demonstrate respect to the workforce in other countries and will solidify the Human Resources professional. Research prior to visits ensures appropriate clothing is worn, as in many cultures clothing and areas of the body to cover, is a sign of respect for the local teams and will inform not only their view of you, but also how they react to and work with you in the future.

Reflection: lastly, it is about the time for reflection after a global visit. With all the aforementioned points linking with the actual role and tasks when visiting teams, it can be exhausting and not everything always goes right. This is where time is allocated to reflect upon what went well and what could have been done better. If a mistake or inadvertent offence was caused to someone or a team, it needs to be acknowledged and rectified. How this is done will depend on the culture of the team and the relationship, but it is recommended to resolve any animosity or challenges as soon as possible.

9.4 Managing Virtually in a Global World

The world is vast and there are not enough hours in the week to see your global teams face-to-face on a regular basis. This is where the Human Resources professional needs to take time to build strong communication with their teams. Things to remember which can often be overlooked when working across multiple countries include:

Time zones: it is easy to sometimes forget that not everybody within the team works in the same time zone, especially when some countries change their clocks at certain times of the year and others do not. When setting deadlines, organising calls, etc. it is vital to keep this in mind. Many online calendars now have the option to add another time zone and this can be an easy way of ensuring effective management consideration.

Public holidays and religious festivals: countries celebrate different things at different times and knowing when teams have celebration days, public holidays, or religious festivals demonstrates knowledge and shows respect to teams and their culture. During such days, it is important to understand what meetings or calls are needed and plan them accordingly. It is advisable to speak to teams and ask them if calls have been scheduled at inappropriate times or during their time off, rather than for them to feel they must log on. Again, this demonstrates mutual respect of the working relationship.

Setting boundaries and agenda of the call: if everyone knows what the call will be covering it helps speed up processes and allows people the time to think and come to the call with examples. The more preparation everyone can do, the more the projects or tasks can be moved forward following the call.

Agree with teams the best way to communicate. In some countries the internet connection can be poor and unstable, so videoconferencing is unlikely to be the best method of communication. Try not to impose your preferred working style on others, but instead compromise and agree on the best solution for all concerned.

As many global relationships are built virtually nowadays, it is important to still get to know the people behind the screen and so icebreakers and starts to all calls can be an important and effective way to achieve this. Ask questions and involve everyone in the call but be mindful of various cultures and how they would view these exercises.

9.5 Managing Global Teams in One Location

Human Resources professionals have become accustomed to working with many nationalities in the one location all coming together for the common goal. This can often be more difficult to navigate than managing global teams as the mix of nationalities, in comparison to a workforce of one nationality, can bring its own challenges.

In this case, Human Resources and managers must be mindful of others and their thoughts and reactions in terms of how messages will be received, about the needs and wants of everyone, their beliefs and values, and their ways of working. If this is kept in the forefront of the mind, it will shape how you act, carry out your role, and how you interact and communicate with others.

It is part of the role in Human Resources and for managers to help others work together to increase levels of tolerance, as well as understanding. Awareness around working with other nationalities is not only the responsibility of Human Resources but the responsibility of the whole workforce, so managers need to create an inclusive, culturally rich, engaged, and motivated workforce to reach business success.

9.6 Diversity, Equality and Inclusion (DE&I)

It is important to understand what DE&I means for the business, what this means for the manager, and what it means for the teams. Human Resources professionals should have DE&I in mind to ensure everyone feels part of and included in the organisation and that they have a purpose and a part to play in the business.

DE&I means different things in different countries, so time should be taken to understand what teams currently feel and how this could be improved, what could be changed, and how it can be ensured that a strategy is in place for the future. As all countries are different, it is essential that not a one-size-fits-all approach is taken, and the actions are tailored to suit everyone in that part of the business and that part of the world to ensure everyone feels they belong.

Robust systems should be in place for the team to be able to declare, without repercussions, that they do not feel included or that they are not being treated equally or fairly. Human Resources must ensure these are followed up in terms of policy and process. This will contribute to a trusting workforce who feel they can openly communicate and know that the company takes DE&I seriously.

Creating a diverse workforce can be a challenge but it is highly rewarding if everyone can bring their own experiences, cultures, and talents together to form a highly performing, open, respectful, and tolerant team. This also complies with global equality laws and requirements in terms of Diversity, Equality, and Inclusion.

As the world is becoming more accessible, teams are becoming more global, and for Human Resources it is vital to get the people-strategy right and to have engaged, motivated, and understood teams who feel a sense of belonging and respect for everyone to work towards a common goal for success.

It is important to be conscious of the cultural lens you are using and the perceptions you hold, and be prepared to flex and adapt, as well as compromise to find the best way forward.

Human Resources professionals or managers must continually develop their skills and learn from mistakes, which in time makes a richer and more all-round key strategic partner in the success of the organisation.

Chapter 10

Communication

10.0 Introduction

Communication is a fundamental part of our everyday working lives, and an essential skill in hospitality, hotel, and events. Communication is essential when delegating tasks, identifying client needs, when confirming bookings and responding to enquiries, and when forming a rapport with team members.

Communication is essentially about one person relaying a message to another, or multiple people, and ensuring it is clear and understood. It also involves using the right channels in which to impart information. Communication can be via a variety of media including verbal face-to-face communication such as in a meeting, or emails, instant messaging apps, letter, or social media as examples.

In a hotel, the operations staff and managers should meet every morning to brief check-outs, check-ins, continuous stays, restaurant reservations, and what events are occurring that day.

In events, communication involves pre-event planning meetings, liaison with clients, venues, suppliers and contractors, contracts being signed, writing and distribution of a function sheet or event management plan, a pre-event briefing, onsite briefings, after-event debrief meetings, and client feedback and post-event evaluation as examples.

DOI: 10.4324/9781003469803-11

In a restaurant, communication is a pre-service briefing, communications between front of house and the kitchen on guest dietary requests, checking quantities of menu items for availability, guest interactions, taking payments, and a de-brief at the end of service as examples of communication during the shift.

According to psychology professor Albert Mehrabian, the spoken word makes up 7 per cent of communication, 55 per cent of non-verbal communication (such as body language and gestures), and is 38 per cent paralinguistic, which is the way things are said. This means communication is multifaceted and can be complicated.

Communication is vital in the workplace but at times can be complex and things can go wrong because communication was not effective. This can result in complaints, mistakes, conflict, loss of custom, and even legal issues as examples.

When communicating, it is important to know what is being communicated, and to consider how and when communication needs to take place.

This chapter identifies different communication types and theories of communication. The staff hierarchy will also be examined with consideration given to lines of authority and communication within different types of staffing structures. Conflict management and team building will then be discussed as part of organisation communication and effectiveness, alongside the role of Artificial Intelligence (AI) in organisational communication.

INDUSTRY VOICE

Dr Philip Berners, Associate Professor in Events Management

I challenge my students to think of a problem or issue that they have faced, trace back what went wrong, and they will find that the root cause is communication: miscommunication; misinterpretation; misunderstanding... whatever went wrong: communication.

10.1 Determining the Medium of Communication

The choice of medium used for communicating is determined by several factors including:

Whether the information needs to be recorded: for example, the minutes of an internal stakeholders' meeting, an annual appraisal, or disciplinary for an employee will need to be recorded, usually on a form or Word document and stored securely. This will usually require a meeting. An email communicating dates of meetings with a calendar invite is useful and serves as a reminder and record of any meetings.

If there is companywide information that needs to reach all employees quickly and efficiently, an all-staff meeting or an email would be chosen, and 'read and received' alerts activated if necessary, demonstrating receipt of the message.

Who needs to receive the information: a marketing campaign targeted at customers is best communicated via direct personalised emails or social media. Cold-calling customers is generally not well received, and customers can choose whether to opt into emails or unsubscribe. If negotiating or communicating with suppliers, an email or phone call would be more appropriate.

Demographics also prefer different forms of communication:

Baby Boomers (born 1946–1964) favour face-to-face conversations or phone calls.

Generation X (1965–1980) prefer email and phone calls.

Millennials or Generation Y (born 1981–1996) and Gen Z (born 1997–2012) prefer digital communication such as instant messaging or social media due to digital fluency.

Different generations prefer different digital platforms: Baby Boomers tend to use Facebook and LinkedIn; Gen Y opt for Facebook, YouTube, Instagram or X (formally Twitter); and Gen Z Instagram, YouTube, Snapchat, and Tik Tok.

Therefore, numerous social media platforms need to be adopted to appeal to different generations.

Confidentiality: an email or one-to-one meeting is appropriate when communicating with an employee involved in a grievance and should be marked as 'private and confidential' in the header. Likewise, client details should be made available to only the staff members who need to access this information and data should not be made available on a companywide database, or should be stored on a password protected device to ensure security. For security and privacy, details of high-profile clients should be shared only with appropriate colleagues and not shared externally.

Nature of the information, length, complexity, and timings: the context of the communication also determines the type of communication chosen, and the relationship to the individual being communicated with. Communication depends on the situation. A new menu, product, or service could be revealed at an all-staff meeting so everyone can receive the information at the same time with demonstrations or examples included. A contract would be sent by email to be signed digitally. A multinational company promotion targeted at customers would be best advertised on television and social media or via a direct mailshot by post. More complex information is best communicated verbally so questions can be asked, and then followed up in writing so it can be referred to and a record kept. Communication also depends on urgency, and a verbal conversation, phone call, or email can ensure timely communication.

Cost of the communication: traditional media used for communication such as billboards, television, and radio are costly platforms. Some advertising and marketing campaigns are more suited to direct emails and social media when promoting special offers and are more cost efficient.

Marriott Bonvoy advertised hotels on Netflix in 2025 for an unknown cost, but being the largest hotel brand in the world it will have flexibility in finances compared to smaller firms. In 2023 Marriott spent $794 million on advertising costs; $635 million in 2022; and $470 million in 2021 (Marriott Annual Report, 2023).

10.2 Artificial Intelligence (AI)

According to a 2024 PricewaterhouseCoopers (PwC) report, almost 73 per cent of businesses are using AI. Examples of AI include software such as *ChatGPT* and *Gemini*, and AI robots and chatbots that can learn and improve with human interactions.

AI can be applied in hospitality, hotels, and events to create competitive advantage. Hilton trialled Connie, an AI robot which interacts with guests; Marriott with Alexa; and Henn-Na Hotel in Japan uses a variety of robots to assist guests, with varying levels of success.

AI can be utilised for content generation to make communications easier. AI can enhance creativity and human skills, and training should be offered where needed to ensure staff using AI have appropriate support, knowledge, and skills to use AI effectively. AI can improve systems, processes, and administration, and provide efficiency, but also requires individuals to understand technology and AI capabilities, and training will be needed to ensure effective use.

AI can assist guests and operations, and at times replace human job roles. Generally, however, staff are also needed, and as jobs evolve alongside innovation, this technology can be used for a variety of functions:

- To generate career paths for employees by highlighting skills required and training plans

- To identify common employee concerns, feedback, and needs. A line manager can submit appraisals or other one-to-one reports to AI to produce data on common themes, patterns, or trends that emerge
- To generate interview questions based on key job criteria
- To create recruitment documents, such as person specifications, job descriptions, and advertisements when key criteria is uploaded
- To create group and individual interview assessment activities to test skills and aptitude, helping determine whether applicants are a good fit for the job
- To write contracts
- To construct policy documents
- To create standard operating procedures (SOPs), KPIs, or targets
- To create forms
- To analyse data

In Human Resources, AI such as *ChatGPT* can be used for shortlisting candidates for interviews, drafting contracts, creating policies, and job profiles. When generating important documents such as contracts or legal processes, specialist legal advice should always be sought, and content must be checked, and preferably authorised by appropriate senior managers.

For example, when recruiting, attitude and whether the candidate would fit into workplace culture is important. Whilst AI is useful for shortlisting against qualifications and a list of skills, it is not able to truly assess personality. Shortlisting applicants using AI can result in the ideal candidate being wrongly excluded from the recruitment process and AI should therefore be used with caution.

If a contract is generated with AI and contains errors or missing information, legal stipulations could be overlooked, leading to legal issues for either party. Such problems can become costly and detrimental to the business, should something go wrong.

All content and capabilities must be trialled, tested, and checked before it is rolled out to customers, or content generated by AI is used within operations or information and relayed to staff, contractors, or other stakeholders.

Standard models of AI such as *ChatGPT* and *Gemini* are built upon information available on the internet, which is not 100 per cent accurate. If a custom AI model is created for the business, it is likely to be more accurate and fit for use.

The European Artificial Intelligence Act came into force in July 2024 which raises issues for Human Resources and managers. The Act, affecting all European businesses, is the first of its kind in terms of regulation of technology identifying risks.

In Human Resources, risks include systems, such as online systems, shortlisting candidates during the recruitment phase, which may create bias. This AI can be used to evaluate applicants and filter applications according to specific parameters or filters, but care must be taken. When used properly, AI can reduce bias and discrimination during the recruitment process if robust controls are in place.

Cyber security and data breaches are a high risk; therefore, data must be protected and safeguarded and when used properly, it mitigates risk. Data Protection laws reinforce this stance.

AI is a useful tool that can assist Human Resources and managers, enhance creativity, and create documents quickly and easily to support efficient work processes, or it can be used to support delivery of the guest experience.

Where used, all content generated through AI should be checked for accuracy and training provided. AI is a tool that can complement operations, but no system is perfect, and care must be taken to protect the business.

10.3 Theories of Communication to Apply in the Workplace

There are theories of communication that can be considered such as Drucker's Fundamentals of Communication; Hofstede's Cultural Dimensions Theory; the Shannon-Weaver Model of Communication; alongside Cutlip and Center's Seven Cs of Communication.

10.3.1 Drucker's Fundamentals of Communication

Peter Drucker, a renowned management theorist provided useful insights into effective communication and the impact on management and organisational success.

Drucker believed that effective communication helps an organisation achieve its strategic goals and, without clear communication, decision-making becomes difficult, job roles or tasks can be misunderstood, and teams might not work effectively. This is due to an increase in mistakes, and co-worker ineffectiveness, and ultimately leads to conflict. Communication needs to be direct, clear, and transparent. Where necessary, recommunication may need to occur to ensure clarity and prevent misunderstanding, depending on the recipient of the information.

Communication is a two-way process, whether during an appraisal, during interactions with clients, or when delegating tasks to a team. Both parties must communicate clearly and listen to one another to effectively communicate their needs, and verbal cues given to demonstrate listening and understanding such as nodding or saying 'yes', or 'I understand' to demonstrate active listening.

Managers should be model communicators, which is essential in achieving desired outcomes, such as team members completing delegated tasks or problem-solving. The same applies to decision-making, and it is helpful to explain reasons behind decisions to clarify and avoid confusion and support team understanding.

Drucker outlined how written communication is important. In hospitality, hotels, and events, written communication is essential for communicating documents such as function sheets, policies, procedures, and the contractual obligations of a new employee. This means documents can be referred to, should there be a need at a later stage to check information.

Staff can become overloaded with communication also, such as sending too many emails, confusing policies, contradicting perspectives, or complicated explanations as examples. Therefore, communication frequency, type of media, and relevant important information should be stipulated.

Considering the range of hotels, events, and other hospitality outlets, plus leisure tourism and travel destinations globally, communication is also dependent upon culture. Whilst Drucker's views on culture may not have been as specific, Drucker acknowledged communication must be culturally sensitive. This is of importance in multinational hospitality organisations such as large hotel and restaurant chains where communication varies according to each geographic area. What works in one location, may not in another, and might be considered disrespectful.

Drucker believed culture impacts communication, and whilst some countries are more respectful of authority than others, there are countries with cultures that have honest, open communication between managers and staff.

This is what Geert Hofstede, a Dutch social psychologist, referred to as 'power distance' in his works on cultural differences between countries.

10.3.2 Hofstede's Cultural Dimensions Theory

In cultures with high power distance, such as in China and India, hierarchical structures are respected and those at the bottom of the hierarchy are more likely to accept inequalities and authority and will rarely be involved in decision-making.

In low power distance countries, authority is more evenly distributed and could be attributed somewhat to more democratic nations. Staff can talk more openly with managers, sharing ideas, and challenging decisions, such as in the United Kingdom, Norway, and Australia.

Hofstede wrote about individualism and collectivism, our tendency to be integrated into groups, or not, with individualistic countries preferring individual achievement and control over their work compared to teamwork and dependency.

He also noted the impact of masculine versus feminine society with more masculine cultures associated with power and control, and more feminine societies linked to cooperation in communication, modesty, and work–life balance.

Hofstede discussed the impact of uncertainty avoidance and how some cultures are more likely to takes risks over others, long-term and short-term orientation such as traditions or change, and indulgence over restraint as to whether people enjoy life more freely and follow their own ideals as opposed to being restrained and following rules.

Cultural norms and values will influence communication effectiveness, so adapting to local culture will prevent miscommunication, misunderstandings, and conflict. Strategies need to be adaptable to these differences because recognising these nuances avoids misunderstandings and builds stronger relationships.

Managers in hospitality, hotels, and events should be highly skilled in delegation, whilst being mindful of their communication styles and respectful of individuals to ensure effectiveness.

Communication from managers and Human Resources becomes especially important when managing change. When going through change, time frames for change, and the impact and justification for change should be communicated to ensure team resilience and successful change management (see Chapter 13).

10.3.3 Shannon–Weaver Model of Communication

The Shannon–Weaver Model of Communication explains how information flows from a sender to a receiver, as penned by Claude Shannon and Warren Weaver in 1948. The theory is also referred to as 'A Mathematical Theory of Communication' and is considered one of the original models of communication.

The Shannon–Weaver model divides communication into five components as outlined in Figure 10.1.

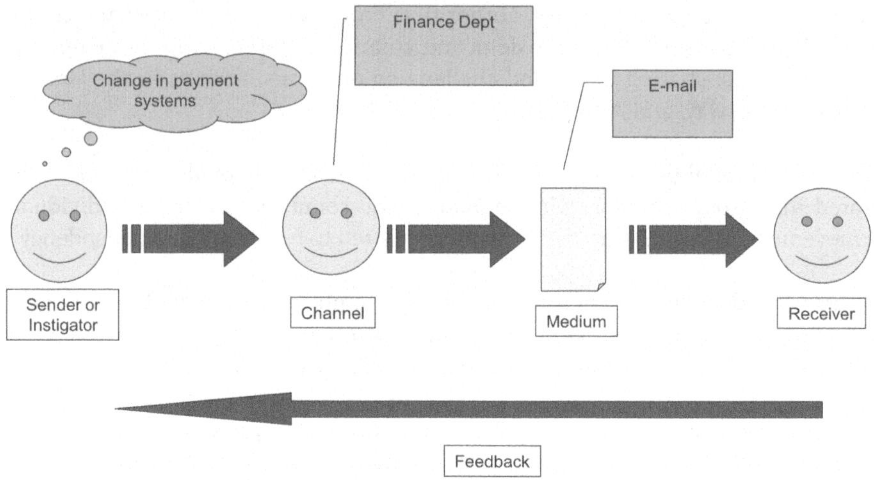

Figure 10.1 Shannon-Weaver Model of Communication
Adapted from Nokia Corporation and AT&T Archives.

The five components are:

Source: the information source who creates the message such as a manager creating a new payment system (a new till system, touch screen device, or contactless payments, for example), or Head Chef who has devised a new menu. This information needs to be communicated and may then be passed onto a 'transmitter' to communicate required information.

Transmitter: the transmitter, also known as the 'encoder', is the person who then translates the message and needs to impart the information. This involves putting the required information into a 'signal' which needs to be transmitted to others. This can mean the message being put into words verbally, put in writing, via images, or other means. In Figure 10.1 this is the Finance Department who need to inform staff of the new payment system.

Channel: this is the way the 'signal' (information) is delivered to those who need to be given this information. In the instance of communicating the new system in Figure 10.1, this is by email (from the Finance Department).

Receiver: the person or persons who are the recipients of the information, for example those who use the payment systems will be sent the information and need to receive this. The receiver is the 'decoder' to interpret and understand what is being communicated. It can be that different interpretations are made, so it is important the original message is clear.

Destination: The person for whom the message was intended.

An additional stage is **feedback**. As communication is not always linear, questions may be asked, concerns raised, or clarification needed, so this involves further communication. A manager may need to hold a training session with staff to demonstrate the new system, to alleviate any concerns, and to ensure the new system is installed and used effectively without causing operational issues or staff resistance.

The model considers **'noise'**, which refers to anything that can prevent the message from being received or understood. Barriers (or noise) to communication include an email failing to send, not hearing instructions, or loud noise preventing hearing, letters being lost in the mail, body language, or the way things are said which may cause different interpretations of the message being received.

Measures need to be taken to reduce 'noise' and ensure messages are received and understood. This can include adding 'read' receipts to emails being sent, information being signed and dated when received, speaking clearly, being mindful of non-verbal communication such as body language and the way things are said, and asking people to repeat back or demonstrate their new knowledge.

INDUSTRY VOICE

Dr Philip Berners, Associate Professor in Events Management

I like the Shannon–Weaver model of communication, and I explain it when teaching students and training those who are already working in the industry.

The model shows the process of sending a message until it is received. The message can be disrupted by 'noise' – but not always physical noise such as a noisy background – so the message can't be heard. It can be other ('noise') disruptions such as an email bouncing back, an email being seen too late, or the receiver misinterpreting the message.

This is why the Feedback loop in the model is so important, because it checks that the message has been received and understood.

The sender needs to always ask for feedback, such as, 'Did you receive my message?', 'Did you understand my instructions?', or 'Did you manage to act upon my request?'

The receiver should always provide feedback, such as, 'I received your email and I've done what you asked', or 'Thank you for your email'.

The model teaches good practice for managers when they communicate: always ask for feedback; always provide feedback.

10.3.4 The 7 Cs of Effective Communication

The 7 Cs of Effective Communication model was created by Scott Cutlip and Allen Center, and was first published in their 1952 book, *Effective Public Relations*.

The Seven Cs of Effective Communication, as outlined in Figure 10.2, is a circle of principles that must be followed to ensure effective communication, so that communication is heard and understood. The 7 Cs are: Clear; Correct; Complete; Concrete; Concise; Considered; Courteous.

Clear: it is important to have a clear message to communicate, with purpose and intent, so that the receiver understands why the message is being communicated. The message itself should be clear, free from jargon and acronyms that might not be understood by others.

Correct: avoid assumptions, and ensure the correct information is being communicated and not misconstrued or open to interpretation. Even a spelling mistake or mispronunciation can be scrutinised and take attention from key messages. Accuracy should be checked before going live with any communication.

Also, it is imperative to provide correct information, such as asking someone to meet a customer in reception, when actually they are waiting in the bar.

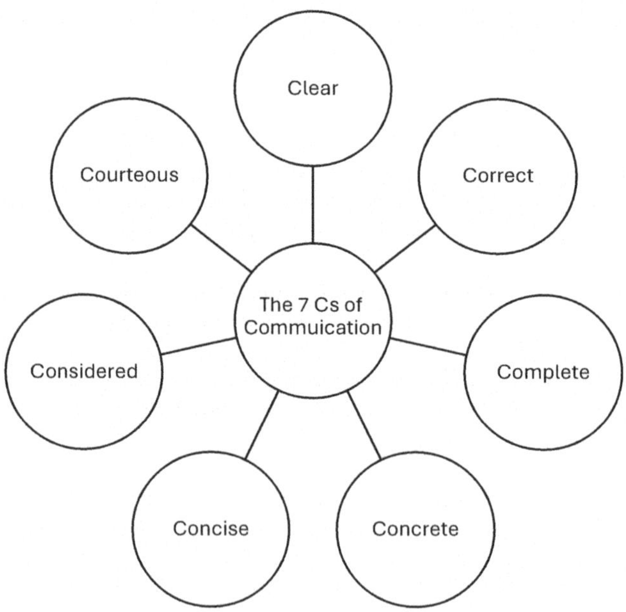

Figure 10.2 Cutlip and Center: The 7 Cs of Effective Communication Model

Complete: there is nothing more frustrating than seeing an event advertised and missing details such as location, how to book, prices, or other missing information. A job advert may not state how to apply, how much information is needed on an application, when to apply, or miss out the salary. Communication must contain all relevant and useful information and any relevant links or enquiry information so action can be taken if needed.

Concrete: as well as messages being specific and accurate, they should be factual and free from bias or opinion where feasible. Information being given should not be open to misinterpretation or misunderstanding. Specific data, visual images of hotel rooms, spa spaces, or events should be given to support arguments such as 'modern facilities' or 'recently refurbished'. This helps reassure recipients of key messages.

Concise: communication should be short and simple, easy to read and understand. Concise language helps identify key information quickly without the receiver having to find the information and avoids loss of attention. If a message is not concise, the core message can be lost among irrelevant information – it may be diluted.

Considered: the flow of communication should be effective, utilising a logical flow of information, and be free from inconsistencies or literacy errors. If the same communication is being promoted across different media such as email, social media, and websites, the style and design should be consistent and the same message evident across all platforms. Also, consider the person receiving the message: how will it affect them; what impacts will it have; will it be received gladly, or unwelcome?

Courteous: being polite and considerate with messages shows respect for the recipients. Humour and sarcasm should only be used when appropriate and must be culturally sensitive also. It helps to be empathetic and to understand what is being communicated from the different perspectives of those receiving it. If a message is arrogant or rude, it will likely be rejected, resisted, or refused. Effective communication means keeping the receiver onside.

CASE STUDY: ONLINE ARGUMENT BETWEEN VENUE AND BRIDE

A wedding venue manager started an argument with a bride within an online bridal forum after a bride who had booked a wedding at the venue, asked questions within the forum about food prices as children's meals were priced the same as adults, whilst also asking about terms of payment.

The venue manager insulted the bride and threatened her with legal action within the forum, despite the venue having never been named.

The argument escalated online with other bride-to-be's jumping to the bride's defence. This resulted in backlash, poor publicity, negative press coverage, and temporary closure of the wedding venue.

Communication can be formal or informal. Formal communication is through established official lines of authority such as the contract of employment, staff handbook, policies, and customer confirmations. Informal communication includes a chat between two members of the team, rumour, gossip, and word of mouth amongst staff.

Whereas formal communication is visible and regulated, informal communication is unseen and uncontrolled. But this does not mean gossip and rumour are bad – an organisation might send a 'rumour' that somebody will be promoted and then watch everybody do their job just that little bit better.

Gossip and chat are also helpful for new employees. This is how they learn informal information and behaviours which are not printed in formal documents.

10.4 Staff Hierarchy

Contributed by Jennifer Kaye, Author; Megan-Ellis Smith, Hotel Management graduate; and Tamsin Parker, Events Management graduate, Edge Hotel School, University of Essex.

Organisational structure, also known as 'management structure/hierarchy' or 'staffing structure/hierarchy', is the way a business is structured to carry out activities, providing a representation of how authority and communication is passed through the organisation.

Organisational structures provide a framework of a business' decision-making processes based on the lines of control, known as 'lines of authority'. Structure will be determined by factors such as business size and scope, geographical spread, its goals and objectives, and the industry it operates within.

Managers at the top of the hierarchy will make decisions and determine strategic direction, organisational goals, policies, rules, and brand standards. They will communicate information down the hierarchy to middle management and eventually to operational staff at the bottom of the hierarchy. This is a traditional top-down approach to management and is considered a centralised approach.

Whilst the top-down structure may be considered bureaucratic, it establishes formal lines of communication to ensure the correct information is passed down to relevant employees to maintain brand standards and quality of service to achieve organisational goals. Decision-making at the top of the organisation is considered as 'centralisation', whereby all decisions are made top-down. This will generally result in 'formalisation' which is the extent of rules, policies, and procedures to follow as dictated by managers within the hierarchy.

Formal, more bureaucratic approaches to management can lead to eventual resistance from staff as they become overwhelmed by rules and policies and are given little flexibility to do their job. For instance, across all service industries such as in hotels and restaurants, if policy dictates all guests are referred to as Mr or Ms, a guest may prefer to have their first name used. In terms of guest complaints there may be a formal procedure to follow, but in situations where clients have urgent needs, or a complaint, things need to be resolved quickly and efficiently and may not allow for the chain of command to be followed.

There should be flexibility and trust in team members to make decisions and to resolve problems effectively and to be adaptable to guest's needs to ensure a more personable service. It is, after all, front-line staff who are serving guests, and they are responsible for delivering guest satisfaction.

The structure or hierarchy is usually communicated to staff during the onboarding of new recruits to ensure they know who to report to, and who they are responsible for in the workplace.

This structure is usually presented in a diagram, identifying managers at the top of the hierarchy, with lines connecting to the job titles they line manage or need to communicate with, who are then connected to staff at the bottom of the structure. This ensures everyone knows who needs to report to up, down, and across the chain of command (lines of authority).

The more people within the structure, the taller and wider it becomes, and the more complex communication becomes.

Communication can go wrong if appropriate lines of authority are not followed and information can be missed.

10.4.1 Span of Control

'Span of control' refers to the number of people someone manages or supervises and is dictated by lines of authority or reporting lines. The number of levels of management is also referred to as the 'scaler chain' or 'chain of command' which is the linear flow of communication from managers down the chain to operational staff and is important because it can affect operational efficiency depending on how complex it is.

Vertical differentiation determines complexity of organisational structures and refers to the number of layers or levels of management within the structure. The more managers, the more authority, the taller the structure, and the more layers which communication needs to pass through to reach the required staff members. This could result in information being lost or miscommunicated at any point. Greater vertical differentiation means a narrower span of control, and this is likely to be seen in tall or wide organisation structures.

A narrow span of control results in a manager with fewer people to manage, which often makes communication, delegation, and task completion easier. This is common in flatter, smaller organisations. However, poor communication skills will still lead to inefficiencies and issues, even in smaller venues.

A large multinational hotel or restaurant chain will have a wide span of control. This results in a manager who has multiple reports (staff to manage). This can often result in loss of control where there are so many staff to communicate with, to train, and be responsible for. Communication skills are essential in maintaining control and ensure delegated tasks are completed and standards are met by all employees.

INDUSTRY VOICE BOX

Dr Philip Berners, Associate Professor in Events Management

The traditional pyramid structure of an organisational chart where the top flows downward is considered out of date. Nowadays, companies recognise the importance of all-inclusive communication across the landscape of the organisation and are thus adopting flexible structures, not rigid reporting, which encourages downward, upward, and across-ways communication.

It always concerns me to look at the 'risk' points: where in the communication processes there is a point for risk in communication. A risk point is usually where communication gets transferred from one person to another, or one department to another. This is why I adopt the one-person management structure (Berners, 2019) where one person has ownership of the event or client from first contact to last contact.

For example, I know a hotel where the sales office handles the enquiry, planning, client liaison, and negotiations until the day of the event. Then, on the day of the event, they hand it over to the operations team. This creates a risk point where the ops team might not have all the information required to satisfy the client. Or information might get misinterpreted. And the client relationship must begin again.

Would it not be better for one person to 'own' the event start-to-finish where the client relationship flows and grows, and the communication is seamless?

10.4.2 Fayol's Scientific Management Theory

According to Henri Fayol's Scientific Management Theory, to ensure clear lines of authority and communication, an employee should never report to more than one manager – which he referred to as 'the chain of command'. For example, a barista might report to one manager to request vacation time, and if not authorised, the barista should not then go to a second manager and undermine the first; this is why it is important to have a clear management structure for all staff to follow. In the instance of the barista, the manager would be undermined by the employee, and the authorising manager may not be aware of the request originally being denied, nor the reasons. It could be that there is already another member of staff who has just had annual leave authorised and would result in staffing shortages.

There are different organisational structures, depending on products and services offered and geographic spread. These structures include functional, product, geographical, and matrix structures and determine lines of authority (span of control). Each, is explained here:

10.4.3 Functional Structures

Functional organisational structures organise a company into departments based on areas of expertise, which may be at Head Office level or within an individual hotel or events venue where departments exist. For a restaurant, bar, or coffee shop chain, a functional structure is likely to be Head Office only, as multiple departments tend not to exist in these services.

Typical functional structures indicate individuals who are responsible for different functions within the business such as Human Resources; Marketing; Finance; Operations at Head Office level or at individual property level for a singular business, for example in a hotel; Rooms Division; Sales; Food and Beverage; Events; and Housekeeping.

Figure 10.3 and Figure 10.4 identify managers or owners at the top of the hierarchy where decisions are made, with lines connecting with secondary managers, supervisors, and operational staff. Managers will then communicate down the chain to their subordinates such as Deputies, Assistant Managers, or Heads of Department, giving them the responsibility to implement processes, rules, and standards to operational employees on the lower levels of the hierarchy in each department.

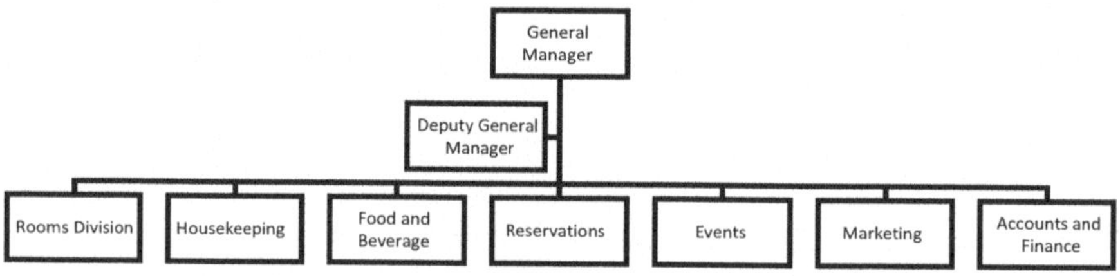

Figure 10.3 Typical Functional Structure in a Small-to-Medium-Sized Hotel

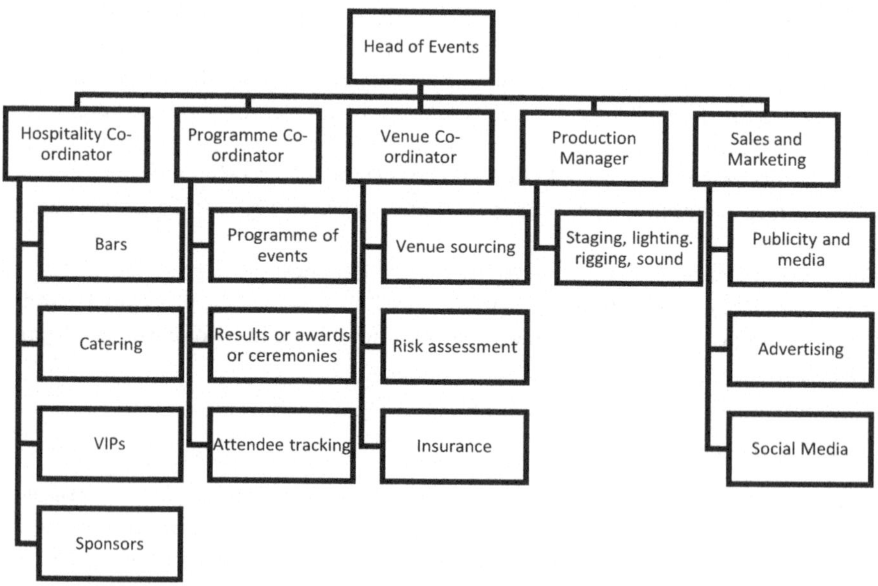

Figure 10.4 Typical Functional Structure in Events

This structure is commonly used to group employees with shared specialist skills and knowledge, performing similar functions to a high level, to improve operational efficiencies using their expertise.

Within events, this varies according to the business type, whether a fixed venue or outdoor, whether ongoing events take place or ad hoc events.

This type of structure is needed on a business-to-business, or-venue-to-venue level to understand the inner workings as each will provide different services and products and will have diverse needs.

10.4.4 Product Structures

Product structures involve creating separate departments for each product or service used by hospitality, hotel, and events organisations. This allows a company to manage each specialist product or service using separate managers in accordance with brand standards. This does, however, require numerous managers, and operations staff may need to be duplicated across the multiple products.

Having a product structure and dedicated team in each division means the brand can respond quickly to changing market conditions and trends and can adapt to the product's specific target market more easily compared to doing this across multiple brands with one team in place for all. The product structure's specialist team for each division can achieve a competitive advantage in their markets as they have bespoke knowledge and understanding of a particular product or service and streamline decision-making in their divisions according to this.

An example product structure has been outlined in Figure 10.5.

Typically, product (or brand) structures exist in multinational firms, whereby they operate multiple brands across different markets such as budget, midscale,

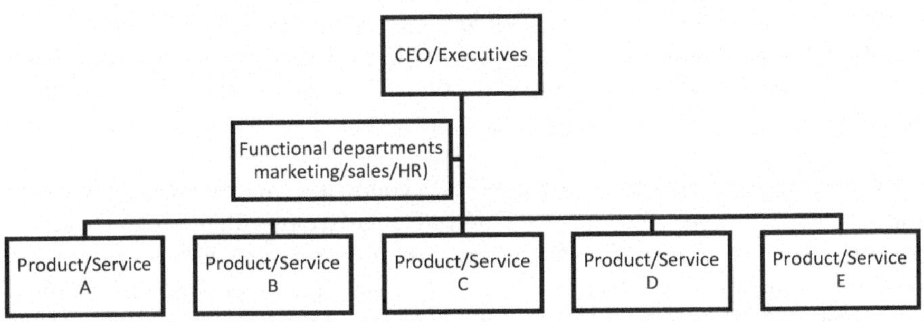

Figure 10.5 Typical Product Structure

and luxury markets. Brands such as Hilton operate Hilton Hotels, Waldorf Astoria, Hilton Garden Inn, and Doubletree as examples, and Marriott with Moxy, Marriott, Renaissance, and Ritz-Carlton as a selection of their brands.

Likewise, some businesses operate events, hotels, and restaurants as their different products. And some event companies might specialise in different event products and services such as weddings, music and festivals, corporate events, and sporting events. A manager will typically be allocated for each brand to help differentiate the products and services being offered between them.

Many of these brands or products might typically be operating in more than one geographical area and thus a geographical structure is also needed.

10.4.5 Geographical Structures

A geographical structure separates the areas of work for a company that operates in more than one region, whether in the same country, or within a multinational firm. A geographical structure helps to operate according to the demands of consumers in that region, which will vary country to country.

Culture, religion, laws, and other external factors determine product success in each region and it is therefore necessary to have regional managers with specialised knowledge in each area to manage the business, compared to an overall manager who is responsible globally and might not understand local market demands. For example, McDonalds do not serve beef in India and have a vegetarian menu, and Virgin Atlantic introduced a gender-neutral uniform policy in 2022, but this policy was suspended for the England World Cup flight to Qatar where homosexuality is still illegal.

When determining regions, The United Kingdom may be divided by England, Ireland, Scotland, and Wales, or England by South East, North, West and so on. A multinational company could have divisions based in each country or continent. Some organisations will also group some regions together such as Europe, Middle East, and Africa (EMEA). Bigger geographical areas can be challenging for one manager to be responsible for, and therefore they would have regional managers for each country who help implement and advise on local markets.

For example, Compass Group operates in 33 countries, McDonald's around 118, and Accor in around 110 countries. Different regulations will apply in these areas, and what is required in Middle Eastern countries will vary from that of Western countries. The effect of this on Compass' functions would be a different set of management for each of these regions, and they may choose to hire these from the region being managed to ensure culture is maintained and amend their policies and procedures incorporating uniform, facilities, services, operating hours, and menus. These managers will have a wide span of control – many employees working under one manager – which could present difficulties with localising entirely to countries and may instead branch out a general change per continent.

Therefore, a geographical organisational structure is the allocation of employees into divisions based on geographic location of each business, enabling businesses to operate their sites according to localised demand in accordance with rules and polices that apply in each area, aligning with regional differences to meet market demand in that area.

See Figure 10.6 for an example geographical structure.

However, this autonomy of decision-making could cause conflicts between the divisions and headquarters as decision-making will become decentralised. Brand standards may therefore vary leading to a loss of centralised control, leading to brand inconsistencies and loss of organisational culture.

A matrix structure may also exist.

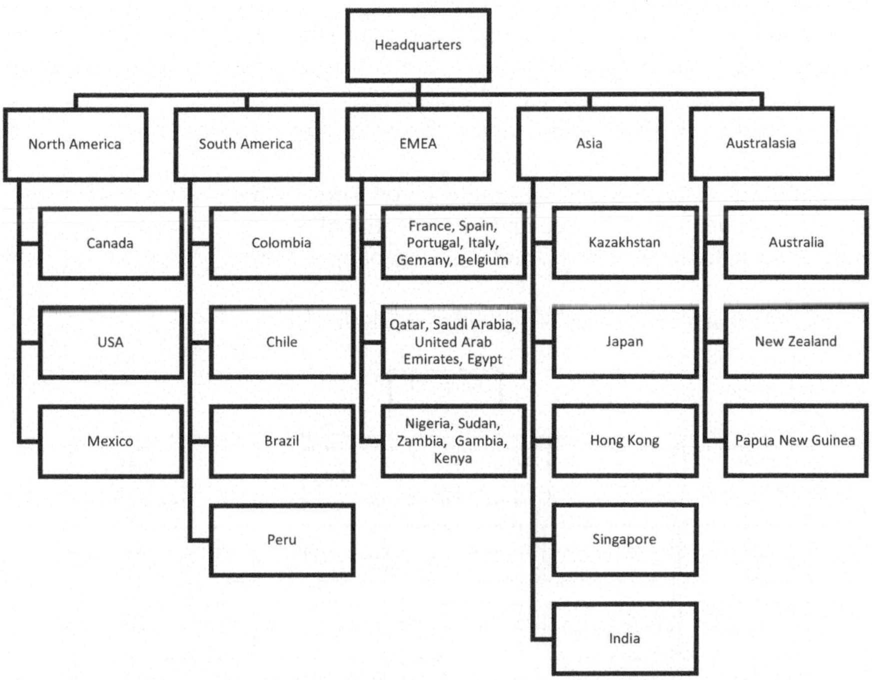

Figure 10.6 Typical Geographical Structure

10.4.6 Matrix Structures

A matrix structure can be used where teams work across multiple projects and therefore individuals report to more than one manager.

Staff may work with a functional manager such as in Marketing, but are also responsible for more than one brand, event, or venue, and therefore report to a project manager, also. This helps a company to operate new brands and services without restructuring teams. In this instance, the Marketing Manager will be responsible for promoting and advertising each event, creating publicity, and launching multiple campaigns and teams at the same time.

This type of structure uses a grid to identify reporting lines, and as there are multiple chains of command, there can be conflicting demands on team members. However, functional specialists such as Human Resources, Marketing, and Sales each have specialist skills that can be utilised across multiple projects which removes the need to have multiple functional teams across the company such as those that might be used in product or geographical structures.

The matrix structure is complex due to having more than one manager and multiple projects. Employees may have conflicting responsibilities and deadlines, leading to operational inefficiencies due to conflict, mistakes, or communication issues and pressure to support multiple projects which may result in burnout. However, the benefits are utilisation of functional departments across projects and more efficient use of resources. Communication can go across, up, and down the chain of command, enabling more efficient communications.

An example of a matrix structure would be in the events industry where there are numerous events being planned and each functional team is involved in planning and organising multiple events, and their day of operation.

An example matrix structure is presented in Figure 10.7.

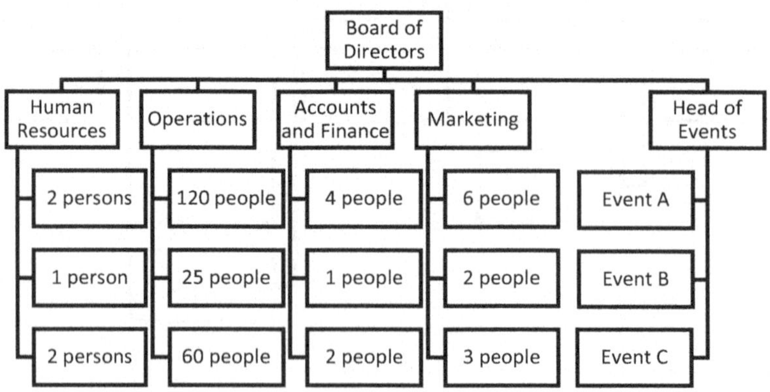

Figure 10.7 Typical Matrix Structure

10.5 Conflict Management

Conflict in the workplace is common, and yet there is no common training offered to managers to help manage conflict. As people in hospitality, hotels, and events work closely in teams, conflict arises when working under pressure, to deadlines, and with factors such as personality clashes.

Much of a manager's and Human Resources' time will be spent dealing with interpersonal issues and conflict within the workplace, detracting from day-to-day operational responsibilities.

Conflict will usually be caused by personal differences, misunderstandings where information is misconstrued, incompatibility with the job role the staff member was employed to do, such as involving skills shortages or lack of experience, and stress arising from work-based activities such as time constraints or resource pressures.

Conflict can be dealt with through collaboration, compromise, through avoidance, through accommodating the needs of others, or through force. Each will have a different impact in the workplace, especially when an individual neglects their own needs to accommodate others, or when force is placed upon someone, which may manipulate or cause harm to another.

Compromise seeks partial satisfaction for both parties, but collaboration is more effective where the concerns of both are considered, and conflict can be overcome mutually by considering a solution together.

Human Resources will often support managers and individual employees through conflict. If conflict leads to communication breakdown and teams are affected, operations may suffer, and it therefore becomes imperative for managers and Human Resources to become involved. Human Resources can train managers and staff members in conflict resolution and act as mediators to resolve problems. Human Resources will need to support employees whilst representing and protecting the company by mitigation.

Conflict can be draining for Human Resources teams dealing with complaints, harassment, victimisation, and discrimination. Much time and resources can be spent investigating issues and attempting to provide satisfactory outcomes for all parties.

Conflict may require the formal disciplinary or grievance procedures to be followed and therefore can lead to a significant workload for Human Resources.

Once a dispute has been reported formally, investigations can begin which require managers, witnesses, the party involved, and perhaps union representatives to attend meetings, and for notes to be taken and checked for accuracy by those involved. Decisions must then be made as to appropriate actions to be taken such as further training, formal warnings, and eventual dismissal.

It is crucial to organisational success that team members and managers can effectively communicate at work to ensure team cohesion, to prevent misconduct and absenteeism, and to retain staff, which influences productivity and customer service.

10.6 Teambuilding (Belbin / Tuckman / team events)

Service industries rely on teamwork for providing excellent customer service, productivity, and staff satisfaction. Well-integrated teams lead to better staff morale, better communication, and less conflict at work, and will result in work being more enjoyable.

When a new employee begins, they will usually be introduced to their department, managers, and peers to help them settle into their role during induction. This ensures an employee knows who to talk to, who to get advice from, and who they report to.

Team relations can be enhanced through team-building activities such as team away days; company socials such as cinema nights, parties, or charity fun days; or sporting activities which enable staff members to socialise and form closer connections on a personable level.

When interviewing individuals or creating teams, managers and Human Resources should consider the range of personality types and traits both current members of the team possess alongside those who are being interviewed. This helps ensure a fit with company culture and teams already in place, being mindful of how individuals can contribute to conflict or a peaceful workplace.

When putting teams together, managers and Human Resources can make use of theoretical frameworks such as Belbin's Team Roles and Tuckman's Stages of Group Development model:

10.6.1 Tuckman's Theory

Bruce Tuckman penned this theory in 1965 to explain how teams form and develop. The theory identified four stages of team development: forming, storming, norming, and performing, later adding a fifth stage: adjourning.

Forming is when a team comes together whether for an individual project or to work generally. The team can be decided through their own choices or allocated by a leader. The team will spend time getting to know one another and individual personalities.

Storming is when the team start to work, collaborating on projects and ideas with varying levels of effectiveness. Individuals will have their own perceptions and values. Conflict may arise, people may be submissive or overly assertive, and relations can break down at this stage whilst others may be getting to know one another and forming bonds.

Norming will occur once team members start to progress out of the storming stage and this should lead to a more harmonious team, starting to build trust and stronger communication and collaboration with one-another. Previous conflict or clashes may be overcome at this stage and personalities accepted. Some team members may naturally take a stronger lead, and others will be more compliant, but some creativity may be lost during this stage. Differences will start to be accepted and resolved to respect the skills and experiences of others.

Performing is when the team establishes how to work effectively to its full potential. Members will feel satisfied with progress and utilise each other's strengths, recognising how teams can perform better in the workplace and be productive together. Team members begin to feel part of a community which will increase satisfaction at work when feeling a sense of belonging, leading to a supportive and productive work environment.

Adjourning is the added stage of Tuckman's model when the team dissolves at the end of a project such as when an event has taken place or when the restaurant closes for the night. Team members might work together on the next project or will shift and go through the process again.

10.6.2 Belbin's Team Roles

Dr Meredith Belbin developed Team Roles theory in the late 1970s believing that teams with different competencies performed better when these skills were utilised when creating teams, as opposed to less balanced teams.

Teams are different from a group of people, as teams work towards common goals, establishing ways of utilising each other's skills to achieve these goals. A group of people can be a group of strangers gathered in a room, students in a classroom, or a restaurant; it does not mean they can work together or perform together.

The team roles Belbin identified are:

Plant: generates ideas and likes to problem-solve

Resource investigator: explores opportunities and networks to support a project

Co-ordinator: clarifies goals, delegates tasks

Shaper: possesses drive and ambition to work on projects and works well under pressure; helps ensure the team stays focussed

Monitor-evaluator: strategic and monitors progress and options

Team worker: cooperates, listens, and gets on with the work and helps ensure teams work effectively together

Implementer: practical and reliable and actions ideas; helps organise work

Completer finisher: conscientious, often the perfectionist who will proofread, check for errors, and perfects the work

Specialist: possesses knowledge, skills, or experiences helpful to the project

When different roles are considered, each person can contribute something different to the team to ensure team cohesion and effectiveness. If there are too many people with the same role, such as co-ordinator, there may be too many leaders leading to clashes.

Belbin's Team Roles can be identified by using the following test: https://www.belbin.com/resources/free-belbin-test-looking-for-a-free-team-roles-test

The benefits of working effectively as a team include reduced conflict, better team cohesion, ability to problem-solve, and working effectively to enhance productivity, wider group construct, gaining knowledge and understanding from one another to develop the team knowledge as a whole, and a happier and more contented workplace.

This will reduce a manager's time dealing with conflict, productivity issues, and communication breakdown, and will lead to better staff retention and a lower administrative burden on Human Resources, and lower the risk of litigation.

Bibliography

Mehrabian, A. (1981). *Silent Messages: Implicit Communication of Emotions and Attitudes*. Belmont, CA: Wadsworth.

Marriott Annual Report (2023). Annual Reports. Available from: https://ir.marriottvacationsworldwide.com/annual-reports/

PwC (2024). *PwC's 2024 US Responsible AI Survey*. Available from: https://www.pwc.com/us/en/tech-effect/ai-analytics/responsible-ai-survey.html/

Belbin.com (no date). *Free Belbin Test*. Available from: https://www.belbin.com/resources/free-belbin-test-looking-for-a-free-team-roles-test/

'Shannon's Model of Communication', *A Mathematical Theory of Communication in 1948*. *Bell Lab Technical Journal*, XXVII(3) July 1948, p. 381. Nokia Corporation and AT&T Archives.

Chapter 11

Employment Law

11.0 Introduction

Employment law is complex and requires organisations to be extremely vigilant to ensure compliance to mitigate legal issues that arise from risks resulting in fines and negative publicity. Human Resources are often mistrusted by employees for this reason, as Human Resources must protect the business, but Human Resources are also tasked with supporting employees, whilst adhering to policy, employment law, and other relevant laws, and it is necessary to avoid bias, discrimination, and unfair treatment of employees and other stakeholders.

Whilst most hospitality, hotel, and events organisations are micro, small, and medium-sized enterprises (SMEs), other organisations will be multinational which brings further challenges in complying with laws across multiple countries which will also vary. Such information should be sought from relevant employment law specialists by Human Resources or business owners and necessary information communicated down the chain of command to ensure compliance, for example to regional managers, general managers, and operations managers.

This chapter provides an overview of what Employment Law covers. However, due to the size and scope of laws globally, it is not possible to analyse all laws herein. Legal advice should always be sought. Equality rights will be covered alongside right to work checks, contracts of employment, working hours, holiday

DOI: 10.4324/9781003469803-12

pay, health and safety, minimum wage, risk management, maternity leave, data protection, investigation, redundancy, sexual harassment, and the role of unions when dealing with employment matters

11.1 Equality Law

One of the key employment laws organisations must follow is fair employment law which aims to protect employees and applicants from discrimination.

Some countries have laws which prohibit discrimination based on 'protected characteristics' such as nationality, race, ethnicity, and religion. Other countries will include disability, age, marital status, sexual orientation, gender reassignment, pregnancy, and maternity. Anti-discrimination laws deter discrimination during the employment process, ensuring employers recruit based on the ideal profile of the candidate and criteria such as qualifications, experience, aptitude, and skills as set out in the person specification, as discussed in Chapter 2.

These laws also protect against discrimination, harassment, and victimisation in the workplace during employment and ensure employees receive fair pay, there is gender equality, and there are equal opportunities for progression and training as examples.

Certain reasonable adjustments may need to be made, work assessments made, or other support put in place. Likewise, all individuals should have the same opportunities for employment, progression, promotion, and reward, and be treated fairly, with differences taken into consideration.

Some of the laws relating to Equality law include:

- Argentina: Law on Discriminatory Acts (no. 23592 of 1988)
- Australia: Age Discrimination Act; Disability Discrimination Act, Racial Discrimination Act; Sex Discrimination Act
- Canada: The Canadian Human Rights Act
- China: PRC Labour Law; PRC Employment Promotion Law; the Regulation on the Employment of the Disabled; the PRC Law on the Protection of the Rights and Interests of Women
- Egypt: No specific employment law in Labour Law, but men and women have the same rights, and employers must not discriminate on pay based on sex, race, language, religion, or creed; and employees must not be dismissed unfairly based on race or sexual orientation, because they are caregivers, or because of pregnancy, religion, or political stance
- Finland: The Non-Discrimination Act (yhdenvertaisuuslaki)

- India: no specific law that governs private businesses. Equal Remuneration; Maternity Benefit Act; Rights for Persons with Disabilities; The Sexual Harassment of Women at the Workplace
- Japan: The Labour Standards Act; The Equal Opportunity Act
- Nigeria: The Labour Act
- Russia: The Russian Labour Code
- Switzerland: Swiss Gender Equality Act; Federal Act on Equal Treatment of Women and Men; Federal Disabled Equality Act
- UAE: Article 4 of the Labour Code
- Ukraine: The Code of Labour Laws of Ukraine 1971
- United Kingdom: The Equality Act 2010
- United States: Title VII of the Civil Rights Act 1964

INDUSTRY VOICE

Dr Philip Berners, Associate Professor in Events Management

Equality law protects against the discrimination of 'protected characteristics' which includes disability in the UK. Under the Equality Act (2010), people with a disability are entitled to 'reasonable adjustments'. Employers have a legal duty to adjust the working environment to allow employees with a disability to do their job.

Some disabilities, of course, are not obvious or visible. Mental health conditions are protected under health and safety laws and under the Equality Act they are classified as disabilities, as a protected characteristic.

Those with physical or mental health issues should have a review of their work environment and 'reasonable adjustments' made. An example I can recollect is when an employee with depression found it a struggle to cope with a hectic environment. In this case, the reasonable adjustment was to relocate the employee to a less busy location where the pace was slower and would not impact anxiety and exacerbate issues.

The job advertisement, person specification, and job description must all comply with this law. Job adverts need to be free from discriminatory language yet capture the key details from the person specification and job description for potential applicants to determine whether they are suitable for the role based on job competencies and skills.

Furthermore, the recruiting team should shortlist applications against the person specification to ensure fair processes, free from bias and discrimination. Candidates are shortlisted against the key criteria such as essential and desirable traits listed in the person specification, as opposed to protected characteristics highlighted under equality law.

Once candidates are invited for interview, any reasonable adjustments should be determined to identify if applicants need hearing loops, braille documents, or disabled access.

During interviews, fair employment practices can be maintained by asking all applicants the same questions based on skills and the ability to do the job, to assess suitability for the role. Candidate answers can then be captured on an interview analysis form and scores given to key competencies and experiences, skills, and qualifications to fairly compare candidates against one another. This provides the organisation with comparatives scores, with the strongest applicant with the highest score offered the position, demonstrating fair recruitment practices and legal compliance.

Once appointed, reference checks are made, normally requiring two references from previous employers, educators, or other organisations the individual may have worked with, volunteered for, or been part of. This helps confirm the individual's identity and experience. Right to work checks are then made to ensure the applicant is eligible to work, such as checking passport or working visa.

11.2 Right to Work Checks

Contributed by Frazer Gander, Assistant Head of People & Culture, De Vere

One of the first stages in the employment lifecycle requires an understanding of right to work legislation. This will vary country to country and has been briefly discussed in Chapter 2.

The UK is a leading example of a country with extensive employment laws. In terms of right to work checks in the UK, it is governed by The Asylum, Immigration, and Nationality Act 2006. This is key legislation which outlines employers' responsibilities in verifying potential or current employees' right to live and work in the UK. This section will discuss UK requirements as an example.

Following the UK's exit from the European Union (EU), right to work compliance has become more complex as the ability to migrate to the UK is more challenging for individuals.

The penalties for non-compliance in this area could have serious consequences for employers. If an employer knowingly employs a worker without the right to work in the UK, they could face unlimited fines or a prison sentence up to five years.

Employers who employ a worker who does not have the right to work in the UK or did not complete the correct checks could face a fine of up to £65,000 per illegal worker and risk their company's name being published by the Home Office.

It is therefore essential that all managers with responsibility for recruitment and the employment of workers have a good understanding of the legal requirements and how they can demonstrate compliance.

Due to the transient nature of hospitality workers with diverse workforces, the hospitality industry can be subject to unannounced inspections by the Home Office to ensure employers are operating compliantly.

There are several ways in which an employer can verify a potential or current worker's right to work in the UK. This may be determined by the worker's nationality or current immigration status.

11.2.1 British Workers

British workers can demonstrate their right to work by producing an original British passport to the employer. The passport does not need to be in date provided that the passport photograph reasonably represents the appearance of the worker. Rules regarding identification documents and expiration will vary country to country.

Alternatively, a worker can provide their full British birth certificate combined with official proof of their National Insurance number (NINO). The birth certificate must be the full A4 page version which includes their parents' details (not the shorter version which only includes a summary of the birth).

Official proof of National Insurance number can include letter correspondence from His Majesty's Revenue & Customs (HMRC) or evidence from a former employer or government agency, such as a previous payslip, P45, or P60. Workers cannot complete a P46 form themselves with their National Insurance number.

If a worker does not have either of these documents, they would be required to obtain a replacement birth certificate from the General Register Office for a small fee.

If an employer relies on the verification of these documents for a British worker, they must follow the three-step process as outlined by the Home Office:

1. **Obtain** – Obtain (not retain) the original version of these documents. Employers must request that the worker provides them with original documents for them to verify.
2. **Check** – Check the validity of the documents in the presence of the holder. The employer needs to be reasonably satisfied that the documents are genuine. The employer also needs to be satisfied that the appearance of the worker is consistent with the document's photograph and date of birth.
3. **Copy** – Make and retain a clear copy including the date that the check was made. This date must be prior to the start date of employment.

11.2.2 Identity Document Validation Technology (IDVT)

Recent changes introduced by the Home Office have allowed employers to use IDVT via the services of an Identity Service Provider (IDSP) to complete a digital verification of right to work checks for British and Irish citizens who hold a valid passport (including Irish passport cards).

Identity Service Providers are outsourced organisations who conduct these identity checks on behalf of the employer. The responsibility to comply with the relevant legislation remains with the employer, therefore if opting to use an IDSP the employer must be satisfied with the competency of their provider. An IDSP must retain appropriate certifications that demonstrate their ability to conduct verification to the required standards set by the Home Office.

11.2.3 Online Right-to-Work Checks

The Home Office have recently simplified conducting checks on non-British workers for all EU or non-EU workers by allowing them to demonstrate their right to work through an online checking service.

It is the employer's responsibility to complete the online check prior to the employee commencing employment. Potential workers provide employers with a nine-character 'share code' which can be verified on the Home Office's online service. This instant check provides employers with details of the individual's right to work in the UK, including any restrictions, and the duration of their eligibility. Employers must retain this evidence in physical or electronic copy for the duration of employment.

British workers are currently unable to use an online right-to-work service to demonstrate their right to work in the UK.

11.2.4 Student Visa

International students studying at a university in the UK are granted a Student Visa which permits them to work for a maximum of ten or 20 hours during termtime. These students provide a great talent pool for hospitality and events who may offer casual contracts in areas such as restaurants, bars, or housekeeping. The healthcare sector is another common employer of students with student work visas. A similar Visa can be grated to work in the European Union.

In the US, international workers can obtain a J-1 Visa for work experience such as an internship or an H-1B Visa for a more permanent role after graduation. Students can also gain a Working Holiday visa or Temporary Skills Shortage Visa for Australia.

Within the UK employers are not permitted to offer a Student Visa for any role that replaces a permanent position. The employer must also closely monitor the student's working hours to ensure they do not exceed 20 hours in any week. The Home Office defines this weekly period as a Monday to Sunday which means venues may need to manually track the working hours if their own rota system operates on a different working week.

11.2.5 Expiring Status

Employers must adopt a rigid tracking system to monitor any employees on a working visa in case these visas are due to expire. Whilst it is the responsibility of employees to maintain their ability to live and work overseas, employers may need to remind their workers of their expiring visa and request updates to maintain their ability to continue working.

Towards the end of their expiring status, these workers will consider which route they intend to take depending on the immigration routes available to them. Whichever route these workers take, the employer must ensure that up-to-date documentation is provided to prevent illegal employment practices.

Most of the leading people systems used within the hospitality industry have functionality to alert employers with the upcoming expiry of right to work. Alternatively, employers should consider manual methods such as adding notes in calendars or diaries to ensure they do not miss these deadlines.

11.2.6 Retention of Information

Employers must establish a thorough administrative process to ensure all right-to-work documentation can be retained throughout a worker's employment and for two years after employment ends. Particular attention must be made to ensuring a full paper-trail of documentation is retained throughout employment and not replaced with any updated documentation.

11.2.7 Visa Sponsorship

Employers may wish to consider the option of applying to the Home Office for a sponsor licence which provides the opportunity to recruit and sponsor non-UK nationals into specific roles within their business. Visa sponsorship is particularly attractive to employers to assist them with filling their hard-to-fill vacancies by opening their talent pool on an international basis.

However, the benefits must be weighed against the initial implementation costs, sponsorship costs, and rigid compliance requirements. The Home Office also provides strict criteria on job suitability for roles that may be sponsored, which mostly includes roles for skilled workers that are restricted by minimum salary requirements or skill levels.

11.3 Issuing Contracts of Employment

It is important that employers provide employees with information relating to minimum terms through a 'written statement of particulars' which ideally must be shared with an employee before they commence employment. The period in which a contract should be issued was discussed in Chapter 4, which identified a general time frame prior to employment, on the first day or within a month of employment. Laws must be checked in the home country to ensure adherence to local laws.

An employer must also provide confirmation of additional terms in a wider written statement. It is usually practical to provide all these points within one document as a written Contract of Employment.

The Contract of Employment contains relevant terms and conditions of employment which both parties must abide by throughout the period of employment. Depending on the terms included within a Contract of Employment, other conditions known as 'post-termination restrictions' apply even after employment has come to an end on areas such as sharing confidential company information or attempting to entice employees of that company to new employment.

As a minimum, a written statement of particulars must contain the following and again will vary globally:

- the employer's name which should include their legal trading entity name
- the employee's name, job title, or a description of their work and start date

- the employee's pay and frequency of receiving their pay
- hours and days of work and if and how they may vary (also if employees or workers will have to work on Sundays, during the 'night period', or take overtime)
- holiday entitlement (and if that includes public holidays)
- the location of work and whether the employee might have to relocate
- if an employee or worker works in different locations, where these will be and what the employer's address is
- how long a job is expected to last (and what the end date is if it is a fixed-term contract)
- the duration and conditions of any probationary period
- any other benefits such as childcare vouchers or lunch provision
- mandatory training, and whether this is paid by the employer
- for employees, it must also include the date of a previous job started if it counts towards a period of continuous employment
- Details of sick pay, paid leave, and notice periods – or information to direct the employee to where they can locate this information

Employers must also provide their employees with additional information about pension schemes, any relevant collective agreements, and the company's disciplinary and grievance procedures.

To avoid additional administration, it is best practice to provide new employees with one set of terms and conditions within a Contract of Employment that includes all these required items as a minimum.

Employers do have flexibility to adapt these terms to suit their business, providing they meet statutory requirements, such as not providing less than the statutory minimum notice period or entitlement to sick pay.

In the UK, the Employment Rights Act (1996) requires that a written statement of particulars must be issued before the commencement of employment or on the first day of employment.

In Europe, the EU Directive on Transparent and Predictable Working Conditions (2019/1152) stipulates that all employees must receive a written statement of employment conditions within seven days of commencing employment.

In France, contracts are governed by the French Labour Code and most jobs require an employee to be issued with a contract of employment. French law stipulates contracts to be issued prior to commencement of employment or on the first day at work. Within seven days the main stipulations must be provided, and within one-month additional written information such as training and paid leave entitlement should be given.

In Germany, whilst a written contract is not necessarily legally required, a written record of the main contractual terms should be issued within one month.

In Poland, an employee is not able to commence employment unless the employer has issued the contract of employment.

In Switzerland, the law enables verbal contracts, but best practice is to issue this in writing. Whilst best practice in Switzerland aligns with most countries by issuing the contract with the offer letter prior to the job role starting, or on the first day of work, a contract must be issued within one month as per the Swiss Code of Obligations that certain employment terms should be provided in writing such as job title, start date, salary and benefits, hours of work, and notice period.

In the United States, there is no federal law that identifies a contract should be issued for all employees, and where contracts are issued this can be when an offer letter is provided and in general many senior job roles are issued with contracts as are those who belong to a union.

Canadian law varies by province and does not always stipulate that a contract should be issued. Best practice, like many countries, is for a contract to be issued in writing prior to the first day of work. But if signed once the job role has commenced, there may be ambiguities, and certain conditions might not be enforceable especially if implied and written terms differ to what was agreed prior to the job role starting.

South American law varies country to country and is broadly consistent with most countries globally. The contract must be issued and signed before the start of employment, including fixed-term contracts and temporary employment.

In Australia, there are certain rules under the Fair Work Act (2009) providing organisations with obligations to outline specific terms and conditions in writing. The National Employment Standards outline minimum conditions which must be met.

Whilst in Malaysia this is normally within the first month of employment or upon offer of employment. This is stipulated within the Employment Act (1955) for some professions.

In China, the Labor Contract Law of the People's Republic of China (2008) outlines strict guidelines and has clearer legal requirements in comparison to other countries. The law encourages employers to issue the contract prior to the employee starting work and, by signing a contract, prevents potential disputes. If not signed prior to commencement of the job role, the requirements are for a contract to be issued within one month of commencement of employment. There are penalties for failing to establish a contract of employment. An employer must pay double the monthly wage as the penalty for each month worked without a contract.

Different rules apply for part-time workers in China, who work less than four hours per day or 24 hours within a working week whereby a contract does not need to be issued but it is still considered best practice to do so.

A summary of when employment contracts should be issued for a sample of countries is listed below in Table 11.1. This should be used for guidance only, as laws may be subject to change or interpretation.

Table 11.1 Summary of When Employment Contracts Should Be Issued

Argentina	Labor Contract Law No. 20,744 (Ley de Contrato de Trabajo): Before or on first day of employment (especially for fixed-term contracts).
Australia	Fair Work Act 2009 and The National Employment Standards: dictate organisations must outline specific terms and conditions in writing but initial contract may be in writing or a verbal agreement and there is no obligation to have a written contract. Try to issue before employment starts.
Bangladesh	Bangladesh Labor Act 2006 and 2015; Labor Rules 2015. Issue a written appointment letter upon recruitment of an employee with a written contract then issued afterwards.
Brazil	Consolidation of Labor Laws 1943 (The Consolidação das Leis do Trabalho): Before first day of work and within 48 hours of first day at work. Written agreement not legally required, but is best to have in writing.
Bulgaria	Bulgarian Labour Code: Contract to be issued before employee starts work and employer should register this with the National Revenue Agency within three days of being signed. Contract must be issued in writing.
Canada	Canada Labour Code: varies by province, best practice to issue prior to first day at work.
Chile	Chilean Labor Code: 15 days for permanent contracts and five days for fixed-term contracts.

(Continued)

Table 11.1 (Continued)

China	The Labor Contract Law of the People's Republic of China (2008): issue contract prior to start date or within one month of commencement of employment. Part-time workers who work less than four hours per day, or 24 hours per week, a contract does not need to be issued, but it is still considered best practice to have a contract in place.
Columbia	Colombian Labour Code (Código Sustantivo del Trabajo): before or on the first day of employment. Fixed-term contracts should be agreed in writing. Verbal agreements can be used, but a contract is better in writing.
Czech Republic	The Czech Labor Code (Zákoník práce): at the commencement of employment or within one month in writing.
Dubai	The UAE Labour Law, or Federal Decree Law No. 33 of 2021: within seven days of commencing employment in writing and all employees must be employed on a fixed-term three-year contract to enhance competitiveness but it can be renewed.
Egypt	Labour Law (Law no.12/2003): issued on first day of employment with wider written statement within two months.
Ethiopia	Labour Proclamation No. 1156/2019: written contract at the start of employment, and employee may still be protected even if not issued.
France	French Labour Code: contracts to be issued prior to commencement of employment or first day at work.
Germany	The Civil Code (Bürgerliches Gesetzbuch, BGB): within one month of starting employment.
Ghana	Labour Act 2003: within two months or at the beginning of employment.
Hungary	The Labour Code: contract to be issued before employee starts work.
India	No single legislation that stipulates law. The Indian Contract Act 1872; Industrial Disputes Act 1947; and Shops and Establishments Act rules conditions of employment and contract law. Best practice is to issue contract as quickly as possible to protect rights.
Iran	The Labour Code of 1990: on first day of employment in writing and wider written terms within two months.
Kenya	Employment Act 2007: contract to be issued before first day of work for those who work more than three months for an employer.
Malaysia	Employment Act 1955: within the first month of employment or upon offer of employment.

(Continued)

Table 11.1 (Continued)

New Zealand	Employment Relations Act 2000: issued before start of employment and the employee should be given sufficient time to review this beforehand. Can lead to penalties for the employer if not issued.
Nigeria	Nigerian Labour Act: contract must be issued within three months, but certain terms must be communicated at the commencement of employment. Best practice is to issue the contract at beginning of employment.
Peru	The Labour Productivity and Competitiveness Law: contract should be issued within 30 days and before first day of work for fixed-term contracts.
Poland	The Polish Labour Code: to be issued before employee starts work, and employee cannot commence employment without this.
Romania	The Romanian Labour Code: contract to be issued before employee starts work and be entered onto the Government database before work commences.
Russia	The Labor Code of the Russian Federation: contract must be signed before the employee starts work or within three working days of the first working day. The probation period must be included in the contract.
South Africa	Basic Conditions of Employment Act: contract to be issued on or before the first day of work. Certain terms must be in writing such as the job description, pay, hours of work, and holiday entitlement.
Spain	Workers' Statute (Estatuto de los Trabajadores): contract to be issued within ten days.
Sweden	The Employment Protection Act (Lag om anställningsskydd): within 30 days of commencing employment.
Switzerland	Swiss Code of Obligations: contract to be issued with the offer letter or prior to the job role starting, or first day of work, and must be issued within one-month, verbal contracts also accepted, but best practice is to issue the contact of employment in writing.
Tanzania	Employment and Labour Relations Act of 2004: upon starting work and for any employees working on projects or employed for more than six months a written contract must be provided.
Uganda	Employment Act 2006: any employee who works for more than four weeks must be issued with a contract. Ideally, issued before employment starts or within four weeks of starting employment.
United Kingdom	The Employment Rights Act 1996: written statement of particulars to be issued before the commencement of employment or on the first day of employment, with a wider written statement of terms within two months.

(Continued)

Table 11.1 (Continued)

United States	The National Labor Relations Act (NLRA): can be issued when the offer letter is issued.
Uruguay	The Code of Commerce 1865: before or on first day of employment (especially for fixed-term contracts).
Zambia	The Employment Code Act of 2019: within one month of starting work. Best practice is to issue the contract at beginning of employment especially for long-term employment.

11.4 Continuous Employment

Contributed by Frazer Gander, Assistant Head of People & Culture, De Vere

An employee maintains their period of continuous employment when working for the same employer without a break in their employment contract. Employees maintain continuous employment if they are absent due to sickness, maternity leave, or when taking annual leave.

However, once an employee departs from the business due to resignation or dismissal, their period of continuous employment will cease.

If an employee chooses to return to an employer after leaving due to resignation, if their employment contract had correctly been terminated, then their employment would recommence on an entirely new period of continuous employment.

The period of continuous employment is an important term to clarify within an employment contract as this may impact other terms of the contract, such as the length of a probationary period, a notice period, or the employee's qualifying period for statutory employment rights.

Employees are generally unable to make a claim for unfair dismissal until they reach two years' continuous employment.

A period of continuous employment should be honoured if an employee changes roles with the same employer or if they have a revised contract of employment issued due to a change in other terms such as their contracted hours. Employers with multiple locations, such as hotel and restaurant groups, would also be required to provide continuous employment if their employees transfer internally within the business.

Continuous normally applies whereby a company is taken over or merges with another, to ensure employment rights and uphold the original contract of employment (revisions can be made if the new owner/s offer more beneficial terms). This is commonly referred to as TUPE covered in section 11.11.

11.4.1 Types of Employment Contract

The Contract of Employment between the employer and employee is a legally binding agreement to outline the terms and conditions of employment. Each party must abide by the terms specified in the contract.

Within the hospitality industry, employers have flexibility to offer a range of types of Contracts of Employment to suit their business operations and their staffing requirements as outlined in Chapter 4.

Here is a summary of the main types of contracts used in hospitality, hotels, and events:

Permanent Full-Time or Part-Time Contracts – these contracts are offered on a permanent basis with a minimum number of working hours per week or month. Employers must ensure they have sufficient work for the employee to fulfil these contractual minimum working hours.

Zero-Hour or Irregular Hours Contracts – these contracts could provide no fixed number of working hours or working hours that may vary over a week or month due to changes in business levels. These types of contracts may be suitable for certain statuses of workers, such as students who have other commitments to balance outside work. However, they do not provide workers with job security so might be considered less attractive.

Fixed-term contracts – to offer employment on a temporary basis for a fixed duration or to complete a project for example, to provide cover to a colleague on maternity leave or for an employee assigned to launching a new Property Management system or other project as examples.

11.5 Working Time and Arrangements

The 24-hour nature of hospitality and hotel environments (and some events) provides employers with further challenges to balance daily business operations with working-time regulations and legal requirements. Some employment law will be stricter in some countries that others.

UK regulations will again be discussed as a given example, and Human Resources, employers, and students would need to research the laws in their home country to confirm requirements when citing information. This includes requirements for rest breaks and working hours.

The key UK legislation which stems from EU law is the Working Time Regulations (1998) which outlines key requirements to protect work–life balance, health and safety, and overall welfare.

The requirements of the working time regulations include:

- Maximum weekly working time – workers are not permitted to work an average greater than 48 hours per week. The average should be calculated based on a 17-week period unless the worker has worked for the employer for less than 17 weeks. It is possible through a written agreement with their employer that a worker can 'opt-out' of this arrangement to permit them to work over the maximum number of weekly hours.
- Length of night work – defined as the period between 23:00 and 06:00, the regulations restrict night working to an average maximum of eight hours within a 24-hour period.
- Night worker health assessment – an employer must also offer a night worker the opportunity of a free health assessment to assess their suitability for night work prior to their work commencing. This requirement also extends to those employed in night work, entitling them to regular assessments. Employers may choose to complete these assessments with their nominated Occupational Health (OH) provider. Records must be retained to demonstrate these health assessments have been offered.
- Daily rest period – adult workers (aged 18 years+) are entitled to a daily rest break no less than 11 hours in each 24-hour period. A young worker is entitled to a daily rest break no less than 12 hours in each 24-hour period.
- Weekly rest period – adult workers (aged 18 years+) are entitled to uninterrupted rest periods of at least 24 hours in each seven-day period. For a young worker this is increased to an uninterrupted rest period of at least 28 hours in each seven-day period.
- Rest breaks – if an adult worker's daily working hours are more than six hours, they are entitled to a rest break which is no less than 20 minutes. If a young worker's daily working hours are more than four and a half hours, they are entitled to a rest break of at least 30 minutes. Rest breaks must be taken in locations away from the worker's work environment such as in a designated canteen or staffroom.

Managers who are responsible for compiling their departmental schedules and managing working time during business hours, therefore, have a wide range of factors to consider in balancing the demands of the business with their team's entitlements.

Collective agreements may exist within certain hospitality, hotel, and events businesses which can adapt the definition of certain terms within the Working

Time Regulations specifically for that business, including the definition of night-time and the duration of daily rest for adult workers.

Employers are required to retain records that demonstrate employees are not working over the 48-hour weekly maximum (unless there is an opt-out agreement) or the limits for night working and young workers.

Employers are not required by the regulations to retain all daily records. However, it is advisable for hospitality employers to do so in a way that is practical for their business. Retaining these records is made simpler if the employer has implemented a time and attendance management system for payroll purposes. Some time and attendance systems have enhanced functionality to alert users to breaches in the regulations such as daily rest, maximum weekly working hours, and relating to young workers.

11.5.1 Holiday Pay (Annual Leave; Vacation Entitlement)

In Europe and the UK, annual leave (or holiday pay) is dictated also by The Working Time Regulations which provide workers with the entitlement to paid annual leave. Workers in the UK are entitled to 5.6 weeks paid holiday each year which can also be calculated in days based on a worker's number of working days per week.

Average annual leave across countries varies between 20 and 30 days but others can be as little as five to ten days, for example. This is discussed in Chapter 4 under Employment Contracts.

Recent developments in employment law in the UK have also outlined a special requirement for workers on Zero-Hours Contracts to receive holiday entitlement equivalent to 12.07 per cent of hours worked within a pay period up to a maximum of 5.6 weeks' holiday entitlement each year.

The calculation method for holiday pay can be complicated due to the ongoing developments in employment law, and each country will be different.

Employers should consider the general concept that workers should not be subject to detriment for time spent on annual leave and therefore their holiday pay should account for an average value of overtime or commission for the period they were on leave.

Managing holiday records and calculating holiday pay is a key feature of many time and attendance systems which can greatly assist employers with these complexities. Employers should also consider clarifying holiday booking processes and required timescales within their contracts of employment, colleague handbooks, or policies.

11.5.2 Health and Safety Regulations

Health and safety laws exist to protect the health, safety, and welfare of all persons entering a premises. All employees and others contracted to carry out work have a legal requirement to protect the health and safety of everybody, including fellow staff, members of the public, contractors, and suppliers. The latter two will also have responsibilities including reporting dangerous occurrences, risks, and accidents and doing everything as practicable as possible to prevent any ill-health, accidents, or death in the workplace.

INDUSTRY VOICE

Dr Philip Berners, Associate Professor in Events Management

Every employee should be made aware of constructing their 'environment of self-learning' (Berners, 2024). This means being aware of learning from what is happening around them. Employees can learn from, as examples; their managers, their colleagues, their clients, their guests, and other businesses such as events and hotels. This is how we all learn, of course – we call it 'experience' which teaches us what works and what needs improving.

But not everybody is aware of the need to construct their environment of self-learning. For example, if an American client checks into a hotel, the staff can learn how Americans behave, and what they like, what they dislike...

In terms of health and safety, the presence of specialists such as health inspectors, is not something to fear – it is something to learn from. I had a health inspector visit my kitchen during an event and my chefs understood this was a learning opportunity, not a hindrance.

Organisations should provide training on any potential risks, including where food is served, such as food hygiene, food handling, food safety, and Hazard Analysis [and] Critical Control Points (HACCP); fire prevention training; training if using chemicals such as the Care Of Substances [that are] Hazardous [to] Health (COSHH); manual handling and lifting; and the using of visual display units (computers).

Protective clothing (PPE) should be provided where necessary such as steel toe-capped boots in kitchens, gloves when handling food, goggles when changing beer kegs, and chain link aprons if butchering meat as examples.

INDUSTRY VOICE

Dr Philip Berners, Associate Professor in Events Management

All hospitality, hotel, and events organisers will be familiar with conducting risk assessments. Everybody should be doing the same in their workplace. Risk assessment is about identifying risks; then rating how likely they are to happen; rating that if they did happen, what would be the severity or impact; then taking actions to lessen the likelihood, lessen the impact, or eliminate the risk.

It is good practice for managers to risk assess their workplace, and for staff to do the same. This manages risk out of the business.

The workplace also has a responsibility to protect, not just physical health, but mental well-being to prevent stress, anxiety, and burnout.

Ultimately, it is the organisation that is responsible for health and safety and a breach can lead to prosecution, fines, and possible imprisonment.

11.5.3 Lone Working

If an employee is required to work alone (lone working), the health and safety regulations require employers to consider their employees' health and safety. Lone working is considered a greater risk to employees as there will be fewer employees around to help in emergencies or to provide training or supervision.

There is no defined duration of 'lone working', therefore employers should consider the nature of roles across their business and the risks to employees if they are working alone. Shift work and unsociable hours are susceptible to lone working in hospitality and events. Common roles within events, hotels, restaurants, cafes, fast food outlets, and bars that may include an element of lone working include night manager, porter, security, housekeeper, bar tender, waiter, office staff, and early or late-shift chef.

Employers must consider lone working when conducting workplace risk assessments to ensure risks are effectively managed before allowing colleagues to work in lone conditions.

Government and health and safety advisors provide useful resources to support employers in managing these risks, including recommendations on methods of communication and plans for dealing with emergencies.

Navigating the ever-changing employment law landscape remains a key challenge for hospitality operators, line managers, or Human Resources professionals. Due to the transient labour market within hospitality, it is key for managers to have a solid understanding of relevant employment law to ensure their departments and teams are working compliantly.

Working in line with the relevant employment law and best practice protects the business from risk or legal claims whilst ensuring employees' best interests are protected.

11.6 Minimum Wage and Living Wage

Minimum wage is a legal minimum that an employer can pay their workers and is determined by the government in the relevant country.

The minimum wage may change every year and rise with inflation and as the cost of living increases. For payroll, this means significant increases in wage costs and can lead to financial strain or business closure during economic uncertainty and where high costs exist with already tight profit margins. Hospitality and events are labour-intensive industries and wages can absorb a high proportion of revenue.

According to the United Nations, over 170 countries have one or more minimum wage requirements within their legislation, with some countries varying this by sector and others having a set standard across all businesses.

There is also a drive to increase wages to align more closely with the rate of inflation which continues to grow above the rate at which wages are rising. Therefore, some countries have also adopted a wage that is closer to the cost of living which may be referred to as a 'living wage', which puts employers under further financial pressure.

However, being a living-wage employer may help attract and retain talented recruits, reducing recruitment costs, improving service, and therefore profitability, reputation, and competitive advantage. There are many benefits to paying a higher wage and it does not always require a business to reduce service quality or raise prices to counteract increased wage costs.

The United Nations and European Commission have been productive in pursuing increases in wages across certain locations globally.

In the US, whilst the Minimum Wage for hospitality workers was \$2.13 (2024) under the Fair Labor Standards Act, each state has implemented different amounts, many of which pay above this. Hospitality employees are generally not entitled to the minimum wage applied to many other industries due to the tipping culture which is common in the US. The wage for those not exposed to tips/gratuities is over $7 in comparison.

Tipped employees must be paid a minimum of $2.13 in the US, but their tips help bridge the gaps with wages in other industries. Due to the tipping culture in the US, many servers would prefer receiving tips over a wage increase. Tips may exceed any minimum wages that can be imposed, and therefore, a change in this culture would be difficult to overturn.

The expectation for restaurant guests, and those drinking in bars, for example, to tip staff, can be off-putting for tourists who are not used to this culture and would expect employers to pay a fairer wage.

Furthermore, US law does not require vacation, severance, or sick pay, rest periods, pay rises, or terminations demands unlike many other countries which further reduces the total remuneration package available, particularly in this country.

Numerous sources online, including *Statista*, report average wages across the globe, with Luxembourg as the highest net minimum wage per month earning $2459, Australia $2150, Ireland $2020, and UK $1937, as some of the highest earners (in US dollars). Some of the lowest earners globally include those in Russia earning a monthly wage of $180, Pakistan $114, India $99, and Nigeria $68 a month.

11.7 Health & Safety, Food Hygiene, Food Safety, Licences

Whilst training is not a legal requirement, there are certain requirements to ensure businesses operating across hospitality, hotels, and events are compliant with the law and to ensure legal mitigation against issues such as food poisoning, allergies, responsible service of alcohol, and the safety of all stakeholders on the premises.

Food safety and food hygiene training prevent the risk of illness or death from food that has not been stored, prepared, handled, or cooked correctly or safely, and prevent cross contamination, food poisoning, and injury resulting from unsafe food or drink.

Food safety inspectors or environmental health officers visit premises serving food to inspect the premises and check records, such as training certificates for food handling, fridge and freezer temperatures, food handling and temperature controls, pest control, and cleaning, and to take samples of food to ensure standards are being met to protect consumers. These standards and processes, where they exist, will vary country to country. They may issue improvement notices, fines, or take legal action, and even enforce business closure.

Alcohol licences ensure the premises and individual workers are legally permitted to sell or provide alcohol, protection of children, informed consumer decision-making as to consumption, and prevention of disorderly behaviour.

Weights and measures ensure that what is being advertised is what is being sold in terms of alcohol measurements and food processes.

Health and safety, hazardous substances, manual handling training is imperative to ensure the health, safety, and welfare of all guests, staff, contractors, and others who are involved in the premises/business. This helps prevent accidents, injuries, near misses, and deaths. Any major incidents need to be reported to government or other officials who may then advise industry-wide on how to prevent dangerous occurrences.

The National Examination Board in Occupational Safety and Health (NEBOSH) provides globally recognised qualifications in health, safety, and environmental qualifications, useful to all events, hotel, and other hospitality practitioners. Human Resources and managers may offer to fund such qualifications.

An accident book is used within the business to report any near misses, accidents, and injuries to outline what action was taken as a result, with the aim to improve health and safety processes and procedures.

Training must be provided when the job involves manual handling, lifting, and carrying.

Training in the use of chemicals or other hazardous substances is needed to prevent contamination, poisoning, explosions, burns, etc. The Care Of Substances that are Hazardous to Health (COSHH) is the relevant procedure here. This includes not dispensing chemicals into other containers, not decanting chemicals into water bottles, not mixing chemicals, the proper use of chemicals, wearing protective gloves and goggles, use of chemicals in ventilated areas, correct ratio of chemicals to water, and using correct cloths for cleaning to prevent contamination.

Visual display units for staff who are required to work on a computer or screen must meet legal requirements in some countries to make assessments of the set-up of screens, keyboards, adjustable chairs, and seating positioning to ensure eyes are protected, alongside prevention of injuries such as Repetitive Strain Injury (RSI).

11.8 Risk Management

Risk management, emergency planning, and crisis preparation is essential for managers. Human Resources may support managers in the planning and training for the occurrence of incidents.

Hospitality and events face challenges from natural disasters such as volcanic eruptions to flooding, and other crises such as fire, bomb threats, crowd safety and overcrowding issues, power failure, gas leaks, chemical hazards, and collapsing structures as examples. Terrorism is a major incident that can impact venues, and it is important to plan for such incidents to reduce the likelihood, impact, and to protect the business, staff, and customers, and to help with post-incident recovery.

There are laws across the globe that determine legal requirements businesses need to follow such as completing Event Management Plans (EMPs), crisis plans, risk plans, or risk assessments.

Such measures help ensure the health, safety, and welfare of all stakeholders, help prevent or reduce risk, and reduce the number of accidents, injuries, or deaths, whilst protecting the reputation of the organisation and reassuring visitors.

Risk is reduced by having clearly signed fire exits, clear escape routes, fire safety precautions, security, safety procedures and training, mock events, guest tracking, keeping staff records, and CCTV.

Events pose further risks where there are large gatherings of people in an unfamiliar environment, leading to potential crowd safety issues, crushes, and heat exhaustion.

Events also involve consumption of alcohol and illegal substances, which impacts customer behaviour and impaired decision-making leading to further risks of violence, accidents, and even death.

Furthermore, events and other hospitality venues may be attended by celebrities, dignitaries, and royalty, who may be under threat from overzealous followers, protestors, or people with political motives, leading to terrorist attacks.

Terrorist attacks are also likely to occur where large gatherings take place and can be targeted in one place for optimum impact. It is necessary to mitigate or reduce these risks.

Incidents are well documented in hospitality and events including the following:

- 1985 Bradford City fire
- 1989 Hillsborough disaster leading to a fatal crowd crush
- 2001 9/11 terrorist attacks in the US, a series of four coordinated terrorist attacks
- 2002 and 2005 Bali bombings
- 2002 Fatboy Slim concert crowd safety incident at a free-to-attend beach concert
- 2005 London bombings
- 2008 Taj Hotel attack in Mumbai
- 2011 Indiana State Fair stage collapse
- 2015 Massacre at the Bataclan in Paris
- 2015 Tunisia shooting spree at a beach resort
- 2015 Islamic State militants targeted a Russian plane over Egypt killing 224
- 2016 Brussels airport and train station attacks
- 2016 Berlin Christmas market attack
- 2017 Manchester Arena suicide bombing at the Ariana Grade concert
- 2017 Mass shooting at an open-air music festival in Las Vegas
- 2018 Novichok chemical attack in a restaurant in the UK
- 2024 Mexican stage collapse at an election campaign
- 2024 German Christmas market attack when a vehicle was driven into crowds
- 2025 New Orleans New Year's Eve attack when a vehicle was driven into crowds

11.8.1 Crisis Management

Crisis management plans and risk assessments provide early identification of potential issues to minimise crises and help determine how organisations should respond to potential issues and crisis.

Crisis management identifies tactics for dealing with emergency situations, prevention, training, evacuation, and post-incident recovery.

All employees should be trained to understand how to respond, such as monitoring behaviour of guests, unattended baggage, fire drills, and how to respond to finding a potential bomb.

All venues must have appropriate insurance policies in place such as public liability, alongside any emergency and crisis plans. Emergency services such as police, ambulance, and the fire service must be notified where relevant and appropriate road closures, medical services, and police or security is required onsite.

11.8.2 Risk Assessment

Risk assessments are imperative in hospitality, hotels, and events. The most common accidents that occur are slips, trips and falls, burns, and cuts. Health and safety must be managed in the workplace and to do this it is necessary to determine what the risks are which might harm people so control measures can be put into place to prevent harm and comply with the law.

INDUSTRY VOICE

Dr Philip Berners, Associate Professor in Events Management

The job of an event organiser is to eliminate, or certainly minimise, risk. It is about managing risk out of the event so that it is not left in to cause harm.

We do this by risk management procedures. Firstly, an assessment is carried out to identify risks: rate how likely each risk is to happen; rate that if it were to happen, what would be the impact; what measures are already in place; and then identify what further measures should be in place to mitigate that risk from occurring or minimise its impact. Finally, the risk assessment shows who is responsible for the actions taken to mitigate each risk.

Remember, risk is not only about physical harm. There are other risks such as the potential to lose money; the damage to reputation; the risk of not selling tickets. It is important to identify all risks and what steps can be taken to manage these out of the event.

Table 11.2 Risk Assessment

Potential hazard:	Who might be harmed and how:	Existing control measures in place:	Further actions required:	Who is responsible for these actions:	Date needed by:	Completion date:
Manual handling -Lifting, carrying of linen and mattresses. -Pushing and pulling of trolley. -Overloading of trolley -Carrying, folding and tucking of linen on bed -Carrying and folding towels -Working quickly due to time constraints -Bending and twisting when cleaning	Housekeeping team	Use trolleys to move heavy loads Do not overload trolley and make sure brakes are applied when not in use Lift using safe manual handling measures Do not overload team with work, and provision of reasonable timings to clean rooms and public areas	Remind staff to maintain good levels of housekeeping	All staff and managers	30/11/25	28/11/25
Slips, trips or falls -Falling or tripping over furniture such as bed, chairs, and tables	Housekeeping team, guests and other staff or visitors	Rooms and public areas designed with space to walk around furniture and fittings	Replace frayed carpet and chipped tiles	All staff and managers	12/08/25	12/08/25

-tripping over cables such as vacuum cord -Slipping on wet bathroom floor -Slips or trips on uneven floors or steps		Ensure cables are covered, tucked away or hazard signs displayed warning people Make sure all tiled and ceramic floors are dried as much as they can be when mopping Report and make safe any loose tiles or steps Provide adequate lighting Remove any obstacles or other hazards				
Chemicals -Misuse of cleaning chemicals causing burns, and gases or fumes that may cause breathing issues	Housekeeping team and any other guests, visitors, or staff	Use chemicals as directed on bottles Do not decant chemicals and other cleaning products into other containers	Housekeeping Manager to purchase gloves	All staff and managers	12/10/25	12/10/25

(Continued)

Table 11.2 (Continued)

		Do not mix chemicals Do not ingest chemicals or cleaning products Wear gloves, masks and any other PPE as required when handling chemicals and other hazardous substances	Housekeeping manager to provide training on COSHH to all new staff			

Table 11.3 Risk Assessment Template

Potential hazard:	Who might be harmed and how:	Existing control measures in place:	Further actions required:	Who is responsible for these actions:	Date needed by:	Completion date:

I place risk as the top priority of an event manager. Higher than profit. After all, if something goes wrong or somebody gets hurt, the profit is impacted anyway – refunds, compensation, legal costs, negative word of mouth, damage to reputation...

A risk assessment (see Table 11.3) identifies potential risk, the level of risk, and preventative measures to help overcome such incidents. Whilst not all risks can be avoided, a business should do everything that is reasonably practicable to prevent dangerous occurrences.
An example of a completed risk assessment for a food-handling business can be found on the UK-based Health and Safety Executive website: https://www.hse.gov.uk/simple-health-safety/assets/docs/foodprep.pdf and a basic example for housekeeping below.

If an accident or near-miss should occur, an accident report form must be completed to ensure the incident does not reoccur, to identify future risks, to protect everyone who engages with the business, and as a record in case of repercussions or delayed symptoms. Depending on the severity, it may also be necessary to inform local government agencies. An example accident report form is presented in Table 11.4.

Table 11.4 Accident Report Template

Accident Report Form			
Details of person involved			
First name			
Surname			
Address			
Phone number		Alt phone number	
Email address			
Employee/guest/contractor?			
About the incident			
What are you reporting? Near miss/ accident/ incident/ dangerous occurrence)			
What happened? Detail the incident			
Detail injuries/illness or disease			
What first aid/ medical treatment / hospital admission was needed?			
Any absences from work as a result? If so, give duration			

When did it happen? (Date)	
Where did it happen?	
Witnesses	
Name and contact details for any witnesses	
Details of person completing form	
Name and contact details	
Date form completed	

11.9 Maternity and Paternity Leave

Some countries will enable mothers to take leave when they have a baby, whether paid, unpaid, or supported by the government. In some instances, both parents can share this leave and/or take time off work together.

The average maternity leave varies from 12 to 26 weeks, with European countries being more generous in the pay and time given. In Australia and Japan this tends to be lower. In the United States there is no national paid maternity leave, but unpaid leave is secured for 12 weeks.

Global law surrounding maternity rights will vary, and in some locations, rights will be extended to partners (paternity leave for fathers) and even adoptive parents. Rights may also vary for same sex parents or LGBTQ+ parents. Laws will vary depending on legal, cultural, and economic factors.

In some countries, such as in the United Kingdom, pay increases are still granted during maternity leave, and holiday entitlement still accrued and protection from redundancy will also exist. In the UK, 52 weeks maternity leave can be taken, and payment will be determined by the employing organisation and the government.

11.10 Data Protection

In accordance with General Data Protection Regulations (GDPR), all employee and client data need to be handled securely and sensitively. Human Resources and managers, as well as other employees, will likely handle client data and employee data. How this is captured, retained, stored, and used is dictated by law.

Data protection is necessary to safeguard data and can be compromised through cyber-attacks, hacking, and theft, leaving people vulnerable to data breaches and data-steals such as bank or credit card details, names, addresses, medical records, or other details being leaked.

For example, when the hiring team are recruiting, the data stored on applicants must be destroyed within certain time frames and only used for its intended purpose, with permission. Contracts of employment, details of pay, and other benefits must be kept secure so other employees cannot access this sensitive personal information. Records such as appraisals and investigations must be kept private, confidential, and secure and be stored on the employee's record so these can be referred to when needed.

Only those who need access to personal data should be given access, and data should be safely stored, password protected, or locked away and used appropriately.

11.11 TUPE

TUPE is the Transfer of Undertakings (Protection of Employment) Regulations (2006) in UK law. Similar laws under different names may exist elsewhere in the world. These regulations protect rights when employment is transferred from one employer to another, such as in a merger or takeover.

The original date of employment will be upheld so employment rights remain and will be classed as continuous service when calculating pay scales and aspects such as notice period, probationary review, or redundancy pay.

The employee's job will transfer to the new employer along with the same employment terms and conditions as per their original contract of employment. If more favourable terms exist, these may be granted, such as pay increases, paid annual leave entitlement, and other benefits.

In the United States, no statute governs the employment relationship when a new business takes over and employees can choose to transfer to the new employer under new conditions. Employees may be entitled to 60 days' notice of termination of employment, however. Employment unions or trade unions may also be able to negotiate terms of behalf of staff.

11.12 Disciplinary and Grievance Procedures

Employee performance will be monitored throughout their tenure, and should the employee underperform, have unreasonable levels of absenteeism, or be consistently late, they may be put through the disciplinary process.

Likewise, if an employee feels aggrieved, is being bullied or victimised, they may raise a grievance with managers and Human Resources.

In these situations, Human Resources will normally have policy and procedures as to how to manage the process.

11.12.1 Disciplinary Processes

The typical process for disciplinary action at work follows a structured procedure to ensure a consistent, fair, and justified process has been followed.

This will typically involve verbal, written, and a final warning. Or in the case of gross misconduct, the employee could be instantly dismissed. Misconduct can involve being under the influence of drugs or alcohol at work, theft, violence, or sexual misconduct as examples.

The process may vary, but this is the general process which should be followed:1.

1. **Informal warning**

   Purpose: This seeks to address issues early in an attempt to prevent the issue progressing.

   Process: A manager will discuss issues privately with the employee to identify causes, clarify expectations, and offer support where needed. It may be that the employee needs further training or processes explained.

2. **Verbal warning**

   Purpose: To formally address behaviour following an informal meeting.

   Process: The issue is discussed between the manager and employee, the manager will provide an explanation and provide any necessary examples or evidence, and improvement expectations provided to the employee. This will be noted on the employee's record but is not considered a written warning.

3. **Written warning**

   Purpose: This addresses repeated issues or more serious actions or behaviours. This will be formally documented.

   Process: The employee will be sent a formal written notice from the manager or Human Resources. This will detail the specific behaviours or actions, any policies that have been breached, and what corrective action is needed. It is usual for the employee to sign a declaration that they have read and understood the warning. It will be recorded on the employee's record. It may form part of an investigation into their behaviour.

4. **Final written warning**

   Purpose: This is the final warning if corrective action is still not taken by the employee. This identifies further non-compliance with policies, inappropriate behaviour, or other issues.

Process: This serves as a final formal warning, held on the employee's record following previous warnings. This provides the employee with a final warning to improve before further action, such as termination of contract of employment.

5. **Suspension or termination**

   Purpose: Suspension may be necessary when an investigation is needed to determine circumstances where more serious performance issues or behaviours are being addressed. Termination may be more appropriate where actions or behaviours are proven due to persistent or serious issues (such as theft of money or stock, drug use on shift, or violent or abusive behaviour towards guests or peers).

   Process: For suspension, the employee is temporarily removed from the workplace (with or without pay) for a specified period. When termination is necessary, all other reasonable warnings and steps have been taken to improve behaviour, or gross misconduct has taken place. The employee is given notice of their termination, may not be able to re-enter the workplace, and may be on paid notice.

During disciplinary action, an investigation may take place in which managers and Human Resources will work together with the employee to ensure a fair process is followed. The individual, if part of a union, may wish to have a union caseworker attend any meetings to provide advice, act as counsel, and establish correct procedures are followed and a mutual outcome achieved.

An employee must be provided with the opportunity to appeal the decision, and each organisation should have an appeals process in place. This is necessary if action taken against an employee is considered unfair or unjust, for example if correct procedures are not followed or the reason for the termination of employment is not given, resulting in wrongful or unfair dismissal.

Unfair dismissal: when a reason for the termination of employment is not given. Law requires an organisation to provide a valid reason such as misconduct, performance issues, or redundancy. There is also a legal obligation to follow a fair process, such as following the disciplinary process, and to enable a full and fair investigation to take place.

Wrongful dismissal: occurs when an employee is terminated in breach of the employment contract and/or is in breach of contractual obligations, such as not subjecting the employee to verbal and written warnings or not honouring an agreed notice period.

11.12.2 Grievances

A grievance procedure in the workplace enables employees to raise concerns or a complaint in case of a dispute related to the work itself, with a colleague or manager, in terms of policies or treatment at work.

The typical procedure will be:

- For the individual involved first to try and resolve the issue at the early stage to avoid escalation.
- If unresolved, to speak with the manager or their superior if it involves the line manager.
- If unresolved, raise the issue with Human Resources.
- Human Resources, if not able to resolve issues informally, may then ask the employee to formally raise a grievance. This will be done in writing, citing dates, times, incidents, and any witnesses. This should be factual and avoid bias or opinion where possible. The desired outcome should also be noted.
- The investigating manager or Human Resources professional needs to acknowledge the complaint. The investigating appointee will then gather relevant facts, have an initial interview with the employee, and interview witnesses. This may take time due to complexities or number of people involved but must done in a timely manner. Notes must be taken, and all parties involved will check the notes as an accurate account and confirm any amendments.
- The employee may be reinvited for a more formal meeting to discuss the situation further where necessary, and the employee is entitled to bring a representative such as a colleague or union representative. Other persons involved may also be invited to further meetings with entitlement to bring a representative.
- Resolution and outcome meetings will then take place. After the investigation has taken place, Human Resources or an investigating manager will write to the employee to inform them of the outcome (this may follow from an in-person or online meeting, also). If upheld, corrective action will be taken by the employer such as disciplinary action against the other party, or a change in policies or procedures. If not upheld, the reasons will be outlined.
- Appeals process. If the employee is not satisfied with the outcome and feels they have grounds for appeal, the employee can appeal. The issue can also be escalated through courts.

11.13 Redundancy

Redundancy or severance pay is compensation offered to employees whose contract is terminated through no fault of their own. This is usually due to economic uncertainties of the company, restructure, or downsizing.

Rights to redundancy pay will be outlined, which may typically be one week's pay for every year of service. However, the law varies between countries. Many countries will also cap the maximum payout, despite how many years' service an employee has completed.

In 2024 within the UK, employees are entitled to redundancy pay if they have been employed for over two years. Many employers will pay 1.5 months' pay per year of service. A new Employment Rights Bill, when implemented, will mean companies must consult with employees if 20 or more redundancies are proposed across the organisation.

In the US, there are no federal laws governing redundancy pay, but there is an agreement between the employer and employee. At the time of publication, eight US states have laws that stipulate severance pay but employers are not obligated to offer this (but it must be paid if promised).

In Germany, redundancy is paid if it is part of the employment contract and typically pays two weeks' salary for each year worked, but there is no legal requirement here.

In Canada, under the Canada Labour Code, redundancy is paid if the employee has been employed for over 12 months and is then entitled to two days' pay for each year in employment.

In Japan, the law is protective of employees and whilst there is no specific requirement, organisations may offer generous severance packages for those who volunteer for redundancy but is typically one month's pay for the first year of service and a further one month for every two years' service after that.

In Australia, the National Employment Standards governs redundancy pay entitlements. Severance pay is four weeks' salary if employed between one and two years, increasing by one to two weeks' salary for each year worked after that.

China generally pays one month's salary per year of service when employed for more than one year (half for 6 months' employment).

CASE STUDY: REDUNDANCY PROCESS

On a Friday afternoon, during the 2008/2009 economic crisis, an employer gave all employees a letter to take home, notifying that redundancies were to take place.

On the Monday, the manager took a colleague to the office. Twenty minutes later, she returned to her desk, crying. The individual had been made redundant and had to leave the office. Over the course of the day, more colleagues were taken into meetings with the same outcome.

Team members were naturally devastated, and managers were also upset. Despite the devastating impact on staff, redundancies were necessary for the survival of the organisation and to secure the employment of the remaining staff.

The nature in which staff were informed was unfortunate whereby it became evident if one was called to the office, their job was no longer viable and their distress seen by everyone in the workplace.

Redundancies cause a lot of stress and harm to teams and managers. It is best to give plentiful notice of redundancies and offer voluntary severance as the first step. Some team members might opt to reduce their hours, retire early, or to leave and source alternative employment. The process should involve consulting staff members, communicating time frames and processes, and involving unions.

11.14 Trade Unions

There is a role for trade unions when there is an employee dispute. A trade union is also known as a worker's union or labour union and is an organisation that can help support workers in terms of improving working conditions. A union is made up of workers within the same organisation or trade sector and is often industry wide.

Representing workers, a union can negotiate on behalf of individuals, organisations, or the entire industry in matters such as pay negotiations, benefits, holiday allowances, health and safety regulations, and safe working conditions, and where there are large-scale redundancies. Unions will be involved in collective bargaining where needed for all staff.

Unions can also support individual workers with issues when they are experiencing workplace disputes, grievance, or disciplinary hearings. They will provide guidance and support as regards procedures and legal requirements and can assist their member by attending meetings and hearings, and notetaking, providing counsel, offering support, and guidance, and ensuring process is followed. Human resources will need to accommodate union representatives within these negotiations and meetings.

It is the choice of the individual employee whether they want to join a union, or leave a union, and they are free to choose which union to belong, even if it is different from the one that normally negotiates with the employer.

An employer cannot force a worker to join or leave a union or dictate which union the employee should join. An employer cannot refuse employment or dismiss a worker due to them being in a union, or not. Employers cannot treat the worker unfavourably because of their union membership.

A worker can join a union for a membership fee, which can be a set fee or determined by a percentage or proportion of salary. A worker should ideally join a union prior to experiencing issues, as limited support may be provided otherwise.

Normally, the member will be assigned a caseworker to support them throughout the process should an investigation or meetings need to occur. The caseworker will need to check the employee's union membership status to determine whether the individual has joined or not, and when the member joined, as limits with providing support can be limited. Members should not sign up when they experience an issue, but rather have an ongoing membership.

A union may support their member by ensuring they have the information they need, including options available to them whether this is a result of a disciplinary, redundancy, or grievance such as bullying by a co-worker. The union is not there to give information, but to help the member obtain that information from Human Resources and managers.

The union representative can raise points during meetings, but primarily must support the member in making their points and stating their case, and act as witness to what is being said in meetings, or emails around meetings. If it should come to a dispute between their member and the employer, the union or the caseworker can act as witness. The union representative will also take notes of key points raised by all parties during meetings and can provide these to the organisation if needed and so both parties can check for accuracy.

A caseworker is not expected to give legal advice, and if a member asks a question, the caseworker can find out the answer, such as to clarify information via the employer and report back to the member. The caseworker may need to talk to officials to get advice and support in branch before reporting back.

In situations of redundancy, union members can arrange for the union to support with negotiations and will likely arrange a consultancy meeting, which can be by email, face-to-face, or via an online meeting. The caseworker will ensure the member has the opportunities to address what they want to cover or discuss and clarify any information provided to the member.

11.14.1 Role of Unions when Preparing with the Member

The member is going to potentially be anxious and will need support. The caseworker will help the employee understand the process and ensure the individual feels comfortable raising any points, concerns, or questions.

The caseworker will ask the employee if they know why redundancies are happening and why, and the process, and if they cannot provide the answers, this information needs to be requested from Human Resources. Information about the redundancy selection process and time frame will also need to be clarified by Human Resources. If this information is not available, Human Resources will need to gather it and disseminate it.

The caseworker will then help the employee to clarify what points they wish to make, such as understanding of processes, options, time frames, and policy.

There may be other suitable alternative work, or continuing roles for which they need to apply, and the caseworker will check if the employee feels options are suitable, and if there are any problems.

Discrimination could apply if the employee feels they have not been treated the same as others due to the protected characteristics under Equality law. Consideration needs to be given as to whether the employee requires reasonable adjustments to be made for them to engage with the meeting – such as access, or a translator, or periodic breaks to ease anxiety.

It is important for Human Resources, managers, and the caseworker to determine how the employee feels about alternatives, severance, reduction in hours, voluntary early retirement, redeployment, job share, or other options provided.

Voluntary severance (when one opts to take redundancy) can be a better termination package, as opposed to forced redundancy. It is important all parties are aware of the terms of both options.

Trade unions must be cautious about providing advice about finances to union members. The member can compare notes with the caseworker, assess severance options, and decide what to do.

In a large organisation and during large-scale restructuring, unions will be involved and be responsible for collective bargaining/negotiations about deals with unions, their members, and the employer. If a member wants something different from the collective negotiation, the member and caseworker need to be able to discuss this.

Individuals normally get a better deal through negotiation, and the caseworker will help negotiate severance pay and terms with the employer.

Union caseworkers will make a list of what a member wants to ask, check what was agreed, and send an email to Human Resources to request this.

If a member or manager becomes distressed, or discussions become heated, the parties can ask for a recess. Human Resources should make allowances for this.

Union members and the caseworker will normally decide on a signal to stop the employee speaking, whereby it may reflect negatively on them with the employer. The employee would be discouraged by the union from agreeing to accept terms immediately but will encourage individuals to consider offers and decide afterwards.

The union will take notes and encourage the employee to do the same. Human Resources should also take their own notes, nominating an administrator or the secretary of the meeting to record key discussions and any key points raised.

11.14.2 Consultation Meeting

In cases of a redundancy meeting, Human Resources will be required to provide managers with a process to follow and will want to ensure a manager follows the correct process. The meeting may be perceived as formal, as managers and Human Resources tend to follow notes and guidance to avoid issues.

The union representative/caseworker can be assertive but should avoid aggression. A caseworker is not there to prevent redundancy, their role is to make sure points are raised that need to be raised and questions asked that need to be asked. All parties should enable the employee to ask questions also, and support if needed will be provided by the caseworker and Human Resources. The caseworker may need to prompt the employee to ask questions: 'You wanted to check if...'

As with the pre-meeting, the employee can request a break to collect themselves, then return to finish the meeting.

If the information needed for the meeting has not been received before or during the consultation meeting, decisions cannot be made, so this must be made available by Human Resources. Failure to provide this information can lead to claims of unfair dismissal.

The consultation meeting should be a fair and meaningful process.

11.14.3 Following up on the Consultation Meeting

After the meeting, the caseworker will ask the employee if they would like to debrief, but the employee may not be ready at this stage if upset or stressed.

The caseworker will ask the employee if there is there anything they would like checking. The caseworker can then check against organisation policy to ensure correct processes and time frames are being followed. Caseworkers can challenge this if they are not being followed and may state what the employee would like to happen in this case.

The caseworker will check if the employee wishes to keep their job, accept voluntary redundancy etc., but the employee may change their mind as time progresses.

The employer should send copies of notes to the caseworker and employee to check for accuracy and can add notes with amendments. If the employer and employee do not agree with the notes, both copies of notes need to be retained.

CASE STUDY: REDUNDANCIES

Due to economic crises, some organisations will need to make staff members redundant for the financial well-being of the firm and to survive in difficult market conditions.

No organisation wants to lay off team members but when the financial climate leaves no choice the process needs to begin.

An employer was in a large financial deficit and sent an all-staff email advising that voluntary severances of over 100 staff was to take place. Due to the large numbers, they also held an all-staff meeting with online access for those who could not attend in person. The employer communicated time frames, financial information, the need, impacts, and process, both during the meeting and in the email, offering opportunities for staff to ask questions.

The union was involved in negotiating the severance package and held meetings so questions could be redirected to senior managers.

Employees were kept informed and sent a range of key documents outlining next steps, key dates, how to apply for voluntary severance, and a calculator to establish the financial package each would receive, based on their salary and length of service. This was helpful in informing staff members to make decisions as to whether to apply.

The key tactics used by this firm included ongoing communication, which was honest, clear, and transparent as to what, when, why, and how. Providing key information assisted employee decision-making, alongside union involvement, following proper processes, and provision of opportunities for staff to ask questions to alleviate concerns and frustrations.

Chapter 12

Policy-Writing

Julia Greenwood

12.0 Introduction

This chapter provides a step-by-step guide on how to write Human Resources policies that are clear, compliant, and aligned with organisational culture. From understanding the role of Human Resources policies to drafting, implementing, and reviewing them, this chapter offers practical insights and best practices for creating policies that will effectively support the organisation and its employees.

This chapter includes the role of policy, the need for policy, and differentiating between policy, procedure, and guidance. The chapter will also outline good practice in policy-writing, act as a guide to what policies an organisation should have, communication and training around policies, and monitoring of policy adoption.

12.1 Understanding the Role of Human Resources Policies

Human Resources policies serve as the foundation on how a wide range of employment issues should be handled within an organisation. Written well, they will support consistency and fairness across an organisation and protect the organisation against legal claims.

Legal compliance is one of the key purposes of effective Human Resources policies to ensure the organisation is fulfilling its legal requirements. By addressing

DOI: 10.4324/9781003469803-13

legal obligations such as safety, confidentiality, and discrimination prevention, Human Resources policies protect the organisation from costly legal claims.

Employment laws are regularly updated, so outdated policies will leave the organisation at risk. Having legally compliant policies demonstrates to employees they will be treated fairly and in accordance with the law. The absence of a written policy on a key employment area is likely to reflect poorly on the organisation in the event of a legal claim.

A well-written Human Resources policy promotes organisational culture and is the vehicle for reinforcing the organisation's strategies, values, and behaviours. Policies should be used to reflect and reinforce the culture being created. Getting this right will have an impact on employee attitude and motivation, and promote the organisation to potential job applicants.

Human Resources policies need to provide clear expectations and consistency as guidance for employees and managers in their roles and responsibilities in the workplace. They give a steer towards accepted behaviours and what the organisation expects. Human Resources policies ensure consistency in decision-making across the organisation, helping prevent the risk of discrimination.

12.2 The Differences Between Policy, Procedure, and Guidance

Before writing a policy, it is worthwhile understanding the differences between policy, procedure, and guidance, each of which are used by Human Resources policy teams.

12.2.1 Policy

Policy is a high-level statement setting out the organisation's position on a topic. It is often brief as it is a statement of intent. A policy is mandatory.

An example of a policy in hospitality, hotels, and events could be guest privacy and confidentiality. The policy would require staff not to talk to their friends or the media about celebrities, VIPs, politicians, and high-profile guests who visit a hotel or restaurant, and to ensure confidentiality for security and privacy purposes. This would also be compliant with data protection regulations.

Staff would be trained not to disclose information to anyone outside the organisation without permission, and training would include data protection laws, protocols, and appropriate communication channels.

Policies build trust in organisations with the customer's safety and privacy being safeguarded, as well as protection for the venue in terms of legal compliance.

12.2.2 Procedure

Procedure is the process or set of stages which employees must follow to comply with the policy. A procedure aims to ensure consistency in how a policy is followed. Procedures tend to be specific but are more likely to be changed over time. Procedure is mandatory and would often include instructional words such as 'must'. Because procedures are in place for a reason, they must be followed every time. There must be no variations or 'get-outs' which would make it a request, not a procedure.

An example procedure, which aligns with guest privacy as previously exampled will contain details such as discreet check-in and check-out procedures away from other guests and performed by a manager, and their own private entrance where feasible.

It might be procedure for only essential staff to have access to guest information and not to disclose information to other parties. Staff would be prohibited from disclosing information, and any breach would result in disciplinary action or termination of employment. Staff might be required to sign privacy agreements or a Non-Disclosure Agreement (NDA).

Code words or a pseudonym is often used to protect high-profile guests, and training will often be provided to staff to ensure compliance of procedures which would include not asking for autographs, taking photos or selfies, or posting information on social media.

12.2.3 Guidance

Guidance is information which is recommended and supportive. Guidance documents provide suggestions for what action an employee could take in a situation. Guidance is appropriate when information is not mandatory. Suggestive words such as 'should' are advisory.

In continuance of the above examples, guidance documents for high-profile guests could include information about pre-arrival, risk assessment, arrival and check-in/out information, room security details, staff conduct, and media protocol.

Pre-arrival planning guidance may include detailing whether confidentiality agreements need to be created, whether individual risk assessments need to be carried out in relation to the guests, and liaison with security, agents, or police as required by the guest.

Guidance may also need to include arrangements for private entrances, private check-in, or guest relations, and whether the guests will be named or use a pseudonym, any security requirements, guidance on staff training and staff conduct, and how to deal with media and risks.

12.3 Identifying the Need for a Policy

Before creating a policy or updating an existing one, it is important to understand why the organisation needs it. It could be in response to legal changes where new legislation makes it obligatory to have a policy or to address changes in the organisation as examples. Considering 'why' will ensure Human Resources policies are not only legally compliant but address the needs and challenges within the organisation.

For example, many organisations offer remote working policies for Working From Home (WFH). Whilst many roles in hospitality and events make WFH impossible, a reservations agent, accountant, or marketing team might have the flexibility to WFH or be employed under hybrid working agreements which enable staff to split their time flexibly between WFH and being in the workplace, policy dependant.

Explaining 'why' behind policies fosters transparency, which builds trust and supports employee engagement. To understand 'why', the following should be considered:

Legal requirements: it is important to keep abreast of employment law to understand the legal 'why' behind certain policies.

Human Resources metrics: periodic analysis and interpretation of the organisation's Human Resources data should take place to give good indication of where policies are needed or where existing policies could be improved. For example, analysing staff turnover rates and conducting exit interview responses allows Human Resources to determine causes for staff to decide to leave.

If staff turnover is high, and exit interviews reveal staff are leaving due to lack of training and support, it will be necessary to communicate policy to managers to ensure training is provided for staff to improve skill set and confidence in the workplace, and for training to be monitored to ensure staff are effectively supported in their employment and to help retain them within the business.

Employee voice (feedback): understanding what employees want and trying to improve their experience and satisfaction is essential. Employee feedback can be collected through employee surveys, focus groups, suggestion boxes, and employee networks. Inviting employees to express their view of the organisation, their experiences, what is important to them, and suggestions for improvement can shape the culture of the business. Engagement with employee networks is important to understand the challenges for particular groups of staff such as chefs, or housekeepers.

A restaurant, hotel, bar, or events venue should question if the policy is having the desired effect. There can be times when employees are following the policy but it is not having the desired effect. For example, a policy on upselling or cross-selling of food and drink when an order is taken: if customers are not ordering extras and increasing the average spend per customer, the policy is not producing results. It will be necessary to understand from employees why this is the case. It could be a training issue, product knowledge issue, or the policy is overly bureaucratic and confusing.

AUTHOR'S VOICE

When we were creating neurodiversity guidance, it was very important for us to learn from the 'lived experience' of our employees who are neurodivergent and from the line managers who manage those neurodivergent individuals. By using employee focus groups to listen to the voices of our employees, we hoped to address the actual needs and challenges of the people who work for us.

12.3.1 Best Practice

It is important to research best practice and trends in the industry and sector to keep a competitive advantage. What are the current issues affecting Human Resources policies? Various resources can be used such as trade publications, newsletters, podcasts, legal updates, webinars, professional networks, industry bodies, and competitor activity to research best practice. There is a growing awareness of menopause, menstruation rights, hybrid working, and gender identity that many hospitality, hotel, and events organisations will increasingly adopt and develop policy for.

12.3.2 Benchmarking Against Competitors

It is helpful to find out what Human Resources policies other companies and competitors have and how they are responding to employment challenges. In the competitive world, everyone is looking to recruit the best candidates for the job. Organisations must be attractive, not only through their competitive salaries or benefits, but through their workplace policies. Employees are more likely to trust and be supportive of policies that are well-researched and benchmarked against leading competitors. Some organisations make their policy documents available online for anyone to view. This is a good starting-point for benchmarking against other organisations and to demonstrate transparency.

12.4 Good Practice in Policy-Writing

12.4.1 Clarity and Simplicity

Using clear and simple language and avoiding jargon or TWAs (Three-Word Abbreviations) is essential when creating Human Resources policy. Overly complicated policies which are difficult to understand can create confusion and misinterpretation among employees, resulting in uncertainty in understanding rights and responsibilities.

Simple policies are more easily navigated and referenced when needed. Employees can save time searching for information and seeking clarification from the Human Resources team. Policy Advisors will spend less time resolving policy misunderstandings.

Another reason not to include too much detail in a policy is because employment tribunals will typically check whether an organisation has followed its own policy when assessing fairness. If the organisation has failed to follow its policy accurately, because it was too complex, it may strengthen the employee's case. To ensure Human Resources policies do not become quickly outdated, avoid references to employee names or organisational teams which are likely to change over time.

12.4.2 Consistency

Ensuring uniformity in design and structure across all Human Resources policies will help employees navigate the documents more easily as they will come to know where to find the information they need. A consistent format will reinforce the Human Resources brand and help employees know they are reading a Human Resources document. When thinking about consistency, consider policy structure, colours, logos, images, and tone of voice.

AUTHOR'S VOICE

When undertaking a full review of our existing employment policies, we realised they all look different in design, layout, and tone. To ensure we have a consistent look we decided to create a policy template that had a recognisable front page (with a picture of our organisation) and banner which used the same colour scheme, font style, and font size so employees would immediately recognise they were reading a Human Resources policy.

We also wanted to ensure our policies were clear by avoiding jargon and having a consistent tone, throughout. The hope is that our employees will feel a sense of familiarity and connection with our policy brand. We also created a template for our guidance documents, displaying a similar look and feel.

12.4.3 Flexibility

In a changing landscape, overly prescriptive policies, which try to account for every possible situation, are likely to become outdated very quickly. Although Human Resources policies should be legally compliant, rigid policies with too much detail can stifle creative decision-making and will not allow for changing circumstances. Whilst it can be tempting and feel reassuring to have every eventuality written down, it is better to construct policies that encourage employees to exercise personal judgement in different circumstances. This will ensure they are relevant and effective and allow managers to exercise their own judgement.

More recently, the trend is moving towards having light-touch principles that can be adapted to different employee needs. For example, rather than having a detailed bereavement policy that specifies the number of days an employee can take depending on their relationship with the individual who passed away, it may be more effective to have a simple policy statement that recognises everybody's situation is different, and that appropriate time and support will be provided.

Lots of rules can signal that the organisation does not trust their employees to use their own common sense. Trusting employees to use their judgement encourages them to take personal responsibility for their work, fostering a sense of autonomy and accountability, establishing a greater level of engagement with the organisation.

Overly prescriptive rules, focusing on what an employee must do in all circumstances can also set a negative tone rather than a positive one and can signal that the organisation is overly concerned about compliance rather than flexibility.

Do not write policies for the minority who occasionally break the rules. Instead, trust that most people will do the right thing and avoid overly bureaucratic rules.

12.4.4 Putting People at the Heart

People-centred employment policies consider the well-being and needs of employees. When constructing policies, consider how the employee would feel and what support they may need during difficult situations. When employees feel genuinely supported by their organisation, they are more likely to be engaged and committed to their work. Supportive employment policies that put people at the heart of everything they do are often seen as progressive and caring and will help to foster a sense of belonging and trust and attract and retain motivated employees. Consider the audience and the appropriate writing style. If trying to create a friendly and supportive environment, use language that is informal, conversational, and inclusive (e.g. 'Us' and 'We').

AUTHOR'S VOICE

One technique that really helps to 'put people at the heart of our policies' and truly understand what motivates employees is through use of employee personas. The use of personas has long been a practice of marketing teams in their desire to better understand their customers. Employee personas are fictional representations of employees which help an organisation to become more employee focused by understanding employee goals, motivations, needs, and frustrations.

By using this technique, it helps to empathise and better understand different employees and to remember that employees are 'real' individuals with challenges and personalities outside work that often impact how they behave in work. For the exercise to work, it is necessary to make characters believable. The more specific the better.

Things to consider when building an employee persona:

What is their name; what age are they; where do they live; do they have a family; what is their job role; how long have they been with the organisation; what motivates them; what is their personality; what do they want from their job; what do they like to do in their spare time; what are their current frustrations?

Once fictional employees are created, consider what they would want from employment policies: are they struggling to manage home and work life, and do they want a supportive flexible working policy? Would they be motivated by having some time away from work to travel and would a career break policy support them?

12.4.5 Accessibility

Accessible Human Resources policies ensure all employees, including those with language barriers or disability needs, can access and understand the information provided. By considering the font style, font size, and the clarity of layout, all employees are more likely to access and understand the information. It is also advised to provide policies in multiple formats, such as electronic documents and braille to ensure inclusivity and accommodate different needs.

12.5 Human Resources Policies an Organisation Should Have

Law dictates that all employers must have a health and safety policy. Employers must also set out their disciplinary and grievance procedures in accordance with legal codes of practice in the home country. In the UK, the Advisory, Conciliation, and Arbitration Service (ACAS) provides guidance on this.

The number, range, and type of Human Resources policies that an organisation will have depends on their specific requirements. A small company such as an independent bar or café might need just a few policies, whereas a larger, more complex organisation such as a multinational hotel chain or large events venue is likely to require more policies.

Common organisational policies are listed here:

Beginning employment – policies in this area will include how an organisation recruits and selects employees; market supplements (a temporary or regular additional payment to retain staff members by supplementing salary when pay may not be competitive); overtime; relocation assistance (for example, when getting an inter-company transfer or moving for the job); probationary period; induction and onboarding; annual leave entitlement; staff search; mobile phones (cell phones); driving; and uniform and dress code.

Health, safety, and well-being – including handling hazardous substances; reporting incidents; manual handling and lifting; food safety and hygiene; and fire prevention.

Managing well-being – family leave policies (including maternity, paternity, adoption, shared parental leave, neonatal leave); alcohol; drugs and substance misuse; menopause; miscarriage; stillbirth and infertility; smoking or vaping; sickness absence management; stress identification and management; compassionate leave; bereavement leave; adverse weather; and time off for public service.

Work–life balance – policies in this area include flexible working; hybrid working; remote working; career break; and job share.

Learning and development – including a training policy; secondments (transfer to another department, branch, or job); payment of professional membership fees to obtain qualifications.

Equality, Diversity, and Inclusion (EDI) – should run through all employment policies. Most organisations have an Equality, Diversity, and Inclusion policy which communicates the organisation's values and commitments. This may then be supported by guidance which covers topics, including transition, non-binary, and gender non-conforming staff; bullying and harassment; tackling misogyny and sexual violence against women; and domestic abuse.

Managing performance – policies in this area include probationary period; appraisals; peer review; personal development; reward; disciplinary; grievance; and capability.

Managing change and ending employment – including redundancy; redeployment; notice period; garden leave; exit interviews; and retirement.

Corporate social responsibility and sustainability – polices surrounding corporate social responsibility (CSR) and sustainability will be written by Human Resources or managers involved with strategy.

CSR policies will incorporate ethical and transparent business practices that align with the *'Three Pillars'* of CSR or *'Triple Bottom Line'* theories. The Three Pillars/Triple Bottom Line models consider economic, environmental, and social aspects of the business. This includes ethical practices surrounding profits of the business and how profit is achieved, the measures the business uses for reducing environmental impact, and investment in people, which may include staff, the wider community, or supporting fundraising projects.

Policy surrounding sustainability and green measures is of growing importance, and globally, legal requirements stipulate measures all businesses have to adopt.

12.6 Drafting Human Resources Policies

Depending on the size of the organisation, reviewing Human Resources policies might be outsourced to an external Human Resources company at a cost. Otherwise, there are organisations offering standard templates to adapt to suit an organisation.

Stakeholder consultation – effective Human Resources policy development should not be created in isolation but requires input from various organisational stakeholders. Stakeholders are likely to be different depending on the policy. For example, it would be unlikely to consult the housekeeping team on payroll systems, whereas Finance, Accounts, or Payroll would be consulted. Likewise, changes in the distribution of service charges or gratuities would be discussed with food and beverage staff.

Main internal stakeholders would be the senior leadership team, employees, employee networks, managers, and the Human Resources team, with involvement from the wider Human Resources team (including employee relations, reward and payroll, resourcing, Equality, Diversity, and Inclusivity (EDI). If applicable, consult union representatives in policy development to hear and address any concerns from union members.

Documenting comments and changes – it is important to ensure all comments and changes are documented in case legal issues arise surrounding a subsequent policy version. Some organisations use a policy repository which stores historical versions of a policy, showing changes over time. It is helpful to appoint a policy owner who is responsible for the policy edits.

Review and approval – the final draft of a policy should be shared with a higher level of management for approval (e.g. the senior management team, governing body, or board of directors). It is advisable to use the services of a legal team to review the policy before it is finalised.

12.7 Policy Communication

Effective communication of Human Resources policy to employees is essential to ensure it is understood. There are several ways an organisation can promote its policies and the most appropriate will depend upon the nature of the policy and the specific company. Depending on the size of the organisation, it is useful to consider a range of communication channels to ensure maximise coverage. The following options could be used:

- **All-employee email:** sending policy information via email to all staff to ensure everyone is aware
- **Newsletters / blogs:** employees could receive a monthly newsletter that contains policy updates
- **Intranet:** if the organisation has an employee intranet, it could be used to communicate updates with employees
- **Team meetings:** Human Resources representatives or managers could update employees on policy changes during all-staff briefings
- **Handbooks:** if policies are contained in company handbooks, ensure these are updated when policy information changes

12.8 Training

Training employees on Human Resources policy is different from communicating the policy and should aim to enhance engagement and understanding. Not all policies will need training to accompany them, so organisations should decide which ones in their Human Resources policy portfolio are particularly current or complex.

Decide the format of training (e.g. face-to-face workshops, webinar, or online course) and who the audience should be (e.g. all employees, managers, senior leaders). Consider who will deliver the training (e.g. employee relations team, policy specialists, legal team), ensuring that the trainer is skilled in training delivery and able to tailor the content to the needs of the individuals being trained.

It is important to remember that the training is not simply for communicating the policy. Effective training should add elements of discussion, case studies, and roleplay that encourages participant engagement. This will ensure the information is understood and retained. All training should include a test of learning – a quiz or demonstration to test the information imparted has been interpreted and understood by the recipients.

Line managers are key to bringing Human Resources policies to life, so consider how to use training to effectively support them so they have a clear understanding of how to implement the policies fairly and sensitively.

12.9 Monitoring

The review process in policy development is an important stage to ensure Human Resources policies remain legally compliant, relevant, and continue to meet organisational needs. Human Resources policies should be live documents that evolve as the organisation changes. Adopting a culture of continuous improvement is key to staying responsive and agile.

Policy review does not always have to involve large changes. Sometimes, it may just need a few small adjustments, or no changes at all.

To ensure policies are still relevant and meet the needs of employees, seek employee feedback through annual surveys or more regular pulse surveys. Organisations that want to be more innovative and responsive do not wait for annual feedback but allow employees to provide their thoughts on Human Resources policies when it suits them, often by emailing a central inbox. Policies should also continue to align with organisational strategy and reflect the organisational culture. If the organisation has access to legal advisors, their services should be sought for compliance with employment law.

There is no law for the frequency of reviewing Human Resources policies. Decide what is a suitable review timeline for the Human Resources policy portfolio and schedule these in. This could be annually, or every three years, say. Some policies will need reviewing more regularly, particularly if legislation changes.

A checklist for what to include in policies is outlined in Figure 12.1 and an example policy template in Figure 12.2.

Preparation
Identify the need for the policy:

- legal changes
- Human Resources metrics
- employee voice (feedback)
- benchmarking

Drafting the policy

- research
- stakeholder consultation
- legal compliance

Review and feedback

- circulate the policy amongst key stakeholders
- consider suggestions and necessary amendments

Approval

- obtain approval from senior management

Communication

- develop a communication plan

Training

- consider how employees will be trained

Monitoring

- consider when and how the policy will be reviewed and how often
- collect feedback on the policy's effectiveness

Figure 12.1 A Checklist to Ensure Consistency in Policy-Writing

Policy Title: Clearly state the name of the policy.

Purpose, aim, or statement: Explain the reason for the policy and its intended outcome. Describe why the policy is needed and how it supports organisational strategy and priorities.

Scope and exclusions: Clearly state who the policy applies to (e.g. all employees, full time, part time, fixed term) and who may be excluded (e.g. employees from subsidiary companies).

Definitions: Provide clear definitions of key terminology used in the policy (e.g. remote working is an employee working at their home, or at some other place that is not the organisation's usual place of business).

Roles and responsibilities: Describe who in the organisation is responsible for what part of the policy or additional support (e.g. employees, managers, Human Resources, occupational health).

Procedure: Provide full details of the policy and explain the process or procedure that employees/managers need to follow to comply with the policy.

Related organisational policies: Provide weblinks to other related organisational policies.

Support and resources: Provide weblinks to employee assistance programmes, or external sources of support (e.g. local drug and alcohol services).

Monitoring: State who has responsibility for monitoring the effectiveness and impact of the policy.

Approval: Document who is the approving individual or approval body (e.g. Human Resources Director, CEO, Board of Directors).

Review process: State who is responsible for the policy review and the date by when it will be reviewed (e.g. annually, or every three years). It is also useful to provide the review history to track when updates were made.

Figure 12.2 A Template for Structuring a Policy

Chapter 13

Change Management

13.0 Introduction

Change is part of everyday life and is a necessary component for organisations that want to be innovative and maintain competitive advantage.

Change is challenging and requires consideration of time frames, resources, key stakeholders, and associated costs. Barriers to change, alongside resistance from staff and customers, can be overcome if change is managed well, resulting in enhanced competitive positioning and operational efficiencies.

This chapter analyses the barriers that can prevent change from being successful, including resistance which can occur from key stakeholders. An analysis is undertaken of the change models that can be used by managers and Human Resources to ensure change is successful and the importance of communication during times of change is emphasised.

13.1 Change Management

Change management is the planning, communication, implementation, and monitoring of change within organisations.

Planning for change involves identifying the need to change, or the need to respond to change, and the impact and the process of adapting. Managing change

DOI: 10.4324/9781003469803-14

involves careful planning, including identification of time frames and communication to key stakeholders, provision of training and support where needed, and control of the process. Once change is implemented, employees may resort to their previous ways of working, so change should continue to be monitored, alongside return on investment or other impacts, and change should be closely monitored to ensure it endures.

When change is managed effectively it is likely implementation and longevity will be a success. Employees and other stakeholders such as customers will buy into the change and a positive response from team members will ensure a smooth transition to a new system, a new way of working, or adapting to a new management structure as examples.

13.2 Drivers of Change

Drivers of change are the factors that necessitate change.

If an organisation can analyse the macro and micro business environment and understand what causes change, opportunities can be identified, and threats mitigated.

There are numerous drivers of change from political, legal, and economic changes, technological advances, increased competitive rivalry, social changes, and increasing awareness of sustainability and environmental preservation. Responding to such changes means the hospitality, hotel, and event industries can remain competitive, increase operational efficiencies, reduce costs, reduce the risk of legal issues, and provide a unique selling point (USP), enhancing position in the market and success.

Hospitality businesses face many changes in a business environment where wage costs continue to rise, increased tax burdens are experienced, alongside rising food costs, ongoing staffing challenges, legislative updates, and fluctuating economic conditions impacting operations. Well-known restaurant brands are closing due to lack of differentiation, high numbers of pubs are closing due to financial challenges, the night-time industry has experienced reduced demand as consumer behaviour evolves, and event attendance has been impacted by the global pandemic driving online meetings instead of in-person conferences.

Many hospitality businesses need to revise costs, scrutinise the supply chain, and reduce staffing numbers to mitigate financial challenges.

However, change can be planned, such as new systems or technology, a new menu, a new site opening, a new product or service, or a new manager. Change, despite its cause, is positive for organisations, especially where operational efficiencies are improved, cost savings can be made, and innovative ideas are adopted to increase competitive advantage and market positioning. Changes can be made to improve the business.

There are both internal and external challenges that necessitate change:

Internal drivers: a new manager or change in the organisational structure, new systems, equipment, or facilities, new products or services, finances, or staffing changes, a revised business strategy, employee turnover, guest feedback, mergers, or takeovers.

External drivers: innovation, competitor activity, economic downturn, legal changes, new government, new minimum wage rates, taxes, changes in rent and rates, suppliers.

Innovative organisations which can evolve, adapt, and overcome are more likely to maintain competitive advantage.

Change is not always planned by organisations, and therefore changes emerge because of external drivers within strategy texts, this what is referred to as 'emergent change'.

Change can also be transformational in that it involves major strategic upheaval in line with a change of strategic intent or the external macro business environment which lends itself to formal change planning considering business and human needs.

Change can be transactional, and whilst the organisation might not need significant strategic updates, smaller and simplistic changes may take place such as a change in menu, payment systems, or processes. This would still require planning and change to be carefully managed.

When an organisation involves team members in change implementation, providing training and support, communicating time frames, then change will be readily accepted and chances of success increase. The aim is to reduce resistance to change and remove any obstacles or barriers which can cause change to fail.

13.3 Barriers to Change

Barriers to change are factors which stop organisational change from being successful or cause delays or other issues. Barriers include budgets, people, legal issues, time constraints, and poor planning or lack of focus.

Prior to change, managers should evaluate key drivers and impacts and manage the process carefully with support from the Human Resources team to mitigate issues.

Many organisations face delays, unplanned costs, and teething issues when change is implemented, and careful planning, analysis of benefits and implications, alongside communication of time frames and impact on teams are necessary to ensure better chances of success. Failure to do this results in change failing and unnecessary stress, cost implications, and potential conflict or reputational damage.

13.3.1 Lewin's Forcefield Analysis

Change planning helps organisations identify why the change is occurring, and the likely impact.

Kurt Lewin created the Forcefield Analysis model in the 1940s; a model to identify why change is happening and the likely barriers or restraining factors to help plan for and overcome change barriers.

Lewin identified driving forces that instigate the necessity for change, including internal and external forces for change such as customer expectations for automation and demand for self- service in hotels, including touchscreen check-ins, touchscreen ordering in fast food restaurants, and ticket scanning in events and airports.

Lewin recognised that with any change, restraining forces will likely occur that prevent the change from being successful. Through identification of both driving forces and restraining forces, the model helps organisations identify strategies to reduce restraining forces, or barriers, and enhance drivers for change.

Hospitality organisations can use this model to identify their own drivers for change and potential restraining factors (barriers). A template of the model is provided within Table 13.1.

Table 13.1 Lewin's Forcefield Analysis

Driving Forces (for change)	Proposed Change	Restraining Forces (against Change)
	Task: Considering the change being proposed – outline the driving forces (why change is happening) and restraining forces (barriers/things that could prevent change from happening).	

13.4 Resistance to Change

When undergoing change, some emotions employees might feel include anxiety, uncertainty, frustration, or fear. These negative emotions may lead to resistance.

At first, teams might worry how change will impact them, which may cause panic, anger, distrust, and stress. Some might leave their job role when uncertainty and risk is experienced. Others will likely be excited for change, accept it more quickly, and help initiate change. Any stakeholder with an interest in the business could share similar feelings, including customers and suppliers, unsure how changes may impact them.

Resistance may spread if colleagues are able to gossip, spread fear or anxiety, or spread negativity about change. This needs to be carefully managed, and can be prevented by communicating the necessity for change, the impact of change, how individuals will be affected, alongside sharing ideas, voicing concerns, and being able to become involved, and time frames communicated from the offset.

The different emotions people feel when exposed to change will vary, whilst some may be change ready, others may not, and individual feelings should be considered. Some people accept change more readily than others, and some may experience anxiety and fear. These emotions are captured in Fisher's Personal Transition Curve.

13.4.1 Fisher's Transition Curve

Fisher's Personal Transition Curve model illustrates different emotions experienced during the change process. The model, which can be found online, shared by Fisher with Businessballs.com, highlights how individuals transition, considering initial responses such as anxiety or elation as change is announced, through to fear, feelings of being threatened, guilt, depression, and even hostility, or gradual acceptance and moving forward with change.

As individuals and in the workplace, we become complacent, so any change can be unsettling. We may question why change is happening or recognise the benefits that change may bring. In these situations, excitement for change may occur, after initial anxiety and people start to 'buy' into the change.

But as the reality of change becomes apparent, the anxiety and excitement may turn to fear; for example, when a new manager is incoming, a merger is occurring, or a new system is adopted. Fear leads to feelings to feeling threatened, and as anger builds some may worry how change will impact them and avoid or resist change.

These emotions give way to guilt, in change avoidance or denial, which leads to contradictory emotions and even depression takes over as change is imminent. This hostility towards the organisation imposing change may lead to individuals quitting their job role.

Hostility gradually gives way to acceptance as change is adopted, eventually leading to the moving forward stage, with mass acceptance across the firm.

The Transition model is outlined in Figure 13.1.

The model recognises that whilst some employees welcome change and enjoy a fresh approach, others will think 'we've been working this way for years, why change?'. To reduce resistance, the push/pull method should be considered, with push being a harder approach to change, and pull a softer more positive approach that focuses on the benefits of change encouraging members to accept change more readily.

Push is an approach that needs managers and Human Resources to communicate the necessity of change, its costs, the risks of not initiating change, the consequences of change not occurring, and the impact on the team and organisation. This can create a level of discomfort.

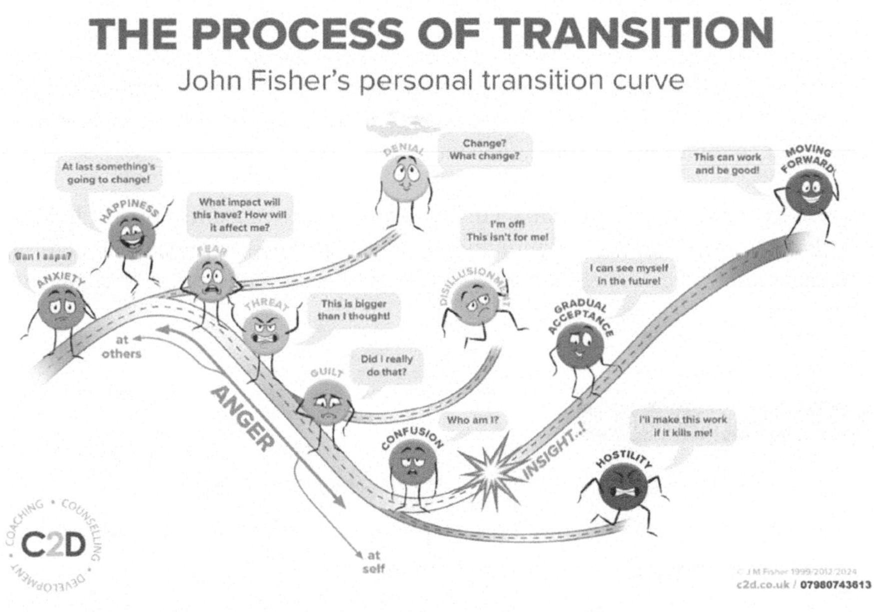

Figure 13.1 The Process of Transition Model
The Process of Transition, John Fisher (2012).

Pull is a more humanistic positive approach to change which encourages team members to accept change and involves highlighting the benefits of changes being made and the outcomes and advantages to work and people. This is more likely to encourage acceptance.

13.4.2 Nudge Theory

Nudge Theory is a modern change management theory that helps individuals make decisions based on small prompts. Nudge theory was created by Richard Thaler and Cass Sunstein in their book, *Nudge: Improving Decisions About Health, Wealth, and Happiness* (2021).

Nudge theory involves creating choices that lead to positive decisions, whilst recognising the unhelpful nudges that guide people's behaviour (which can be considered as barriers). The theory involves offering tactful choices, that lead to desired behaviours and outcomes (i.e. change), rather than imposing change on people. It is more subtle through guidance, the stipulation of benefits and impact, leading by example, and use of a no-pressure approach that encourages participation in change.

An example of Nudge Theory at a music festival is to erect signs that stipulate 'Do Not Drop Litter', whereas if litter bins are provided, it would nudge people to dispose of their litter without the need for instructional signage.

Employees become contented with ways of working. As organisations adapt and evolve, continuous change is necessary. As planned and emergent change occurs, people will evolve through the 'four rooms' and stages of denial, confusion, renewal, and contentment as the cycle continues.

Regardless of how change is managed, it is important to recognise that individuals will respond differently and individualistic experiences, attitudes, personality type, and communication should be considered to ensure resistance to change is minimised.

INDUSTRY VOICE

Dr Philip Berners, Associate Professor in Events Management

Employers tend to be frightened of change because it is fraught with risks and errors. But it is all about communication.

Managers need to consider how to communicate the change; when to communicate; and ensure the impacts on all employees are considered.

Employees will resist change if they do not have the full information, or their concern about impacts has not been thought through and addressed.

After all, resistance happens for a reason: it is a consequence of fear, nervousness, or rejection – each of which can be addressed with communication.

13.5 Managing Change (Models of Change)

There are numerous models of change to guide those who need to manage change. Each model is useful, but there is no single perfect approach or model for managing change. John Kotter's book on change, *Leading Change*, estimated 85 per cent of change in organisations fails, as leaders fail to create a vision for change and an environment which encourages innovation.

Model or theories of change support leaders through change. Kurt Lewin and John Kotter are just two authors of theories which can be used by organisations to guide the changes process, alongside the ADKAR model explained in Section 13.5.3.

13.5.1 Kurt Lewin's Model of Change

Kurt Lewin in the 1940s proposed a change model with three stages: unfreeze, change, refreeze – using an ice-cube to illustrate the change process.

The **unfreeze** stage involves communicating why change is necessary to all affected individuals, and to respond to any concerns they have. The **change** stage happens as people start to accept change is happening. Here, the benefits should be communicated to gain support and time frames provided to keep individuals informed of the process and help them adjust. The **refreeze** stage occurs when change has become part of company culture and individuals are provided with support and training to support progression towards change. Managers, alongside Human Resources, will reinforce these actions, and progress towards change is monitored to ensure successful implementation.

The firm will need to ensure change is sustained and continues to be enforced.

Lewin's model provides an awareness of the need to communicate, promote the idea, the benefits, and time frame of change to reduce resistance and build resilience for change through training and mentorship.

13.5.2 John Kotter's Eight-Stage Process

Kotter identifies how models can 'oversimplify reality'. There is no best model to guide change, instead they can be used to identify good practice, which Kotter categorises into eight sequential steps or stages:

1. Establishing a sense of urgency

   This involves analysis of the business environment and competitive rivalry and identifying potential crises or opportunities.

2. Creating a guiding coalition

   Putting an authoritative steering group together to manage the change process and initiate the change process.

3. Developing a vision and strategy

   Creating a vision to identify the firm's further desired state which helps identify a sense of direction. Strategies to manage the change will also need to be formulated.

4. Communicating the change vision

   Communicate the vision via meetings, in-person where feasible, emails, and other forms to ensure everyone can understand the outcomes of change. A change champion can be nominated to communicate change and to demonstrate model behaviours to team members to encourage participation. Change Champions will be individuals who demonstrate positivity towards change and are well connected within the organisation as these individuals will help ensure change participation spreads.

5. Empowering broad-based action

   This involves overcoming barriers and reducing the forces that prevent change from being successful. People should be encouraged to act and share ideas.

6. Generating short-term wins

   Monitor, recognise, and reward progress towards change implementation, celebrate and announce these 'wins'.

7. Consolidating gains and producing more change

   As change gains momentum, changes can be implemented and systems/processes updated to support the vision. Any further hires or promotions of team members that can enforce change can be actioned and continue to communicate and promote change.

8. Anchoring new approaches in the culture

   Monitor and measure change success, continuously monitor for change to be upheld and the connection between change and organisational success.

13.5.3 The ADKAR Model

The ADKAR (Awareness, Desire, Knowledge, Ability, Reinforcement) relates to understanding the needs of others and the type of support needed when individuals undergo change.

The ADKAR model considers the individual emotions associated with change, and both Lewin's and Kotter's models outline the process of change.

A: Awareness

When new technology, for example, is being introduced to a property, staff might worry that their jobs are at risk of being replaced by technology or worry about the impact on service and user issues. Therefore, staff may resist change.

Communicating to staff as to why change is occurring will lead to a more positive reaction as awareness is raised and seeks to eliminate assumption and worry.

AUTHOR'S VOICE

When working as a reservation's agent, the manager announced that our office was being relocated to another area further away. The initial reaction was negative, worrying about a longer commute, additional fuel costs, or a longer train journey. This is when a team meeting was called to explain the move, and managers drove us in groups in their own cars to the new offices. The offices were a beautiful modern upgrade, a new build, in the countryside, and was just an additional 10-minute journey and near to a train station. The team then became really excited about the move and no longer felt anxious.

D: Desire

Human Resources and managers should be mindful that change leads to resistance and staff may lack motivation or desire to undergo change. An employee's response to change and reasons for resisting change are personal and might not be linked to the change itself. A line manager who works alongside these individuals can coach the team through change to encourage positive engagement.

K: Knowledge

Once teams are motivated to embrace change, and are aware of the need for change, Human Resources can offer training and support to make change happen. If training is offered prior to this, it is not as effective, as staff have not yet bought into the change.

A: Ability

Once staff have knowledge about their new way of working, a new system, process, or manager, for example, this might not necessarily mean they are capable, competent, or confident. The employees need to be able to apply the new knowledge. Further guidance, coaching, and support from managers at this stage is useful. If the change involves technology, team members need to be able to test the new system. When a new menu is launched and a menu tasting is provided, staff will be confident in making recommendations to guests as they have experienced the dishes.

R: Reinforcement

The final stage of the ADKAR model of change is Reinforcement. Teams might adopt change in the interim, but then revert to previous ways of working. Managers and Human Resources should monitor team engagement with change, and the change itself to ensure success.

Change models can help guide change, and whilst Lewin, Kotter, and the ADKAR models can be used as guides, the reality of change is very different.

When undergoing change, hospitality, hotel, and event firms should gather the team for a face-to-face meeting or online to communicate change within the organisation in a timely manner and communicate the need for change, time frames, and impacts on individuals and the organisation.

It is not just employees who may be affected, other stakeholders such as suppliers, customers, law enforcers, local governments, and the wider community might need to be informed of change.

A steering group should be formed to manage the change, and change champions utilised to communicate positively about change to encourage mass participation and buy-in.

People will react and respond differently to change and will need training, support, and encouragement to embrace it.

Recognition should be given where recognition is due, rewards given, and achievements celebrated. Individuals should be praised as well as team efforts, and this is best done publicly to encourage others to adopt change, as well as giving regular feedback when monitoring progress so teams can see progress and successes.

13.6 Case Studies

The Royal Air Force Club has provided the two following case studies – the first demonstrates the change process adopted when implanting a new payroll system, and the second case study explains the implementation of a new staffing structure.

CASE STUDY 1: CHANGE MANAGEMENT – IMPLEMENTING A NEW PAYROLL/HUMAN RESOURCES SYSTEM

Contribution from Holly Lockyear, People and Culture Executive, The Royal Air Force Club

Having a reliable, trustworthy, and employee friendly payroll/Human Resources system is essential. Before I joined the company, there had been talks about implementing a new payroll/Human Resources system. One reason for changing the system was because the existing system was not accessible via employee's phones. This limitation resulted in employees not being able to request annual leave or access their payslips easily.

These documents should be accessible but with the existing system they could only be accessed via a computer. Today, everything should be accessible via mobile devices as it is the easiest way to communicate with employees. Besides, not everyone owns a computer.

The implementation of this change for the company was challenging in the first few stages. The company was required to research available products on the market and the first few did not meet the Club's requirements. Once a compatible service provider was found which met the requirements, a new payroll/Human Resources system was approved, and its implementation began.

Under the guidance of the implementation team from the new service provider, we set about collating and entering all employees' personal data into the new system. Once the background information was correctly set up and the personal data had been transferred, we launched the app to our employees.

As Human Resources professionals, it is essential to always provide clear and effective communication to employees about changes that will be implemented. Providing initial training and being prepared for any questions from employees has reduced anxiety.

We then released the link and verification process to our employees for them to access the new system. However, the provider of our new system had not mentioned that employees only had two hours to use the verification link. This led to some difficulties at the start when asking employees to download the app.

We spent a few days getting all employees to access the app, and we carried out a Head of Department (HOD) walk-round with branded cupcakes to encourage excitement among employees for the new system. This activity enabled us to listen to any questions and concerns the employees wanted to voice.

Once everybody had accessed and logged into the new app, we began employee training.

We started by training our HODs in how to input the rota to the time and attendance feature within the app. This is linked to payroll, which helps streamline the job of the payroll team.

Training was delivered to managers and Human Resources by the provider as there were some unexpected technical difficulties. This led to some confusion amongst our HODs about the new system, particularly with those who manage large teams.

The Human Resources team remained calm and met HODs on a one-to-one basis to provide training and tackle any resistance to the change in system. This worked well. It enabled thorough and personalised training, and we ensured all questions the HODs had were answered. We ensured clear communication throughout and provided support where necessary. We acknowledged that we had language barriers with some employees and differences in abilities to technology. We created training and Standard Operating Procedures for HODs to ensure they had a guide to refer to for the time and attendance system.

We then began employee training; for example, how to request annual leave or view payslips using the mobile app. Most employees were able to use the app straight away and picked up how to request leave and view payslips. For some others, we encouraged employees to come to the Human Resources office for a demonstration how to use the app. We also printed help sheets for the staff canteen to ensure clear and effective communication to our employees on how to use the app. This included images to ensure we overcame any language barrier.

From my experience implementing a companywide change which affects everyone, there are some factors which Human Resources should implement when bringing change. Human Resources must emphasise why the change is being implemented, what is the main reason the change has been put in place, and how this will benefit employees and managers within their professional and personal lives. In our case, the new system was implemented to provide employees with a user and mobile friendly app where payslips can be accessed, annual leave requested, and personal details updated and changed easily.

I recommend encouraging feedback and questions from employees, without which, we would not have resolved the initial issues we encountered. We always want to give employees a voice, and any feedback is something we can learn from when implementing future changes within the Human Resources department and the Club itself.

The Human Resources team consistently showed commitment to the new system, highlighting the positives and solutions to queries which arose. We still encourage employees to send emails to us and visit us regarding the new system. We encourage clear communication as employers to and from our employees. It is essential to the problem-solving process and building trust in our teams.

CASE STUDY 2: CHANGE MANAGEMENT – NEW STAFFING STRUCTURE AS OUR CLUB MANAGER RETIRES AFTER WORKING AT THE CLUB FOR 38 YEARS

Contribution from Rachel Matthews, Director of People and Culture, The Royal Air Force Club

Much like a general manager within a hotel, our Chief Executive and Club Manager work hard to ensure the culture within the workplace is positive, fair, and consistent. The CEO and Club Manager work closely and are involved with the employees at the Club.

We have a special and 'one-of-a-kind' culture at our Club. The CEO and Club Manager like to get to know employees, ensuring the employees are happy at work, and show that open communication and support is always available to the team.

The CEO and Club Manager are involved with the recruitment and selection of new employees into the business. They know everyone by name, and we hold an open-door policy within the Club to further encourage communication between all employees.

The Club Manager had worked within most roles within the Club, beginning their career journey with the Club as a Food and Beverage Assistant, and working their way up to Club Manager.

The Club Manager played a fundamental role in creating the positive and welcoming working culture we enjoy. It is an important role, reporting to the Chief Executive Officer (CEO) and offering support through their strong working relationship. The Club Manager also has numerous managers reporting to them, such as Meetings and Events, Membership, Front Office, and Housekeeping.

The Club Manager impacts the employees' positive experience within the workplace, and offers them support, and is well known amongst members. The Club Manager attends many board and member events and regularly has catch-ups with members who ask to see the Club Manager specifically. All in all, they are at the very core of the Club.

With the Club Manager nearing retirement, a new role has been created for a Director of Operations to replace the current Club Manager role. This new role will cover not only the responsibilities the Club Manager had, but the reporting lines of managers. This will result in managers having a new line manager, which could be the cause of uncertainty among the team.

The recruitment process for this job role is panel interviews with the Head of Human Resources, Club Manager, and CEO. The shortlisted candidates will then proceed to a second interview stage with the Chairman of the Club.

We always show candidates around the Club as this shows the facilities which are open to our members, as well as the history and artwork of the Club. We also highlight the work-related culture of the Club and the service we provide to members. This enables candidates to meet with current employees and see the natural connections the team have with each other.

To tackle uncertainty around the new Director of Operations role, the current Club Manager has worked to provide a lengthy handover to the team and to the Club in general. The Club Manager also ensured open communication, providing updates to the team regarding their successor. This includes recruitment updates of interview progress and brief details of the candidate specialities. This sharing of information instils trust throughout the restructure.

The Human Resources team have an open-door policy and so if any questions arise, we follow up and provide relevant support. The Human Resources team also provide updates about the vacancy within the daily morning meeting, outlining the stage we are at when it comes to recruiting the Club Manager's successor.

It is essential for employees to be kept up to date throughout the process as this job role will directly affect them and their reporting manager. Any unanswered questions could lead to further doubt and worry about what the future holds.

Once a successful candidate was found, a handover week was planned, where both the current Club Manager and the new Director of Operations would work alongside each other. This way, the new Director of Operations will have a well-structured handover and induction to the Club and get to know their reporting managers more easily and smoothly.

The key factors for Human Resources to consider when implementing a change regarding roles within an organisation, is clear, consistent, and open communication towards current team members. This is essential as it ensures our current team feel reassured throughout the process of receiving a new manager and member of the executive team.

Bibliography

Fisher, J. (2021). *The Process of Transition. Available from:* https://www.c2d.co.uk/techniques/process-of-transition/

Prosci Inc (no date) *The Prosci ADKAR Model*. Available from: https://www.prosci.com/methodology/adkar

Thaler, R.H., and Sunstein, C.R. (2021). *Nudge: The Final Edition*. London: Allen Lane an imprint of Penguin Books.

Index

Note: **Bold** page numbers refer to tables and *italic* page numbers refer to figures.

For Product Safety Concerns and Information please contact our EU representative GPSR@taylorandfrancis.com Taylor & Francis Verlag GmbH, Kaufingerstraße 24, 80331 München, Germany

Printed and bound by CPI Group (UK) Ltd, Croydon, CR0 4YY
06/02/2026
02049560-0018